MAJOR CASES IN CLIMATE LAW

Climate change is one of the great problems facing humanity; this book introduces readers to major rulings from around the world that centre on climate change as a core focus.

In addition to including general considerations, discussion, and analysis of major climate cases, the book engages with specific case studies. A range of major rulings from around the world are examined in detail: The *Heathrow Runway Case* (UK); The *Urgenda Case* (Netherlands); The *Colombian Amazon Case* (Colombia); The *Centre for Oil Pollution Watch Case* (Nigeria); The *Gloucester Resources Case* (Australia); *Climate Case Ireland* (Ireland). The reader is taken through relevant facts, issues, law and commentary pertinent to each case, and a clear, critical and evaluative account of each ruling is provided.

Climate law has emerged more recently than many other established branches of law, yet it is fast becoming one of the most discussed and studied areas of law around the world. This introduction to important cases in the area is essential reading for students, lawyers, and researchers engaged with climate law and policy in educational and practical settings.

Major Cases in Climate Law

A Critical Introduction

Thomas L Muinzer

•HART•
OXFORD • LONDON • NEW YORK • NEW DELHI • SYDNEY

HART PUBLISHING
Bloomsbury Publishing Plc
Kemp House, Chawley Park, Cumnor Hill, Oxford, OX2 9PH, UK
1385 Broadway, New York, NY 10018, USA
29 Earlsfort Terrace, Dublin 2, Ireland

HART PUBLISHING, the Hart/Stag logo, BLOOMSBURY and the Diana logo are trademarks of Bloomsbury Publishing Plc

First published in Great Britain 2025

First published in hardback, 2025

Paperback edition, 2026

A catalogue record for this book is available from the British Library.

A catalogue record for this book is available from the Library of Congress.

Library of Congress Control Number: 2024949695

ISBN: PB: 978-1-50998-027-7
ePDF: 978-1-50998-029-1
ePub: 978-1-50998-030-7

Typeset by Compuscript Ltd, Shannon

for Tara Blue

FOREWORD

Dr Muinzer's book is a study in applied juristic method. American legal realist Karl Llewellyn described juristic method as 'the *ways* of handling "legal" tools to law-job ends, and of the on-going upkeep and improvement of both ways and tools'.[1] It is the craft of lawyering. The legal tools to which Llewellyn referred included both substantive law and adjective law. Substantive law includes, in domestic law, constitutional and administrative law, human rights law, planning and environmental law, and climate law, and in international law, environmental and climate change conventions. Adjective law in domestic law includes the law of court practice and procedure, evidence and remedies.

Llewellyn acknowledged that the craft of lawyering of course requires knowledge of substantive and adjective law, but he argued that this knowledge of the law is merely 'the precondition of our work' as lawyers. There needs also to be knowledge of juristic method, of the 'craft of doing and getting things done with the law'.[2] In relation to judicial decision making, this requires study of not merely '*what* courts have decided' but also '*how* they go about deciding cases, and *how* they use the authorities *with* which they work, and how and why those authorities themselves came into existence'.[3]

This is the aim of Muinzer's study of six seminal climate cases. Muinzer does describe *what* the courts decided, but more importantly he critically analyses *how* they went about deciding the cases. This analysis includes identifying the authoritative legal instruments and judicial decisions with which the courts worked, and how and why those authorities themselves came into existence. Muinzer demonstrates the juristic method the courts used to adjudicate the climate cases.

The first and last chapters of the book provide an overview of major climate litigation and its adjudication by courts, while the six chapters in between provide in-depth case studies of the six seminal climate cases. The first chapter explores the relationship between climate law as a general field and climate litigation as a component of that field. The courts' adjudication of climate litigation develops legal doctrine, building a body of climate law jurisprudence. The final chapter draws together the learnings and findings of the six case studies, offering insights and lessons for climate litigation in the future.

[1] Karl Llewellyn, 'The Normative, the Legal and the Law-Jobs: The Problem of Juristic Method' (1940) 49 *Yale Law Journal* 1355–1400, 1392.

[2] Karl Llewellyn, *Jurisprudence: Realism in Theory and Practice* (University of Chicago Press, 1962) 318.

[3] ibid.

The six chapters in between these two chapters provide in-depth case studies of six landmark rulings in both the Global North (the UK, Ireland, the Netherlands and Australia) and the Global South (Colombia and Nigeria). These chapters identify and analyse the adjudicative process employed by each court to reach its decision. This includes identifying the applicable law and facts for the central issues in each case, and the legal reasoning the court employed to decide the case. The cases, as seminal cases, have received significant discussion in case notes and journal articles. Muinzer's analysis draws on this literature to provide a coherent and consolidated account of the state of knowledge and understanding of each case. This close technical and critical analysis of complex court judgments makes real the process of adjudication of climate litigation.

In so doing, Muinzer has woven tapestries of climate law and litigation. He has teased out the threads of the law and authorities used to reach each decision and explicated the ways in which those legal threads are woven together, by the legal reasoning employed, to form the warp and weft of the decision. The resultant book is an exhibition of six tapestries of climate law jurisprudence and juristic method. And like any successful art exhibition, the whole is greater than the sum of its parts. There are synapses and synergies between each case study, allowing for a deeper and holistic understanding of how courts employ juristic method to adjudicate climate cases.

In these ways, Muinzer's book provides valuable instruction in the 'craft of doing and getting things done' with climate law and litigation. Llewellyn would have approved.

The Honourable Justice Brian Preston
Chief Judge, Land and Environment Court of New South Wales

PREFACE

In Chapter 1 of this book, the following observations are made:

> Climate change is one of the great problems facing humanity. As concern over the issue has mounted over recent years, courts around the world have started to deliver rulings that are increasingly sensitive to climate matters. While climate issues often remain a background concern even in these sorts of cases, a number of major 'climate law' rulings have emerged that centre on climate change as a core focus. These cases have engaged the issue of climate change in detail while at the same time exerting a strong, leading-edge influence on shaping an emerging and discernible branch of 'climate law' in the courts.

This book introduces readers to the kind of major climate ruling referred to here, providing what at the time of writing is the first individually authored book-length introduction to the early landmark climate litigation rulings that have started to emerge around the world. The first and last chapters (Chapter 1 and Chapter 8) are focused on the *broader* consideration, discussion and analysis of major climate cases, and the chapters in between (Chapters 2–7) are focused on *deeper* consideration; these middle chapters provide deep-dive explorations of specific leading-edge judgments from around the world.

Chapter 1 focuses in part on the significance of the relationship between 'climate law' as a general field and 'climate litigation' as a component of that field. Here, climate litigation rulings can be viewed as interacting with, and feeding into, a broader field of 'climate law' in interesting and significant ways. Relatedly, the chapter also hones in on climate litigation in narrower terms, exploring the concept of cases that engage significantly with climate change issues; major rulings in this vein have started to arise with increased frequency and prominence in recent years. Like Chapter 1, the final chapter (Chapter 8) takes a relatively broad approach, drawing together learnings and findings from the major case study chapters that precede it (Chapters 2–7), so that insights and lessons for climate litigation in going forward can be identified.

Chapters 2–7 provide deep-dive studies of landmark cases drawn from the UK, the Netherlands, Colombia, Nigeria, Australia and Ireland. These chapters take the reader through the relevant facts, issues and law, engage with scholarly and other commentary pertinent to each major case, and provide a critical and evaluative commentary. This work employs primary and secondary source analysis, doctrinal legal analysis and policy analysis, and places an emphasis on close technical analysis of complex court judgments. Given that this is an introductory book, this work is partly descriptive, outlining and clarifying complex cases for the reader. Further, these chapter analyses employ critical thinking, which involves analysis of the law and related facts in concert with objective consideration of evidence and arguments, in order to provide analysis and judgement for the reader based on the application of rational and bias-free evaluation.

Most of the major cases addressed over Chapters 2–7 have received significant discussion across a range of journal articles and case notes. As Justice Preston notes in the Foreword, this book 'draws on this literature to provide a coherent and consolidated account of the state of knowledge and understanding of each case'. The cases have been chosen largely on the basis of being the first major breakthrough climate law cases in the relevant jurisdictions to reach the highest courts in the land and to deal explicitly and substantially with climate-specific issues. They have also been selected to reflect exemplary cases from both the Global North and the Global South.

Dr Thomas L Muinzer
Reader in Energy Transition Law
University of Aberdeen

ACKNOWLEDGEMENTS

Many people have assisted me over the course of this book's preparation in various ways, and I extend my thanks and appreciation to all of them.

Special thanks to Anna-Marie McAlinden (Partner, Mills Selig solicitors) and the Honourable Justice Brian Preston (Chief Judge, Land and Environment Court of New South Wales).

In relation to Latin America, my particular thanks to Judge Luis Armando Tolosa Villabona (Supreme Court of Justice of Colombia), Dr Paola Villavicencio Calzadilla (University Rovira i Virgili) and Dr Camila Bustos (Pace Law School). In the Netherlands, particular thanks to Professor Jonathan Verschuuren (Tilburg University), Professor Kars de Graaf (University of Groningen), Roger Cox and the Urgenda Foundation. In relation to Nigeria, particular thanks to Dr Uzuazo Etemire (University of Port Harcourt), Dr Smith Azubuike (Durham University) and Dr Pedi Obani (University of Bradford). In Ireland, particular thanks to Dr Suryapratim Roy (Trinity College Dublin), Fred Logue (FP Logue LLP), Dr Andrew Jackson (University College Dublin), Dr Orla Kelleher (Maynooth University) and Dr Peter Doran (Queen's University Belfast). In Australia, particular thanks (again) to the Honourable Justice Brian Preston and his team, and Professor Jacqueline Peel (Melbourne Law School). In the UK, particular thanks to Emeritus Professor Gavin McLeod Little (University of Stirling), Dr Robert Taylor (University of Aberdeen) and Professor Annalisa Savaresi (University of Stirling).

Special thanks are also due to Dr Alina Averchenkova and Dr Joana Setzer at the Grantham Research Institute and Isabella Kaminski (editor, *The Wave*).

Also, I extend sincere gratitude to: my colleagues at my research institution, the University of Aberdeen, Scotland, particularly Professor Greg Gordon, Dr Eddy Wifa and Dr Tomi Akanle Eni-ibukun; Professor Seita Vesa and Dr Kaisa Huhta at the University of Eastern Finland; and the team involved with this book at Bloomsbury-Hart Publishing, especially Roberta Bassi, Verity Stuart and Jon Lloyd.

The analyses, comments and views that appear across this book are those of the author's alone.

CONTENTS

TABLE OF CASES

TABLE OF LEGISLATION

1

Major Cases in Climate Law

Climate change is one of the great problems facing humanity. As concern over the issue has mounted over recent years, courts around the world have started to deliver rulings that are increasingly sensitive to climate matters. While climate issues often remain a background concern even in these sorts of cases, a number of landmark 'climate law' rulings have emerged that centre on climate change as a core focus. These cases have engaged the issue of climate change in detail while at the same time exerting a strong, leading-edge influence on shaping an emerging and discernible branch of 'climate law' in the courts. This text provides a study of these major cases.

This first chapter explores 'climate law' and landmark climate litigation in broad terms. Chapters 2–7 then proceed to hone in on specific climate cases, with each chapter providing a deep-dive case study of a leading landmark case. Chapter 8 concludes the book by drawing learnings from the foregoing chapters together to yield new insights. The case study chapters take the reader through the facts, issues and law pertaining to each landmark case, engage with scholarly and other commentary, and provide a critical, evaluative account of the jurisprudence.

This book assumes that climate litigation rulings are important features of 'climate law'. This first chapter therefore begins by endeavouring to clarify the notion of 'climate law' itself in order to elucidate the broader shaping context in which climate litigation jurisprudence operates. It then addresses climate litigation more narrowly and engages with landmark climate cases directly. This includes the cases to follow in the case study chapters, which are briefly summarised.

I. Climate Litigation as an Element of 'Climate Law'

Over the last two decades, 'climate law' has come to be identified increasingly as a free-standing branch of law, and one that continues to grow in content and robustness as more and more explicit 'climate' legislation is created, targeted 'climate cases' increase in courts around the world and so on.[1] This pace of development

[1] In 2008, Peel observed that in the immediate years leading up to 2008, it was possible to identify an emerging trend towards the *organisation of legal rules and principles around the central problem* of climate change. This was an important observation because it meant that one could endeavour to investigate the scope and content of the rules and principles consolidating around the issue, and that

comes from a relatively standing start; prior to the turn of this century, detailed studies and articles engaging 'climate law' were in short supply. In a survey of the literature on climate litigation produced in 2018 and covering 2000–18, Setzer and Vanhala have found that studies in the field have 'proliferated' over this period.[2] According to Mayer and Zahar, the earliest books on climate law 'with the exception of one outlier' appeared over 2005-2010, 'at a rate of one or two per year',[3] and the first climate law courses were 'not offered much earlier than 2008'.[4] Individual 'climate lawyers' themselves were also in short to non-existent supply until recent times, as were teams of overt climate law specialists, such as the team that has emerged at the respected non-governmental organisation (NGO) ClientEarth.

The new millennium heralded a shift, as public, media and governmental concern relating to anthropogenic climate change started to grow exponentially across the world, driven in part by the publication of an increasing number of alarming, high-profile scientific reports, notably the outputs of the Intergovernmental Panel on Climate Change.[5] However, this is not to say that a very significant body of 'climate law' did not exist prior to the millennium. Insofar as climate law pertains to or encompasses any law engaging anthropogenic climate change in some significant way, laws engaging climate change either directly or indirectly prior to this period can be said to be 'climate laws', strictly speaking. In the author's view, it is helpful to limit the presumed meaning of 'climate law' to climate-relevant law created in the period in which people acquired scientific understanding and awareness of the phenomenon of anthropogenic climate change (or, at least, began to acquire such understanding and awareness meaningfully).[6] Thus, legislating to place taxes on coal in the UK today in order to assist the country in meeting in its 2050 Net Zero target[7] by depressing coal emissions can be interpreted as falling within the sphere of 'climate law' on these grounds. The application of targeted taxes to coal in the UK in the Victorian period, such as the taxes applied to coal export that Robert Peel ultimately abolished in 1845,[8] fall outside the meaning of 'climate law' here.

it was not unreasonable to describe such law as 'climate law'. Peel made early inroads into this work in 2008, providing valuable insights in the process. See further: Jacqueline Peel, 'Climate change law: the emergence of a new legal discipline' (2008) 2(3) *Melbourne University Law Review* 922–79.

[2] Joana Setzer and Lisa C Vanhala, 'Climate Change Litigation: A Review of Research on Courts and Litigants in Climate Governance' (2019) 10(3) *Wiley Interdisciplinary Reviews: Climate Change* e580.

[3] Benoît Mayer and Alexander Zahar (eds), *Debating Climate Law* (Cambridge University Press, 2021) 1.

[4] ibid 2.

[5] See, eg, IPCC Third Assessment Report, *Climate Change 2001: The Scientific Basis* (Working Group I); *Climate Change 2001: Impacts, Adaptation, and Vulnerability* (Working Group II); *Climate Change 2001: Mitigation* (Working Group III).

[6] See further, eg, Jill Jäger and Tim O'Riordan, 'The History of Climate Change Science and Politics' in *The Politics of Climate Change* (Routledge, 2019) 1–31.

[7] Climate Change Act 2008 (UK), s 1(1).

[8] See further Charles-François Mathis, 'King Coal Rules: Accepting or Refusing Coal Dependency in Victorian Britain' (2018) XXIII(3) *Revue Française de Civilisation Britannique/French Journal of British Studies* 23.

It is helpful at this stage to pose and face the following question: 'What laws are "inside" and what laws are "outside" the meaning of "climate law"?' Although, as noted, it is helpful to face this question, it must also be concluded that this is a question with no correct answer. It is correct to say that '2 + 2 = 4', and it is incorrect to say that '2 + 3 = 4'. However, it is not correct or incorrect to place a particular law inside or outside of the meaning of 'climate law'. This is because the placing of a law inside or outside of the meaning is a matter of choice. '2 + 2= 4' is not a matter of choice, whereas it is a matter of choice whether or not one decides to interpret the Victorian taxes on coal exports noted above as 'climate law' (the author has chosen not to). As Hilson correctly highlighted back in 2010, 'all manner of litigation could conceivably be characterised as related to climate change'.[9] This insight extends beyond litigation to law more generally. It is up to the lawyers and law firms working in practice, the university deans, professors and administrators designing programmes and courses, and the academics and analysts working on the content and parameters of the subject to determine where they place their boundaries around climate law as a branch of the legal profession.

The author's primary interest in this discussion is doctrinal law, often described as 'black letter law'. McConville and Chui summarise that:

> '[B]lack-letter law' … focuses heavily if not exclusively upon the law itself as an internal self-sustaining set of principles which can be accessed through reading court judgments and statutes … Deriving principles and values from decided cases and re-assembling decided cases into a coherent framework in the search for order, rationality and theoretical cohesion has been the fodder of traditional legal scholarship.[10]

However, it is noteworthy that the implications of the fact that there is no 'correct answer' to the question of 'what laws are "inside" and what laws are "outside" the meaning of "climate law"' extend beyond the categorisation of doctrinal law, to pervade climate law as an intellectual field, and as a collection of past, current and developing laws, legal principles, practices and norms. A brief example will be taken as an illustration of such broader dimensions. The example concerns the work practices of lawyers and the way in which such lawyerly activity is perceived and categorised.

Let us say that a lawyer, Ms X, is based in a commercial law firm, and she is working on an onshore wind turbine transaction. She is doing legal work for a client who is developing a wind turbine that will generate electricity from renewable wind energy, and the turbine is to be sited on land owned by a farmer. This involves arranging for a lease to be taken by her client for the turbine on the farmer's land. A property lawyer may view the wind turbine lease being put in place

[9] Christopher J Hilson, 'Climate Change Litigation: A Social Movement Perspective' (April 2010), 2, https://ssrn.com/abstract=1680362.

[10] Mike McConville and Wing Hong Chui, 'Introduction and Overview' in Mike McConville and Wing Hong Chui (eds), *Research Methods for Law* (Edinburgh University Press, 2017) 1.

between the developer (ie, the client) and the landowner as a fundamental 'property law'/'land law' transaction. This would be unsurprising, given that leases are a common feature of property law. Let us also say that another lawyer at Ms X's firm, Mr Y, is working on this case as well. He is dealing with a green financial subsidy that the Government has introduced in order to incentivise wind turbine development, where a small subsidy will be paid from the Government to the developer for each unit of electricity that the developer goes on to generate once the turbine is built.[11] The subsidy arrangements that Mr Y is working on for the client take the form of a contract between the developer and the Government. Mr Y may view this as an application of 'contract law', which would be unsurprising, given that a contractual arrangement is at issue. Indeed, all of this should seem especially unsurprising if we are informed that Ms X presents herself as a 'property lawyer' and Mr Y presents himself a 'contract lawyer' in their professional dealings, that they have specialised across their training and careers in property and contract law respectively, and that Ms X is part of the law firm's property department and Mr Y is part of the law firm's contracts department.

An 'environmental lawyer', however, may interpret the wind turbine arrangements that have been outlined as a classic instance of 'environmental law' in action, and including the separate component parts of the transaction that have been noted (leasing, green finance contracts). On any reasonable analysis, harnessing the natural energy of the wind through renewable energy technology in order to generate power in an environmentally friendly way is surely a legitimate domain of the environmental lawyer. An 'energy lawyer' may also view this type of wind energy transaction as falling naturally within her or his purview. Indeed, Ms X (the 'property lawyer' working on the lease) and Mr Y (the 'contract lawyer' working on contractual green finance) might just as easily consider themselves *not* to be property and contract lawyers. Perhaps their law firm is about to rebrand them publicly as 'environmental lawyers' for marketing purposes in a move to diversify and extend the firm's client base. For related purposes, perhaps Ms X and Mr Y are due be moved from their respective property and contracts departments, and relocated to a new 'environmental' department, which will be opening in order to cohere workstreams and boost the firm's visibility in the environmental space. Yet Mr Z, another lawyer of a new and emerging kind, might object that in his experience, Ms X and Mr Y are in fact 'climate lawyers', insofar as Mr Z's legal training and the perspective he has derived as a solicitor at a climate-focused NGO has reinforced his understanding that wind turbine development and the subsidisation of wind energy by the Government are headline 'climate' measures intended to bring down national greenhouse gas emissions.

So, whose view is correct here? Is the work of Ms X and Mr Y on the turbine climate law, property law and/or contract law, environmental law or energy

[11] Such renewables subsidies are common (the subsidy noted here is framed in simple terms for the purposes of the example).

law – or indeed something else? In fact, there is no 'right answer' to this question. The element that remains stable and fixed in this example is *the legal work that Ms X and Mr Y do* on the wind turbine transaction. The perspective that is applied to that work and the way in which it is categorised by participants, observers, departments and markets remains in flux. There is no 'correct answer' as to whether the wind turbine transaction is a 'climate law' transaction or not. The perspective and categorisation one applies to the fixed set of legal activities is a matter of choice.

Returning to the subject of actual laws themselves, it has been noted that conventional doctrinal law is of primary interest in this discussion, namely Acts of Parliaments/national assemblies, court judgments, binding national constitutions and so on. The discussion is not concerned directly with what Kulovesi has described as the 'deformalization of climate law', accounting for the wider reach of soft law and phenomena like informal collaboration, voluntary regulatory initiatives and so forth (although such related matters are of course worthy objects of study in their own right).[12] The conceptualisation of doctrinal (climate) law is under consideration and it is assumed that binding judgments arising from climate litigation are an important constituent of this field.

While it has been identified that the designation of laws that are and laws that are not 'climate law' is a matter of choice, it is submitted that this choice should not be left completely open; rather, it should be constrained within *reasonable limits*. This makes it possible to structure a body of law that can be subjected to intelligible study in a manner that allows insights to be derived. If one accepts this position, it begs the question as to what the parameters of such 'reasonable limits' are or ought to be. This is difficult to specify in precise terms, but in the author's view it is helpful to posit that a particular law ought to link either *directly*, or *indirectly* but distinctly, to the issue of climate change if it is to be classified as 'climate law'.[13] If a law sits beyond these bounds, it can be interpreted as having strayed beyond 'reasonable limits', thus indicating that it is not climate law.

In summary, this position pre-supposes the application of three categories, which are as follows:

(1) Laws that are within the reasonable limit of the meaning of 'climate law' because they link directly to the issue of climate change.

[12] Kati Kulovesi, 'Exploring the Landscape of Climate Law and Scholarship: Two Emerging Trends'. in Erkki J Hollo, Kati Kulovesi and Michael Mehling (eds), *Climate Change and the Law* (Springer, 2013) 31–62.

[13] The terms 'direct' and 'indirect' arise occasionally as useful referents and descriptors in scholarly climate law discourse and analysis; see in particular Joana Setzer and Catherine Higham, *Global Trends in Climate Change Litigation: 2023 Snapshot* (Grantham Research Institute on Climate Change and the Environment and Centre for Climate Change Economics and Policy, London School of Economics and Political Science, 2023). See also Eloise Scotford and Stephen Minas, 'Probing the Hidden Depths of Climate Law: Analysing National Climate Change Legislation' (2019) 28(1) *Review of European, Comparative & International Environmental Law* 67.

(2) Laws that are within the reasonable limit of the meaning of 'climate law' because they link indirectly but distinctly to the issue of climate change.
(3) Laws that are outwith the reasonable limit of the meaning of 'climate law' because of an insufficient connection to the issue of climate change.

Here, categories (1) and (2) encompass laws that are 'climate law', and category (3) encompasses all other laws.

Much could be said about each of these categories in broad terms. However, the focus of this book is on climate litigation, where rulings arising from such litigation are understood to be an important element of climate law, and so these features will be dealt with relatively briefly. A short specific example of litigation and legislation in the case of each category can be drawn as a concise illustration of the sorts of laws that the author interprets as falling within their scope.

Category 1: Laws Directly within the Reasonable Limit of the Meaning of 'Climate Law'

Example, litigation – a binding court judgment that rules directly on a Government's climate mitigation objectives (as arises with the *Urgenda* ruling, examined in this volume).

Example, legislation – the UK's Climate Change Act 2008 (which arises as an important consideration in the *Heathrow Runway Case*, examined in this volume).

Category 2: Laws Indirectly within the Reasonable Limit of the Meaning of 'Climate Law'

Example, litigation – a binding court judgment that rules directly on non-climate issues to expand court standing rules, serving to expand standing rules for climate-related litigation indirectly in the process (as arises with the *Oil Pollution Watch* ruling, examined in this volume).

Example, legislation – provisions in the Environmental Planning and Assessment Act 1979 (New South Wales, Australia) requiring an Environmental Impact Statement to be submitted with a development application where it is deemed likely that a development will significantly impact the environment, thereby indirectly providing a forum for climate change considerations to be addressed if relevant (this arises as a consideration in the *Gloucester Resources Case*, examined in this volume).

For category 3, concerning laws outwith the sphere of climate law, a single indicative example will be taken and discussed briefly, as follows.

Category 3: Laws Outwith the Reasonable Limit of the Meaning of 'Climate Law' Due to an Insufficient Connection

Legislation stating that a landlord must give a residential tenant a minimum of one month's notice before the landlord ends a tenancy.

This category 3 example is clearly far removed from mainstream climate concerns. However, it might be pointed out that the domestic sector is typically a substantial source of greenhouse gas emissions in countries around the world, that a landlord's house is part of the domestic sector, and that a legal arrangement relevant to that house – here, concerning eviction notices – therefore has direct relevance to a building that is ultimately relevant to emissions. Based on this line of thinking, one might endeavour to assert that this item of housing legislation is also climate law. While the logic just stated that points towards this conclusion is not incorrect, in the author's view an example of this kind stretches the connection between the item of law and the applicable meaning of 'climate law' too far beyond a reasonable limit. As such, according to the criteria outlined above, the example cited here does not classify as 'climate law'.

The author accepts that there is no rigidly determinable distinction between each of the three categories – including the boundary between 'direct' and 'indirect' climate laws, which is contestable[14] – and so individual cases may likely arise in which the category that a particular law might be most suitably placed into can be disputed.[15] Further, one is arguably compelled to assess whether a law is 'inside' or 'outside' the field of climate law (ie, whether or not it is a category 3 law) on a somewhat pragmatic basis. There is no clear '2 + 2 = 4' general principle that can make this absolutely plain in all cases.

As noted, climate litigation rulings are understood here to be nested within the field of 'climate law' under discussion, as one of its core elements. Peel and Osofsky have provided a sophisticated examination of the concept of 'climate change litigation' and related problems of definition, advancing a number of definitional categories in the process. In their framing, cases that can be said to amount to climate litigation in a robust and clear way will include cases that are 'about' climate change very directly; here, litigation involves climate change as a central issue.[16] In addition, the authors suggest that '[l]itigation with climate change as a peripheral issue' can also be construed legitimately as climate change litigation.[17] One can also move further away from such explicit and semi-explicit recognition of 'climate change', to encompass '[l]itigation with climate change

[14] Scotford and Minas (n 13) also recognise a conception of direct and indirect climate laws, linking them to what they describe as 'legal cultures'.

[15] Bearing this in mind, it is notable that climate law has been characterised as 'legally disruptive' and polycentric; see further Elizabeth Fisher, Eloise Scotford and Emily Barritt, 'The Legally Disruptive Nature of Climate Change' (2017) 80(2) *Modern Law Review* 173–201.

[16] Jacqueline Peel and Hari M Osofsky, 'Climate Change Litigation' (2020) 16 *Annual Review of Law and Social Science* 21–38, 23.

[17] ibid 24, adapted from Figure 1. The authors depict climate change litigation as a number of concentric circles, with litigation that involves climate change as a central issue positioned at the 'core' of the circles; see ibid.

as one motivation but not raised as an issue, e.g., cases against coal brought on environmental grounds'.[18] And one can move further away still, to incorporate '[l]itigation with no specific climate change framing but with implications for mitigation or adaptation, e.g., fracking cases'.[19] These four fields provide a thoughtful framework that allows for the identification and interpretation of climate litigation in a meaningful way.[20] The framing also accommodates characteristic complexities arising across climate law as a general field, in which climate litigation is nested; as discussed above, climate law will not necessarily engage with climate change in direct or overtly clear terms, and the work of Peel and Osofsky accommodates this problem.[21]

Returning to the identification of the characteristics of 'climate law' as a broader field in order to sharpen an understanding of the body of law that enmeshes and shapes climate litigation, it is notable that climate law engages with a problem that is global in scale,[22] and it can also reasonably be held that climate law has a common tendency to concern itself with *anthropogenic* climate change (where climate mitigation is concerned, at the least). For example, it has been pointed out that the first example of 'national framework climate legislation',[23] the UK Climate Change Act 2008, is 'explicitly concerned with anthropogenic emissions'.[24] The United Nations Framework Convention on Climate Change has served to cement an anthropogenic orientation at the international level, defining its 'objective' in the following terms:

> The ultimate objective of this Convention and any related legal instruments that the Conference of the Parties may adopt is to achieve … stabilization of greenhouse gas concentrations in the atmosphere at a level that would prevent *dangerous anthropogenic interference* with the climate system. (Emphasis added)[25]

This orientation towards anthropogenic emissions appears to make logical sense, insofar as anthropogenic emissions are emissions that humanity is directly

[18] ibid.

[19] ibid.

[20] Hilson has also noted that what he describes as 'proactive' and 'reactive' cases can be usefully distinguished and subjected to targeted examination. He construes proactive litigation as involving civil proceedings, whether public law (judicial review) or private law (tort)-based, and reactive litigation as involving criminal proceedings brought by the Crown. See further Christopher J Hilson, 'Climate Change Litigation: An Explanatory Approach (or Bringing Grievance Back in)' in Fabrizio Fracchia and Massimo Occhiena (eds), *Climate change: la riposta del diritto* (Editoriale Scientifica, 2010) 421–36.

[21] For useful further discussion of the classification of climate litigation, see pages 687-700 (particularly pages 687–695) in Jacqueline Peel and, Jolene Lin, 'Transnational Climate Litigation: The Contribution of the Global South' (2019) 113(4) *American Journal of International Law* 679–726.

[22] Ivano Alogna, Christine Bakker and Jean-Pierre Gauci (eds), *Climate Change Litigation: Global Perspectives* (Brill, 2021).

[23] See further Thomas L Muinzer, 'What are National "Climate Change Acts"?' (2021) 39(4) *Journal of Energy & Natural Resources Law* 419–438.

[24] Thomas L Muinzer, *Climate and Energy Governance for the UK Low Carbon Transition: The Climate Change Act 2008* (Springer, 2018) 49.

[25] United Nations Framework Convention on Climate Change, Article 2, 'Objective'.

responsible for and that it can directly govern, such that controls reflected in laws tend to proceed naturally from this circumstance. In sum, in engaging with greenhouse gas emissions, 'climate law' exhibits a tendency or *orientation* towards the anthropogenic.

In addition to exhibiting an anthropogenic orientation, it is also possible to distinguish what could be described as particular *strands* or *components* of climate law. Here, attention is projected onto certain core themes/issues; laws, principles and legal discourses proceed to cluster around these themes or issues. The strands or components of climate law that emerge include *mitigation* and *adaptation* most particularly. Romppanen and Huhta write that '[c]limate law, in broad terms, addresses climate change and the main responses to it, which are essentially mitigation and adaptation'.[26] Thus, addressing climate litigation, Banda and Fulton have written:

> [C]limate litigation in national courts has gone beyond the traditional confines of environmental litigation … to include a variety of disputes addressing climate change issues both directly and indirectly … These disputes can broadly be categorized as (a) litigation involving climate mitigation measures – efforts designed to reduce or prevent emissions of greenhouse gases (GHGs), and (b) litigation involving climate adaptation measures – efforts designed to build resilience and reduce the negative impacts of climate change on communities and ecosystems.[27]

This distinction between *mitigation* and *adaptation* is certainly important because, as McDonald's work has shown, certain characteristics of climate change and its associated impacts make law-making for adaptation uniquely challenging.[28]

As well as *mitigation* and *adaptation*, these sorts of identifiable 'strands' or 'components' may include further examples, notably (climate) *finance*. In outlining 'The Subject Matter of International Climate Change Law',[29] Bodansky et al include a fourth, internationally focused strand in addition to *mitigation*, *adaptation* and *finance*:

> International climate change law focuses on four basic issues: (1) *mitigation* of climate change – that is, limiting it or preventing it from happening; (2) *adaptation* to climate change, in order to limit its harmful effects; (3) *financial* and other means of support for mitigation and adaptation; and (4) *international oversight* to promote implementation, compliance, and effectiveness. (Emphasis added)[30]

[26] Seita Romppanen and Kaisa Huhta, 'The Interface between EU Climate and Energy Law' (2023) 30(1) *Maastricht Journal of European and Comparative Law* 45–62, 51.

[27] Maria L Banda and Scott Fulton, 'Litigating Climate Change in National Courts: Recent Trends and Developments in Global Climate Law' (2017) 47 *Environmental. Law Reporter* 10121, 10132.

[28] Jan McDonald, 'The Role of Law in Adapting to Climate Change' (2011) 2(2) *Wiley Interdisciplinary Reviews: Climate Change* 283–295.

[29] Daniel Bodansky, Jutta Brunnée and Lavanya Rajamani, 'Introduction' in *International Climate Change Law* (Oxford University Press, 2017) 11–17.

[30] ibid 11.

For Hollo et al, *technology* and *capacity building* embody further identifiable strands of climate law that have emerged: 'The emphasis of climate law has traditionally been on *mitigation*, but *adaptation*, *finance*, *technology* and *capacity building* have recently asserted their place as key elements of climate change law and policy' (emphasis added).[31]

Additionally, the author has suggested elsewhere that another relevant feature of climate law is that it has an interactive relationship with three very particular challenges. These challenges arguably impact climate law, and thus contribute to the shape and character of the field in which climate litigation is enmeshed. These have been stated as follows:

> First … climate change is one of the great problems of our times and therefore the stakes are unusually (and extremely) high in terms of finding appropriate solutions, meaning in turn that the stakes are abnormally high for climate law itself.[32]
>
> Second, climate law is compelled unavoidably to engage with very complex headline issues, due to the fact that anthropogenic climate change is highly complex in its own right and also due to the fact that its resolution involves (amongst other things) complex economy-wide decarbonisation transitions. These complexities, which are to some extent in-built into the issue, mean that climate law has very substantial challenges that it must inherently rise to.[33]
>
> Third, climate change poses novel problems for technical/doctrinal law, insofar as it is a unique problem that law has comparatively little experience in grappling with in direct terms. For example, one might contrast the newly emerging sphere of 'climate law' that is crystallising in order to tackle the problem with conventional English criminal law; English criminal law, while being as current and contemporary as any other branch of law one may seek to identify in practice, stretches back in its direct and conscious development over hundreds of years. The novel character of the climate change problem, combined with law's inexperience in managing it directly, leads to newly identifiable practical legal problems that the law must endeavour to cope with effectively.[34]

In summary, this book understands climate litigation jurisprudence to operate in the context of the parameters, forces and constraints pertaining to 'climate law' that have been sketched out above. Here, it has been advanced that there is no 'correct answer' to the question of what laws fall inside and what laws fall outside of climate law, and that it is a matter of choice. It has been postulated that this choice should be constrained within *reasonable limits*, and in order to structure those reasonable limits, three categories have been advanced that serve to classify 'climate law' (categories 1 and 2) and law beyond the range of its meaning (category 3). The category 1 and 2 laws exhibit some *orientation* towards anthropogenic concerns, and predominant *strands/components* can be identified within

[31] Hollo et al (n 12) 2.

[32] Thomas L Muinzer (ed), *National Climate Change Acts: The Emergence, Form and Nature of National Framework Climate Legislation* (Hart: Publishing, 2020) 21.

[33] ibid 22.

[34] ibid.

the field: *Mitigation – Adaptation (– Finance) (– etc)*. Three novel and substantial challenges also confront and impact the field, which is engaging with a problem that is global in scale, and these have been outlined (in summary: *the stakes are high*; *inbuilt complexity*; *engagement with a unique problem, with little historical experience of doing so*).

II. Spotlight on Climate Litigation

Hilson has noted that virtually all litigation could be conceived of as climate litigation, and therefore choices have to be made that bring some degree of deliberate framing to bear on the issue, so that it can be studied in a meaningful way that can yield insights.[35] A scientist endeavouring to understand some aspect of the human body cannot merely study 'the body'; he or she must place some narrowing framework upon the body in order to investigate some point of interest systematically and draw lessons. This includes an aspect of the human body such as the immune system, which runs throughout the body and cannot be isolated for study in the way that, for example, the human eye can be isolated. Something similar can be said by way of analogy for the study of climate law and, within that, climate litigation. The overall body of law that confronts the analyst contains climate-relevant material running throughout that body of law in all directions – much like the immune system in the human body – and a narrowing framework of inquiry must be brought to bear on it in order to investigate it in a meaningful and systematic way that can yield insights. Thus, substantial framing has been applied by the author to 'climate law' in the preceding section, which in turn moderates the study of climate litigation within that field.

In 2010, Hilson also noted that '*there must be some agency* in the way in which litigation is framed which deliberately brings out a climate change element in the way the case is put forward. In other words, *to count as climate change litigation, cases must be framed as such*' (emphasis added).[36] In highlighting the role of active agency and active framing here, Hilson's comments should sound a cautionary note for researchers conducting collective analyses of climate litigation (including the present author). Where one may perceive an 'objective' data set based on identifiable climate cases, that data set has been influenced by quasi-subjective participation to some significant degree, insofar as the agency behind the definitional choices and the framing of what has been included and omitted has played some determinative role in the data's construction. This includes but is not limited to so-called 'mapping' exercises that attempt to map climate litigation cases.[37]

[35] See further Hilson (n 20).

[36] Hilson (n 9) 2.

[37] See further Kim Bouwer, 'The Unsexy Future of Climate Change Litigation' (2018) 30(3) *Journal of Environmental Law* 483–506, 484 fn 3, 502.

These circumstances are potentially subject to a further degree of refraction in instances where researchers draw on such mapped data, databases and similar by screening the data further in order to isolate and interpret cases, trends or themes of interest to them within the dataset.[38]

Further, Kysar has noted that by forcing law to engage with outlying or novel issues due to the novel character of anthropogenic climate change itself, the climate challenge exerts some degree of shaping force on law in its own right, recalibrating it in the process.[39] While he finds this process to be a complicating factor, he also suggests that this shift can be viewed in a positive light, as it suggests that the momentum is compelling law to adapt and become responsive to the needs posed by the issue.[40] Such a view is arguably illustrated in a direct way by the climate case *Bushfire Survivors for Climate Action v Environment Protection Authority* (2021).[41] Here, the Land and Environment Court of New South Wales, Australia, found that the Environment Protection Authority's statutory duty to develop policies relating to environmental protection included a duty to ensure that these policies adapt in response to environmental challenges as necessary, particularly climate change.[42]

This book understands climate litigation to involve legal action (litigation) that engages climate change issues,[43] and its case study chapters are concerned with judgments engaging climate change directly (category 1 climate law),[44] with the exception of the chapter examining *Oil Pollution Watch*, where the engagement is indirect (category 2 climate law).[45] The cases have been selected largely on the basis of being the first major breakthrough climate law cases in the jurisdictions engaged to both (a) reach the highest courts in the land, and (b) deal explicitly and substantially with climate-specific issues. Thus, for example, the *Heathrow Runway Case* was the first case in the UK to (a) reach the UK Supreme Court, and (b) deal explicitly and substantially with climate-specific issues at that top court level. As noted, the *Oil Pollution Watch* case provides a category 2 exception, where climate issues are engaged indirectly in terms of the actual facts of the case. In the *Gloucester Resources Case*, the highest court in the relevant jurisdiction is engaged

[38] Osofsky has also clarified that it is possible to conceptualise climate litigation as occurring across multiple complex scales of governance; see further Hari M Osofsky, 'The Continuing Importance of Climate Change Litigation' (2010) 1(1) *Climate Law* 3–29.

[39] Douglas A Kysar, 'What Climate Change Can Do about Tort Law' (2011) 41 *Environmental Law* 1.

[40] ibid.

[41] *Bushfire Survivors for Climate Action v Environment Protection Authority* (2021) 250 LGERA 1, [2021] NSWLEC 92.

[42] ibid.

[43] As with litigation in general, it is notable that climate litigation itself is a form of *adjudication*, and adjudication can be interpreted as being subject to various merits and demerits, and capacities and limitations, in its assorted guises: see further Lon Fuller's exploration of this matter in his classic paper 'The Forms and Limitations of Adjudication' (1978) 92(2) *Harvard Law Review* 353). This suggests that adjudication as a decision-taking process in such a polycentric area (ie, that of climate governance) may serve a very useful role while remaining subject simultaneously to deceptively complex demerits and limitations. On polycentricity, see further Fisher et al (n 15).

[44] Category 1 climate law has been outlined in the previous section.

[45] Category 2 climate law has been outlined in the previous section.

(New South Wales, Australia), but the highest court in Australia itself is technically the High Court of Australia. Cases have also been selected to reflect exemplary major cases from both the Global North and the Global South.

In their informative 2017 paper addressing climate litigation and the role played by national judiciaries, Banda and Fulton have highlighted the relatively recent focus emerging around climate law, the field's wide-ranging character, and the impact that climate litigation has had in expanding it and driving it forward:

> The developing field of 'climate law' – which has emerged over the past decade through an explosion in climate change litigation – comprises a wide range of legal disputes before a variety of judicial, administrative, and arbitral institutions at the domestic, regional, and international levels.[46]

In their 2023 policy paper *Global Trends in Climate Litigation*,[47] researchers at the Grantham Institute reporting on climate litigation cases distinguish cases that have 'direct judicial outcomes that can be understood as favourable to climate action' and those that have 'significant indirect impacts on climate change decision-making beyond the courtroom'.[48] The report employs what it describes as 'a fairly narrow definition' of climate litigation based on the approach adopted by the Sabin Center for Climate Change Law at Columbia Law School, which runs a substantial online climate law database.[49] It 'consider[s] such litigation to include cases before judicial and quasi-judicial bodies … that involve material issues of climate change science, policy, or law'.[50]

This strand of work makes the important point that '[s]cholarly and media attention on climate litigation tends to focus on cases that seek to advance climate action … However, not all climate litigation is filed with that aim in mind'.[51] Setzer and Higham usefully employ the terms 'climate-aligned' and 'non-climate aligned' litigation.[52] The latter category includes 'cases in which litigants challenge the introduction of regulations or policies that would lead to greenhouse gas emissions reductions or other "positive" climate outcomes'.[53] Rather than being limited to cases that are clearly filed with the intention of 'delaying or obstructing climate action',[54] it may be that such cases 'might not have opposition to climate action as their main objective', but yet impact on climate governance in some significant way

[46] Banda and Fulton (n 27).
[47] Setzer and Higham (n 13).
[48] ibid 2.
[49] ibid 8.
[50] ibid. The definition appears to be slightly circular, as 'litigation' will involve 'issues of … law' by definition.
[51] Joana Setzer and Catherine Higham, *Global Trends in Climate Change Litigation: 2022 Snapshot* (Grantham Research Institute on Climate Change and the Environment and Centre for Climate Change Economics and Policy, London School of Economics and Political Science, 2022) 7.
[52] ibid 6–7.
[53] ibid 7.
[54] ibid.

nevertheless.[55] Additionally, some cases 'might not object to climate action, but rather to the way in which such action is carried out or its impacts'.[56]

The deep-dive case studies in this book are in the 'climate-aligned' tradition, in the Setzer-Higham sense just noted, insofar as their emphasis generally falls on efforts seeking to advance climate action rather than obstruct or reverse it.[57] Returning to the work of Peel and Osofsky, it has also been discussed in the previous section that these authors carefully delineated 'climate change litigation' categories in 2020.[58] This work drew on previous detailed scholarship by the authors from 2015.[59] The case study chapters in this book fall into the Peel-Osofsky category of litigation that involves climate change as the central issue,[60] with the exception of the Nigerian case study. It appears that the Nigerian case study might fall within the Peel-Osofsky category of '[l]itigation with no specific climate change framing but with implications for mitigation or adaptation',[61] due to *Oil Pollution Watch*'s expansion of standing to bring climate litigation in the Nigerian courts. Alternatively, the case might sit within the category of '[l]itigation with climate change as a peripheral issue',[62] insofar as Justice Aka'ahs does raise the issue of climate change explicitly in his judgment.[63]

[55] ibid. In relation to these categories taken overall, it is possible that the excellent work from Grantham in this area could be usefully complimented by research undertaken with reference to a further category of litigation, concerning litigation that does not directly engage climate issues and that is not intended to do so (so far as one is aware), but that impacts substantially on climate issues nevertheless. This is a hard category to research because the import for climate governance is not initially clear and must be investigated and calculated.

[56] ibid. In 2023 the authors developed their 'climate-aligned' and 'non-climate aligned' taxonomy by introducing a further category of cases, which they describe as 'just transition litigation'. Cases falling within this category are distinguished as follows: 'These are cases that challenge not the lack of climate action but the manner in which that action is being taken … In our 2022 report we classified such cases as a sub-category of non-climate-aligned litigation. However, as our understanding of the issues involved in these cases evolves, it is evident that this is too simplistic a way of understanding the complex issues raised.' Thus, 'the objective of just transition litigation is not to undermine climate action. Often, the applicants' aim is to strike a better balance between the actions taken to advance the transition and the rights of communities impacted by those actions' (Setzer and Higham (n 13) 9).

[57] The *Gloucester Resources Case* is slightly distinct, as it involves an appeal against a refused planning consent for an open cast coalmine; see further ch 6.

[58] Peel and Osofsky (n 16) 23–24.

[59] Jacqueline Peel and Hari M Osofsky, *Climate Change Litigation* (Cambridge University Press, 2015).

[60] Peel and Osofsky (n 16) 23. The case study cohort in this volume also places some emphasis on public interest state-oriented litigation. For useful targeted discussion of corporate cases, see further Setzer and Higham (n 13), where, inter alia, Setzer and Higham highlight the increase in 'climate-washing cases' such as *KlimaAllianz v FIFA* (2022, Fair Advertising Commission, Switzerland), and the increase in cases brought against financial institutions, such as *R (on the Application of Friends of the Earth Ltd) (Appellant) v Secretary of State for International Trade/UK Export Finance (UKEF) and Another (Respondents)* UKSC 2023/0026 (which was ultimately unsuccessful).

[61] Peel and Osofsky (n 16) 24.

[62] ibid 24.

[63] *Centre for Oil Pollution Watch v Nigerian National Petroleum Corporation* [2019] 5 NWLR (Pt 1666) 518, 580. See further ch 5.

A. Landmark Climate Cases

Before turning to the case studies directly, which are of assistance in exploring the details of landmark climate cases in analytical and critical depth, the breadth of landmark climate litigation should be reflected on further. Major climate rulings are slowly increasing as a growing number of cases continue to arise. As the number of cases increases around the world, so too does the level of geographical and doctrinal diversity.[64] In the landmark Pakistani ruling *Asghar Leghari v Federation of Pakistan* (2015),[65] the Lahore High Court accepted arguments that governmental failures to address climate change violated the plaintiff's rights. This case forms part of a body of climate change-related cases that incorporate rights-based arguments, and indicates a growing receptivity of courts to this type of framing.[66] Here, the Government of Pakistan had passed a National Climate Change Policy 2012 and a Framework for Implementation of Climate Change Policy (2014–30). However, the plaintiff (an agriculturist and law student) argued that the Government had failed to implement these, and that this failure amounted to a violation of his rights. He based this argument on his Article 9 constitutional right to life, and his Article 14 right to a healthy and clean environment and to human dignity, connecting these rights to climate change, which presents serious threats to water, food and energy security in Pakistan. The plaintiff submitted that priority items under the Framework had not been complied with and action had not been taken by the relevant governmental actors to develop adaptive capacity and resilience to address climate change.[67] The Court agreed, as Barritt and Sediti summarise:

> In two linked court orders, that read like the scolding of naughty children, Mr Justice Mansoor Ali Shah criticises 'the delay and lethargy of the State in implementing the Framework' and the impact of this on the fundamental rights of the citizens of Pakistan. In the first order of 4 September 2015, he mandates the creation of a Climate Change Commission to monitor the progress of the Framework. He also compels the appearance of the Joint Secretary for Climate Change, who had recently been transferred to another region, and requires that each ministry, department and authority appoint a Climate Change Focal Person to attend and assist at the next hearing. In the second order of 14 September, he examines the Framework and Policy in detail, constitutes the Climate Change Commission and sets expectations for that Commission, retaining a supervisory jurisdiction for the court over the activities of the Commission.[68]

[64] Wolfgang Kahl and Marc-Philippe Weller (eds), *Climate Change Litigation* (Beck, 2021).

[65] *Asghar Leghari v Federation of Pakistan* (2015) WP No 25501/201 (Lahore High Court, Pakistan).

[66] On the development of rights-based litigation, see further Annalisa Savaresi and Joana Setzer, 'Rights-Based Litigation in the Climate Emergency: Mapping the Landscape and New Knowledge Frontiers' (2022) 13(1) *Journal of Human Rights and the Environment* 7–34.

[67] See further *Asghar Leghari* (n 65).

[68] Emily M Barritt and Boitumelo Sediti, 'The Symbolic Value of *Leghari v Federation of Pakistan*: Climate Change Adjudication in the Global South' (2019) 30(2) *King's Law Journal* 203–10, 204–05.

In its judgment of 25 January 2018, the court opined that: 'Climate Justice … moves beyond the construct of environmental justice. It has to embrace multiple new dimensions like Health Security, Food Security, Energy Security, Water Security, Human Displacement, Human Trafficking and Disasters Management within its fold. Climate Justice covers agriculture, health, food, building approvals, industrial licenses, technology, infrastructural work, human resource, human and climate trafficking, disaster preparedness, health, etc.'[69]

Moving focus from the Global South to the Global North, in the landmark case *Neubauer et al v Germany* (2021),[70] the young plaintiffs argued that Germany's binding greenhouse gas reduction trajectory under its Federal Climate Protection Act ('Bundesklimaschutzgesetz' or 'KSG') was insufficient and violated the German Basic Law (the Constitution). The KSG contained a requirement for a 55 per cent reduction in greenhouse gas emissions by 2030, but no specific provisions as to how Germany would continue to reduce emissions post-2030. Amongst other matters, the plaintiffs argued that the extant targets under the KSG were inadequate to limit the increase in global temperature in line with the requirements of the international Paris Agreement, and that the lack of detail in the KSG for the post-2030 period inequitably placed the burden of heavier emissions reductions and combating climate change onto future generations, breaching fundamental rights. The Court broadly agreed, finding that the existing KSG targets would offload major emission reduction burdens onto periods after 2030, impacting on the freedoms of future generations. The Court ordered the German Government to correct and improve existing climate law provisions, including requiring it to make specific provisions for reduction targets from 2031 onwards by the end of 2022.[71] In response to the decision, the German Parliament reacted very quickly. Just two months later, it approved significant amendments to the KSG which introduced more ambitious emission reduction targets. Preston CJ (writing in a non-judicial capacity) has summarised that: 'Fundamental rights under the Basic Law protected the complainants against threats of freedom caused by greenhouse gas emissions reduction burdens being unilaterally offloaded onto the future. The [Constitutional Court held that] provisions of the Climate Protection Act have an adverse interference-like effect on the freedoms.'[72]

In the year prior to this German ruling, the Norwegian Supreme Court also delivered its first landmark climate judgment: *Greenpeace Nordic Association*

[69] *Asghar Leghari* (n 65) 23, para [22].

[70] *Neubauer et al v Germany* (2021) 1 BvR 2656/18, 1 BvR 78/20, 1 BvR 96/20, 1 BvR 288/20 (Federal Constitutional Court, Germany).

[71] ibid 6, para [4] (English translation provided by the German courts service). For an unsuccessful claim brought against the German Government, where organic farming families and Greenpeace argued that the Government had breached its constitutional rights in failing to meet a 2020 emissions reduction target, see *Family Farmers and Greenpeace Germany v Germany* VG 10 K 412.18 (31 October 2019).

[72] Brian J Preston, 'Changing Climate Law and Governance: A Multi-level Perspective' (2023) *Global Policy* 1–12, 7.

v Ministry of Petroleum and Energy (2020).[73] The Court considered a claim that petroleum licences, issued by the Norwegian Government, were in violation of the 'right to a healthy environment' contained in the Norwegian Constitution. It rejected the claim and held that the constitutional protection of the environment applies as a substantive constraint on governmental action only in very limited circumstances.[74] In the following year, the important EU case *Carvalho and Others v European Parliament and Council* (2021)[75] also proved unsuccessful. Here, 10 families from a variety of countries argued that the EU's emissions reduction trajectory was too weak and that a milestone emissions reduction target established for 2030 required mandatory strengthening in order to avoid dangerous climate change and adequately protect their fundamental rights; however, the Court held that the case was inadmissible due to a lack of standing.

The plaintiffs in the landmark Dutch case *Milieudefensie v Royal Dutch Shell* (2021) were considerably more successful.[76] Here, in a case taken against a large corporation rather than the state, the environmental group Milieudefensie (Friends of the Earth Netherlands) and its co-plaintiffs alleged that Shell was not doing enough to reduce greenhouse gas emissions and prevent serious climate damage, thereby breaching its duty of care under Dutch law and human rights obligations. Shell was ordered by the court to limit or cause the limitation of 'the aggregate annual volume of all CO_2 emissions into the atmosphere (Scope 1, 2 and 3) due to the business operations and sold energy-carrying products of the Shell group'.[77] This order applied to Shell 'both directly and via the companies and legal entities it commonly includes in its consolidated annual accounts and with which it jointly forms the Shell group'.[78] The court ordered the volume of emissions to be 'reduced by at least net 45% at [the end of] 2030, relative to 2019 levels'.[79] Substantial climate litigation has also broken through nearby in France in *Notre Affaire à Tous and Others v France*.[80] Here, the Paris Administrative Court held in February 2021 that the French Government had not undertaken sufficient action to mitigate greenhouse gas emissions under French and EU law, giving the

[73] *Greenpeace Nordic Association v Ministry of Petroleum and Energy* Case No 20-051052SIV-HRET, 22 December 2020 (Supreme Court, Norway).

[74] The Court found that the petroleum exploration licences should be granted notwithstanding Norwegian constitutional protections, as the link between granting the licences and the increase of future greenhouse gas emissions was too uncertain to constitute a real and immediate threat to the right to life, and the right to respect for private and family life; see further ibid. The plaintiffs referred the case to the European Court of Human Rights on 15 June 2021. It has not been heard at the time of writing.

[75] Case C-565/19 P *Carvalho and Others v European Parliament and Council* ECLI:EU:C:2021:252.

[76] *Milieudefensie v Royal Dutch Shell*, Hague District Court, ECLI:NL:RBDHA:2021:5337, 26 May 2021 (the Netherlands).

[77] ibid para [5.3].

[78] ibid.

[79] ibid. This decision was at the District Court only, and unsurprisingly Shell has appealed the decision at the time of writing; however, the District Court's decision is provisionally enforceable, so Shell is obliged to meet reduction obligations whilst the appeal is ongoing.

[80] *Notre Affaire à Tous and Others v France* (No 1904967, 1904968, 1904972, 1904976/4-1).

Government two months to disclose the steps it would take to ensure that climate targets would be met.

Influential landmark climate litigation has also arisen in the US, notably in *Massachusetts v Environmental Protection Agency* (2007),[81] which focused on statutory interpretation in assessing whether the US Environmental Protection Agency (EPA) had abused its discretion by refusing to regulate greenhouse gas emissions under the Clean Air Act, with a Supreme Court majority ruling against the EPA. In subsequent litigation, young plaintiffs have endeavoured to argue that the Federal Government has violated their constitutional rights by causing dangerous carbon dioxide concentrations in the atmosphere.[82] The American experience can be juxtaposed with developments in neighbouring Canada, notably the Supreme Court of Canada's landmark decision in *References re Greenhouse Gas Pollution Pricing Act* (2021), which involved a carbon pricing scheme.[83] Here, in a majority decision, the Court interpreted climate change as meeting the threshold of a national concern and held that that the Greenhouse Gas Pollution Pricing Act 2018 was constitutional under Parliament's residual power to make laws for 'peace, order, and good government'.[84]

Over the period of this book's production, some much-awaited judgments of the European Court of Human Rights have also been issued recently. In *Verein Klimaseniorinnen Schweiz and Others v Switzerland*,[85] involving a complaint by four elderly women and a Swiss association, the Court's Grand Chamber ruled by a majority of 16:1 that Article 8 of the European Convention on Human Rights[86] covers a right to effective protection by the state from the serious adverse effects of climate change on life, health, well-being and quality of life. The Court found that the elderly female applicants' complaints were inadmissible, as they did not attract victim status under Article 34 of the European Convention; however, the applicant association was held to be entitled to bring a complaint on behalf of individuals who could arguably claim to be subject to threats or adverse effects of climate change. The Court found that the Swiss state had positive obligations under Article 8 to take steps to safeguard individuals from climate change and that it had failed to put in place an adequate framework for doing so. It also ruled that Article 6 of the Convention had been violated, as the Swiss courts had not considered the merits of the applicants' complaints (which the Grand Chamber held to include a need to take account of compelling scientific evidence). By contrast, in *Duarte Agostinho and Others v Portugal and 32 Others*,[87] six young Portuguese nationals

[81] *Massachusetts v Environmental Protection Agency* 549 US 497 (2007) (US Supreme Court).

[82] *Juliana v United States* 217 F Supp 3d 1224 (D Or 2016).

[83] *References re Greenhouse Gas Pollution Pricing Act* (2021) SCC 11 (Supreme Court of Canada).

[84] ibid.

[85] *Verein Klimaseniorinnen Schweiz and Others v Switzerland*, Grand Chamber, European Court of Human Rights (Application No 53600/20), 9 April 2024.

[86] Engaging the right to respect for private and family life.

[87] *Duarte Agostinho and Others v Portugal and 32 Others*, Grand Chamber, European Court of Human Rights (Application No 39371/20), 9 April 2024.

were unsuccessful in a complaint concerning the present and future effects of climate change, where they argued that Portugal and 32 other respondent states bore responsibility for the problem. The Grand Chamber deemed their case inadmissible, as the applicants had not engaged legal avenues available in Portugal and the possibility for domestic remedies had not been exhausted. Similarly, in *Carême v France*,[88] a former resident and mayor of the Grande-Synthe municipality in France, who complained that the state had not taken sufficient steps to prevent climate change, was unsuccessful. The Grand Chamber found that the applicant failed to attract victim status under Article 34 of the Convention, in significant part because he no longer lived in Grand-Synthe or permanently at that point in France.

B. Landmark Climate Case Studies

The deep-dive case studies in this book begin at Chapter 2[89] with a detailed study of the *Heathrow Runway Case*, a 2020 Supreme Court of the United Kingdom ruling: *R (on the Application of Friends of the Earth Ltd and Others) v Heathrow Airport Ltd* (2020).[90] This first landmark climate case to reach the UK's highest court involved contestation of the UK Government's support for the proposed expansion of runway capacity at Heathrow Airport, England. Such expansion was likely to result in a growth of aviation activity that would add significantly to UK greenhouse gas emissions, and it was argued that the UK Government had breached legal obligations by neglecting to factor climate change considerations into its decision-making process adequately. The case has a rich seam of climate law running through it, including consideration of the Paris Agreement, the UK's Climate Change Act 2008 and provisions pertaining to climate change in the UK's Planning Act 2008.

As explored in Chapter 2, the Divisional Court that first heard the case ruled in favour of the UK Government's support for runway expansion,[91] which had been articulated in an official national policy statement;[92] however, this decision was emphatically reversed by the Court of Appeal, which criticised the Government for what it interpreted as a failure to take the Paris Agreement into account adequately.[93] This decision was reversed in turn by the Supreme Court. In some sense, the case that came before the Supreme Court embodied a challenge to

[88] *Carême v France*, Grand Chamber, European Court of Human Rights (Application No 7189/21), 9 April 2024.

[89] See ch 2.

[90] *R (on the Application of Friends of the Earth Ltd and Others) v Heathrow Airport Ltd* [2020] UKSC 52.

[91] *R (on the Application of Spurrier) v Secretary of State for Transport* [2019] EWHC 1070 (Admin).

[92] Department for Transport, *Airports National Policy Statement* (UK Government, 2018).

[93] *Plan B Earth v Secretary of State for Transport* [2020] EWCA Civ 214 (27 February 2020).

the UK Government, since the Government's policy statement affording support for the runway expansion was at issue; however, the Government itself was not involved directly as an appellant by this stage because it was the owner of the airport (Heathrow Runway Ltd) that had appealed the Court of Appeal's decision. The respondents in the case were the environmental NGOs Friends of the Earth and Plan B Earth.

In having ruled against the NGOs after their success at the Court of Appeal, the Supreme Court decision may be difficult news for environmentalists, although on legal grounds the Court arguably provides a cogent rationale for its decision based on applicable law. Nevertheless, it is advanced over the course of analysis in Chapter 2 that the Court at best overstates (and at worst arguably misinterprets) the extent to which the UK's domestic Climate Change Act 2008 can be said to implement the international Paris Agreement. It is also advanced that the Court appears to misinterpret the extent to which the Secretary of State in the UK Government took the Paris Agreement into account. Further, the chapter analysis identifies arguable imprecision arising in the conceptual distinctions drawn by the Court between statute law, treaty law, and policy. It also appears that the Secretary of State could have done more to address non-CO_2 emissions as part of his relevant considerations. An advance leak of the Supreme Court judgment in draft form by an activist environmental barrister is also discussed, which resulted in the barrister coming before the Supreme Court again after the case had been concluded, where he was held in contempt.[94]

The *Urgenda Case* is examined next in Chapter 3,[95] involving the Supreme Court of the Netherlands: *State of the Netherlands v Urgenda Foundation* (2019).[96] This is the most renowned and influential landmark case in climate law to have arisen to date. It involved the efforts of Dutch NGO the Urgenda Foundation and almost 900 Dutch citizens participating as co-plaintiffs to compel the Dutch Government to reduce national greenhouse gas emissions by a minimum of 25 per cent below 1990 levels by 2020. In 2019 the Dutch Supreme Court ruled in favour of the plaintiffs, ordering the government to increase its lower reduction ambitions to the 25 per cent minimum level advocated by the plaintiffs, with the minimum reductions to be achieved by the end of 2020 at the latest. This major ruling was the first successful climate case of its kind.

At the District Court where the case was first heard, and where the plaintiffs had also been successful, the lower court's reasoning had been based primarily on the Dutch tort of hazardous state negligence.[97] This ruling had been appealed to the Court of Appeal, which had also ruled in the plaintiffs' favour, but in doing so it

[94] *Her Majesty's Attorney General v Crosland* [2021] UKSC 15.

[95] See ch 3.

[96] *State of the Netherlands v Urgenda Foundation*, ECLI:NL:HR:2019:2006 (English translation ECLI:NL:HR:2019:2007), Judgment (Sup Ct Neth, 20 December 2019) (Neth).

[97] *Urgenda Foundation v The State of the Netherlands*, ECLI:NL:RBDHA:2015:7145 (English translation ECLI:NL:RBDHA:2015:7196), Judgment (Dist Ct, The Hague, 24 June 2015) (Neth).

had also applied Articles 2 and 8 of the European Convention on Human Rights.[98] Here, the Court of Appeal afforded climate protections by applying Article 2 (the right to life) and Article 8 (the right to private and family life) of the Convention. This connection of climate change to human rights law and its application to the Government's obligations was followed by the Supreme Court.

Among other elements, Chapter 3 considers the extent to which the *Urgenda* case, and its approach to the European Convention on Human Rights in particular, might extrapolate to, or influence, climate litigation in other countries. Particular attention is accorded to the Supreme Court's integration into its reasoning of the United Nations Framework Convention on Climate Change and international scientific standards, as embodied by the major scientific reports of the Intergovernmental Panel on Climate Change. This element of the case may provide inspiration and guidance for climate litigation in other jurisdictions. Yet it is also seen that arguable difficulties underlie aspects of the Court's reasoning in this area. Indeed, it is pointed out that the international standards that the Court works to are arguably dated by 2019, and, if anything, might have compelled the application of a higher minimum reduction figure than 25 per cent for 2020 if the Court had been in a position and was willing to factor more recent developments in directly.

Arguable tensions arising between the Supreme Court's domestic reasoning and aspects of EU climate law are also pointed out, as is a missed opportunity for the plaintiffs to have pushed for a minimum reduction greater than 25 per cent via the framing of the appeal (they had done so at the District Court). Tensions between the separation of powers between the courts, the executive and parliament also arise and are explored. Commentary in the abundant literature generated by the case is also addressed, and the question of what the Supreme Court's new self-declared facility to apply national mitigation targets based in part on international and scientific standards means for the Netherlands going forward is raised as a point of interest.

Chapter 4 moves the focus of attention to the Global South and Latin America,[99] with consideration of the *Colombian Amazon Case*: *Andrea Lozano Barragán et al v Presidencia de la República et al* (2018).[100] This case came before the Supreme Court of Justice of Colombia and involved a challenge to negative climate impacts occasioned by the ongoing deforestation of Colombia's Amazon rainforest. A total of 25 plaintiffs aged between 7 and 25 sought a court order compelling the Government to fulfil existing national and international climate mitigation and deforestation reduction commitments. The case was brought against a number of governmental actors, including the President of Colombia, and the NGO Dejusticia provided support to the plaintiffs over the duration of the

[98] *State of the Netherlands v Urgenda Foundation*, ECLI:NL:GHDHA:2018:2591 (English translation ECLI:NL:GHDHA:2018:2610), Judgment (Ct App The Hague, 9 October 2018) (Neth).

[99] See ch 4.

[100] *Andrea Lozano Barragán et al v Presidencia de la República et al*, Sentencia de la Corte Suprema de Justicia del 5 de Abril de 2018, MP Luis Armando Tolosa Villabona, STC4360-2018 (Colom).

action. The judgment was handed down in 2018 in favour of the plaintiffs. Given that climate harm occasioned by deforestation sat at the heart of the of the case, a significant point that the Court was required to determine was whether a sufficient causal link between climate change and the progressive unlawful reduction of the Amazon existed. It found clearly in the affirmative.

Chapter 4 accords significant attention to the type of action at issue, called an *acción de tutela*, which the Court partly expanded in this ruling. A *tutela* involves judicial review in the interests of fundamental rights protection, and technical points including the Court's approach to fundamental and individual rights are examined. The Supreme Court also affords recognition to the intrinsic value of nature, and interprets the Amazon rainforest itself as being possessed of rights. The ruling contributes to the development of a rich strand of eco-centric jurisprudential philosophy and doctrine in Colombia, which is outlined and considered. This emerging eco-jurisprudential heritage is traced through the Colombian Constitution,[101] the green jurisprudence of the Constitutional Court (most particularly the *Tierra Digna* case)[102] and the jurisprudence of the Supreme Court (culminating in the *Colombian Amazon Case* itself). The principle of intergenerational equity also features prominently in the ruling, and the Court's reasoning in relation to present, future and unborn generations is considered. It is submitted that greater clarity would be helpful from the Court regarding its doctrinal position on unborn future generations.

The orders issued by the Supreme Court are also discussed, which are extremely robust and extensive in comparison to more typical orders arising in climate litigation judgments. In addition to ordering governmental actors to create and implement plans to counteract the rate of deforestation in the Amazon and associated climate impacts, a range of other directions are issued, including an order for the Government and other relevant parties to produce and implement an *Intergenerational Pact for the Life of the Colombian Amazon* within a specified timeframe. The analysis highlights research that has been conducted on the implementation of the orders, which finds that progress has been made, but that more remains to be done.

Chapter 5 moves to Africa and hones in on Nigeria,[103] where the *Oil Pollution Watch* case is examined: *Centre for Oil Pollution Watch v Nigerian National Petroleum Corporation* (2018).[104] This ruling by the Supreme Court of Nigeria is not an explicit example of landmark climate litigation in the way that the other case studies in this volume are, but it is of major importance for climate litigation due to its substantial widening of the standing rules that permit climate-focused cases

[101] Political Constitution of Colombia 1991.

[102] *Tierra Digna v Presidencia de la República y otros*, del 10 de Noviembre del 2016, sentencia de la Corte Constitucional de Colombia, T-622 del 2016.

[103] See ch 5.

[104] *Centre for Oil Pollution Watch v Nigerian National Petroleum Corporation* [2019] 5 NWLR (Pt 1666) 518.

(and other environmental damage cases) to be brought to court in Nigeria. Climate change is engaged in the judgment, but the central issue concerns environmental damage resulting from extensive and prolonged spillage from a ruptured oil pipeline in an area of Abia State. Oil from this spillage was discharged into streams and the surrounding environment over an extended period, and when it was finally contained, the contamination that remained was not adequately remediated.

The litigation was initiated by an NGO, the Centre for Oil Pollution Watch, on behalf of the affected communities. It sought reinstatement, restoration and remediation of the contaminated environment, and the provision of fresh water and medical facilities for those impacted. The respondent was the Nigerian National Petroleum Corporation, which operates oil installations and infrastructure across Nigeria. As examined in Chapter 5, the key legal element of the case turned on the issue of locus standi, that is, the question of whether the NGO had the standing or ability to bring a lawsuit of this kind before the courts. The Federal High Court[105] and the Court of Appeal[106] had found that the Centre for Oil Pollution Watch did not have the requisite standing to bring the case; however, the Supreme Court overturned these decisions in 2018. In doing so, the Supreme Court actively and carefully expanded of the scope of locus standi in Nigeria.

The ruling has paved a way for climate litigation to be brought by NGOs and others acting in the public interest that would otherwise have been precluded. Chapter 5 highlights that the opinion of Justice Aka'ahs connects the major environmental problems posed by climate change to the legal imperative of recognising the entitlement of environmental NGOs and public spirited individuals to bring public interest litigation.[107] It is notable that the Supreme Court initiated this liberalisation of the traditional rules on locus standi without any statutory enactment, and the case is seen to highlight the power of courts to produce important and far-reaching determinations that can facilitate (or constrain) climate litigation practices and outcomes.

Chapter 6 moves to Australia,[108] for examination of the *Gloucester Resources Case*: *Gloucester Resources Limited v Minister for Planning* (2019).[109] This case came before the New South Wales Land and Environment Court, in the Australian state of New South Wales, and the Court's decision was issued in 2019. The inclusion of this important climate case as a case study takes a liberal approach to this volume's guideline selection criteria, where chapters are chosen 'on the basis of being the first major breakthrough climate law cases in the jurisdictions engaged to … a) reach the highest courts in the land'.[110] The Land and Environment Court

[105] Federal High Court, Lagos.
[106] *Centre for Oil Pollution Watch v Nigerian National Petroleum Corporation* [2013] 15 NWLR 556.
[107] *Centre for Oil Pollution Watch v Nigerian National Petroleum Corporation* [2019] 5 NWLR (Pt 1666) 518, 577–81 (Aka'ahs, JSC).
[108] See ch 6.
[109] *Gloucester Resources Ltd v Minister for Planning* [2019] NSWLEC 7.
[110] Quoting from the text given in section II above.

is a powerful court within the hierarchy of the New South Wales court system, equivalent to the Supreme Court in a case of this kind, and so it is the highest court in the jurisdiction. Technically, however, the highest court in Australia as a whole is the High Court of Australia.

The case involved an application for consent to construct an open-cut coal mine. The mine was expected to result in the production of 21 million tonnes of coal over 16 years, and was anticipated to generate high levels of greenhouse gas emissions via the construction and operation of the mine and the combustion by other parties of the coal that it would produce. The Minister for Planning had refused to grant development consent on grounds unrelated to climate change. This refusal was appealed by the applicant, Gloucester Resources Limited, to the Land and Environment Court. This court upheld the Minister's refusal, but based its own refusal on the project's anticipated negative contribution to anthropogenic climate change, in concert with a number of other prohibitive factors.

Climate considerations form an extensive and detailed portion of the judgment, where many significant issues are addressed. These include argumentation advanced by Gloucester Resources Limited engaging *carbon leakage*, *market substitution* and a range of other points of technical importance that are examined in the chapter. The Court's treatment of 'greenhouse gas emissions' is also explored, where a *causal link* is identified between the proposed development's projected emissions and climate change, and the significance of the project's individual contribution to cumulative atmospheric emissions is addressed. It is seen that greenhouse gas emissions are broken down into *Scope 1*, *Scope 2* and *Scope 3* emissions in an influential way by the Court in its reasoning. The notion of *ecologically sustainable development* also receives significant integration. Chapter 6 also discusses the influence of the United Nations Framework Convention on Climate Change and the Paris Agreement, as well as the Court's consideration of the concept of a *global carbon budget*. The notion of 'public interest' and a range of other socio-cultural and economic considerations that arise are also addressed. This includes interesting reference to *solastalgia* (a type of place-based distress that can arise as a consequence of environmental change), *distributive inequity* and other points of note.[111]

Chapter 7, the final case study chapter,[112] is devoted to the Irish case *Climate Case Ireland: Friends of the Irish Environment v Government of Ireland* (2020).[113] Here, a legal challenge was brought by environmental NGO Friends of Irish Environment against the Government of Ireland. It was argued before the Supreme

[111] For a subsequent example of a prominent climate case in Australia, see *Minister for the Environment v Sharma* [2022] FCAFC 35. Here, the lower courts had held that a duty of care in negligence was owed by the federal Environment Minister to protect young persons from harms related to climate change when utilising certain powers, and the Federal Court of Australia overturned this. For the Federal Court first instance decision, see *Sharma and Others (by Their Litigation Representative Sister Arthur) v Minister for the Environment* [2021] FCA 560.

[112] See ch 7.

[113] *Friends of the Irish Environment v Government of Ireland* [2020] IESC 49.

Court of Ireland that the Government's 2017 *National Mitigation Plan*[114] that had been adopted under Ireland's national Climate Change Act[115] was invalid. The Irish Government was required to produce a plan of this kind on a rolling basis within five-year periods for the purpose of 'enabling the State to pursue, and achieve, the transition to a low carbon, climate resilient and environmentally sustainable economy by the end of the year 2050'.[116] In 2020, the Supreme Court ruled against the Government and quashed this *National Mitigation Plan*. It is clarified in the chapter that the Irish Climate Change Act mandating these plans was passed in 2015 and has since been amended significantly in 2021, after the 2020 ruling. The amended version of the Act is similar in spirit and substance to the original, such that the Supreme Court judgment continues to assist in the interpretation of important aspects of Ireland's current domestic framework.

In ruling in favour of Friends of the Irish Environment, the Supreme Court held that the Government's *Plan* did not adequately explain how the Government intended to meet the 2050 national transition objective quoted above. This was in breach of the relevant legislation, which required the Government to 'specify' such detail. This meant in turn that the reasonable and interested observer would be unable to know how the Government intended to achieve its statutory 2050 objective. The Court duly quashed the *Plan*, and the Government was required to produce a new one (which was to be wholly new rather than a republished version of the current *Plan* with some minor adjustments).

As explored in the chapter, the Court provides a good deal of consideration of rolling climate policy plans, discussing their conception, form and content, and including discussion of the extent to which such policy documents might be expected to provide policy specificity into the future where a long-term transition objective is relevant (here, pegged to the date 2050). The chapter also addresses efforts by Friends of the Irish Environment to rely on constitutional and human rights law, which proved unsuccessful. Detailed commentary provided by the Supreme Court on whether or not a constitutional right to a healthy environment can be said to be derived from the Irish Constitution is also engaged. Such a right had previously been accepted by the lower courts,[117] but the Supreme Court rejected this. Elements of the rationale underlying this aspect of the judgment are criticised.

[114] Department of the Environment, Climate and Communications, *National Mitigation Plan* (2017).
[115] Climate Action and Low Carbon Development Act 2015.
[116] ibid s 3(1).
[117] *Friends of the Irish Environment v Fingal County Council* [2017] IEHC 695.

2

The UK

The Heathrow Runway Case

> An expansion of airport capacity in the South East would involve a substantial increase in CO_2 emissions from the increased number of flights which would take place as a result. The proposals for such expansion have therefore given rise to a considerable degree of concern as to the environmental impact it would be likely to have on global warming and climate change … At the heart of the challenge … is the Paris Agreement … which acknowledged that climate change represents 'an urgent and potentially irreversible threat to human societies and the planet.
>
> *Heathrow Runway Case*, UK Supreme Court, paragraphs 8 and 70

I. Emerging Legal Issues and Themes Prior to the Case

In the UK, the first landmark climate case to reach the country's highest court – the UK Supreme Court – has been *R (on the Application of Friends of the Earth Ltd and Others) v Heathrow Airport Ltd* (2020), often described as the *Heathrow Runway Case*.[1] By this time in 2020, the UK had already started to develop a significant seam of overtly climate-oriented case law, due in part to the influence of the UK's Climate Change Act 2008. In passing the 2008 Act, the UK Parliament was the first national parliament in the world to apply economy-wide long-term legally binding national emissions reduction targets to its country in law.[2] The duty to achieve the targets was placed on the Secretary of State, a senior member of the UK Government.[3] This pioneering example of 'national framework climate legislation'[4] had exerted an influence on the 2010 ruling *R (on the Application of London Borough of Hillingdon and Others) v Secretary of State for Transport*

[1] *R (on the Application of Friends of the Earth Ltd and Others) v Heathrow Airport Ltd* [2020] UKSC 52. Hereafter cited as 'Judgment'.

[2] Thomas L Muinzer, *Climate and Energy Governance for the UK Low Carbon Transition: The Climate Change Act 2008* (Palgrave Macmillan, 2019).

[3] Climate Change Act 2008, ss 1(1), 4(1)(b), 5(1)(a).

[4] Thomas L Muinzer, 'What are National "Climate Change Acts"?' (2021) 39(4) *Journal of Energy & Natural Resources Law* 419–38.

(hereafter the '*Hillingdon Case*'),[5] doing so in a way that prefigured certain themes that would arise in the *Heathrow Runway Case* some years later.

The *Hillingdon Case* concerned the UK Government providing support for planning permission to develop a third airport runway at Heathrow Airport in England. Heathrow expansion has been a controversial and contested issue in the UK for many years. In her book on the subject, journalist Celeste Hicks writes that 'Heathrow expansion has been like a zombie. On several occasions since the 2000s the idea has raised its head, been beaten down and apparently killed off, only to resurface in a different form a few years later'.[6] In the *Hillingdon Case*, the Secretary of State had indicated in 2003 in a policy document that if certain specified conditions could be met, the Government could support the development of a third runway.[7] The Secretary of State went on to declare that the conditions could be satisfied, but by this time the Climate Change Act 2008 had been passed and it was argued at the Administrative Court that the Secretary of State was in error.[8] Climate change considerations had been incorporated into the 2003 conditions that the Government had outlined, and the court held that those conditions that the Secretary of State was basing his runway support on would need to be reviewed in light of the subsequent Climate Change Act 2008 developments in order for support for a third runway development to be valid.[9]

The UK's Climate Change Act 2008 applies a Net Zero target for 2050, meaning that emissions of UK greenhouse gases governed by the 2008 Act need to be reduced by 100 per cent from 1990 emissions levels by 2050.[10] This figure originally sat at an 80 per cent reduction on 1990 levels for 2050, until it was amended upwards to a 100 per cent reduction in 2019.[11] The 2008 Act does not include emissions from international aviation within the UK Net Zero target directly at the time of writing;[12] however, the UK Government does report on these emissions and take them into account.[13] The UK Government has also endeavoured to leave headroom in carbon budgets to incorporate aviation emissions.[14] Prior to

[5] *London Borough of Hillingdon and Others, R (on the Application of) v Secretary of State for Transport and Another* [2010] EWHC 626 (Admin) (26 March 2010).

[6] Celeste Hicks, *Expansion Rebellion* (Manchester University Press, 2022) 4–5.

[7] Department for Transport, *The Future of Air Transport* (UK Government, 2003). This is a 'White Paper', that is, a type of formal policy document produced by the UK Government.

[8] *Hillingdon Case* (n 5).

[9] The court held that a National Policy Statement on airports that was due to be produced under s 5 of the Planning Act 2008 in this period would involve a review of the relevant matters, including climate change issues, and that the Secretary of State could not limit the debate on climate change in the meantime. For further detail and comment on the *Hillingdon Case* in the context of airport expansion litigation, see Richard Burnett-Hall and Brian Jones, *Burnett–Hall on Environmental Law*, 3rd edn (Sweet & Maxwell, 2012), paras [7-046]–[7-048].

[10] Climate Change Act 2008, s 1(1).

[11] Climate Change Act 2008 (2050 Target Amendment) Order 2019.

[12] Climate Change Act 2008, s 30.

[13] ibid ss 30 and 10(2)(i).

[14] On this approach in relation to s 30 of the Climate Change Act 2008, see 'Government's Decision with Respect to Section 30 of the Act' in *International Aviation and Shipping Emissions and the UK's Carbon Budgets and 2050 Target* (UK Government, 2012) 11–12 at para [6].

the 2008 Act's 2019 amendment, the environmental charity Plan B Earth endeavoured to argue in the courts that the Secretary of State in the UK Government had a legal obligation to amend the 80 per cent figure upwards.[15] This was in large part because the UK had now become a signatory to the 2015 Paris Agreement since the original 80 per cent figure was set.[16] The Paris Agreement, informed by important developments in scientific understanding that also post-dated the 2008 Act, called for a strengthening of climate mitigation objectives. The 2008 Act's original reductions had been calculated based on the scientific understanding that it was necessary to keep average global warming to 2°C maximum over pre-industrial levels, but the subsequent Paris Agreement, in alignment with the most current consensus scientific understandings of the problem, now asserted that the UK and other signatories must pursue efforts to keep average global warming to 1.5°C maximum above pre-industrial levels.[17]

Thus, in *R (Plan B Earth and Others) v Secretary of State for Business, Energy and Industrial Strategy*,[18] an application was made to the Administrative Court for permission to bring a judicial review action against the Secretary of State. Permission to proceed to judicial review was refused on two occasions due to a lack of foreseeable success,[19] and permission to appeal this was also refused.[20] As Paterson and the author have noted, this refusal was unsurprising.[21] The UK Climate Change Act 2008 does enable the Secretary of State to utilise 2050 target amendment powers where 'it appears to the Secretary of State that … significant developments in scientific knowledge about climate change, or … international law or policy' have taken place;[22] however, the Secretary of State's power to amend the 2050 target is expressed in *discretionary* rather than mandatory terms, and as such the courts' refusal of permission to proceed to judicial review was unsurprising.[23]

[15] *Plan B Earth and Others, R (on the Application of) v Secretary of State for Business, Energy and Industrial Strategy* [2018] EWHC 1892 (Admin) (20 July 2018). Plan B Earth, joined by a number of private citizen claimants, argued that the failure to amend the target was ultra vires, based on an error of law, irrational, in violation of elements of human rights law and in breach of s 149 of the UK's Equality Act 2010.

[16] UNFCCC, *Adoption of the Paris Agreement*, Report No FCCC/CP/2015/L.9/Rev.1. The UK ratified the Paris Agreement in 2016.

[17] Paris Agreement, art 2(1)(a): 'This Agreement … aims to strengthen the global response to the threat of climate change … by [h]olding the increase in the global average temperature to well below 2°C above pre-industrial levels and pursuing efforts to limit the temperature increase to 1.5°C above pre-industrial levels.'

[18] *Plan B Earth and Others* (n 15).

[19] *Plan B Earth and Others v Secretary of State for Business, Energy and Industrial Strategy*, 14 February 2018, CO/16/18; *Plan B Earth and Others v Secretary of State for Business, Energy and Industrial Strategy*, 20 July 2018, CO/16/18.

[20] Court of Appeal, Civil Division, *Plan B Earth and Others v Secretary of State for Business, Energy and Industrial Strategy*, 25 January 2019, C1/2018/1750.

[21] Thomas L Muinzer and John B Paterson, 'La Ley de Cambio Climático y Energía en Reino Unido' ('The Law of Climate Change and Energy in the United Kingdom') in José Francisco Alenza García and Lorenzo Mellado Ruiz (eds), *Estudios Sobre Cambio Climático y Transición Energética* (*Studies on Climate Change and Energy Transition*) (Marcial Pons, 2022) 743–60, 754 (in Spanish).

[22] Climate Change Act 2008, s 2(2)(a)(i)–(ii).

[23] Muinzer and Paterson (n 21) 754.

It is also notable that, where the Secretary of State *does* order an amendment, that order still requires the approval of the UK Parliament.[24]

Yet, taken more broadly, the case does seem to have had a positive impact in terms of encouraging the Secretary of State's subsequent amendment of the 2050 target from 80 per cent to Net Zero in 2019.[25] During the period of the Plan B Earth judicial review applications, the Secretary of State requested advice regarding the viability of an increase in ambition to Net Zero from the UK Government's independent advisory body, the Committee on Climate Change (CCC).[26] The CCC released its reply in the form of a major report entitled *Net Zero – The UK's Contribution to Stopping Global Warming*.[27] Appearing in May 2019, a day after the UK Parliament passed a motion declaring a climate and environmental emergency (1 May 2019), the report recommended an increase of the 2050 target to Net Zero, and these recommendations were followed by the Secretary of State, resulting in the amendment of the Climate Change Act 2008.[28]

The most successful case to date at the time of writing in terms of a positive and substantial outcome for environmental NGOs in the UK is the 2022 case *R (on the Application of Friends of the Earth Ltd) v Secretary of State for Business, Energy and Industrial Strategy*.[29] The case was brought by Friends of the Earth, ClientEarth and the Good Law Project, and involved the UK Government's *Net Zero Strategy*.[30] Here, the High Court ruled that the Secretary of State had failed to comply with obligations under sections 13 and 14 of the Climate Change Act 2008,. It found that the strategy issued by the Government did not explain how the Government's proposals and policies would meet the UK's emissions targets,[31] and that the Secretary of State had made relevant decisions without being appraised of the adequate information needed to do so.[32] The court thus ordered that the strategy had to be suitably updated by the Government within eight months. The case bears some resemblance to the quashing of the Irish Government's mitigation plan in *Climate Case Ireland*.[33] It can be interpreted as a 'landmark' UK court ruling in its own right; however, the landmark *Heathrow Runway Case* preceded the *Net Zero Strategy* case, and in a sense cleared the way for it. The *Heathrow Runway Case* was also subject to more contestation, twists and turns within the UK court

[24] Climate Change Act 2009, s 2(6).

[25] Richard Macrory and Thomas L Muinzer, 'The UK's Climate Change Act', in Thomas L Muinzer (ed), *National Climate Change Acts: The Emergence, Form and Nature of National Framework Climate Legislation* (Hart Publishing, 2021), ch 3, 69–92, 86.

[26] 15 October 2018, via a publicly available formal letter to the CCC.

[27] Committee on Climate Change, *Net Zero – The UK's Contribution to Stopping Global Warming* (2019).

[28] Climate Change Act 2008 (2050 Target Amendment) Order 2019.

[29] *R (on the Application of Friends of the Earth Ltd) v Secretary of State for Business, Energy and Industrial Strategy* [2022] EWHC 1841 (Admin).

[30] *Net Zero Strategy: Build Back Greener* (UK Government, 2021).

[31] Climate Change Act 2008, s 14.

[32] ibid s 13.

[33] See ch 7.

system, and, unlike the *Heathrow Runway Case*, the *Net Zero Strategy* case did not make it to the Supreme Court.

II. The Supreme Court and Lower Courts

The *Heathrow Runway Case* was adjudicated at the UK's Supreme Court by Lord Reed (President of the Supreme Court), Lord Hodge (Deputy President), Lady Black, Lord Sales and Lord Leggatt. It was heard on 7 and 8 October 2020, and judgment was given on 16 December 2020. The appellant in the case was Heathrow Airport Ltd, the owner of the airport that was promoting the third runway development. Respondents in the case were Friends of the Earth and Plan B Earth.[34] The judgment was delivered jointly by Lord Hodge and Lord Sales, with Lord Reed, Lady Black and Lord Leggatt agreeing with them, such that the decision was unanimous. Bell and Fisher have highlighted the importance of the case: 'as the first time the UK Supreme Court has engaged directly with the legally disruptive nature of climate change, *Heathrow* warrants reflective scrutiny'.[35]

The case involved a finding from an independent commission that was established in 2012 to consider possible airport expansion options in the south-east of England,[36] with the commission concluding that additional runway expansion at Heathrow Airport would be an appropriate way to cater to air travel demand and foster the national economy.[37] The UK Government accepted the general case made by the commission,[38] and announced that the option of building an additional runway at Heathrow was the Government's preferred course.[39] The Government announced that it would use a policy framework statement document, called a *National Planning Statement*, to establish the framework for the consideration of applications by developers.[40] The Government's power to issue such statements was enabled under the Planning Act 2008.[41] The final version of the *Airports National Policy Statement* (*ANPS*) was laid before the UK Parliament by the Secretary of State on 5 June 2018.[42] It was approved by the Parliament by a large majority (415 votes to 119) on 25 June 2018,[43] and was designated as national

[34] The Supreme Court summarises that 'FoE is a non-governmental organisation concerned with climate change. Plan B Earth is a charity concerned with climate change'. Judgment (n 1) para [14].

[35] Joanna Bell and Elizabeth Fisher, 'The Heathrow Case in the Supreme Court: Climate Change Legislation and Administrative Adjudication' (2023) 86(1) *Modern Law Review* 226–37, 227.

[36] The Airports Commission, chaired by Sir Howard Davies.

[37] Judgment (n 1) paras [3]–[4].

[38] ibid para [5].

[39] ibid para [9]. Alternative options identified by the Airports Commission as credible but ultimately less preferable included extending the existing northern runway at Heathrow and building a new runway at Gatwick Airport.

[40] ibid para [5].

[41] Planning Act 2008, s 5.

[42] Department for Transport, *Airports National Policy Statement* (UK Government, 2018).

[43] Judgment (n 1) para [11].

policy by the Secretary of State the next day via section 5(1) of the Planning Act 2008. Over the course of its judgment, the Supreme Court points out that an 'expansion of airport capacity … would involve a substantial increase in CO_2 emissions from the increased number of flights which would take place as a result',[44] and notes that the 'proposals for such expansion have therefore given rise to a considerable degree of concern as to the environmental impact it would be likely to have on global warming and climate change'.[45]

Prior to the appeal reaching the Supreme Court, the case had proceeded through the Divisional Court and the Court of Appeal. Hawkins has characterised the lively initial phase at the Divisional Court as follows:

> In 2019, a rollercoaster of a judicial review process began: four claims were dealt with in a rolled-up hearing during which ten claimants raised a total of 22 grounds of challenge in relation to the designation of the ANPS (and the favouring of the Heathrow third runway). None of these grounds were successful at the [Divisional] Court.[46]

In a dramatic ruling, the Court of Appeal went on to hold that the Secretary of State's decision in June 2018 to support the development of a new runway at Heathrow Airport via the *ANPS* was unlawful: see *R (on the Application of Plan B Earth) v Secretary of State for Transport*.[47] In doing so, the Court of Appeal reversed the decision of the Divisional Court that first heard the case.[48] As will be seen below, the Court of Appeal's ruling was reversed in turn by the Supreme Court.[49]

In contrast to the Divisional Court, the Court of Appeal held that the UK Government had not taken the Paris Agreement into account when it was obligated to do so because its commitment to the Paris Agreement amounted to a policy consideration within the scope of the Planning Act 2008 that the Government was required to take into account.[50] Similarly, in neglecting the relevance of the Paris Agreement, the Court of Appeal held that the Government had failed to take account of a necessary material consideration under the Planning Act 2008.[51]

[44] ibid para [8].

[45] ibid.

[46] Joanne Hawkins, 'A Lesson in Un-creativity: (*R (on the Application of Friends of the Earth Ltd and Others) v Heathrow Airport Ltd* [2020] UKSC 52' (2021) 23(4) *Environmental Law Review* 344–349, 345.

[47] *R (on the Application of Plan B Earth) v Secretary of State for Transport* [2020] EWCA Civ 214 (27 February 2020).

[48] For the original ruling at first instance, see *R (on the Application of Spurrier) v Secretary of State for Transport* [2019] EWHC 1070 (Admin).

[49] For a detailed and thought-provoking consideration of the Court of Appeal case that benefits from being produced prior to the Supreme Court ruling, and is thus able to dive into the judgment in isolation without being diverted by the Supreme Court developments, see Joanna Bell and Elizabeth Fisher, 'The "Heathrow" Case: Polycentricity, Legislation, and the Standard of Review' (2020) 83(5) *Modern Law Review* 1072–85.

[50] *Plan B Earth v Secretary of State for Transport* (n 47).

[51] ibid paras [234]–[238]. After the Court of Appeal decision, Gordhan commented in the *Journal of Environmental Law* that it was 'particularly notable' in being 'the first time that a UK Court has identified the direct applicability of the Paris Agreement, an unincorporated treaty, to the climate change provisions of the Planning Act 2008. Given the Court's relatively brief reasoning on this issue, Supreme

These technical elements will be outlined and considered below, in the context of the Supreme Court's treatment of the law.

While the Court of Appeal ruling might be seen as somewhat radical,[52] this should not be overstated, not least given that the court was dealing with *procedural* elements of law; the Court did not, for example, overturn the Government's *substantive* support for runway expansion at Heathrow. Thus, in juxtaposing the ruling with the *Urgenda* case,[53] Heyvaert comments that the Court of Appeal decision 'stands as a beacon of hope in perilous times, and the desire to celebrate it as a game-changing silver bullet is deeply understandable';[54] however, it 'is far more judicially conservative, and much more deferential to executive discretion [than the *Urgenda* ruling]. It is, by no stretch of the imagination, an activist judgment'.[55] The *Heathrow Runway Case*, then, has a relatively sharp procedural focus that is not preoccupied with the substantive aspect of Heathrow runway expansion,[56] and it is significant that this procedural framing sets the focus across all of the relevant hearings and judgments, from the Supreme Court downwards. As Adelmant et al note, 'the concern is … whether the policy documents comply with the appropriate process'.[57] The case was appealed to the Supreme Court by Heathrow Runway Ltd, but not by the Secretary of State.[58] The Supreme Court noted that Heathrow Airport Ltd 'has already invested large sums of money in promoting the … [s]cheme and wishes to carry it through by applying for a DCO [ie, a Development Consent Order] in due course and then building the proposed new runway'.[59]

III. Issues and Outcomes

The Supreme Court case divides into five grounds of appeal, (i)–(v); however, it was not necessary for the Supreme Court to consider ground (v) in the end,

Court consideration of this important issue in environmental law would be welcome'. See Sonam Gordhan, '*Plan B Earth v Secretary of State for Transport*: Airport Expansion, the Paris Agreement and the Planning Act 2008' (2020) 32(3) *Journal of Environmental Law* 559–75, 573. As noted above, the Supreme Court went on to reverse this decision.

52 David Campbell, 'Temperature Tantrum' (2021) 137 *Law Quarterly Review* 380–84.

53 *State of the Netherlands v Urgenda Foundation*, ECLI:NL:HR:2019:2006 (English translation ECLI:NL:HR:2019:2007), Judgment (Sup Ct Neth 20 December 2019) (Neth); see also ch 3 in this volume.

54 Veerle Heyvaert, 'Beware of Populist Narratives: The Importance of Getting the Heathrow Ruling Right', *British Policy and Politics at LSE*, 1–3, 1, http://eprints.lse.ac.uk/104190/1/politicsandpolicy_getting_the_heathrow_judgment.pdf.

55 ibid 3.

56 In addition to the contrast drawn above by Heyvaert between this case and *Urgenda*, its procedural focus can also be contrasted with the substantive focus of the Land and Environment Court in the *Gloucester Resources Case* considered in this volume: see ch 6.

57 Victoria Adelmant, Philip Alston and Matthew Blainey, 'Human Rights and Climate Change Litigation: One Step Forward, Two Steps Backwards in the Irish Supreme Court' (2021) 13(1) *Journal of Human Rights Practice* 1–23, 14.

58 Judgment (n 1) para [17].

59 ibid para [17].

because this concerned the issue of whether the Court of Appeal should have granted the relief that it did. In what has been described as a 'disappointing blow to environmentalists,'[60] the Supreme Court overturned the Court of Appeal across grounds (i)–(iv), so the matter of relief was no longer relevant. These four grounds of appeal engaged the following: *ground (i)* concerned the interpretation of section 5 of the Planning Act 2008; *ground (ii)* concerned the application of section 10 of the Planning Act 2008; *ground (iii)* concerned obligations under the EU's Strategic Environmental Assessment Directive and associated Regulations implementing that Directive in the UK; *ground (iv)* engaged additional matters pertaining to section 10 of the Planning Act 2008.

The UK's Planning Act 2008 and Climate Change Act 2008, which were enacted by the UK Parliament on the same day, are important to the case, as is the international Paris Agreement. In summarising key aims of the Planning Act 2008, Bell and Fisher note:

> The PA 2008 is an ambitious legislative scheme … Its main aim was to introduce a novel two-stage procedure – involving the designation of National Policy Statements (NPS) followed by the grant of Development Consent Orders (DCO) – to streamline decision-making about nationally significant infrastructure projects.[61]

The Planning Act 2008 ensures that, where the UK Government is producing a National Policy Statement (NPS),[62] it is required to 'include an explanation of how the policy set out in the statement takes account of Government policy relating to the mitigation of, and adaptation to, climate change' (section 5(8) of the Planning Act 2008).[63] The UK Government is also required to 'have regard to the desirability of mitigating, and adapting to, climate change'(section 10(3)(a) of the Planning Act 2008).[64] In this case, in designating the *ANPS*, the UK Government had taken account of the Climate Change Act 2008, but it had not taken account of the Paris Agreement. Indeed, in the preparation stages, the UK Government had received legal advice expressly advising that it was not required to take the Paris Agreement into account directly in this context.[65] As outlined above, the Court of Appeal had held that the Paris Agreement amounted to a policy consideration and a necessary material consideration within the scope of the Planning Act 2008, and as such the UK Government was required to take it into account.[66] Therefore, a declaration

[60] Laura Hughes-Gerber, 'A Third Runway for Heathrow? To Build or Not to Build? A Brief Review of the Supreme Court's Recent Judgment' (2021) 46(2) *Air and Space Law* 309–14, 309.

[61] Bell and Fisher (n 35) 228–29.

[62] The Court of Appeal summarises this as follows: 'National policy statements are the statements of national planning policy for "nationally significant infrastructure projects" in England and Wales under the statutory regime in Parts 2 and 3 of the Planning Act.' *Plan B Earth v Secretary of State for Transport* (n 47) para [37].

[63] Planning Act 2008, s 5(8).

[64] ibid s 10(3)(a).

[65] *Plan B Earth v Secretary of State for Transport* (n 47) para [227].

[66] ibid.

that 'the *ANPS* has no legal effect unless and until the Secretary of State decides to conduct a review' had been issued by the Court of Appeal.[67]

The four grounds at issue in the case that have been noted above will be examined one by one below. First it will be useful to take a short look at the Planning Act 2008 in a little more detail, given its importance to the grounds. It will also be useful to acknowledge the role of Strategic Environmental Assessment (SEA) in the UK planning process, raised by *ground (iii)*.

A. The Planning Act 2008, SEA

As indicated above, the Planning Act 2008 establishes the UK development consent procedure for 'nationally significant infrastructure projects', including the airport-related development at issue in the case, with relevant functions being exercised by the Secretary of State. The content of an NPS is covered in section 5(5)–(8) of the Planning Act 2008,. Section 5(7)–(8) asserts that an NPS must 'give reasons for the policy set out in the statement'[68] and the 'reasons must (in particular) include an explanation of how the policy set out in the statement takes account of Government policy relating to the mitigation of, and adaptation to, climate change'.[69] Section 10, headed 'Sustainable development', asserts that:

> (1) This section applies to the Secretary of State's functions under sections 5 and 6.[70]
> (2) The Secretary of State must, in exercising those functions, do so with the objective of contributing to the achievement of sustainable development.
> (3) For the purposes of subsection (2) the Secretary of State must (in particular) have regard to the desirability of—
>
> (a) mitigating, and adapting to, climate change.[71]

The NPS, then, 'sets the policy framework within which any application for a DCO must be determined'.[72] Application for development consent is made to the Secretary of State.[73]

When the Secretary of State is producing a draft NPS an obligation also exists to carry out an SEA, with the requirement having originated in EU law[74] and having been transposed into UK law by domestic regulations.[75] This involves assessment of the environmental impact of plans and programmes. In this case, the *ANPS*

[67] ibid para [280].
[68] Planning Act 2008, s 5(7).
[69] ibid s 5(8).
[70] Section 6 of the Planning Act 2008 concerns the review of NPSs by the Secretary of State.
[71] ibid s 10(1)–(3).
[72] Judgment (n 1) para [31].
[73] Planning Act 2008, s 37.
[74] Directive 2001/42/EC (SEA Directive) of the European Parliament and of the Council of 27 June 2001 on the assessment of the effects of certain plans and programmes on the environment [2001] OJ L197/30.
[75] Environmental Assessment of Plans and Programmes Regulations 2004 (SI 2004/1633).

required strategic environmental assessment under the EU SEA Directive and the implementing Regulations. This involves, amongst other things, the production of an environmental report on the matter.[76] Article 5 of the Directive asserts that 'an environmental report shall be prepared in which the likely significant effects on the environment of implementing the plan or programme, and reasonable alternatives taking into account the objectives and the geographical scope of the plan or programme, are identified, described and evaluated'.[77] The perspective adopted by the British courts on SEA is that it is a relatively broad process and that an environmental report is produced as part of this broader process – ie, evaluation of an SEA is not purely reducible to the environmental report itself.[78] (The UK is no longer a member of the EU. The law is discussed in this chapter as it applied at the time of the case.)

B. Ground (i)

This ground appealed the following element of the Court of Appeal's decision:

> The Secretary of State breached his duty under section 5(8) of the PA 2008 to give an explanation of how the policy set out in the ANPS took account of Government policy, which was committed to implementing the emissions reductions targets in the Paris Agreement.[79]

Section 5 of the Planning Act 2008 is dealt with chiefly in paragraphs [101]–[113] of the judgment. As noted above, section 5(7)–(8) of the Planning Act 2008 asserts that the NPS is required to explain how it has 'take[n] account of Government policy relating to the mitigation of, and adaptation to, climate change',[80] and the Supreme Court differed from the Court of Appeal in its interpretation of this element. The Court of Appeal had understood commitment to the Paris Agreement to fall within the purview of the term 'Government policy' here, and thus held that it should have been taken into account in relation to the NPS. The Supreme Court emphasised that statements from Government ministers concerning adherence to the Paris Agreement were considered to be relevant to this line of reasoning by the Court of Appeal, in addition to the Government's adherence to the Paris Agreement as construed more narrowly through the UK's ratification of that agreement:

> The court [of appeal] held that section 5(8) of the PA 2008 simply required the Government to take into account its own policy. The statements of Andrea Leadsom MP and Amber Rudd MP in March 2016 … and the formal ratification of the Paris

[76] SEA Directive 2001/42/EC, art 2(b).

[77] ibid art 5(1).

[78] *Cogent Land LLP v Rochford District Council* [2012] EWHC 2542 (Admin); *No Adastral New Town Ltd v Suffolk Coastal District Council* [2015] EWCA Civ 88.

[79] Judgment (n 1) para [15].

[80] Planning Act 2008, s 5(8).

> Agreement showed [in the Court of Appeal's opinion] that the Government's commitment to the Paris Agreement was part of 'Government policy' by the time of the designation of the *ANPS* in June 2018.[81]

The Supreme Court did not accept this, applying a more restricted interpretation of 'Government policy' in the context of the 2008 statute:

> In our view the phrase is looking to carefully formulated written statements of policy such as one might find in an NPS, or in statements of national planning policy (such as the National Planning Policy Framework), or in government papers such as the Aviation Policy Framework.[82]

The Supreme Court outlined that this view makes logical sense in the context of UK political-legal culture and practice:

> For the subsection to operate sensibly the phrase needs to be given a relatively narrow meaning so that the relevant policies can readily be identified. Otherwise, civil servants would have to trawl through Hansard[83] and press statements to see if anything had been said by a minister which might be characterised as 'policy'. Parliament cannot have intended to create a bear trap for ministers by requiring them to take into account any ministerial statement which could as a matter of ordinary language be described as a statement of policy relating to the relevant field.[84]

The Supreme Court took the opportunity to underscore and reinforce criteria deriving from UK case law that assists in the interpretation of what does and does not qualify as 'policy': 'a statement qualifies as policy only if it is clear, unambiguous and devoid of relevant qualification'.[85]

This framing was linked to the examples of the statements from Andrea Leadsom MP and Amber Rudd MP noted above, which Plan B Earth had sought to rely on as evidence that the Paris Agreement amounted to 'Government policy'. The Supreme Court held that those statements, and statements like them, did not satisfy those criteria:

> Their statements were not clear and were not devoid of relevant qualification in this context. They did not refer to the [Paris Agreement] temperature targets at all and they both left open the question of how the Paris Agreement goal of net zero emissions would be enshrined in UK law.[86]

Thus, the Court clarified not only that 'the Paris Agreement itself is not Government policy', but that the sorts of statements made by Leadsom and Rudd do not amount to Government policy within the parameters of the Planning Act 2008 either.[87]

[81] Judgment (n 1) para [104].
[82] ibid para [105].
[83] Hansard is the official report and record of UK parliamentary debates.
[84] Judgment (n 1) para [105].
[85] See, eg, *Inland Revenue Commissioners v MFK Underwriting Agents Ltd* [1990] 1WLR 1545, 1569; *R (Gaines-Cooper) v Commissioners for Her Majesty's Revenue and Customs* [2011] UKSC 47, [2011] 1 WLR 2625, 28, 29, 70.
[86] Judgment (n 1) para [106].
[87] ibid para [112].

In reversing the Court of Appeal decision, the Supreme Court also emphasised that ratifying a treaty – here, the Paris Agreement – does not give rise to direct obligations within UK domestic law.[88] In the UK's dualist legal system, international law is not automatically binding by virtue of ratification, and domestic legislation is required if it is to be incorporated into the domestic legal order. Thus, the Court emphasised that: 'Ratification does not constitute a commitment operating on the plane of domestic law to perform obligations under the treaty.'[89] The Supreme Court's observations confirmed the Divisional Court's correct summary of the Paris Agreement's position in relation to UK law, where it lacks significant legal applicability because it is:

> [W]ell-established that English law is a dualist legal system under which international law or an international treaty has legal force at the domestic level only after it has been implemented by a national statute … Therefore, [since it has not] been incorporated [by a national statute], any obligation imposed on the UK Government by the Paris Agreement has no effect in domestic law.[90]

In the author's view, given the scale of the climate emergency and the importance of the Paris Agreement in tackling it, the Agreement should have a much stronger direct presence and applicability within the UK legal order; however, while this is *desirable*, it is true that it is not the case in actuality. The Supreme Court and Divisional Court's statement of the legal position is correct. As is so often the case in climate litigation, a correct statement of the legal position here is revealing of weaknesses inherent in international climate law.[91]

[88] ibid para [108]; *R (Miller) v Secretary of State for Exiting the European Union* [2017] UKSC 5, [2018] AC 61, para [55].

[89] Judgment (n 1) para [108].

[90] *Spurrier* (n 48) para [606]. See further: *JH Rayner (Mincing Lane) Ltd v Department of Trade and Industry* [1990] 2 AC 418, 500; *R v Secretary of State for the Home Department ex p Brind* (1991) 1 AC 696, 747 F–H. The Paris Agreement obligations permit states to determine their own Nationally Determined Contributions to emissions reduction, and its objectives are relatively generalised. The primacy of the UK's domestic political-legal order and the broad nature of the Paris obligations suggest that even if the Secretary of State *was* required to take the Paris Agreement directly into account in the manner envisaged by the Court of Appeal, he may not have had to act in accordance with it. The Court of Appeal appears to acknowledge this problem at *Plan B Earth v Secretary of State for Transport* (n 47) para [238]. Ghaleigh comments that: 'The Court of Appeal held that the Government erred by not taking the Paris Agreement and attendant policy explicitly into account. It was careful to make clear that the Secretary of State was not required to act in accordance with any particular policy, even the Government's own stated policy.' See Navraj Singh Ghaleigh, 'Climate Constitutionalism of the UK Supreme Court' (2021) 33(2) *Journal of Environmental Law* 441–47, 442.

[91] The Supreme Court also dispensed with last-ditch efforts from Plan B Earth to raise an argument under s 3 of the UK's Human Rights Act 1998 in relation to arts 2 and 8 of the European Convention on Human Rights, which are applied via this 1998 Act in the UK. The Supreme Court noted that an argument in this line had been raised before the Divisional Court and rejected by that court, had not been appealed to the Court of Appeal, and thus was not part of the formal considerations before the Supreme Court. The Supreme Court commented that if this line of argument had been raised credibly in relation to s 5(8) of the Planning Act 2008, it was the case that potential impact on the lives and family life of those affected by climate change would not stem from the *ANPS* designation itself, but rather, if such impacts could be said to arise, from the making of a Development Consent Order. This case was concerned with the *ANPS*, and no Development Consent Order had yet been issued, such that this line of argument would not have been successful. See further Judgment (n 1) para [113].

Paterson and the author have dealt with related matters arising here and have emphasised that a further issue is also at play, beyond a treaty's applicability in domestic law. This pertains to the fundamental legal distinction between *treaties* and *policies*, which are distinct phenomena in their own right. We have commented that:

> [I]t is questionable whether it is sensible and coherent to conflate 'Government policy' (s.5(8)) – which in a technical sense points to just that, *policy* – with an international treaty, which, in a technical sense, is just that (an international *treaty*). Thus, when the Court of Appeal … asserts that 'In our view, the Government's commitment to the Paris Agreement was clearly part of 'Government policy' by the time of the designation of the *ANPS*',[92] this is at best questionable.[93]

Regardless of a particular treaty's applicability, we find that it is unhelpful to muddy the distinction between *treaties* and *policies*, which are distinct things by definition. In summarising her impressions of the Court of Appeal's reasoning, Gordhan, drawing in part on the Court's phrasing, notes as follows: 'Regardless of the Paris Agreement's effect on the designation of the ANPS, the duty was to consider the UK's commitment to it as part of "Government policy" – which the Secretary of State had failed to do.'[94] This emphasises the subtle distinction of the *commitment* to the treaty amounting to a policy (rather than the treaty itself amounting to policy), but any treaty that is ratified is committed to in this sense, and the treaty–policy distinction seems too unclearly and unhelpfully drawn in the Court of Appeal's reasoning, sailing very close to the wind of merely conflating treaties and policies as being one in the same.

Paterson and the author note that Friends of the Earth, which had joined Plan B Earth on the appeal and was seeking to succeed against the Secretary of State, did *not* appear to accept the general line of reasoning put forward by Plan B Earth here based on section 5(8):

> [C]ounsel for Friends of the Earth (Mr David Wolfe QC) expressly distanced himself from the submissions … based on section 5(8) [of the Planning Act], accepting the relevant policy was no more and no less than that set out in the Climate Change Act.[95]

We have also emphasised that, as with certain difficulties arising where one conflates 'policy' with a 'treaty' (here, the Paris Agreement), the position of Friends of the Earth as summarised here, which locates 'the relevant policy' as 'that set out in the Climate Change Act', presents a similar problem.[96] In other words, one runs into a similar conceptual problem posed by casually conflating 'law' (here, a statute, the Climate Change Act 2008) with 'policy' ('the relevant policy') as if

[92] *Plan B Earth v Secretary of State for Transport* (n 47) para [228].
[93] Muinzer and Paterson (n 21) 756.
[94] Gordhan (n 51) 568.
[95] Muinzer and Paterson (n 21) 756; *Plan B Earth v Secretary of State for Transport* (n 47) para [191]; see further *Spurrier* (n 48) paras [605], [636].
[96] Muinzer and Paterson (n 21) 756–57.

a statute and policy were one and the same thing. Such conflation of statute law and policy also arises in expert commentary on the case (unsurprisingly, given that it is chiefly following the Court's reasoning), as where Hawkins discusses 'the Government's consideration of *the Climate Change Act (CCA) 2008 (the only established government policy* on climate change at the date the ANPS was designated in June 2018)' (emphasis added).[97]

Thus, in trying to clarify and emphasise some degree of bright-line distinction between 'treaty/policy' in this case in relation to the Planning Act 2008, the Supreme Court seems to risk muddying the conceptual waters between a 'statute/policy' distinction in the process. This does not seem particularly helpful. Nonetheless, Paterson and the author conclude that it is clear that the Climate Change Act 2008 sets a framework policy direction for the UK through the medium of domestically binding law, and so in practice the semantic disjunction between 'statute-policy' is mild enough to be fairly negligible in this particular setting. In the specific context of this case, which involves novel national framework climate legislation, one might summarise the perspective that is assumed to apply to the statute–policy distinction as follows (or as something equivalent): *policy is to be in accordance with the policy direction represented by the statute.* In sum, concluding simply that a 'statute' (the Climate Change Act 2008) is 'policy' seems to open a conceptual can of worms that is unhelpful and should be avoided by the courts in the interest of clarity. Gordhan has commented in relation to the Divisional Court ruling that this court 'emphasised the 'entrenched' character of *the UK's climate change policy produced under the Climate Change Act 2008*, concluding that this *legislatively mandated policy* was the only relevant policy that the Secretary of State was required to take into account' (emphasis added).[98] Distinguishing policy produced *under the 2008 Act* in this way from the 2008 Act itself seems helpful.

C. Ground (ii)

This ground appealed the following element of the Court of Appeal's decision:

> The Secretary of State breached his duty under section 10 of the PA 2008, when promulgating the ANPS, to have regard to the desirability of mitigating and adapting to climate change, in that he failed to have proper regard to the Paris Agreement.[99]

Section 10 of the Planning Act 2008 is entitled 'Sustainable development'. The UK's National Planning Policy Framework[100] incorporates a definition of sustainable development that includes 'meeting the needs of the present without

[97] Hawkins (n 46) 347.
[98] Gordhan (n 51) 567.
[99] Judgment (n 1) para [15].
[100] Ministry of Housing, Communities and Local Government, *National Planning Policy Framework* (UK, July 2018).

compromising the ability of future generations to meet their own needs'.[101] This interpretation follows the classic definition of sustainable development outlined in the Brundtland Report.[102]

It is significant that the Climate Change Act 2008 certainly *had* been taken into account by the Secretary of State when designating the *ANPS*, including its emissions reduction targets and carbon budgets, and this was reflected in the *ANPS*.[103] The Paris Agreement is a different matter, as it does not feature in the *ANPS* at all. It appears on the face of it, then, that there could be a strong basis for the argument advanced by Friends of the Earth, namely that the Secretary of State failed to have proper regard to the Paris Agreement in the context of the sustainable development requirement in section 10 of the Planning Act 2008 to 'have regard to the desirability of mitigating, and adapting to, climate change'.[104]

However, the Supreme Court found that 'the UK's obligations under the Paris Agreement are given effect in domestic law, in that the existing carbon target under section 1 of the Climate Change Act 2008 and the carbon budgets under section 4 of that Act already meet (and, indeed, go beyond) the UK's obligations under the Paris Agreement to adhere to the NDCs notified on its behalf under that Agreement'.[105] This is true in some sense, but it does not appear to read accurately in sharp legal terms. The Climate Change Act 2008 preceded the Paris Agreement and was not designed in any way to give effect to the Paris Agreement, which was not created until 2015. It is also notable that section 1(1) of the Climate Change Act 2008, which applies a 100 per cent emissions reduction target based on 1990 levels (ie, a 'Net Zero' target), initially sat at 80 per cent over 2008–19, and the Paris Agreement (2015) was ratified by the UK in this 80 per cent era (2016).

When section 1 of the 2008 Act was increased from 80 per cent to 100 per cent through an amendment in 2019,[106] it is true that this amendment was influenced strongly by the Paris Agreement, but it was also influenced significantly by other factors, notably scientific reports,[107] litigation,[108] and the advisory outputs of the Committee on Climate Change.[109] So it does not seem particularly helpful in strict legal terms to construe the Climate Change Act 2008–Paris Agreement relationship as one where 'the UK's obligations under the Paris Agreement are given effect in domestic law' by the Climate Change Act 2008. Indeed, given the facts of this particular case, it seems odd that there is arguable confusion around this, as the

[101] Judgment (n 1) para [115]; Ministry of Housing, Communities and Local Government (n 100) 5.
[102] Report of the World Commission on Environment and Development, *Our Common Future* (1987) (Brundtland Report).
[103] See, eg, Judgment (n 1) para [123]; Department for Transport (n 42) paras 5.71–5.73.
[104] Planning Act 2008, s 10(3)(a).
[105] Judgment (n 1) para [122]. 'NDCs' refer to the Paris Agreement's 'Nationally Determined Contributions' – see n 90 above.
[106] Climate Change Act 2008 (2050 Target Amendment) Order 2019.
[107] Intergovernmental Panel on Climate Change, *Global Warming of 1.5°: An IPCC Special Report*, (IPCC, 2018).
[108] See, eg, Macrory and Muinzer (n 25) 86.
[109] Committee on Climate Change (n 27).

Secretary of State himself clarified directly that he did *not* take the Paris Agreement into account in his considerations, which the Supreme Court acknowledges: 'the Secretary of State accepted that, in designating the *ANPS*, he took into account only the Climate Change Act 2008 carbon emission targets and *did not take into account* either *the Paris Agreement* or otherwise any post-2050 target or non-CO_2 emissions' (emphasis added).[110] Nonetheless, the Supreme Court found that the 'duties under the CCA 2008 clearly were taken into account when the Secretary of State decided to issue the *ANPS*'[111] and that the Paris Agreement was thus taken into account, since, as noted above, in the Court's view, 'the UK's obligations under the Paris Agreement are given effect in domestic law' to an extent by the Climate Change Act 2008.[112]

According to this line of reasoning, in conjunction with the observation that the Secretary of State took advice on whether to include the Paris Agreement and also afforded opportunity for the Paris Agreement to be engaged with during public consultation, the Court held that the Secretary of State *did* give consideration to the Paris Agreement and that the real question must therefore be whether *sufficient weight* was given to it:

> [T]his is not a case in which the Secretary of State omitted to give any consideration to the Paris Agreement; nor is it one in which no weight was given to the Paris Agreement when the Secretary of State decided to issue the *ANPS*. On the contrary, the Secretary of State took the Paris Agreement into account and, to the extent that the obligations under it were already covered by the measures under the CCA 2008, he gave weight to it and ensured that those obligations would be brought into account in decisions to be taken under the framework established by the *ANPS*.[113]

As suggested above, and as generally supported by the judgments of the Divisional Court[114] and the Court of Appeal,[115] in the author's view, the basis of this reasoning is not strictly speaking correct. Again, as noted above, the Supreme Court correctly recognised that 'the Secretary of State accepted that, in designating the *ANPS*, he took into account only the Climate Change Act 2008 … and did not take into account … the Paris Agreement'.[116] In principle, the fact that the Paris Agreement may have been raised in some representations during the consultation stage does not necessarily mean that the Government actively considered it. Moreover, the Agreement might not have been raised substantially at all, the Government was at liberty to respond in significant part to the consultation process as it saw appropriate, and, at any rate, the thrust of section 10 of the Planning Act 2008 is to compel the Government to take the initiative and address relevant matters

[110] Judgment (n 1) para [126].
[111] ibid para [122].
[112] ibid.
[113] ibid para [125].
[114] *Spurrier* (n 48).
[115] *Plan B Earth v Secretary of State for Transport* (n 47).
[116] Judgment (n 1) para [126].

when promulgating the *ANPS* (as opposed to relying on general members of the public via consultation). Additionally, and importantly, acknowledging the Paris Agreement in order to receive advice on whether to take it into account or not, then setting it aside due to receiving advice that it is not necessary to take it into account, does not in itself amount to taking the Paris Agreement into account on any serious or credible basis in the context of promulgating the *ANPS*. For one thing, it entirely ignores the *content* of the Paris Agreement.

The following example demonstrates some arguable degree of underlying illogicality here. Take a hypothetical scenario where the Government is required to take the Freedom of Information Act 2000 into account. Let us say that the Secretary of State asks his relevant advisors whether the Freedom of Information Act must be taken into account in the case in question, is advised that it is not necessary to do so, and sets the Act aside. This omission is then challenged in court:

- Secretary of State: Am I required to take the Freedom of Information Act into account in this context?
- Advisors: No.
- Secretary of State: In that case, I shall set it aside.
- Claimant: In failing to take account of the Freedom of Information Act, the Secretary of State is in breach of an obligation to do so.
- Defendant (the Secretary of State): That is incorrect. In deciding not to take account of the Act, I had to take account of it in order to set it aside!

The defendant's argument seems somewhat absurd, yet the treatment of the Freedom of Information Act in this example appears to echo aspects of the Supreme Court's underlying approach to the account taken of the Paris Agreement by the Secretary of State in the *Heathrow Runway Case*.

In sum, the Supreme Court reasoned that the Climate Change Act 2008 is clearly represented in the *ANPS*, and that this Act covers the headline mitigation requirements of the Paris Agreement and gives effect to them. It has been suggested above that this line of reasoning is somewhat misjudged; the Paris Agreement is an international treaty, the Climate Change Act 2008 is a domestic statute that preceded it and does not directly apply it,[117] and the Paris Agreement was not taken into account directly by the Secretary of State in the *ANPS*. However, even if the Supreme Court had adopted this position, it would have been unlikely to change the fundamental outcome of the case, namely resulting instead in a finding in favour of the appellant Heathrow Airport Ltd. Even where it is accepted that the Secretary of State failed to take the Paris Agreement into account, the Secretary of State appears to have no requirement to do so directly under UK law in this setting. The Paris Agreement is an international treaty that has not

[117] Ghaleigh has commented: 'Note that the UK government ratified the Paris Agreement on 17 November 2016, but that the treaty remains unincorporated. As such, obligations imposed on the UK Government by the Agreement *eo ipso* have no legal effect in domestic law'. Ghaleigh (n 90) 441–42.

been directly incorporated in UK law, and (per the previous section above) it falls outside the purview of 'Government policy' (per section 5 of the Planning Act 2008). As summarised by Hawkins, based on the reasoning of the two judges co-delivering the Supreme Court judgment: 'Lords Hodge and Sales … made clear that a ratified international agreement, in this case the Paris Agreement, was an unincorporated treaty which did not give rise to direct domestic law obligations and rights. Nor … did it constitute Government policy.'[118] As Lord Oliver asserts in *JH Rayner*, 'a treaty is not part of English law unless and until it has been incorporated into the law by legislation'.[119]

Based on the above logic, the Court proceeded to reframe matters as follows: 'On proper analysis the question is whether the Secretary of State acted irrationally in omitting to take the Paris Agreement *further into account*, or give it *greater weight*, than in fact he did' (emphasis added).[120] (For the reasons given above, in the author's view this is an incorrect basis on which to proceed.) The Court found that the robust climate standards in the Climate Change Act 2008, which meet and exceed aspects of the Paris Agreement requirements, provided a sufficient basis for the Secretary of State's consideration, and covered relevant Paris Agreement standards. Therefore, the Secretary of State did not act irrationally in relying explicitly on only the Climate Change Act 2008 in the *ANPS* rather than both the Climate Change Act 2008 and the Paris Agreement.[121]

Thus, the Court concluded that 'it is not necessary to decide the different question whether, if the Secretary of State had omitted to think about the Paris Agreement at all … as an unincorporated treaty, that would have constituted an error of law'.[122] Again, in the author's view, the Paris Agreement was not taken into account in the *ANPS* itself (as the Secretary of State himself conceded). This is so in spite of the fact that its headline emissions reduction requirements happen to be supported by the Climate Change Act 2008's relatively strong emissions reduction standards. As respectfully submitted above, if the Supreme Court had correctly interpreted this as an omission, it is not clear to the author that this would have changed the overall outcome of the case, given that the Paris Agreement is an unincorporated treaty, the Secretary of State has a substantial degree of discretion in relation to the factors he considers,[123] and the free-standing Climate Change Act 2008 is in place, with the result that a vacuum in headline climate standards does not occur.

[118] Hawkins (n 46) 347.

[119] *JH Rayner (Mincing Lane) Ltd v Department of Trade and Industry* [1990] 2 AC 418, 500.

[120] Judgment (n 1) para [125].

[121] The Supreme Court draws on the UK's *Wednesbury* standard for 'irrationality' (see eg, ibid paras [119], [152]). On this standard of review in UK law, see further: *Associated Provincial Picture Houses Ltd v Wednesbury Corporation* [1948] 1 KB 223; *Council of Civil Service Unions v Minister for the Civil Service* [1985] AC 374, 410–11. In technical legal terms, the Supreme Court's determination that *Wednesbury* is the applicable standard of review here means that the respondents have a hard test to satisfy that affords the decision maker substantial discretion.

[122] Judgment (n 1) para [134].

[123] See, eg, ibid paras [116]–[121].

D. Ground (iii)

This ground appealed the following element of the Court of Appeal's decision:

> The Secretary of State breached his duty under article 5 of the Strategic Environmental Assessment Directive … to issue a suitable environmental report for the purposes of public consultation on the proposed ANPS, in that he failed to refer to the Paris Agreement.[124]

The SEA Directive[125] is an item of EU law that applied in the UK prior to 'Brexit', that is, the UK's exit from the EU (completed 31 January 2020) and during a 'transition period' where EU law still applied afterwards (ending 31 December 2020).[126] The SEA process requires potential environmental impacts from plans and proposals for major development projects to be taken into account prior to a development being undertaken. The *ANPS* is a plan falling within its scope, and so an environmental assessment and environmental report were required under the UK's SEA regime.

The environmental report was published by the Secretary of State, and Friends of the Earth, supported by Plan B Earth, argued that it was inadequate due to a failure to refer to the Paris Agreement. Again, the Climate Change Act 2008's 2050 target and carbon budgets *were* referred to, and there was a familiar effort by the appellant, Heathrow Airport Ltd, to argue that this therefore covered any Paris Agreement requirement.[127] In keeping with the themes emerging under the *ground (ii)* and *ground (i)* strands of the argument, it was asserted that the Secretary of State had been advised that explicit reference to the Paris Agreement was not necessary.[128]

Under UK law, the Secretary of State has a significant degree of discretion in relation to relevant environmental information included in a report of this kind.[129] The UK courts take a relatively conservative approach that militates against court interference, applying a *Wednesbury* standard of review,[130] which affords the decision maker (here, the Secretary of State) a significant range of discretion in the exercise of his powers in order to prevent the Court indirectly substituting its own view for that of the lawful decision maker.[131] The Supreme Court noted that as part of the domestic SEA process, the Secretary of State carried out an *Appraisal*

[124] ibid para [15].
[125] SEA Directive, 2001/42/EC.
[126] The UK voted via a referendum to leave the EU on 23 June 2016 by way of a 52 per cent Leave majority against a 48 per cent Remain minority.
[127] Judgment (n 1) para [140].
[128] ibid, referring to formal advice provided by the CCC.
[129] SEA Directive, 2001/42/EC, art 5(2), (3); *Shadwell Estates Ltd v Breckland District Council* [2013] EWHC 12 (Admin).
[130] *Wednesbury* (n 121).
[131] As outlined by the Court of Appeal in this case, at *Plan B Earth v Secretary of State for Transport* (n 47) para [136]. The Supreme Court draws on this outline in Judgment (n 1) para [144].

of Sustainability[132] in relation to the draft National Planning Statement[133] and engaged in public consultation;[134] the Court observed that 'the public was able to comment on the Paris Agreement in the course of the consultation and … their comments were taken into account in the environmental assessment required by the SEA Directive'.[135] The author has been critical of the weight given to the consultation process under the *ground (ii)* heading (see above), but in the differing context of SEA procedure, where the content of the environmental report is subject to significant discretion and the report arises within the SEA framework, the court's position seems more cogent.

In keeping with the relationship drawn earlier between the Climate Change Act 2008 and the Paris Agreement, with the 2008 Act, which was overtly taken into account in the statement, being construed as providing coverage of the Paris Agreement, the Supreme Court asserted as follows:

> [I]n compiling the [*Appraisal of Sustainability*] as the environmental statement required under the SEA Directive the Secretary of State decided to follow the advice of the CCC to the effect that the UK's obligations under the Paris Agreement were sufficiently taken into account in the UK's domestic obligations under the CCA 2008, which were referred to in the *ANPS* and the [*Appraisal of Sustainability*]. Further reference to the Paris Agreement was not required. As we have already held above, this was an assessment which was plainly rational and lawful.[136]

Thus, it was held by the Supreme Court that the *Appraisal of Sustainability* covered the necessary SEA environmental report obligations pertinent to the *ANPS* and that its lack of overt reference to the Paris Agreement was not unlawful.[137] This reversed the Court of Appeal's determination that a breach of SEA requirements had occurred.

E. Ground (iv)

This ground appealed the following element of the Court of Appeal's decision:

> The Secretary of State breached his duty under section 10 of the PA 2008, when promulgating the ANPS, in that he failed to have proper regard to (a) the desirability of mitigating climate change in the period after 2050 … and (b) the desirability of mitigating climate change by restricting emissions of non-CO_2 impacts of aviation, in particular nitrous oxide.[138]

[132] Department for Transport, *Appraisal of Sustainability: Airports National Policy Statement* (2018).
[133] Required under s 5(3) of the Planning Act 2008.
[134] Required under ibid s 7.
[135] Judgment (n 1) para [147].
[136] ibid para [149].
[137] ibid para [150].
[138] ibid para [15].

Like *ground (ii)*, the post-2050 and non-CO_2 emissions elements engaged section 10 of the Planning Act 2008 pertaining to 'the objective of contributing to sustainable development' and, in the course of this, 'hav[ing] regard to the desirability of … mitigating and adapting to, climate change'.[139] Here, the Secretary of State was again subject to a significant margin of appreciation, ie, a significant degree of discretion, in carrying out his duties, and 'the *Wednesbury* irrationality test' would again be the applicable court standard.[140]

The post-2050 strand of legal argument contended that it is inadequate to consider the impact of emissions from aircraft using the proposed new runway capacity in relation to a 2050 target only, as embodied by the UK's 2050 Net Zero target under section 1(1) of the Climate Change Act 2008. This is because this approach neglects the impact on sustainability *after* 2050; notably, the Paris Agreement takes a longer view via its objective for global emissions to reach Net Zero in the second half of this century. The Supreme Court noted that modelling up to 2085/2086 informed the *Appraisal of Sustainability* that accompanied the *ANPS*.[141] Hicks summarises that:

> [F]or the purposes of the ANPS, the economic benefits of Heathrow expansion had been assessed up to 2085, but not the climate or carbon impacts. FoE [ie, Friends of the Earth] argued that by choosing to assess the ANPS against the CCA 08, which set climate targets only up to 2050, the Secretary of State had again breached his section 10 duty: 'climate change will not just stop in 2050', said the FoE trial briefing documents.[142]

Friends of the Earth's position does not entirely reflect the full facts of the matter, with the Supreme Court noting as follows:

> Lord Anderson points out, and FoE accepts, that the Airports Commission assessed the carbon emissions of each of the short-listed schemes over a 60-year appraisal period up to 2085/2086 and that the same appraisal period was used in the AoS which accompanied the ANPS. The Secretary of State therefore did take into account the fact that there would be carbon emissions from the use of the North West Runway after 2050 and quantified those emissions.[143]

Given these factors, in combination with the Secretary of State's discretion, and the fact that the Development Consent Order that would need to be applied for in order to develop the runway and other devices could be used reactively in going forward, it was held that 'the Secretary of State did not act irrationally in not attempting in the *ANPS* to assess post-2050 emissions against policies which had yet to be determined'.[144]

[139] Planning Act 2008, s 10(2), (3).
[140] Judgment (n 1) para [152]. On the *Wednesbury* test, see n 121 above; see also Judgment (n 1) paras [119]–[120].
[141] Judgment (n 1) paras [155], [156].
[142] Hicks (n 6) 113.
[143] Judgment (n 1) para [155].
[144] ibid para [156].

The *non-CO_2 emissions* strand of legal argument involved consideration of particular emissions. The Court summarised that:

> [A]ircraft emit nitrogen oxides, water vapour and sulphate and soot aerosols, which combine to have a net warming effect. Depending on atmospheric humidity, the hot air from aircraft exhausts combines with water vapour in the atmosphere to form ice crystals which appear as linear condensation trails and can lead to cirrus-like cloud formation.[145]

Although these emissions tend to be 'short-lived'[146] and the full extent of the negative impact of non-CO_2 emissions is scientifically unclear at this time, it is evident that some significant climate warming *does* arise via these gases.[147] The *Appraisal of Sustainability* only took CO_2 emissions into account, due to the scientific uncertainty concerning measurement and impact assessment.[148] It is notable that the Court of Appeal drew on the precautionary principle (and so-called 'common sense')[149] to conclude that scientific uncertainty was not a reason for not taking non-CO_2 emissions into account at all; thus, it directed non-CO_2 emissions to be taken into account in the revised *ANPS* that it ordered.[150] In contrast, the Supreme Court found that the precautionary principle 'adds nothing to the argument in this context'[151] in legal terms, in particular because the correct test is whether it was *irrational* for the Secretary of State to address only CO_2 emissions, and, on inspection, his approach could not be said to amount to irrationality in the technical legal sense of the word.[152]

The Supreme Court summarised the Secretary of State's overall approach with approval as follows, noting that it was in keeping with expert advice the Government had received:

> This approach of addressing the question of capacity by reference to CO_2 emissions targets, keeping the policy in relation to non-CO_2 emissions under review and requiring an applicant for a DCO to address such impacts by reference to the state of knowledge current at the time of the determination of its application was consistent with the advice of the CCC to the Airports Commission and to the Secretary of State.[153]

[145] ibid para [159] (drawing on an expert witness statement).

[146] ibid para [159].

[147] The UK Government's Department for Transport published a report on the condition of scientific knowledge in this area in 2018: David S Lee, *The Current State of Scientific Understanding of the Non-CO_2 Effects of Aviation on Climate* (Department for Transport:, 2018). See further Judgment (n 1) paras [159]–[161].

[148] Department for Transport (n 132) para 6.11.11: 'There are likely to be highly significant climate change impacts associated with non-CO_2 emissions from aviation, which could be of a similar magnitude to the CO_2 emissions themselves, but which cannot be readily quantified due to the level of scientific uncertainty and have therefore not been assessed.' See further Judgment (n 1) para [160].

[149] See Judgment (n 1) para [165].

[150] *Plan B Earth v Secretary of State for Transport* (n 47) para [258]; Judgment (n 1) para [164].

[151] Judgment (n 1) para [165].

[152] See further the summary of the Court's conclusions on this point at ibid para [166].

[153] ibid para [161].

The DCO noted by the Court here refers to the 'Development Consent Order' that the UK Government uses to issue planning permission, often with other relevant licences, modifications and conditions attached. In seeking a DCO, an applicant would be required to produce an environmental assessment as part of the application process.[154] Thus, application for a DCO provides an opportunity for non-CO_2 emissions to be factored into considerations more fulsomely if the understanding of measurement and impact has progressed to a point where this is feasible by the time the application is being made. On this line of reasoning, Hawkins has summarised that the 'ANPS was not the end game, and the role of the DCO allowed for flexibility in relation to updated standards/commitments'.[155]

The Court's position might seem logically sensible; however, Westaway has made observations that challenge this view: 'it might be said to be illogical to leave a matter as important as whether or not airport expansion is compatible with climate targets until the determination of a DCO application'.[156] He elaborates:

> The ANPS establishes that there is a pressing need for new airport capacity in the south east of England and that need should be met by a third runway to the north west of Heathrow. Arguably, Government should have addressed whether or not such expansion was compatible with any future targets necessitated by the Paris Agreement before it set down those matters as unassailable national policy.[157]

This seems like a reasonable observation and thus an arguably reasonable criticism. As such, Westaway notes that there 'accordingly remains some force in the view expressed in the Court of Appeal's judgment,[158] rejecting the argument that reliance on a subsequent DCO stage could compensate for what it considered to be the disregard of the Paris Agreement in the ANPS' itself.[159]

In the author's view, and in spite of the uncertainty concerning measurement of the extent of negative non-CO_2 gas impacts, some degree of non-CO_2 appraisal of the effects of warming should have been incorporated meaningfully, if only in a highly qualified way. As the Appendix to the *Appraisal of Sustainability* itself notes: 'Evidence suggests that the global warming impact of aviation, with these sources included, could be up to two times that of the CO_2 impact by itself.'[160] This matter is too significant to minimise or set aside. That said, in strict legal terms, the Supreme Court's decision appears to be correct – ie, the Secretary of State's decision does not appear to breach the UK's irrationality test and the point is correctly decided. It is the Government that should exercise the perspicacity to include some form of meaningful recognition of these emissions, which it can do within the broad bounds of its permitted discretion.

[154] ibid para [163].
[155] Hawkins (n 46) 347.
[156] Ned Westaway, 'Friends of the Earth: Implications for Planning Law' (2021) 33(2) *Journal of Environmental Law* 455–59, 456.
[157] ibid 456.
[158] See further *Plan B Earth v Secretary of State for Transport* (n 47) para [275].
[159] Westaway (n 156) 457.
[160] Department for Transport (n 132), Appendix A-9, para 9.11.5.

IV. Contempt of Court

The Plan B Earth and Friends of the Earth teams foregrounded different legal emphases in their submissions. Tim Crosland, a qualified barrister and Director of Plan B Earth, opted to represent Plan B Earth himself. Plan B Earth emphasised the narrower 'Government policy' strand discussed above (section 5 of the Planning Act 2008), while Friends of the Earth emphasised the broader sustainable development strand (section 10 of the Planning Act 2008) and the lack of incorporation of non-CO_2 emissions. This led to some tension as Plan B Earth sought for the legal submissions to push the envelope of the argument, while the Friends of the Earth team sought to adhere to what they saw as safer and more winnable grounds.[161] Ultimately, Crosland went on to commit contempt of court by leaking the draft Supreme Court judgment, which had been circulated privately to the parties involved in draft form a week prior to being delivered publicly by the Supreme Court.

Circulation of a draft in this way is standard UK Supreme Court procedural practice. It is done so that counsel can 'check the judgement for typographical errors and minor inaccuracies', and, in rare cases of 'apparent error or ambiguity in the judgement', notify the judicial support section of the Supreme Court as soon as possible.[162] Crosland waited six days until the day prior to the judgment being handed down before emailing the Press Association that morning to disclose the outcome of the appeal. He included the following comments:

> I have taken the decision to break the embargo on that decision as an act of civil disobedience. This will be treated as 'contempt of court' and I am ready to face the consequences.[163]

Later that morning, he published a statement on Twitter, including the following comments:

> I am breaking the court embargo on Heathrow to protest against the injustice of the verdict, which is a betrayal to the younger generation and those on the frontline of the crisis in the UK and around the world.[164]

Requests to remove the Tweet by the Supreme Court's Registrar were ignored. These outputs caused a flurry of attention and coverage prior to the judgment being handed down by the Court the next day.

Crosland was held in contempt of court by the Supreme Court[165] and was subsequently disbarred by a separate tribunal brought by the Bar Standards

[161] See Hicks (n 6) ch 3, 'The Paris Agreement's Day in Court'.

[162] Supreme Court, *Practice Direction 6*, para 6.8.4.

[163] Neil Parpworth, 'Breaching an Embargo on the Publication of a Judgment: A Criminal Contempt of Court? *Her Majesty's Attorney General v Crosland* [2021] UKSC 15' (2021) 85(6) *Journal of Criminal Law* 466–470, 466.

[164] ibid 467.

[165] *Her Majesty's Attorney General v Crosland* [2021] UKSC 15.

Board.[166] The application for committal for contempt at the Supreme Court was heard by Lord Lloyd-Jones, Lord Hamblen and Lord Stephens, no doubt chosen in part because none of them had sat in the *Heathrow Runway Case*. Crosland represented himself. The Court had a capacity to apply a penalty of imprisonment for up to two years and an unlimited fine,[167] but opted for a comparatively light fine only of £5,000. Parpworth summarises:

> It was accepted that greater clemency was normally required to be shown in cases of civil disobedience than in other cases. With Article 10 of the ECHR in mind,[168] a fine of £5,000 was a necessary and proportionate penalty for the purpose of maintaining the authority of the judiciary and its judgments.[169]

Parpworth construes the brief embargo on a judgment that exists when it is circulated amongst parties in draft form as 'highly desirable' insofar as it helps to prevent the publication of judgments containing unwelcome and potentially serious errors.[170] The brief period of confidentiality also prevents 'much confusion' arising from different versions of a judgment in the same case becoming publicly available, or from where 'selected passages from a judgment or a person's interpretation of them were to be published in advance of the judgement itself'.[171] Additionally, in the author's view, it is notable that Crosland had been taking cases himself for Plan B Earth as the group's lead lawyer since the group's inception. It does not appear to make sense in the context of that strategy for the Director and lead lawyer to put himself wilfully in a position of contempt of court and disbarment in this way, given that he can no longer use his considerable legal skills to fight for the group's environmental aims in court to the extent he did previously.

V. Concluding Thoughts

The UK is a common law jurisdiction with a rich tradition of case law,[172] but in this particular case, scholars have noted that 'the arguments before the Supreme Court focused closely on legislation, specifically, climate change legislation'.[173] In overturning the decision of the Divisional Court, the Court of Appeal ruled that the *ANPS* would not have legal effect until it was reviewed in light of the court's

[166] Bianca Castro, 'Barrister Who Flouted Supreme Court Embargo Disbarred', *Law Society Gazette*, 21 January 2023.
[167] Contempt of Court Act 1981, s 14(1)–(2).
[168] Article 10 of the European Convention on Human Rights protects freedom of expression.
[169] Parpworth (n 163) 467.
[170] ibid 469.
[171] ibid 470.
[172] Though note that the substate jurisdiction of Scotland has a partially distinct hybrid common law and civil law system.
[173] Bell and Fisher (n 35) 228.

findings by the Secretary of State. The Supreme Court reversed this; as Hawkins puts it, the *ANPS* 'stands steadfast' following the judgment of the Supreme Court.[174]

It is notable that the issues arising cannot be extricated fully from constitutional questions about the proper relationship between the courts, the executive and national Parliament.[175] Moreover, and as with many major climate cases,[176] the frequently overlooked elements of *time and timing* should be acknowledged. In a policy report on UK judicial review, Haddon et al have rightly flagged the impact of this dimension:

> The second concern is about the time taken for the court process to play out when a challenge is brought. The decision on a third runway at Heathrow airport was ruled unlawful in February 2020, 20 months after MPs had voted in favour of the project. The Supreme Court subsequently overturned this decision 10 months later. As one official argued, because you 'might not get a JR [ie, judicial review] decision for three years after the policy work has been completed … it inevitably feels like a block on action rather than a useful feedback mechanism'.[177]

It is also clear from the analysis in this chapter that particular note should be taken of the UK courts' nuanced approach to the Paris Agreement. Martin has commented as follows in relation to the Supreme Court stage: 'As for the implications of ratification of the Paris Agreement, it is notable that neither respondent sought to support the conclusion of the Court of Appeal' – ie, it was accepted that ratification of the international Paris Agreement did not amount to a statement of Government policy in its own right.[178] Commenting at the Court of Appeal stage prior to the Supreme Court, Mitchell noted that the ruling 'might have important implications for the designation of other NPSs if the court's judgment suggests that the Secretary of State should consider international commitments to which the Government has expressed a "policy of adherence"'.[179] This is an apt comment from Mitchell, but the judicial reasoning that it flags betrays something of a paradox latent within the Court of Appeal's thinking that the Court did not unpack or resolve in relation to treaties; is one to assume that a *policy of non-adherence* is in place where the UK ratifies an international treaty, unless a policy of adherence has been expressed directly in a form other than ratification? A treaty may be a weak instrument (in the UK at least), but this seems to be a startling assumption. In the first place, it raises the question of why the UK should ratify treaties at all if some

[174] Hawkins (n 46) 344.

[175] Joanna Bell, Sanja Bogojević and Olivia Hamlyn, 'Friends of the Earth & Legal Interdisciplinarity: Introduction by the Analysis Editors' (2021) 33(2) *Journal of Environmental Law* 437–40, 439.

[176] See further, eg, the discussion of time and timing in this volume in chs 3 and 5.

[177] Catherine Haddon, Raphael Hogarth and Alex Nice, *Judicial Review and Policy Making: The Role of Legal Advice in Government* (Institute for Government, 2021) 10.

[178] Stevie Martin, 'Friends of the Earth: "Government Policy", Relevant Considerations and Human Rights'. (2021) 33(2) *Journal of Environmental Law* 449–54, 451.

[179] Edward Mitchell, 'Climate Change and Nationally Significant Infrastructure Projects: *R (on the Application of Plan B Earth) v Secretary of State for Transport*' (2020) 22(2) *Environmental Law Review* 125–32, 132.

form of entrenched culture of potential non-adherence exists as a matter of default upon ratification, in the absence of a statement to the contrary.

As a concluding point, the Supreme Court judgment appears to be slightly misleading insofar as it asserts that 'Section 1 of the CCA 2008 sets a target that relates to carbon only', while 'Section 24 enables the Secretary of State for BEIS to set targets for other greenhouse gases, but subject to similar conditions to which an amendment to the section 1 target is subject'.[180] Section 1 actually covers the targeted gases incorporated within the 'net UK carbon account',[181] which are carbon dioxide, methane, nitrous oxide, hydrofluorocarbons, perfluorocarbons and sulphur hexafluoride.[182] The gas nitrogen trifluoride (NF_3) was also added to this list in 2023,[183] after campaign pressure compelled the amendment of the 2008 Act.[184] Thus, when one reads references to 'the amendment of the statutory CO_2 target in section 1(1) of the CCA 2008' at paragraph [97] of the judgment, this appears to be somewhat misleading as to the range of gases at issue in law.[185] However, the adjustment of this technical detail would not alter the fundamental reasoning that led to any of the Court's conclusions.

[180] Judgment (n 1) para [44].
[181] Climate Change Act 2008, s 1(1).
[182] ibid ss 24, 92.
[183] Climate Change (Targeted Greenhouse Gases) Order 2023 (SI 2023/118).
[184] 'Climate Legislation Amended Following SCELN's Seventh Gas Campaign', *Scottish Legal News*, 13 March 2023.
[185] Judgment (n 1) para [97].

3

The Netherlands

The Urgenda Case

The question whether the State is in breach of its duty of care for taking insufficient measures to prevent dangerous climate change, is a legal issue which has never before been answered in Dutch proceedings and for which jurisprudence does not provide a ready-made framework.

Urgenda Case, District Court, paragraph 4.53

I. The Importance of *Urgenda Foundation v State of the Netherlands*

The case of *Urgenda Foundation v State of the Netherlands* (hereafter the *Urgenda Case* or *Urgenda*) was first heard in the Netherlands at the District Court.[1] The outcome of this initial ruling was appealed, and a ruling from the Court of Appeal followed.[2] That ruling was appealed in turn to the Supreme Court of the Netherlands, which gave its judgment in December 2019.[3] The Dutch Government was unsuccessful in all three courts. A variety of interesting and important legal points and issues were engaged with over the course of this landmark climate case.[4]

[1] *Urgenda Foundation v The State of the Netherlands*, ECLI:NL:RBDHA:2015:7145 (English translation ECLI:NL:RBDHA:2015:7196), Judgment (Dist Ct The Hague, 24 June 2015) (Neth) (hereafter cited as 'District Court Judgment').

[2] *State of the Netherlands v Urgenda Foundation*, ECLI:NL:GHDHA:2018:2591 (English translation ECLI:NL:GHDHA:2018:2610), Judgment (Ct App The Hague, 9 October 2018) (Neth) (hereafter cited as 'Court of Appeal Judgment').

[3] *State of the Netherlands v Urgenda Foundation*, ECLI:NL:HR:2019:2006 (English translation ECLI:NL:HR:2019:2007), Judgment (Sup Ct Neth, 20 December 2019) (Neth) (hereafter cited as 'Supreme Court Judgment').

[4] The author is working from the formal translations into English of the *Urgenda* judgments, provided to the public by the Dutch courts service. As the Dutch-language judgments are the authentic formal texts, these translations are technically unofficial. The Supreme Court paragraph citation numbers in the English-language translation are less granular/detailed than the demarcations in the Dutch-language Supreme Court version.

The Urgenda Foundation, a Dutch NGO, summarises that it commenced this litigation with '886 Dutch citizens' who participated as 'co-plaintiffs'.[5] The central intention was to compel the Dutch Government, described in the judgment and hereafter in this chapter as 'the State', to take stronger and more responsible climate mitigation action in response to anthropogenic climate change.[6] Initially, the State was steering a course to limit greenhouse gas emissions to approximately 17 per cent below 1990 levels by 2020,[7] but the courts held this to be insufficient, finding that it did not amount to a fair commitment towards holding the global average temperature to a maximum rise of 2°C post-industrial warming this century. Instead, the courts ruled that the State must limit greenhouse gas emissions to a minimum of 25 per cent below 1990 levels by the end of 2020. The Sabin Center for Climate Change Law has commented that this 'is the first decision by any court in the world ordering states to limit greenhouse gas emissions for reasons other than statutory mandates'.[8] The Sabin Center seems to adapt these words from the work of de Graaf and Jans, who phrase the point slightly more softly: '*this case seems to be* the very first decision by any court in the world that orders a state to limit GHG emissions for reasons other than statutory mandates' (emphasis added).[9] So far as the author is aware, this is indeed the first case of this kind.

Viewed socio-culturally, *Urgenda* is the most renowned and impactful example of landmark climate litigation to have arisen in the world to date. Cumulatively, the rulings from the Supreme Court and the other courts involved received a large degree of coverage from national and international media outlets, with the case becoming known across the environmental sector, and beyond it, around the world. Social scientists have demonstrated that the substantial media coverage directly influenced and augmented the level of political attention accorded to related climate issues.[10] It is notable that the case attracted a wide degree of interest from the District Court stage onwards, such that attention was in no way limited to the Supreme Court ruling only. Thus, at the relatively early District Court stage, the case was leading to legal commentaries

[5] Urgenda Foundation, 'Landmark Decision by Dutch Supreme Court', press release, https://www.urgenda.nl/en/themas/climate-case; District Court Judgment, para [2.4]: 'In these proceedings, Urgenda also acts on behalf of 886 individuals who have authorised Urgenda to also conduct these proceedings on their behalf.'

[6] The District Court clarifies its terminology thus: 'The term "the State" refers to the legal person that is party to these proceedings, while the term "the Netherlands" refers to the same entity in an international context. The government is the State's executive body.' District Court Judgment, para [4.2].

[7] ibid para [4.33].

[8] Sabin Center for Climate Change Law, *Climate Case Chart: Urgenda Foundation v State of the Netherlands*, https://climatecasechart.com/non-us-case/urgenda-foundation-v-kingdom-of-the-netherlands.

[9] Kars J de Graaf and Jan H Jans, 'The Urgenda Decision: Netherlands Liable for Role in Causing Dangerous Global Climate Change' (2015),27(3) *Journal of Environmental Law* 517–27, 527.

[10] Anke Wonneberger and Rens Vliegenthart, 'Agenda-Setting Effects of Climate Change Litigation: Interrelations across Issue Levels, Media, and Politics in the Case of Urgenda against the Dutch Government' (2021) 15(5) *Environmental Communication* 699–714.

with titles like 'Potential Implications for the United States of the Urgenda Foundation v Netherlands Decision',[11] speaking to a significant level of international interest and an associated international impact on legal thinking. Ellemers and de Glider observe that the 'broad publicity' generated by the case has 'inspired other groups of citizens' to engage with climate issues.[12]

O'Neill and Alblas have gone so far as to describe the *Urgenda Case* as 'the current climate litigation archetype'.[13] Writing as early as 2016 in the wake of the District Court ruling, legal experts noted that: 'The decision has been considered to be a "landmark" judgment, and it seems that unlike other unsuccessful class action lawsuits on climate change, Urgenda appears poised for being viewed as a global precedent.'[14] Viewed in legal terms, *Urgenda* can be described as the most renowned and impactful landmark climate law ruling to have arisen to date for reasons including the following:

- reference to the decision arises in climate cases around the world;[15]
- the outcome of the ruling has had a concrete bearing on the Netherlands' contribution to anthropogenic climate change mitigation (raising the State's minimum emissions reduction ambitions for 2020);
- the decision illustrates the potentially substantial changes that can be achieved via public interest climate litigation.

On the second of these three points – the concrete impact of the ruling – it is worth emphasising that in ordering a minimum increase in the State's greenhouse gas emissions for 2020, the court order was increasing an economy-wide target to 25 per cent. The ruling therefore engages the decarbonisation of the Netherlands' socio-economy in broad terms. Here, then, it might be noted from a lawyerly perspective that the courts have departed from the resolution of the sorts of relatively narrow technical or perhaps even pedantic low-impact points of law that can often arise in litigation, instead producing a more broadly impactful ruling with a socio-economically transformative character.[16]

[11] Robert B McKinstry, 'Potential Implications for the United States of the Urgenda Foundation v Netherlands Decision Holding That the UNFCCC and International Decisions Required Developed Nations to Reduce Emissions by 25% from 1990 Levels by 2020', 17 July 2015, https://ssrn.com/abstract=2632726> or <http://dx.doi.org/10.2139/ssrn.2632726.

[12] Naomi Ellemers and Dick de Gilder, *The Moral Organization: Key Issues, Analyses, and Solutions* (Springer Nature, 2022), 253.

[13] Sadhbh O'Neill, and Edwin Alblas, 'Climate Litigation, Politics and Policy Change: Lessons from Urgenda and Climate Case Ireland' in David Robbins, Diarmuid Torney and Pat Brereton (eds), *Ireland and the Climate Crisis* (Palgrave Macmillan, 2020) 57–72, 58.

[14] Suryapratim Roy and Edwin Woerdman, 'Situating Urgenda v the Netherlands within Comparative Climate Change Litigation' (2016) 34(2) *Journal of Energy & Natural Resources Law* 165–89, 166.

[15] See, for example, acknowledgement of the case at the Supreme Court of Ireland in *Climate Case Ireland* and the New South Wales Land and Environment Court in the *Gloucester Resources Case*, examined in this volume.

[16] However, the scale of the transformative character should not be over-estimated. See further section III.E below.

II. *Urgenda* at the District Court and the Court of Appeal

As noted earlier, the *Urgenda Case* began at the District Court.[17] Here, the court expanded the Dutch tort of hazardous state negligence, interpreting inter alia Article 162 of Book 6 of the Dutch Civil Code to find that the State's greenhouse gas reduction objectives for 2020 were insufficient.[18] The District Court summarised the State's 2020 target objectives at this stage of the litigation as follows:

> In the period 2007–2009, the Netherlands initially focused its climate policy on a reduction target of 30 per cent in 2020 compared to 1990, which was therefore higher than the EU's target of 20 per cent. However, this reduction target deviated at a later stage. In these proceedings, the State has stated that the Dutch climate policy is based on a minimum reduction target of 16 per cent in 2020 (compared to 2005) for the non-ETS sectors and 21 per cent in 2020 (compared to 2005) for the ETS sectors.[19] At the hearing, the State confirmed that the combined reduction for both sectors is expected to be 14 to 17 per cent in 2020 compared to 1990.[20]

The court held that the State's emissions reduction objective for 2020 must be increased to a 25 per cent minimum target, because a lesser target would prevent the Netherlands from making a permissible contribution to climate mitigation based on current scientific understanding and international standards.[21] In finding for the Urgenda Foundation, the District Court reached its determination on grounds of tort law,[22] rejecting attempts from the NGO to rely on human rights law. In the Netherlands, provisions in treaties that the Dutch State is party to, including the European Convention on Human Rights (ECHR), can apply with direct effect. Here, the District Court found that Article 34 of the ECHR, concerning admissibility of individual applications, acted as a barrier to the application of Article 2 ECHR (the Right to Life) and Article 8 ECHR (the Right to Private and Family Life).[23] de Graaf and Jans have highlighted that 'since Urgenda was not claiming compensation of damages but a court order, the existence of present damage was not required. The threat of future damage was sufficient'.[24] In the wake of the District Court ruling, the Government

[17] This section takes account of the rulings of the lower courts, but saves much consideration of key issues for the discussion of the Supreme Court's judgment that follows below.
[18] District Court Judgment (n 1).
[19] This refers to the EU's Emissions Trading Scheme.
[20] District Court Judgment (n 1) para [4.26]; see also paras [4.85]–[4.86].
[21] ibid para [4.31].
[22] Useful coverage of the technical peculiarities of Dutch tort law is provided (with reference to *Urgenda*) in Jonathan Verschuuren, 'Climate Change and the Individual in the Netherlands' in Sindico Francesco and Makane Moïse Mbengue (eds), *Comparative Climate Change Litigation: Beyond the Usual Suspects* (Springer, 2021) 75–90.
[23] District Court Judgment (n 1) para [4.45].
[24] de Graaf and Jans (n 9) 519.

announced that it would commence implementation of the ruling, but that it would also file an appeal.[25]

The District Court ruling was duly appealed to the Hague Court of Appeal. With the EU implementing a minimum 20 per cent greenhouse gas emissions reduction for 2020 relative to 1990 levels, the Court of Appeal summarised that: 'For the Netherlands, this translates to a minimum reduction target of 16 per cent for the non-ETS sector and 21 per cent for the ETS sector … During the plea hearing in the first instance, the State declared that it expected both sectors to have achieved a reduction of 14 per cent to 17 per cent by 2020, relative to 1990.'[26] The higher court upheld the outcome of the District Court's decision, holding that a minimum 25 per cent reduction for 2020 was appropriate in law.[27] Although the Court of Appeal affirmed the District Court's decision, it took the view that Article 34 ECHR should not be interpreted as a barrier to the application of Articles 2 and 8 ECHR.[28] Here one observes a broadening of the law, where it is seen to initially move on a tortious track at the District Court before broadening to incorporate a human rights track at the Court of Appeal.[29] This shift is particularly significant due to the fact that Dutch tort law is particular to the Netherlands, whereas the ECHR is not; the ECHR is a convention with multiple state signatories.[30] At the time of writing, the Council of Europe includes the Netherlands and 45 other member states, all of whom are ECHR signatories.

[25] ibid 526. Concerningly, however, Verschuuren writes that '[d]espite promises made by the government immediately after the 2015 District Court's decision in the Urgenda case, to already implement that decision while awaiting appeal, it was recently shown by journalists that in fact, the government did not pursue any additional measures to comply with the 2015 judgment': Jonathan Verschuuren, 'The State of the Netherlands v Urgenda Foundation: The Hague Court of Appeal Upholds Judgment Requiring the Netherlands to Further Reduce its Greenhouse Gas Emissions' (2019) 28(1) *Review of European, Comparative & International Environmental Law* 94–98, 98. See further H van Santen and E van der Walle, 'Hoe Urgenda een Levensgroot Probleem Werd' (NRC Handelsblad, 19 December 2018). According to Mayer, in spite of the Government's commitment to implement both the District Court and Court of Appeal rulings, 'it did not actually take any measures until 2019': Benoit Mayer, 'The Contribution of Urgenda to the Mitigation of Climate Change' (2023) 35(2) *Journal of Environmental Law* 167–84, 172.

[26] Court of Appeal Judgment (n 2) para [3.7].

[27] It seems that the constitutional implications of the case, which are addressed below in the context of the Supreme Court judgment, were a particularly important driver of the appeal. Verschuuren writes that '[t]he Government of the Netherlands appealed the decision, mainly because it objected to the interference of the Court with the making of government policies, which it argued should be discussed in Parliament rather than in courts, pursuant to the principle of balance of powers.' Verschuuren (n 25) 95.

[28] Court of Appeal Judgment (n 2) para [35].

[29] Verschuuren has observed that '[t]he court concluded that the State had failed to fulfil its duty of care pursuant to Articles 2 and 8 of the ECHR by not reducing its emissions by at least 25 percent by the end of 2020. The judgment, therefore, seems to replace the duty of care under the Dutch Civil Code referred to by the Hague District Court, with the duty of care under Articles 2 and 8 ECHR, thus essentially turning the Urgenda case into a human rights case'. Verschuuren (n 25) 96.

[30] See further Bernadette Rainey, Pamela McCormick and Clare Ovey, *Jacobs, White, and Ovey: The European Convention on Human Rights* (Oxford University Press, 2021).

On the one hand, it is true that the way in which the Netherlands chooses to apply the ECHR within the context of its own domestic legal order will be unique and particular to the Netherlands to some significant extent. For one thing, the ECHR has direct effect in the Netherlands, whereas in the other European countries examined in the case study chapters in this book (the UK and Ireland), it does not.[31] As Leijten has noted, a 'variety of human rights norms' may be 'invoked in climate litigation, and jurisdictions differ considerably as to their standing requirements and methods of interpretation'.[32] Spoelman summarises that: 'While the ECHR applies to all European nations, the Dutch … Court's interpretation of the ECHR in Urgenda is not binding outside the Netherlands.'[33] On the other hand, it is also the case that certain limits are placed upon the uniqueness of the ECHR's application in the Dutch setting, both by the parameters of the ECHR itself and by the jurisprudence of the international European Court of Human Rights (ECtHR), which supports the Council of Europe by interpreting the ECHR at the international level.[34] Given, then, that the ECHR is an instrument common to many countries, it can be argued that the *Urgenda Case*'s interpretation of elements of the ECHR in the context of climate law has at least some degree of direct relevance for all ECHR signatories as a potentially influential point of reference where pertinent ECHR points arise in the context of climate litigation within their jurisdictions.[35] Indeed, this is a line of reasoning that Friends of the Irish Environment advanced at the Irish Supreme Court in *Climate Case Ireland*.[36] Utilisation of *Urgenda* as a persuasive authority was rejected by the Irish Supreme Court insofar as the Court found that it was not directly pertinent to the relevant Irish law and facts at issue.[37] Taking the word 'influence' in its broadest sense, however, it *could* be argued that the *Urgenda* perspective on the ECHR *was* of some influence in the Irish case insofar as *Urgenda* was raised, considered and some commentary on the matter was provided in the

[31] The Human Rights Act 1998 and the European Convention on Human Rights Act 2003 give effect to the ECHR via primary legislation in the UK and Ireland respectively.

[32] Ingrid Leijten, 'Human Rights v Insufficient Climate Action: The Urgenda Case' (2019) 37(2) *Netherlands Quarterly of Human Rights* 112–18, 114.

[33] Naomi Spoelman, 'Urgenda: A How-to Guide for Enforcing Greenhouse Gas Emission Targets by Protecting Human Rights' (2020) 47 *Ecology Law Quarterly* 751–60, 751.

[34] Angelika Nussberger, *The European Court of Human Rights* (Oxford University Press, 2020).

[35] This observation harmonises with the work of Roy and Woerdman, who conceptualise the *Urgenda* ruling as having characteristics that can 'diffuse' to other jurisdictions. They also suggest such diffusion operates in a climate law context where the *Urgenda Case* itself has been subject to the influence of 'diffused' law from other jurisdictions, writing of 'elements that were 'diffused' from outside the Netherlands and elements that are diffusible in future instances of climate litigation': Roy and Woerdman (n 14) 167. Barritt is of the view that the case has had 'a significant global impact in fostering a body of transnational climate change jurisprudence', believing it to have 'undoubtedly helped to shape the growing body of transnational climate change litigation'; see further Emily Barritt, 'Consciously Transnational: Urgenda and the Shape of Climate Change Litigation: The State of the Netherlands (Ministry of Economic Affairs and Climate Policy) v Urgenda Foundation' (2020) 22(4) *Environmental Law Review* 296–305, 305.

[36] See ch 7 in this volume.

[37] ibid; *Friends of the Irish Environment v Government of Ireland* [2020] IESC 49.

Irish Supreme Court's judgment. Admittedly, the commentary was dismissing the ruling's direct pertinence, but this level of consideration is influence of a kind in itself.

Over the course of the Court of Appeal's reasoning, interesting consideration was afforded to the issue of the extent to which EU climate law obligations might amount to some form of floor or ceiling that is placed on the extent to which EU Member States are at liberty to crystallise mitigation targets in domestic law and policy. In the case itself, the date of 2020 was at issue. Previously, the State had adopted a policy approach that was intended to lower emissions by a minimum of 30 per cent up to that time,[38] but it had gone on to reduce this target in light of minimum requirements that were brought in by the EU, which strived for a 20 per cent minimum EU emissions reduction for 2020.[39] It is notable that Article 192 of the Treaty on the Functioning of the European Union (TFEU) states as follows:

> The European Parliament and the Council, acting in accordance with the ordinary legislative procedure and after consulting the Economic and Social Committee and the Committee of the Regions, shall decide what action is to be taken by the Union in order to achieve … [its environmental] objectives referred to in Article 191.[40]

Article 193 TFEU states that: 'The protective measures adopted pursuant to Article 192 shall not prevent any Member State from maintaining or introducing more stringent protective measures.'[41] Thus, as David Hart KC summarises: 'The underlying difficulty in all of this lay in the EU Treaty, which in Article 192, expressly reserves the rights of states to act more ambitiously than EU measures may require.'[42] Unsurprisingly, then, the Court rejected the State's argument that a formal 25 per cent target for the Netherlands would inappropriately exceed a lower level of EU ambition.

While this element is interesting in the context of climate law in general, the State's argument seems foolish on a point of general principle. In essence, it attempts to construe EU targets that demarcate a *minimum* standard of action, and that are intended to spur Member States onwards towards the achievement of improved climate progress, as a heavy constraint on superior climate progress in instances where it seems possible for a Member State to formalise and implement such superior standards in law and policy for specific time periods (here, 2020).[43]

[38] Court of Appeal Judgment (n 2) paras [52], [66], [72].
[39] ibid paras [17], [18].
[40] TFEU, art 192(1).
[41] ibid art 193.
[42] David Hart KC, 'Climate Change Human Rights Claim Wins in the Dutch Courts', *UK Human Rights Blog*, 14 October 2018, https://ukhumanrightsblog.com/2018/10/14/climate-change-human-rights-claim-wins-in-the-dutch-courts.
[43] For a persuasive legal explanation as to why in principle the adoption of a higher target by an EU Member State in this type of setting renders neither EU targets nor the distributed responsibility to meet them unlawful, see further Suryapratim Roy, 'Distributive Choices in Urgenda and EU Climate Law.' in *European Energy Law Report XI* (Intersentia, 2017), 47–68. It is sensible that this is so, given that EU climate law applies minimum rather than maximum mitigation targets. The District

Interpreted narrowly in the Dutch setting itself, the State's argument seems equally foolish, because the State had set a 49 per cent reduction goal for 2030 that exceeded its requirements under EU law for that year;[44] it does not make reasonable sense to argue that the State *cannot* endeavour to exceed the objectives of EU climate law for 2020 when it *is* endeavouring to exceed those objectives for 2030.[45]

In addition, it will be seen below that the Supreme Court upheld the Court of Appeal's general application of human rights law. It is notable, however, that the Court of Appeal applied what would currently tend to be seen in a legal context as a broad interpretation of human rights law (although this may change gradually over time as courts continue to develop their jurisprudence in the face of the climate challenge).[46] In the UK, for example, the capacity to mount climate-oriented human rights-based challenges was limited by the courts in their early stages in the *Plan B* case.[47] Here, in an application for judicial review that was ultimately refused by the courts because it was considered to be unarguable, the UK High Court opined as follows:

> The fourth ground [of argument] is that the Secretary of State's refusal to amend the 2050 [greenhouse gas emissions reduction] target [contained in the UK Climate Change Act 2008] constitutes a violation of the Claimants' human rights. The Claimants rely on the rights conferred by Articles 2 and 8 of the ECHR, and by Article 1 of the First Protocol,[48] both individually and in conjunction with Article 14[49] … I reject this submission. The Government is committed to set a net zero emission target at the appropriate time … [T]his is an area where the executive has a wide discretion to assess the advantages and disadvantages of any particular course of action, not only domestically but as part of an evolving international discussion. The Secretary of State [in the UK Government] has decided, having had regard to the advice of the Committee [on Climate Change], that now is not the time to revise the 2050 carbon target. That decision is not arguably unlawful, and accordingly the human rights challenge is not sustainable.[50]

Court deals carefully with the State's attempt to argue that the EU ETS imposes an 'emission ceiling' that constrains higher climate ambition, and the arguments that flow from this such as impermissible 'carbon leakage': District Court Judgment (n 1) paras [80]–[82].

[44] Court of Appeal Judgment (n 2) para [25]: 'In its Coalition Agreement, the government writes that it is the duty of the Netherlands to do everything in its power to achieve the Paris goal, for which reason the Netherlands has raised the bar higher than the EU, since the 40% reduction in 2030 is not enough to achieve the 2° C target, let alone the ambition of 1.5°C target.' Such policy positions expose the vacuous nature of the State's argument that 'the State is bound to the European ETS system and cannot do more than is permitted in the context of that system'; Court of Appeal Judgment (n 2) para [30]; see also paras [46], [58].

[45] See further Verschuuren (n 25) 97.

[46] This has occurred to a partial extent in the context of ECtHR jurisprudence while this book has been in its production publication; see *Verein Klimaseniorinnen Schweiz and Others v Switzerland*, Grand Chamber, European Court of Human Rights (Application No 53600/20), 9 April 2024.

[47] *Plan B Earth and Others, R (on the Application of) v Secretary of State for Business, Energy and Industrial Strategy* [2018] EWHC 1892 (Admin).

[48] This article concerns 'Protection of Property'.

[49] This article concerns 'Prohibition of Discrimination'.

[50] *Plan B Earth* (n 48) paras [48]–[49].

It has been argued on legal grounds that the application of human rights law has been drawn too widely in the *Urgenda Case*,[51] highlighting that while the case may be embraced by many around the world as a positive step forwards, many lawyers and legal systems may be very cautious about the extent to which it should be accorded wider practical legal influence, especially in instances where legal systems sit outside of the ECHR framework.

At any rate, the Urgenda Foundation's success at the Hague Court of Appeal resulted in a judgment being handed down requiring the upward adjustment of the State's minimum greenhouse gas emissions reduction target for 2020, moving from an EU-inspired target of at least 20 per cent[52] to a more stringent target of at least 25 per cent, measured from 1990 emissions levels. It has been noted above that the Court of Appeal affirmed the District Court's order, but went beyond the lower court in its reasoning to find that the State had breached its Articles 2 and 8 ECHR duty of care. Unlike the District Court, the Court of Appeal did not interpret Article 34 ECHR as a barrier to the application of Articles 2 and 8.[53] So far as the author is aware, this is the first example in the world of a senior court compelling a national Government to increase a state-wide emissions reduction target without the existence of a statutory mandate.[54] The Dutch State submitted its grounds for appeal to the Supreme Court on 8 January 2019, and the Urgenda Foundation submitted its written defence on 12 April 2019.[55] Hearings at the Supreme Court commenced on 24 May 2019.[56] 'Hopefully', Leijten commented in expert Dutch legal commentary after the Court of Appeal ruling, 'in hindsight, we can say that Urgenda was a first, still somewhat wobbly, judicial step toward [the] effective protection' of rights in the context of climate change.[57] On the face of it, it seemed highly uncertain that the Urgenda Foundation's arguably 'wobbly' success would hold up at the Supreme Court. By September, however, the mood-music sounded very positive for the NGO and its supporters, as the deputy Procurator General and Advocate General published a formal Opinion on 13 September 2020 recommending that the Supreme Court should rule against the Government.[58]

[51] Benoit Mayer, 'Climate Change Mitigation as an Obligation under Human Rights Treaties?' (2021) 115 *American Journal of International Law* 409.

[52] Court of Appeal Judgment (n 2) para [46]: 'the State does not want to commit to more than the 20% reduction relative to 1990 by 2020, as agreed at the EU level'.

[53] ibid para [35].

[54] See de Graaf and Jans (n 9) and text to the note.

[55] Urgenda Foundation, 'Climate Case Explained – Timeline', https://www.urgenda.nl/en/themas/climate-case/climate-case-explained.

[56] ibid.

[57] Leijten (n 32) 118.

[58] *Conclusion, State of the Netherlands (Ministry of Economic Affairs and Climate Policy) v Urgenda Foundation*, FF Langemeijer and MH Wissink, 13 September 2020, ECLI:NL:PHR:2019:1026. English translation.

III. The Supreme Court Ruling

A. The Decision: Placing Human Rights at the Heart of Climate Mitigation

The *Urgenda Case* reached the Supreme Court as an appeal in cassation, meaning that the Court was required to determine whether the Court of Appeal applied the law in a correct, comprehensible and adequately substantiated way. Therefore, as Wewerinke-Singh and McCoach emphasise, 'it is important to note that [the Supreme Court judgment] is based on the facts as established by the Court of Appeal – which were not disputed by either party in cassation'.[59] As noted above, the Dutch deputy Procurator General and the Advocate General released an Opinion advising the Supreme Court to reject the State's appeal.[60] The Urgenda Foundation had instituted its claim under an Article of the Dutch Civil Code enabling interest groups to bring class actions,[61] with the claim being pursued on behalf of the interests of the inhabitants of the Netherlands.[62] As discussed earlier, the Urgenda Foundation had contended that the minimum emissions reduction target set in place by the State for 2020 violated the due care that was part of the State's duty of care to Dutch inhabitants under the Dutch Civil Code.[63] The Court of Appeal had determined that the Urgenda Foundation could rely directly on ECHR provisions in this context, and the Supreme Court upheld this position: 'Since individuals who fall under the State's jurisdiction may rely on Articles 2 and 8 ECHR, which have direct effect in the Netherlands, Urgenda may also do so on behalf of these individuals, pursuant to Article 3:305a DCC [Dutch Civil Code].'[64]

The Netherlands is a party to the United Nations Framework Convention on Climate Change (UNFCCC) and the Paris Agreement, and the State did not dispute the broad principle that anthropogenic climate change is a serious concern, and that it requires significant action to be taken in response. It has been noted that the ECHR has direct effect in the Netherlands, where Dutch courts are required to apply the ECHR's provisions.[65] The Netherlands is subject to the jurisdiction of

[59] Margaretha Wewerinke-Singh, and Ashleigh McCoach, 'The State of the Netherlands v Urgenda Foundation: Distilling Best Practice and Lessons Learnt for Future Rights-Based Climate Litigation' (2021) 30(2) *Review of European, Comparative & International Environmental Law* 275–83, 276.

[60] *Conclusion, State of the Netherlands* (n 58).

[61] Dutch Civil Code, art 3:305a.

[62] Supreme Court Judgment (n 3) para [2.2.1]. The Supreme Court notes that the availability of standing in this case is 'in line with Article 9(3) in conjunction with Article 2(5) of the Aarhus Convention, which guarantees interest groups access to justice in order to challenge violations of environmental law'; para [5.9.2].

[63] Dutch Civil Code, art 6:162(2).

[64] Supreme Court Judgment (n 3) para [2.3.2], summarising the Court of Appeal's position; Court of Appeal Judgment (n 2) para [36].

[65] Dutch Constitution, arts 93 and 94.

the ECtHR,[66] and Dutch courts are required to interpret the ECHR in harmony with the ECtHR.[67] The Supreme Court noted in its judgment that the ECtHR had not issued a landmark climate law judgment to date, and so there was a dearth of direction on the central issue of climate change from the ECtHR itself.[68] However, the Supreme Court also declined to request what it described as a 'possible but not compulsory' advisory opinion from the ECtHR, preferring to decide the case itself and being of the view that 'the answer to this question [of whether Articles 2 and 8 engage climate protections is] … sufficiently clear'.[69]

According to Meguro, another challenge was 'that ECtHR case law has only considered environmental harm that does not cross borders'.[70] Drawing on a report of the Office of the UN High Commissioner for Human Rights,[71] she adds that: 'What is more, "human rights violations are normally established after the harm has occurred", while the threat of climate change largely concerns a problem of risk – anticipated harm.'[72] On this point, concerning climate change largely involving anticipated harm rather than actual harm, it is true that a tendency arises in this and many other landmark cases to view harm arising from anthropogenic climate change as something that will occur in the future; however, on a point of general principle, this quasi-legal norm is founded on inaccuracy – demonstrable harm is occurring on a gradual basis continually, including at the present (and in the past).[73] Wewerinke-Singh and McCoach pick up on this frequently neglected but crucial point, unpacking it in Part 3 of their paper 'The State of the Netherlands v Urgenda Foundation: Distilling Best Practice and Lessons Learnt for Future Rights-Based Climate Litigation'.[74] They stress that the Supreme Court's 'assumption that dangerous climate change is exclusively a future concern remains problematic'.[75] (Indeed, one can go beyond this – more than

[66] ECHR, art 32.

[67] Supreme Court, 16 December 2016, ECLI:NL:HR:2016:2888, para [3.3.3]; Supreme Court Judgment (n 3) endnote 33.

[68] Supreme Court Judgment (n 3) para [5.6.3].

[69] ibid para [5.6.4].

[70] Maiko Meguro, 'State of the Netherlands v Urgenda Foundation' (2020) 114(4) *American Journal of International Law* 729–35, 732.

[71] Report of the Office of the UN High Commissioner for Human Rights [OHCHR] on the Relationship Between Human Rights and Climate Change, UN Doc A/HRC/10/61 (15 January 2009).

[72] Meguro (n 70) 732.

[73] As clearly summarised, for example, by the IPCC's reporting on the 'Observed Impacts from Climate Change': 'Human-induced climate change, including more frequent and intense extreme events, has caused widespread adverse impacts and related losses and damages to nature and people, beyond natural climate variability … Across sectors and regions the most vulnerable people and systems are observed to be disproportionately affected. The rise in weather and climate extremes has led to some irreversible impacts as natural and human systems are pushed beyond their ability to adapt': IPCC, 'Summary for Policymakers' in: IPCC, *Climate Change 2022: Impacts, Adaptation and Vulnerability. Contribution of Working Group II to the Sixth Assessment Report of the Intergovernmental Panel on Climate Change* (H-O Pörtner, DC Roberts, M Tignor, ES Poloczanska, K Mintenbeck, A Alegría, M Craig, S Langsdorf, S Löschke, V Möller, A Okem, B Rama (eds) (Cambridge University Press, 2022) 9.

[74] Wewerinke-Singh and McCoach (n 59) 280–82.

[75] ibid 280.

being problematic, it is incorrect.) They find that 'notably absent from the judgement is any reference to climate change impacts already being experienced'.[76] They also raise the point that in failing to recognise current impacts in the context of such a globalised problem, this neglects not only impacts within the Netherlands in Europe, but also impacts around the world: 'Specifically, the Supreme Court failed to recognize the extent to which climate change has already reached dangerous proportions in many parts of the world, notably including the Dutch Caribbean.'[77]

The commencement of the Supreme Court judgment is not particularly helpful because it states that 'the facts established by the Court of Appeal in paras 3.1–3.26 … of its judgement can be taken as a starting point';[78] the Court of Appeal judgment does not contain a paragraphs 3.1–3.26 section (it runs from paragraphs 3.1 to 3.9).[79] Other inaccuracies include discussion of 'The Fourth IPCC Assessment Report (hereafter 'AR4') from 2004', but this report was from 2007.[80] At any rate, the Supreme Court judgment does provide a considered and logical summary of the condition of climate change based on what is understood from climate science.[81] It clarifies the consensus scientific understanding that global warming must be limited to 2°C maximum on pre-industrial levels this century and, according to the most recent consensus scientific work, 1.5°C if possible.

It has been noted above that the District Court accepted that the State had a pertinent duty of care to act, but rejected the Urgenda Foundation's human rights strand of argument.[82] The Court of Appeal, by contrast, found that Articles 2 and 8 ECHR are directly applicable law under the Dutch Constitution in this context, and that this provides a direct basis for the duty of care.[83] It has also been noted that Article 2 ECHR requires protection of the 'right to life' and Article 8 ECHR

[76] ibid 281.

[77] ibid 283. For more on this matter, see Laura Burgers and Tim Staal, 'Climate Action as Positive Human Rights Obligation: The Appeals Judgment in Urgenda v The Netherlands' in *Netherlands Yearbook of International Law*, vol 49 (TMC Asser Press, 2019), 223–44, 228.

[78] Supreme Court Judgment (n 3) para [2.1].

[79] See Court of Appeal Judgment (n 2) para [3].

[80] Supreme Court Judgment (n 3) para [2.1].

[81] ibid paras [4.1]–[4.8].

[82] As summarised by the Supreme Court, the District Court found that '[t]he legal obligation of the State towards Urgenda cannot be derived from Article 21 of the Dutch Constitution, the "no harm" principle, the UNFCCC with associated protocols, Article 191 TFEU, or the ETS Directive and Effort Sharing Decision based on Article 191 TFEU'; ibid para [2.3.1]. See further District Court Judgment (n 1) paras [4.36]–[4.44] and [4.52]. For the EU ETS Directive and the Effort Sharing Decision, see respectively: Directive 2003/87/EC of the European Parliament and of the Council of 13 October 2003 establishing a system for greenhouse gas emission allowance trading within the Union and amending Council Directive 96/61/EC (as amended); and Council Decision 406/2009/EC [2009] OJ L140/136 (the Effort Sharing Decision, since developed into Regulation (EU) 2023/857, the 'Effort Sharing Regulation').

[83] The Supreme Court made reference to the congruity of this position in Dutch law with the doctrine of 'positive obligations' applied under the ECHR, which the ECtHR has drawn on in its jurisprudence in relation to environmental issues; Supreme Court Judgment (n 3) para [5.8].

requires protection of the 'right to respect for private and family life'.[84] Article 13 ECHR requires national law to provide an effective legal remedy where a violation of those rights has occurred, or where an imminent violation is due to occur.[85] Thus, the national courts must have the facility to afford effective legal protection in the event of ECHR breaches. The Supreme Court upheld the Court of Appeal's position, drawing on the ECHR to determine that the weaker mitigation minimum advanced by the State for 2020 could not meet requisite Article 2 and 8 positive obligations to protect the life of the Dutch.[86]

B. The Influence of the UNFCCC and the IPCC

The judgment engages significantly with the UNFCCC, which is addressed by the Supreme Court and factored into its thinking.[87] The Court makes notable reference to the worldwide 'carbon budget', echoing a preoccupation with this concept in the *Gloucester Resources Case*, although it features less prominently in the *Urgenda* judgment.[88] It is also notable that the Court of Appeal had ground-cleared a range of the State's arguments in advance of the Supreme Court ruling, roundly rejecting them.[89] Following on from the reasoning of the District Court,[90] the Court of Appeal had been unpersuaded that the 'waterbed effect' would arise within the EU if the Netherlands reduced particular greenhouse gas emissions,[91] where it was purported that such reductions would cause emissions to rise outside of the Netherlands in other EU countries by enabling those countries to increase their emissions under the EU's Emissions Trading Scheme (ETS).[92] It had also been unpersuaded that 'carbon leakage' would likely cause companies to move operations to alternative countries where greenhouse gas reduction obligations are less strict.[93]

[84] Article 2 protections can incorporate both shorter-term risks and risks that may only occur over the longer term; ibid para [5.2.2]. Article 8 protections can incorporate the need for reasonable and appropriate measures to be taken to protect individuals against possible serious damage to their environment; ibid para [5.2.3]. Thus, both Articles as developed by the ECtHR contain strands that harmonise with and bolster the *precautionary principle*, a principle that is particularly useful in climate litigation, which often (as in this case) requires a long-term view.

[85] On these human rights elements, see generally ibid paras [5.2.1]–[5.5.3].

[86] Note that where 'a state has taken reasonable and suitable measures, the mere fact that those measures were unable to deter the hazard does not mean that the state failed to meet the obligation [ensuing from Articles 2 and 8 ECHR] that had been imposed on it', such that an emphasis falls on the measures to be taken rather than the guarantee of an envisaged result; ibid para [5.3.4].

[87] ibid paras [5.6.1]–[5.8].

[88] ibid para [2.1]: 'When viewed in light of the maximum concentration level of 430 or 450 ppm in the year 2100 and the current concentration level of greenhouse gases (401 ppm), it is clear that the world has very little leeway left when it comes to the emission of greenhouse gases. The total worldwide leeway that now remains for emitting greenhouse gases is referred to as the "carbon budget".'

[89] The Court of Appeal Judgment also recognised the global 'carbon budget'; Court of Appeal Judgment (n 2) paras [3.5], [44].

[90] District Court Judgment (n 1) para [4.81].

[91] Court of Appeal Judgment (n 2) paras [56].

[92] ibid para [57].

[93] ibid para [57]. See further Supreme Court Judgment (n 3) para [2.3.2].

The Supreme Court clearly distinguishes between UNFCCC Annex I and non-Annex I parties: 'The parties to the UNFCCC are referred to as Annex I countries and non-Annex I countries. The Annex I countries are the developed countries, including the Netherlands.'[94] The position advanced by the State arguing that the Netherlands' emissions are relatively modest in the global context, meaning that reduction measures would be similarly modest and therefore of little importance,[95] is disposed of in part within the parameters of the UNFCCC.[96] The logical consequence of such an argument is that no country takes any significant action at all.[97] The Supreme Court highlighted that each country has a responsibility for its own share of emissions; the UNFCCC apportions a responsibility to take action to all countries.[98] In the global context, this can be described as a State's 'partial responsibility'.[99] The Court also highlighted that the burden to lead in the reductions drive is placed by the UNFCCC on developed nations (which includes the Netherlands).[100] In the Supreme Court's view, Articles 2 and 8 ECHR reinforce this position, because if the State does not act, the life and welfare of people become endangered.[101] Here, then, the UNFCCC and the ECHR can be seen to overlap and come together in a mutually reinforcing way in the Supreme Court's reasoning.

Within the parameters of these UNFCCC-ECHR considerations, the Supreme Court took particular account of the work of the Intergovernmental Panel on Climate Change (IPCC), notably its Fourth Assessment Report of 2007[102] that presented the importance on scientific grounds of limiting average global temperature rise to a maximum of 2°C above pre-industrial levels this century.[103] Both the generally accepted scientific understanding of the climate change challenge and the presence of international standards intended to engage with the problem fed directly into the Court's interpretation of the State's Article 2 and 8 ECHR obligations. Linking scientific understanding, and particularly the work of the IPCC, to international standards, the Supreme Court found that in order to adequately contain dangerous temperature rise, it is generally accepted that UNFCCC Annex I countries need to reduce their emissions for 2020 by a minimum level of 25–40 per cent, and their emissions for 2050 by a minimum

[94] Supreme Court Judgment (n 3) para [2.1].

[95] This is sometimes known in climate discourse as the 'drop in the ocean' argument. See further, eg, Jolene Lin, 'The First Successful Climate Negligence Case: A Comment on Urgenda Foundation v the State of the Netherlands (Ministry of Infrastructure and the Environment)' (2015) 5(1) *Climate Law* 65–81.

[96] Supreme Court Judgment (n 3) para [5.7.7].

[97] An alternative logical consequence of this line of reasoning is that only those states responsible for a comparatively enormous quantity of emissions would be understood to have any obligation to act. The three largest emitters are China, the US and India.

[98] Supreme Court Judgment (n 3) paras [5.7.3], [5.7.5].

[99] Mcguro (n 7) 730–31; Supreme Court Judgment (n 3) paras [5.7.1]–[5.8].

[100] UNFCCC, art 4(2).

[101] Supreme Court Judgment (n 3) paras [5.6.1]–[5.8].

[102] *Fourth Assessment Report: AR4 Climate Change 2007* (IPCC, 2007).

[103] Supreme Court Judgment (n 3) paras [6.1]–[7.3.6].

of 80–95 per cent, with both reductions measured from 1990 levels.[104] The primary origin of this assertion is the IPCC's Fourth Assessment Report, which found that Annex I countries to the UNFCCC would need to reduce greenhouse gas emissions by 25–40 per cent for 2020 if the scientific 'parts per million' (ppm) measurement of harmful greenhouse gases in the atmosphere was going to be kept to a level by 2100 that could likely contain pre-industrial temperature rise within the 2°C warming limit.[105] This became a statistical basis for the Supreme Court's decision to uphold the 25 per cent reduction obligation that had been placed upon the State by the lower courts for 2020.[106]

Viewed from a doctrinal legal perspective, the robust way in which the Supreme Court chose to integrate these factors into its application of domestic law might appear to be something of a stretch in the eyes of some, because, as the Court itself correctly noted: 'The State rightly argues that this target [of a 25–40 per cent emissions reduction for 2020] is not a binding rule or agreement in and of itself.'[107] On the other hand, however, the Court reasoned that '[t]he question for the Court is … whether this target nevertheless binds the State' via the assistance it provides in fleshing out the content of the perceived duty on the State that emerges from the ECHR provisions.[108] Further, in addressing Zahar's belief that the court has mistakenly reasoned from what Zahar characterises as 'physical necessity' rather than from strict legal obligations,[109] Roy points out that 'the IPCC Report does not specify whether the 25–40 percent target is to be achieved by the Netherlands individually or by the EU (and other Annex I countries) collectively',[110] meaning that the Supreme Court may have made a

[104] ibid.

[105] ibid para [2.1]; see further *Fourth Assessment Report* (n 102). See also Court of Appeal Judgment (n 2) para [12].

[106] Mayer seems to suggest that it might be possible to argue on the basis of the IPCC's *Fourth Assessment Report* itself that a minimum standard of 10 per cent rather than 25 per cent might be appropriate for 2020; see Benoit Mayer, 'The State of the Netherlands v Urgenda Foundation: Ruling of the Court of Appeal of The Hague (9 October 2018)' (2019) 8 *Transnational Environmental Law* 167–92, 181–82. Box 13.7 of the relevant report sketches out that a 10 per cent minimum reduction for 2020 and a 40–90 per cent reduction span for 2050 associated with it likely places atmospheric greenhouse gas measurement this century within a 550 ppm scenario range. This is dangerously high: IPCC, *Climate Change 2007: Mitigation. Contribution of Working Group III to the Fourth Assessment Report of the Intergovernmental Panel on Climate Change* (B Metz, OR Davidson, PR Bosch, R Dave, LA Meyer (eds)) (Cambridge University Press, 2007) Box 13.7, 776.

[107] Supreme Court Judgment (n 3) para [7.1].

[108] ibid para [7.1]. It is notable that the Court found that the general 25–40 per cent consensus target has *collective* international relevance for countries, but also *individual* relevance for countries. Thus, in the Court's view, it has individual relevance for the Netherlands, and it is translated into a factor pertinent to the Court's application of arts 2 and 8 ECHR within the domestic parameters of the Dutch legal order: see Supreme Court Judgment (n 3) paras [6.1]–[7.3.6]. The Court of Appeal's rationale for taking a collective target as a starting point for an individual Annex I country (here, the Netherlands) is outlined at Court of Appeal Judgment (n 2) para [60].

[109] Alexander Zahar, 'The Urgenda Appeal Decision and the Argument from Physical Necessity', 3 December 2018, https://ssrn.com/abstract=3285076.

[110] Suryapratim Roy, 'Urgenda II and its Discontents' (2019) 13(2) *Carbon& Climate Law Review* 130–41, 140. See also the comments above at n 108.

tenuous leap in the eyes of some in pinning a minimum 25 per cent reduction figure on the Netherlands so precisely and directly in the way that it did.

Indeed, in an insightful commentary, Meguro has been somewhat critical of aspects of the Court's approach to the UNFCCC,[111] pointing out that the Supreme Court drew on the 'no harm' principle from international law and the UNFCCC in a manner that arguably raises some uncertainty in legal terms:

> In establishing this individual state obligation to counter climate change, the Court also applied the no harm principle to climate change. While the principle refers to a state's due diligence obligation to prevent transboundary harms from activities within its jurisdiction, the Court did not elaborate how the no harm principle provides the guidance to interpret ECHR Articles 2 and 8 in the context of climate change. *The relevance of the principle remains unclear, given that it is only a rhetorical reference in the preamble and not a guiding principle of the UNFCCC.* (Emphasis added)[112]

This is a legitimate observation. As to the way in which international law assisted the Supreme Court in reaching the pinpoint 25 per cent minimum reduction figure that it applied, Meguro explains that this conclusion is arguably problematic in legal terms because 'the UNFCCC *explicitly avoided* defining an individual lowest rate of reduction as an international legal standard' (emphasis added).[113] Moreover, she explains, the Paris Agreement moves international law even further away from the UNFCCC-driven interpretation adopted by the Court:

> Contrary to conceptualization by the Court, individual state obligations under the Paris Agreement adopted within the framework of the UNFCCC are not understood as a part measured against the whole. For the Paris Agreement, the obligation is not premised on any direct causal link between a state's emissions and the individual obligation of reduction. Nor does violation of the Paris Agreement give rise to state responsibility for not doing its part as 'allocated' based on the particular 'total' GHG amount to be reduced. While the Paris Agreement's temperature target is collectively pursued by the member states, it is neither legally linked to nationally determined contributions nor used as the threshold to evaluate the lawfulness of the content of a state commitment.[114]

Based on the objective international legal architecture, this is a reasonable criticism. Meguro thus highlights some of the arguable difficulties underlying the Court's reasoning.

At any rate, in reaching its decision, the Supreme Court arguably attends to the somewhat problematic aspect of the (at best) relatively soft law character of some of the material it relies on (the IPCC reports are not law at all) reasonably well in legal terms via the application of human rights law, as adapted to the Dutch domestic legal setting.[115] In an analysis produced after the District Court ruling and prior

[111] Meguro (n 70).
[112] ibid 732–33.
[113] ibid 733.
[114] ibid.
[115] As discussed previously – see in particular section III.A above.

to the Court of Appeal ruling, Roger Cox, who acted for the Urgenda Foundation at the District Court, has also reflected on the crucial role tort law played in establishing the initial foundations of the litigation.[116] Here, he highlighted the role that tort law could potentially play in other climate cases and opined that:

> As long as the claimant in a climate case bases its argumentation on the IPCC findings, there is little to nothing a national government can do from a legal perspective to contest these findings. This puts the judge in an easier position to pass judgment and reach a verdict.[117]

Without those findings being embedded directly in law in some manner, this seems to be overstated.[118] Thus, for example, it is perhaps unsurprising to find commentary from respected legal scholars Roy and Woerdman highlighting that the District Court ruling seemed to pay somewhat scant regard to aspects of EU climate law.[119] The authors comment that: 'We were puzzled … as to why the international (the IPCC) was identified as a preferred benchmark for allocation of climate targets over the supranational (the EU).'[120] The authors are commenting here after the District Court ruling and prior to the Court of Appeal ruling. Tracking the implications of this observation forward, it appears that what might have been the potentially sharper edge of EU climate law was blunted by the District Court's approach,[121] and therefore the framing of the issues at the Court of Appeal took a similar shape. This in turn generated the primary frame of reference that the Supreme Court's reasoning entered into, bearing in mind that this was an appeal in cassation.[122]

An additional difficulty that troubles the Supreme Court's reasoning, and which the Court does not deal with very convincingly – if at all – pertains to the fact that the Fourth IPCC Assessment Report of 2007 and its 25–40 per cent 2020 figure has become outdated. Since 2007, and prior to the Court of Appeal ruling, further analysis in the scientific sphere,[123] and, linked to that, further major developments in international standards under the Paris Agreement, have moved beyond an intention to limit average warming this century to a 2°C increase on pre-industrial levels. Instead, the requirement is to pursue efforts to limit average

[116] Roger Cox, 'A Climate Change Litigation Precedent: Urgenda Foundation v The State of the Netherlands' (2016) 34(2) *Journal of Energy & Natural Resources Law* 143–63, 146.
[117] ibid 146.
[118] Writing prior to the Supreme Court's ruling, Verschuuren emphasised that: 'Some scholars have … criticized the District Court's judgment for elevating scientific research findings to a legally binding legal norm: "Should the unwritten standard of due care that the State has to observe in society and the court-ordered reduction target be derived directly from scientific data in the IPCC reports?"' Verschuuren (n 25) 95, quoting the work of de Graaf and Jans (n 9) 526.
[119] Roy and Woerdman (n 14).
[120] ibid 189.
[121] See, eg, District Court Judgment (n 1) para [4.44].
[122] On cassation, see section III.A above.
[123] The IPCC's Fifth Assessment Report was published in 2013–14: *Fifth Assessment Report: AR5 Climate Change 2013 & 2014* (IPCC, 2013–14).

warming to 1.5°C.[124] This amounts to a significant shift in the headline goal embedded in the IPCC scientific consensus and international standards.[125] In summarising the Court of Appeal ruling, the Supreme Court notes as follows:

> The IPCC report which states that a reduction of 25–45% by the end of 2020 is needed to achieve the two-degree target (AR4) dates all the way back to 2007. Since that time, virtually all COPs (in Bali, Cancún, Durban, Doha and Warsaw) have referred to this 25–40% standard and Annex I countries have been urged to align their reduction targets accordingly. This may not have established a legal standard with a direct effect, but it does confirm the fact that a reduction of at least 25–40% in CO_2 emissions is needed to prevent dangerous climate change.[126]

Again, this was predicated on limiting temperatures to 2°C in the second half of this century; 1.5°C has since been advanced by the scientific consensus and reflected in the leading-edge international standards embodied by the Paris Agreement. A logical analysis therefore suggests as follows: if a minimum 25 per cent figure has been generated by a specific temperature target and if that temperature target has since been tightened significantly, this indicates that the minimum 25 per cent figure generated by the original target also needs to be tightened. In terms of timing, it is notable that the IPCC's Fifth Assessment Report was published over 2013–14 and the Paris Agreement was adopted at COP21 in Paris in 2015,[127] some years prior to the Court of Appeal ruling in 2018. It is also notable that each of the COPs that the Supreme Court refers to in the quotation above precede this period: Bali, 2007; Cancún, 2010; Durban, 2011; Doha, 2012; and Warsaw, 2013.[128]

[124] Paris Agreement, art 2(1)(a).

[125] In legal terms, it is also notable that the Supreme Court referred to the 2010 COP 16 in Cancún, where the Kyoto Protocol parties 'stated that the [UNFCCC] Annex I countries had to continue to take the lead in counteracting climate change and that, given AR4, this "would require Annex I Parties as a group to reduce emissions in a range of 25–40 per cent below 1990 levels by 2020"': Supreme Court Judgment (n 3) para [2.1]. The judgment continues: 'At the climate conference in Doha in 2012 (COP-18), all Annex I countries were called on to raise their reduction targets to at least 25–40% in 2020. An amendment to the Kyoto Protocol was adopted, in which the EU committed to a reduction of 20% in 2020 compared to 1990, and offered to reduce emissions by 30% if other countries were to undertake the achievement of similar reduction targets. This condition was not met. *The Doha Amendment did not enter into force*': Supreme Court Judgment (n 3) para [2.1], emphasis added (also highlighted in the Court of Appeal Judgment (n 2) para [11]). In terms of international law, then, it is notable that the Doha Amendment designed to increase Annex I party targets towards the 25–40 per cent threshold was not actually brought into force at the international level in this period. The following comment from the Supreme Court is also telling: 'the emission reduction agreements made at the various climate conferences are not legally binding in themselves': Supreme Court Judgment (n 3) para [6.2]. Mayer has suggested that because COP decisions tend not to specify an emissions reductions range explicitly, this actually reflects 'more than anything else, the *absence* of a global consensus on the 25–40% emissions reduction target': Mayer (n 106) 187.

[126] Supreme Court Judgment (n 3) para [2.3.2].

[127] The Paris Agreement entered into force on 4 November 2016.

[128] 'Conference of the Parties (COP)', sessions timeline hosted online by the UNFCCC Secretariat at: https://unfccc.int/process/bodies/supreme-bodies/conference-of-the-parties-cop.

In practical terms, according to current scientific understanding, this shift means greenhouse gases are required to be capped in the atmosphere at 430 ppm[129] rather than at the 2°C 450 ppm levels that the Supreme Court and Court of Appeal worked to in their respective December 2019 and October 2018 rulings.[130] Again, it appears to follow logically that a material change in ppm levels would seem to necessitate a change in a target percentage directly linked to those levels. Indeed, the Supreme Court itself notes that: 'Climate change conferences after 2015 no longer explicitly addressed or referred to the reduction target of 25-40% by 2020.'[131] This is hardly a surprise, given that it has been superseded by a shift from 2°C headline efforts to 1.5°C.[132] Thus, the Supreme Court is incorrect to conclude that 'contrary to what the State argues, this does not mean that [IPPC Fourth Assessment Report] AR4's reduction scenario for 2020 has become outdated'.[133]

On a point of principle, however, this conclusion does not assist the State's position at all; if anything, it assists the Urgenda Foundation's side of the argument, because international standards have become *more* stringent since 2007 based on the Paris Agreement and the work of the IPCC. Therefore, in principle the implication is that fixing a target for 2020 on these grounds should likely result in a higher minimum target than the reduction percentage articulated by the bottom of the 25–40 per cent range, that is to say, a higher target than the outcome minimum 25 per cent reduction applied by the Court. The approach adopted by the District Court in this line seems more reasonable given that this initial case was in preparation prior to 2015 – according to lead counsel for the Urgenda Foundation Roger Cox, the legal action was brought after more than two years of preparation[134] – and the court issued its ruling on 24 June 2015, prior to the drafting of the Paris Agreement later that year. Yet, in the era of the Court of Appeal (2018) and the Supreme Court (2019) rulings, things have since moved on, betraying an unreactive quality underlying the court system that should be guarded against in future wherever possible in order to allow climate litigation to keep pace with the world.

[129] 'Parts per million' or 'ppm' is a measurement of the concentration of greenhouse gases in the atmosphere. For example, if carbon dioxide is at 424 ppm, this means there are 424 carbon dioxide particles in 1,000,000 particles of air.

[130] Thus, although it worked from AR4, in discussing the content of AR5 the Court of Appeal noted that 'studies … [have] looked at scenarios that lead to a limitation of global warming to 1.5°C. Such scenarios assume concentrations of less than 430 ppm in 2100'. Court of Appeal Judgment (n 2) para [12].

[131] Supreme Court Judgment (n 3) para [7.2.3].

[132] The Supreme Court acknowledges this itself as follows (but does not go on to give the point meaningful weight in its reasoning): 'the 2015 Paris Agreement explicitly stipulates that the states will endeavour to limit warming to 1.5°C, "recognising that this would significantly reduce the risks and impacts of climate change" (art 2(1), opening words and (a), of the Agreement). This necessitates a greater reduction in greenhouse gas emissions than is necessary for a target of no more than 2°C.' Supreme Court Judgment (n 3) para [7.2.8].

[133] Supreme Court Judgment (n 3) para [7.2.4]. The Supreme Court's questionable position here followed on from similar shaky reasoning from the Court of Appeal: 'The Court of Appeal's finding that the 25–40% target has not been superseded by AR5 is … understandable and serves as a starting point in cassation.' Supreme Court Judgment (n 3) para [7.2.5].

[134] Cox (n 116) 143.

Relatedly, Wewerinke-Singh and McCoach have identified a further legal miscalculation, which they describe as a 'missed opportunity',[135] whereby the Urgenda Foundation team failed to challenge the District Court's 25 per cent target finding at the Court of Appeal. Here, the Court of Appeal noted that 'Urgenda did not put forward grounds of appeal against … the rejection of a reduction of more than 25%. This means that in these appeal proceedings, a reduction of more than at least 25% by 2020 cannot be awarded'.[136] This also restricted the consideration of augmentation to the 25 per cent figure at the Supreme Court. Wewerinke-Singh and McCoach write:

> [O]n appeal, Urgenda had not challenged the District Court's finding that the Netherlands' discretionary power prohibited the Court from ordering a reduction of more than 25 percent. This was a missed opportunity as such an order might well have been justified based on equity and CBDRRC [i.e., the UNFCCC principle of Common but Differentiated Responsibilities and Respective Capabilities], in light of the Netherlands' greater responsibility for causing climate change and greater capacity to address it than most other Annex I States.[137]

Indeed, it is notable that Robiou du Pont and Meinshausen, in examining and assessing national commitments under the Paris Agreement from a scientific perspective, have found that '[c]urrent NDCs[138] individually align, at best, with divergent concepts of equity and are collectively inconsistent with the Paris Agreement'.[139] They add that:

> In a recent climate case, the District Court of The Hague ruled that the Dutch government has to reduce 2020 emissions to at least the least-ambitious end of the range recommended by the IPCC-AR4 for the Annex I country group … [S]ystematic court decisions that governments must follow the least-ambitious end of an equity range would be insufficient to achieve the Paris Agreement.[140]

This raises an interesting point. The *Urgenda Case* currently stands out amongst landmark climate cases as the most pronounced and immediate driver of national mitigation to date. Hypothetically, if an equivalent form of ruling was rolled out by courts across the Annex I countries, the work of Robiou du Pont and Meinshausen suggests that those courts' adherence to 'minimum' standards could likely produce rulings that are too low to secure the headline Paris Agreement temperature targets. This line of thinking appears to underscore Wewerinke-Singh and McCoach's argument that a useful opportunity was missed by the Urgenda Foundation when it did not challenge the District Court's determination that

[135] Wewerinke-Singh and McCoach (n 59) 278.
[136] Court of Appeal Judgment (n 2) para [3.9].
[137] Wewerinke-Singh and McCoach (n 59) 2278.
[138] This refers to the Nationally Determined Contributions that signatories to the Paris Agreement are required to produce every five years, which include mitigation targets.
[139] Yann Robiou du Pont and Malte Meinshausen, 'Warming Assessment of the Bottom-up Paris Agreement Emissions Pledges' (2018) 9(4810) *Climate Change Nature* 1–10, 1.
[140] ibid 2.

the courts could not exceed the application of a 25 per cent minimum target due to impermissible intrusion on the State's discretion.[141]

C. Reduction Targets and the Pace of Change

A further somewhat subtle but nevertheless important point arising from the judgment concerns the fact that the State did accept the need to reduce emissions, but disagreed before the Supreme Court with the Court of Appeal's view on the necessary speed of the reductions.[142] The State formerly had a relatively ambitious policy of reducing emissions by 30 per cent on 1990 levels in place until 2011,[143] but as the EU set about implementing its *20-20-20* climate plan, which was based on the requirement of a 20 per cent emissions reduction for 2020 for the EU as a whole,[144] the State apparently took this as an opportunity to lower its target, reducing it substantially to 20 per cent for 2020.[145] As the Court of Appeal put it, '[u]p to the year 2011, the Netherlands … started from a reduction target of 30% for 2020 relative to 1990'; however, thereafter 'the Dutch reduction target was adjusted … to align with the EU-wide reduction of 20% for 2020'.[146] In the author's view this is poor, not least as the Supreme Court emphasises that a 'letter dated 12 October 2009 from the Minister of VROM shows that the State itself was convinced that a scenario with a reduction of less than 25%–40% in 2020 would lack credibility to keep the two-degree target within reach'.[147] Despite this, '[t]he Dutch reduction target for 2020 was subsequently adjusted downwards' and 'a substantiation based on climate science was never given' for the change.[148] This clearly suggests that the Government took what it perceived as an opportunity afforded by EU law and policy to slacken national emissions reduction standards in order to gain an easier ride over the short term, leaving future Dutch Governments over the years from 2021 to 2030 to bear the additional emissions reduction burden.

One reason that one can conclude in very explicit terms that by the Supreme Court stage of the *Urgenda* litigation the State was endeavouring to load future Governments falling within the 2021–30 bracket with a heavier burden is that the State explicitly intended to speed up the reductions process greatly after 2020, applying a mandatory 49 per cent target for 2030 (followed by a 95 per cent

141 Wewerinke-Singh and McCoach (n 59).

142 Supreme Court Judgment (n 3) paras [7.4.1]–[7.5.3].

143 See above n 38 and text to the note; Supreme Court Judgment (n 3) para [2.1].

144 Thomas L Muinzer, 'The 20-20-20 Climate and Energy Package', s 4.2 in 'An Evaluation of the Implications of EU Climate and Energy Governance for the UK in Light of Brexit' (2017) 23(2) *European Journal of Current Legal Issues*. See further Supreme Court Judgment (n 3) para [2.1] (24–26).

145 Supreme Court Judgment (n 3) para [2.1].

146 Court of Appeal Judgment (n 2) paras [19]–[20].

147 Supreme Court Judgment (n 3) para [2.3.2].

148 ibid para [2.3.2].

target for 2050).[149] These 2030 and 2050 targets had been set down by Parliament in a Dutch Climate Act (passed after the Court of Appeal ruling),[150] and the more distant 95 per cent target reflected the State's longstanding acceptance that a minimum 80–95 per cent reduction would be necessary for 2050.[151] Thus, a nuance of this case that tends to get lost in commentary is that the Urgenda Foundation and the State both accepted the utility of a minimum 49 per cent 2030 target and an 80–95 per cent 2050 target based on current scientific understanding and international standards, such that *the pace of the transition* – via the 2020 target – was at the heart of the dispute.[152] A more stringent 2020 target requires swifter progress to be made by that time towards the 2030 49 per cent target, while a more lax 2020 target loads a greater burden onto the years 2021–30 and, commensurate with that, places an equivalent burden to deliver this upon the Government(s) in place over the 2021–30 period (and society as a whole). The State did not provide adequate reasons for this substantial slowing of pace, which placed the country out of the 25–40 per cent range sketched out by scientific and international standards, and which would permit more dangerous emissions to aggregate over time in the atmosphere in advance of the 2020 target deadline than would otherwise occur.[153] These aspects assisted the Supreme Court in finding that the Court of Appeal could reach the conclusions it did validly.

D. Constitutional Issues

Lively Dutch constitutional issues were also raised in the case, requiring resolution by the Supreme Court. The State argued that the Dutch courts are not entitled to engage in decisions of this kind because they are the proper domain of the Dutch Government and Parliament.[154] The Supreme Court's approach was broadly in harmony with that of the Court of Appeal.[155] The State argued at the Supreme Court

[149] ibid paras [7.4.1]–[7.5.3].

[150] ibid para [7.4.5].

[151] Thus, the Supreme Court highlighted that '[t]he end goal is clear and is not disputed between the parties … Nor do the parties hold differing opinions as to the required interim target of 80–95% reduction relative to 1990 by 2050'; ibid para [2.3.2].

[152] This point, which can tend to get lost in the jurisprudence, was insightfully and concisely captured by the District Court: 'The dispute between the Parties … does not concern the need for mitigation, but rather the pace … at which the State needs to start reducing greenhouse gas emissions'; District Court Judgment (n 1) para [4.32].

[153] Such delays have serious negative practical consequences in relation to greenhouse gas build-up in the atmosphere, an issue alluded to by the Court of Appeal: 'A delay would, after all, allow greenhouse gas emissions to continue in the meantime; greenhouse gases which linger in the atmosphere for a very long time and further contribute to global warming.' Court of Appeal Judgment (n 2) para [47].

[154] Supreme Court Judgment (n 3) paras [8.1]–[8.3.5].

[155] David Hart KC has summarised the treatment of this issue by the Court of Appeal as follows: 'A … formidable argument was that it was not for the courts but for the democratically legitimised government as the appropriate body to make the attendant policy choices. The Court responded that this did not apply in a rights violation case, but in any event the order left the State sufficient room to decide how it can comply with the order.' Hart KC (n 42).

that the Dutch Government and Parliament have broad latitude to take these sorts of decisions in the Netherlands – here, in relation to the 2020 emissions reduction marker. The role of the courts is not to craft the substance of such a decision, the State argued, but rather to ensure that the Government and Parliament have taken the relevant decision within the bounds of the law. On the face of it, this does seem to be a potentially legitimate criticism in legal terms, as it is typically within the purview of the Government to set such policies in the modern European legal context, which flows from a tradition that has been heavily influenced by texts like Montesquieu's *The Spirit of the Laws*[156] and that is characteristically subject to a relatively distinct 'separation' or 'balance' of powers between the executive, parliamentary and judicial branches of the State.[157] This separation is reflected in the Dutch legal setting by the doctrine of *trias politica*.[158] Part of the logic on which the system rests involves a recognition that, unlike the courts, the Government has been elected by the people in order to advance and implement policies, doing so with the support of the civil service and other Government-specific resources that assist in the purpose.[159] While the Court of Appeal arguably decided this issue correctly, it did rather a weak job of attending to the State's *trais politica* defence in doctrinal legal terms, dismissing it in a rather off-hand way over a short five-sentence paragraph.[160]

As discussed earlier, the Supreme Court held that the State's weaker target of 20 per cent for 2020 could not meet Article 2 and 8 ECHR positive obligations to protect the life of the Dutch. It has also been noted that the Dutch Constitution requires the courts to apply the ECHR, and to do so in keeping with the ECtHR's interpretation of the ECHR's provisions. On the one hand, it might conceivably be viewed as rather a stretch to engage a right to life provision and a right to family life provision that are ill-drawn in relation to an explicit right to a healthy environment,[161] that afford signatory states a substantial margin of appreciation concerning their implementation,[162] and that had not been ruled on by the

[156] Charles de Montesquieu, *Montesquieu: The Spirit of the Laws* (Cambridge University Press, 1989 [1748]).

[157] Anneli Albi and Samo Bardutzky, *National Constitutions in European and Global Governance: Democracy, Rights, the Rule of Law: National Reports* (Springer Nature, 2019).

[158] Chuka Nwanazia, 'The Trias Politica: Dutch System of Government and Why it Matters' *Dutch Review*, 17 March 2021, https://dutchreview.com/culture/society/the-trias-politica-dutch-system-of-government.

[159] Lando strongly suggests in an analysis of *Urgenda* that the courts overstepped the bounds of law and ranged into the policy sphere, a domain ill-suited to the mechanisms of legal adjudication: Henrik Lando, 'Should Courts Decide Climate Policies? A Critical Perspective on the Urgenda Verdict', *Copenhagen Business School, CBS LAW Research Paper* 22-08, 19 October 2022, https://ssrn.com/abstract=4252823.

[160] Court of Appeal Judgment (n 2) para [69].

[161] See further Environmental Rights Recognition Project, *The Right to a Healthy Environment in the United Kingdom: Supporting the Proposal for a New Protocol to the European Convention on Human Rights* (King's College London, 2022). Note that this case preceded climate rulings from the ECtHR such as *Verein Klimaseniorinnen Schweiz and Others v Switzerland*, Grand Chamber, ECtHR (Application No 53600/20), 9 April 2024.

[162] As emphasised by the Court of Appeal in its judgment: (n 2) para [42].

ECtHR in relation to climate issues, yet to conclude nonetheless that the courts can legitimately construct a precise minimum 25 per cent policy-esque target via this channel and impose it on the Government. On the other hand, in dealing with arguable separation of powers issues arising from this approach, the Supreme Court emphasised that the Court of Appeal imposed the lowest minimum limit of an internationally endorsed standard (25 per cent), and the practical policy measures and/or legislative measures required to realise the target in practice are left entirely up to the State, being wholly free from prescription from the Court.[163] Thus, it was held by the Supreme Court that the District Court's order, which was affirmed by the Court of Appeal, could legitimately stand, namely that the State is directed to reduce greenhouse gas emissions by at least 25 per cent based on 1990 levels by the end of 2020.[164]

The courts' approach to the separation of powers had been a hot-button issue in commentary on the case from the District Court ruling onwards.[165] As de Graaf and Jans emphasise: 'Setting mitigation targets and finding efficient and effective instruments to achieve those targets is generally considered a matter of policy.'[166] Writing in 2015 in the wake of the *Urgenda* District Court ruling and drawing on *Waterpakt v The Netherlands*, in which the Supreme Court held that the Dutch courts could not order the State to introduce formal legislation,[167] de Graaf and Jans quite reasonably suggested that 'one could argue that, as a matter of Dutch law and based on the Waterpakt Ruling, the District Court should have refrained from going further than issuing a declaratory decision. This argument is convincing and it seems unlikely that the court's order will survive an appeal.'[168] As has been seen, to the surprise of some, the court order was upheld by both the Court of Appeal and the Supreme Court. Returning to de Graaf and Jans' observation that '[s]etting mitigation targets and finding efficient and effective instruments to achieve those targets is generally considered a matter of policy',[169] it might be noted that there is a practical distinction that may be drawn here between the element of 'setting mitigation targets' and the element of 'finding efficient and effective instruments to achieve them'. David Hart KC notes that 'the district court correctly considered that Urgenda's claim is not intended to create legislation, either by parliament or lower government bodies, and that the State retains complete freedom to determine how it will comply with the order',[170]

[163] Supreme Court Judgment (n 3) paras [8.1]–[8.3.5].

[164] For a spirited and erudite defence of the position that the courts did *not* overstep their constitutional bounds in the context of Dutch law, see Christina Eckes, 'The Urgenda Case is Separation of Powers at Work' in de Boer, N Nieuwenhuis A Michael, B and Reestman, J-H (eds), *Liber Amicorum Besselink (Amsterdam, 2021), Amsterdam Law School Research Paper* 2021–39 (2021).

[165] At the District Court stage, see, eg, Jonathan Verschuuren, 'Spectacular Judgment by Dutch Court in Climate Change Case' (Tilburg University Blog, 26 June 2015).

[166] de Graaf and Jans (n 9) 523.

[167] *Waterpakt v The Netherlands*, Dutch Supreme Court (21 March 2003), ECLI:NL:HR:2003:AE8462.

[168] de Graaf and Jans (n 9) 524.

[169] ibid 523.

[170] Hart KC (n 42).

meaning that the ruling engages the first of the two elements in the de Graaf and Jans statement directly (mitigation targets), while it avoids encroaching directly on the second (the practical instruments that achieve mitigation targets). This allows the latter element to remain within the purview of the executive and Parliament. On the first element – the mitigation target – the District Court found that if it imposed a percentage obligation *above* a 25 per cent minimum, it would intrude on the State's discretion, and therefore it limited itself here, applying only the lowest standard, again as a means of constraining court intrusion into governmental and parliamentary territory.[171] The Supreme Court validated this general approach. Thus, while one may question the courts' approach to the separation of powers, it is not the case that the courts were devoid of sensitivity to the matter or of careful reasoning.

IV. Concluding Thoughts: Taking Stock

Commenting on the decision after the District Court ruling, de Graaf and Jans find that '[a]lthough the reasoning is questionable from a legal perspective, the judgment is nothing short of ground-breaking'.[172] After the Supreme Court judgment had bedded in, Mayer endeavoured to assess 'how Urgenda has contributed to the mitigation of climate change' in terms of actual reductions achieved.[173] 'To assess the emission reductions achieved because of the case', he writes, 'this article identifies and, whenever possible, quantifies the effects of Urgenda on greenhouse gas emissions, by comparison with a counterfactual baseline scenario without Urgenda'.[174] This results in a highly speculative and ultimately unpersuasive exercise. Mayer notes, for example, that a large drop in emissions over 2019–20 was driven by the impact of COVID-19 reducing travel, and by depressed gas prices rendering gas a cheaper energy option than more heavily pollutant coal.[175] Such global shifts sit outside the immediate influence of a comparatively narrow court order, and the speculative, partial and insufficient evidence put forward across the study does not support the author's finding that 'there is no reason to assume that [the *Urgenda Case*] has translated into momentum for climate action more than it has hindered new policy developments'.[176] It is true that the world is a complex place and that economies can be subject to both foreseen and unanticipated shocks and impacts, but this does not change the fact that a State obligation to secure a minimum 25 per cent reduction for 2020 acts as a stronger driver for mitigation than a significantly lower target.

[171] District Court Judgment (n 1) para [4.86].
[172] de Graaf and Jans (n 9) 527.
[173] Mayer (n 25) 168.
[174] ibid 168.
[175] ibid 172.
[176] ibid 167.

In terms of doctrinal law, some of the legal argumentation from the State is amongst the most foolish arising in the major climate cases. For example, it is noted in the Supreme Court judgment that 'the State asserts that the threat … relates to the environment, which the State argues is not protected as such by the ECHR'.[177] This is a foolish assertion in a high-level case of this kind, as it was well and clearly established at this time by the ECtHR that the ECHR affords environmental protection, in particular under Articles 2 and 8 (the primary rights articles at issue in the case).[178] A human rights framework that ignored the protection of humanity's environment in the manner implied would be a weak one indeed. The State also argued 'that it meets its obligations under Articles 2 and 8 ECHR by taking adaptation measures, whether or not in combination with mitigation measures already taken and proposed, and that it therefore does not have to meet the 25–40% target'.[179] It is not sensible to argue in legal terms that adaptation measures in effect cover mitigation measures, because adaptation and mitigation are related and mutually complimentary yet fundamentally distinct features of climate law.[180] This distinct character is driven by the distinction between the issues themselves.[181] In the context of a

[177] Supreme Court Judgment (n 3) para [5.1]. Admittedly, there is nuance to this matter. Discussing the Court of Appeal ruling prior to the Supreme Court ruling, Verschuuren has emphasised that: 'The Court of Appeal … confirmed that, when so asked by individuals or NGOs, courts are obliged to assess government action, including policies, against human rights obligations. Here, Dutch law goes beyond what is required by the ECHR, as under case law by the European Court of Human Rights (ECtHR) environmental NGOs cannot invoke human rights in an attempt to defend the environment as a general interest.' Verschuuren (n 25) 96.

[178] Writing in 2020, Pedersen noted that the ECtHR 'has over decades developed a rich body of case law on environmental rights. It could even be argued that the environmental case law from the ECtHR stands out as one of the central doctrinal sources underpinning the link between human rights and environmental protection simply by reference to the sheer number of environmental cases from the Court, which stands at nearly 200'., Ole W Pedersen, 'The Networks of Human Rights and Climate Change: The State of the Netherlands v Stichting Urgenda, Supreme Court of the Netherlands, 20 December 2019 (19/00135)' (2020) 22(3) *Environmental Law Review* 227–34, 228. Since the Supreme Court's judgment in *Urgenda*, the ECtHR has provided further guidance on ECHR environmental protections with specific reference to climate change in *Verein Klimaseniorinnen Schweiz and Others v Switzerland*, Grand Chamber, ECtHR (Application No 53600/20), 9 April 2024.

[179] Supreme Court Judgment (n 3) para [7.5.2].

[180] Thus, the Paris Agreement treats the issues separately, engaging mitigation at art 4 and adaptation at art 7. See also the discussion of *strands/components* of climate law in ch 1, section I.

[181] In its *Fourth Assessment Report* phase, the IPCC cited distinct definitions drawn from its previous *Assessment Report* phase as follows: 'Mitigation: An anthropogenic intervention to reduce the sources or enhance the sinks of greenhouse gases'; 'Adaptation: Adjustment in natural or human systems in response to actual or expected climatic stimuli or their effects, which moderates harm or exploits beneficial opportunities'. RJT Klein, S Huq, F Denton, TE Downing, RG Richels, JB Robinson and FL Toth, 'Inter-relationships between adaptation and mitigation', *Climate Change 2007: Impacts, Adaptation and Vulnerability. Contribution of Working Group II to the Fourth Assessment Report of the Intergovernmental Panel on Climate Change*, ML Parry, OF Canziani, JP Palutikof, PJ van der Linden and CE Hanson (eds) (Cambridge University Press, 2007) 745–777, 18.1.2. Most recently at the time of writing, IPCC AR6 operates two different working groups looking at adaptation and mitigation respectively: Working Group II – Climate Change 2022: Impacts, Adaptation and Vulnerability; and Working Group III – Climate Change 2022: Mitigation of Climate Change.

discussion on the characteristics of climate legislation, Macrory and the author have summarised as follows:

> Two major thematic elements … can be usefully identified: *mitigation* and *adaptation*. Mitigation, pertaining to the mitigation of greenhouse gases, can be summarised in basic terms as concerning the 'reduction of emissions' or their 'removal' from the atmosphere. Adaptation pertains to the need to 'adapt to the tangible problems and severities arising as a consequence of climate change', and the practices and processes surrounding the issue.[182]

Clearly, mitigating a source (the release of greenhouse gases) that is driving a problem (anthropogenic climate change) is distinct from the process of adapting to the impacts of the problem. Indeed, taken as a point of general principle, where the source of a potentially impactful problem is adequately mitigated from the outset, there will be no negative impact to adapt to, such that a branch of law attending to mitigation fulsomely can hypothetically quash a need for the emergence of a branch of law attending to adaptation in the first place.

The Supreme Court swiftly disposed of this poor argument[183] (as did the Court of Appeal).[184] The Court did so, however, with a rather confusing rhetorical flourish, opining as follows:

> [A]lthough it is correct that *the consequences of climate change can be mitigated by taking adaptation measures*, it has not been demonstrated or made plausible that the potentially disastrous consequences of excessive global warming can be adequately prevented by such measures. (Emphasis added)[185]

To talk of climate impacts being '*mitigated* by *adaptation*' in a technical legal judgment in this way is unhelpful rhetorically, because mitigation and adaptation are technical terms with distinct meanings.[186] One may strive to mitigate emissions to within a 25–40 per cent range for 2020 based on 1990 levels; meanwhile, and as distinct from this, one may (or may not) strive to adapt to the current and/or projected impacts arising from the effects of emissions into the atmosphere. This underlying distinction is correctly emphasised in the Court of Appeal judgment:

> Global warming can be prevented or reduced by ensuring that less greenhouse gases are emitted into the atmosphere. This is known as 'mitigation'. In addition, measures can be taken to counter the consequences of climate change, including raising dikes to protect low-lying areas. This is called 'adaptation'.[187]

[182] Richard Macrory and Thomas L Muinzer, 'The UK's Climate Change Act' in Thomas L Muinzer. (ed), *National Climate Change Acts: The Emergence, Form and Nature of National Framework Climate Legislation* (Hart Publishing, 2021), 69–92, 70.
[183] Supreme Court Judgment (n 3) para [7.5.2].
[184] Court of Appeal Judgment (n 2) para [59].
[185] Supreme Court Judgment (n 3) para [7.5.2]. This discussion draws on the English translation of the judgment (see further at n 4 above).
[186] As recognised in the District Court Judgment (n 1) paras [2.17], [4.75].
[187] Court of Appeal Judgment (n 2) para [3.6].

To talk of 'mitigating by adaptation' (or indeed 'adapting by mitigation') in technical legal documents is therefore rhetorically unhelpful as it confuses the technical distinction between the issues. In the particular case of *Urgenda*, it also risks bolstering the State's attempt to obfuscate matters in arguing (incorrectly) that adaptation measures can absolve a need to meet distinct mitigation objectives.

A. Good News or Bad News?

In a practical sense, this judgment is happy news for those concerned about the planet, insofar as it thankfully compels stronger action to be taken by the Dutch State in the face of the climate change challenge. In legal terms, it is a fairly radical judgment, as it stretches the Dutch Constitution and human rights law to the point that the courts can impose a specific target upon the Government (directly) and Parliament (indirectly), which amounts to a radical outcome in a conventional legal sense. The practical implications of the target itself are fairly modest; as the Supreme Court notes, '[w]hen the Court of Appeal rendered its judgment, it was expected that the Netherlands would achieve a reduction of 23% in 2020'.[188] Adjusting the outcome for the end of 2020 upwards to 25 per cent hardly amounts to a seismic shift in practical terms. While the Urgenda Foundation was successful, a 25 per cent reduction on 1990 levels was the lowest minimum reduction level that it had sought, having initially proposed the imposition of minimum reductions up to 40 per cent on 1990 levels.[189]

Taken broadly, however, it is also unclear from this case where precisely the Supreme Court's self-declared facility to apply targets based on scientific and international standards ends. Hypothetically, one presumes that any new governmental (and potentially parliamentary) efforts in the future to significantly lower target standards for such milestone dates as 2030 and 2050 will be rejected by the Court, which now seems to hold the primary authority to set minimum standards for targets in going forward, generating them from consensus scientific and international standards interpreted in concert with the State's duty of care under Dutch law and its associated human rights obligations. While this is good news for the planet, it is debatable whether it manifests an optimum balance of power between the courts and the elected governmental and parliamentary branches of the State.

B. Literature and Research on the Case

While a substantial body of erudite and insightful work on the *Urgenda Case* exists, it is notable that the litigation stimulated a vast outpouring of scholarly,

[188] Supreme Court Judgment (n 3) para [2.1]. Expectations were lower at the District Court stage as a more current measurement method had not been implemented at that time; see further para 2.1 (31).
[189] District Court Judgment (n 1) para [3.1]; Court of Appeal Judgment (n 2) para [3.8].

academic and related legal commentary that was unprecedented in terms of quantity for a climate law ruling. A general difficulty arising from this is that this vast array of work tended to be highly descriptive, with more and more accounts being produced that merely described the case, thus re-treading ground that rapidly became old without much or sometimes anything new being added in the process. Where research moved beyond mere description, it had a tendency to reiterate familiar points that had already been made elsewhere many times, for example, in relation to the difficulty in striking a balance concerning the separation of powers, the difficulty in articulating the scope of Dutch human rights law and ECHR law, and similar. Again, intellectual ground became rapidly re-treaded in a partially unhelpful way. Key opportunities to engage with gaps in knowledge tended to be overlooked in the process.

For example, a newly elected Dutch Government announced the introduction of a Climate Bill in June 2018.[190] The Dutch Climate Act entered into force on 1 September 2019, some months prior to the Supreme Court's judgment being handed down.[191] The framework contains two particularly important milestone targets, requiring the State to reduce Dutch greenhouse gas emissions by at least 49 per cent by 2030 and at least 95 per cent by 2050, with both reductions measured from 1990 emissions levels. Although the Act had not been engaged at the Court of Appeal stage and the Supreme Court case was a cassation appeal dealing with the lower court's application of the law, the Supreme Court made reference to the Act in its judgment.[192] The State had also produced an important Climate Agreement containing some distinct targets of its own in June 2019.[193] Interpreting *Urgenda* in this broader context, then, an important outcome of the case is that it resulted for the first time in a country receiving important and distinct climate targets from the courts (via *Urgenda*), Parliament (via the Climate Act) and the executive (via the Climate Agreement).[194]

In 2019, Verschuuren made the important observation that: 'The current government seems to believe that with this new piece of legislation [ie, the Dutch Climate Act], and given the far-reaching 2050 target and the wide political support for the bill, it has effectively disabled future Urgenda-like lawsuits.'[195] This important feature flagged by Verschuuren received little detailed consideration in the *Urgenda* literature,[196] namely the manner in which legislation might be employed as a shield against the courts sketching out the State's primary minimum emissions reduction targets in future, via the *Urgenda* precedent. Indeed, such little analytical attention had been afforded to this new and

[190] Verschuuren (n 25) 98.
[191] The Dutch Climate Act, or 'Klimaatwet'.
[192] Supreme Court Judgment (n 3) para [7.4.5].
[193] Dutch Government, *Kllimaatakkoord*, 28 June 2019.
[194] The Urgenda Foundation made significant reference to the (at that time pending) Climate Agreement over the course of its constitutional argumentation at the Court of Appeal stage; cited in Court of Appeal Judgment (n 2) para [68]. It is not referred to in the Supreme Court Judgment (n 3).
[195] Verschuuren (n 25) 98.
[196] At least in the extensive body of literature available to English-language readers.

complex circumstance, and to the broader implications of primary mitigation target drivers crystallising across the three major branches of the executive-Parliament-courts for the first time that, when the volume *National Climate Change Acts*[197] was in preparation, the authors of a chapter that was intended to provide an in-depth analysis of the Dutch Climate Act (Spijkers and Oosterhuis) and I (the editor) took a decision to expand the work beyond its intended parameters in order to interrogate the relationship between the Act, *Urgenda*, the Dutch Climate Agreement and the implications flowing from them.[198] This seemed like a necessary adjustment in order to assist in filling what was by that time a fairly gaping hole in the literature.[199]

Care also needs to be taken in commentary and the scholarly literature to recognise that the *Urgenda* ruling is law; the Dutch courts passed a legally binding judgment. Legal expert Wegener notes in the abstract to his thoughtful consideration of the *Urgenda* litigation[200] that 'the specific "Urgenda"-decision is legally not convincing'[201] – one may take the view that the decision is legally unconvincing, but the decision *is* a legal ruling. The judgment is law. Conversely, one must also be careful not to overstate its doctrinal influence. In 2020 Antonopoulos suggested that '[a]ll signs show that the Urgenda decision will be replicated in other jurisdictions';[202] however, the decision currently remains a novel one and it has not cut through in jurisdictions around the world in the pronounced way that some might have expected. Indeed, research has suggested that the decision appears to remain relatively novel within the Netherlands itself, with Krommendijk having researched this issue in detail and found that the 'turn to rights has so far had a limited substantive impact in the Netherlands in environmental and climate cases beyond *Urgenda*'.[203]

A further difficulty arising in the literature is an occasional tendency towards an unhelpful, highly abstract philosophical approach to issues. This is demonstrated in the following commentary on the Court of Appeal ruling by Mayer:

> [N]o effort whatsoever on the part of the Netherlands is strictly 'necessary' for achieving a global temperature objective as the GHG emissions from the Netherlands make

[197] Muinzer (ed) (n 182).

[198] Otto Spijkers, and Sofie Oosterhuis, 'The Dutch Response to Climate Change: Evaluating the Netherlands' Climate Act and Associated Issues of Importance' in ibid 175–98.

[199] See further ibid, in particular pt V, 'The Climate Act and the Agreement and the *Urgenda* Litigation', 192–97. See also on this matter Gerrit A van der Veen and Kars de Graaf, 'Climate Change Litigation in the Netherlands: The Urgenda Case and Beyond' in Wolfgang Khal and Marc-Philippe Weller (eds), *Climate Change Litigation: A Handbook* (Bloomsbury, 2021), 363–77.

[200] Published after the Court of Appeal ruling but prior to the Supreme Court ruling.

[201] Bernhard W Wegener, 'Urgenda – World Rescue by Court Order? The 'Climate Justice'-Movement Tests the Limits of Legal Protection' (2019) 16(2) *Journal for European Environmental & Planning Law* 125–47, 125.

[202] Irene Antonopoulos, 'The Future of Climate Policymaking in Light of Urgenda Foundation v The Netherlands' (2020) 22(2) *Environmental Law Review* 119–24, 124.

[203] Jasper Krommendijk, 'Beyond Urgenda: The Role of the ECHR and Judgments of the ECtHR in Dutch Environmental and Climate Litigation' (2022) 31(1) *Review of European, Comparative & International Environmental Law* 60–74, 73.

> very little difference at the global scale: climate change could effectively be resolved through international cooperation without any mitigation effort by the Netherlands.[204]

This type of overly philosophical thinking occasionally arises in the literature. This might be fine in an abstract seminar discussion, but it has little or nothing of value to add to the understanding of a pressing real-world problem (anthropogenic climate change) and the important concrete legal questions attaching to it (for example, concerning the extent to which the law does or could engage with the climate problem, and the degree to which it enables or constrains action). Related to this, a tendency to smuggle outlandish claims into otherwise intelligible technical legal criticism of the judgment can arise. Bergkamp, for example, who describes the decision as 'a perversion of the law',[205] summarises that: 'Like all precautionary rhetoric, the *Urgenda* case *assumes what should be proven*, namely that emissions from The Netherlands contribute to dangerous climate change and that further emission reductions by The Netherlands by 2020 will likely prevent this danger' (emphasis in original).[206] There is no question that the Netherlands' emissions do contribute to anthropogenic climate change. Reductions from the Netherlands for 2020 assist the Netherlands in providing a contribution to mitigating this problem. There is no issue here.

A further aspect of the case that has tended to be overlooked in the abundant commentary pertains to the pace at which the court process moved, a problem that the author flagged in print during the transition from the Court of Appeal to the Supreme Court rulings:

> [A] … procedural aspect pertinent to the *Urgenda* litigation that is rarely addressed meaningfully … [is] the issue of *timing*. While it is not unusual for substantial litigation to range across a number of years, the facts of the *Urgenda* case are unusually time-sensitive, involving a target year of 2020.[207]

In the same article, I emphasised a number of key dates:

> Some of the litigation's most important milestone dates include as follows: 24 June 2015, District Court judgement; 9 October 2018, Court of Appeal judgement; 24 May 2019, Supreme Court hearings; 20 December 2019, indicative date of the final Supreme Court judgement.[208]

Bearing in mind that this is a time-sensitive case with key issues pinned to 2020, it is notable that the first judgment was issued many years prior to 2020 at the

[204] Mayer (n 106) 185.

[205] Lucas Bergkamp, 'A Dutch Court's Revolutionary Climate Policy Judgment: The Perversion of Judicial Power, the State's Duties of Care, and Science' (2015) 12 *Journal of European Environmental and Planning Law* 241–63, 263.

[206] ibid 262.

[207] Thomas L Muinzer, 'A Climate of Change? Taking Stock of the Urgenda Case with a Supreme Court Ruling on the Horizon' *UK Human Rights Blog*, 8 October 2019, https://ukhumanrightsblog.com/2019/10/08/a-climate-of-change-taking-stock-of-the-urgenda-case-with-a-supreme-court-ruling-on-the-horizon/#:~:text=This%20case%2C%20brought%20by%20the,law%20to%20assist%20in%20grappling.

[208] ibid.

District Court in 2015.[209] Writing in the wake of the Court of Appeal ruling, Verschuuren pointed out that: 'The Court of Appeal took three years to reach the conclusion that the District Court's ruling in the Urgenda case should stand. The Dutch Government now only has two years to substantially reduce its emissions by the end of 2020, in accordance with the judgment.'[210] A final outcome judgment was not handed down at the end of the Supreme Court stage until less than two weeks prior to the commencement of 2020. In a target-specific climate case where a target date of 2020 is crucial, this gaping timespan is unsuitable. It is notable that the Supreme Court hearings were completed as early as May 2019, but in spite of the case's time-sensitivity, the Court did not hand down its judgment until the eleventh hour at the end of 2019. Where climate law cases are pinned in a critical way to limited time-specific markers, it is incumbent on courts in general to do better to prioritise such cases and move them through the court process with a suitable degree of urgency.[211]

On the other hand, the case has prompted some stand-out examples of insightful, thoughtful research. In addition to a range of work drawn upon throughout this chapter, this includes Maxwell et al's interesting 'Standards for Adjudicating the Next Generation of Urgenda-Style Climate Cases'.[212] Here, drawing on scientific and international legal standards, the authors endeavour to construct a practical *Urgenda*-influenced framework that litigants and courts can refer to in order to assess the legality of a given State's mitigation efforts. The framework employs the concept of the duty of care as manifested in human rights and/or tort law, and the authors argue that it can both assist litigants in bringing 'systemic mitigation cases' to court and assist courts themselves in interpreting the lawfulness of a State's mitigation efforts. The authors explain that they 'describe these as "systemic" cases because they focus on a State's overall mitigation efforts, rather than on a specific project or initiative with GHG emissions implications'.[213]

Working at a narrower Dutch and EU-specific range, Peeters has produced a concise, erudite analysis that draws out issues and arguable tensions particular to EU law, where she suggests that a preliminary reference from the Dutch

[209] It has also been noted earlier in this chapter that Roger Cox, who acted for the Urgenda Foundation at the District Court, has stated that the legal action itself was brought '[a]fter more than two years of preparation'; Cox (n 116) 143. This is a lengthy but unsurprising amount of time, given the huge task in bringing a complicated case like this together, and to the very high standards achieved by the lawyers and parties involved.

[210] Verschuuren (n 25) 98.

[211] Thus, my commentary quoted above celebrated the *Urgenda* litigation in certain respects as a shining example of what might be achieved through the courts, but it also found that on the issue of timing, 'this important case looks much less of a success story'. Muinzer (n 207).

[212] Lucy Maxwell, Sarah Mead, and Dennis van Berkel, 'Standards for Adjudicating the Next Generation of Urgenda-Style Climate Cases' (2022) 13(1) *Journal of Human Rights and the Environment* 35–63. All three authors are associated with the Climate Litigation Network, a project of the Urgenda Foundation.

[213] ibid 38.

courts to the Court of Justice of the European Union would have been advisable.[214] Writing in the wake of the District Court ruling, she also opines that 'it is remarkable that a national lower civil court finds that, if the State would act in conformity with EU law, it would act unlawfully', bearing in mind that the District Court's (and ultimately the Supreme Court's) order required the Dutch State to exceed the EU's own 2020 target.[215] Indeed, one can press this point further. Backes and van der Veen point out that the EU set down a '20% reduction obligation for 2020' for itself in law, 'rather than the 25–40% emissions cut that is the "absolute minimum" and "evidently" necessary' based on the Supreme Court's interpretation of international law and standards.[216] Following this line of thinking through logically, they suggest that the decision implies 'that not only the State of the Netherlands has acted in "evident" … violation of international law, but that the EU has done this as well'.[217] Of course, in doctrinal legal terms the Dutch Supreme Court does not have the jurisdiction to rule that the EU has breached the law in this way and order it to change a milestone target, but in addition to questioning the internal logic of the Court's reasoning, the underlying implication of Backes' and van der Veen's insight underscores a need to recognise that this is a Dutch case that should not be over-extrapolated in relation to other jurisdictions. In this respect, depending on one's view, this strand of reasoning may provide a challenge to Maxwell et al's interesting work, which looks towards the wider extrapolation of a *Urgenda*-style framework.[218]

* * *

Taking the *Urgenda* litigation broadly, it is possible to view the case as a highly successful example of public interest litigation for the protection of the environment,[219] thus highlighting to other public interest lawyers and groups around the world what is conceivably possible. In this respect, this landmark case can justly be described as inspirational.

[214] Marjan Peeters, 'Urgenda Foundation and 886 Individuals v The State of The Netherlands: The Dilemma of More Ambitious Greenhouse Gas Reduction Action by EU Member States' (2016) 25(1) *Review of European, Comparative & International Environmental Law* 123–29.

[215] ibid 129.

[216] Chris W Backes, and Gerrit A van der Veen, 'Urgenda: The Final Judgment of the Dutch Supreme Court' (2020) 17(3) *Journal for European Environmental & Planning Law* 307–21, 316.

[217] ibid 316.

[218] Maxwell et al (n 212).

[219] Otto Spijkers, 'The Urgenda Case: A Successful Example of Public Interest Litigation for the Protection of the Environment?' in Christina Voigt and Zen Makuch (eds), *Courts and the Environment* (Edward Elgar, 2018), 305–44.

4

Colombia

The Colombian Amazon Case

The protection of fundamental rights not only involves the individual, but implicates the 'other'. The neighbor is otherness; its essence, the other people that inhabit the planet, also include other animal and plant species. But in addition, this includes the unborn, who also deserve to enjoy the same environmental conditions that we have.

Colombian Amazon Case, Supreme Court of Justice of Colombia, part 2 paragraph 5.2

I. The *Colombian Amazon Case*

Concern over increased deforestation of the Colombian Amazon rainforest lies at the heart of *Andrea Lozano Barragán et al v Presidencia de la República et al* (hereafter the *Colombian Amazon Case*).[1] The case was filed and ruled on by Colombia's highest court in 2018. In scientific work published in that year, Murad and Pearse clarified that the Amazon rainforest is the largest rainforest in the world in terms of size and diversity, with 10 per cent of its territory belonging to Colombia, covering approximately 35 per cent of the country's total area.[2] The applicants' framing of the case brought climate law and policy to the fore, and a number of legal issues flowing from it. Rich consideration is afforded in the case to environmental and

[1] *Andrea Lozano Barragán et al v Presidencia de la República et al*, Sentencia de la Corte Suprema de Justicia del 5 de Abril de 2018, MP Luis Armando Tolosa Villabona, STC4360-2018 (Colom).

Versions of the Judgment: Dejusticia, the Colombian NGO supporting the plaintiffs in this case, has selected and translated key excerpts of the Supreme Court judgment into English for the public. Where this chapter refers to this version of the judgment, the reference is marked 'Judgment (Dejusticia)'. The author has also translated the judgment into English for the purposes of this study. Where the translation is the author's, it is marked 'Judgment (author)'. In instances where scholars or other commentators have provided their own translations of elements of the judgment that are integrated into this chapter directly, these are marked 'Judgment (author name(s))'. The author has prioritised using the translations from Dejusticia and others over his own translation where he can.

[2] Cesar Augusto Murad and Jillian Pearse, 'Landsat Study of Deforestation in the Amazon Region of Colombia: Departments of Caquetá and Putumayo' (2018) 11 *Remote Sensing Applications: Society and Environment* 161–71.

constitutional rights, including the extent to which future generations and nature itself might attract rights protections.

The litigation involved a *tutela* action, filed on 29 January 2018 against governmental actors including the President of Colombia, the Ministries of Environment and Agriculture, the National Parks and regional autonomous corporations, and mayors and governments of the Colombian Amazon.[3] The plaintiffs sought to halt ongoing extensive deforestation in the Amazon basin through recognition of their constitutional rights, which they argued were placed under threat by rainforest reduction, particularly through the substantial increase in greenhouse gas emissions arising as a result. This included seeking a court order compelling the Government to fulfil its national and international climate mitigation commitments via the reduction of deforestation.

The civil division of the High Court of the Judicial District of Bogota[4] ruled against the *tutela* on procedural grounds on 12 February 2018, such that the case did not proceed to substantive consideration. On 16 February 2018, the plaintiffs appealed the ruling to the Supreme Court of Justice of Colombia, which ruled in favour of the *tutela* on 5 April 2018.[5] The case was heard by a bench of seven judges, with Judge Luis Armando Tolosa Villabona delivering the leading judgment.[6] Colombian *tutela* actions typically move at a relatively swift pace. In Chapter 3, which explored the Dutch *Urgenda* case – a time-sensitive climate case involving a dispute over a national mitigation target linked to the year 2020 – the author has pointed out some difficulties relating to timing.[7] It is noted that an initial District Court judgment was issued by the Dutch courts in 2015.[8] After that, Verschuuren notes that '[t]he Court of Appeal took three years to reach the conclusion that the District Court's ruling in the Urgenda case should stand',[9] thus leaving two years to reach the mitigation target required by the close of 2020. Next, a judgment was handed down by the Dutch Supreme Court less than two weeks prior to the commencement of 2020, even though the Supreme Court hearings were concluded as early as May 2019. The author has commented that this sort

[3] Summarised by Paola Villavicencio Calzadilla, 'A Paradigm Shift in Courts' View on Nature: The Atrato River and Amazon Basin Cases in Colombia' (2019) 15 *Law, Environment and Development Journal* 1–11, 5.

[4] Tribunal Superior del Distrito Judicial de Bogotá- Sala Civil (hereafter the 'High Court').

[5] The judgment was approved in session on 4 April 2018 and the judgment itself is formally dated 5 April 2018.

[6] The judges were: Judge Aroldo Wilson Quiroz Monsalvo (President of the Chamber), Judge Luis Armando Tolosa Villabona (delivering the leading judgment), Judge Margarita Cabello Blanco, Judge Octavio Augusto Tejeiro Duque, Judge Álvaro Fernando García Restrepo, Judge Luis Alonso Rico Puerta and Judge Ariel Salazar Ramírez.

[7] See in particular sections III.E and III.G in ch 3 in this volume.

[8] *Urgenda Foundation v The State of the Netherlands*, ECLI:NL:RBDHA:2015:7145 (English translation ECLI:NL:RBDHA:2015:7196), Judgment (Dist Ct, The Hague, 24 June 2015) (Neth).

[9] Jonathan Verschuuren, 'The State of the Netherlands v Urgenda Foundation: The Hague Court of Appeal Upholds Judgment Requiring the Netherlands to Further Reduce its Greenhouse Gas Emissions' (2019) 28(1) *Review of European, Comparative & International Environmental Law* 94–98, 98.

of gaping timespan is unacceptable in a target-specific climate case where a time sensitive target date (here, 2020) is crucial.[10]

Villavicencio Calzadilla writes that prior to the commencement of the *Colombian Amazon* litigation in 2018, '[u]nder the Paris Agreement (adopted by way of [Law] 1844 of 2017) and the national Law 1753 of 2015, the Government had committed, inter alia, to reduce to zero the deforestation net rate in this region by 2020', and therefore 'at the time the case was filed, [there] only remained two years to comply with this target'.[11] The plaintiffs sought to hold the Government to this commitment, which had relatively little time remaining. In relation to the brief sketch of the case's procedural elements provided above, it is notable that: the High Court ruled against the *tutela* on 12 February 2018; the plaintiffs appealed the outcome to the Supreme Court on 16 February 2018; and the Supreme Court issued its judgment on 5 April 2018.[12] In contrast to *Urgenda*, here one witnesses a best-practice pace from the court system, and appropriate prioritisation of time-sensitive climate litigation in the context of the courts' general caseload.

II. The *Tutela* Element of the Case

In Colombia, an *acción de tutela* for the protection of rights can be raised in the courts in certain circumstances,[13] involving judicial review in the interest of fundamental rights protection.[14] The plaintiffs engaged this channel in the *Colombian Amazon Case*. As part of this process, the plaintiffs drew on constitutional rights law, arguing that the right to a healthy environment,[15] the right to life[16] and the right to health[17] had been infringed. They also drew on other rights, including the right to nutrition and the right to water. In its judgment, the Supreme Court clarified that 'Article 86 of the Political Charter establishes that the *tutela* action is a defense mechanism by which any person may claim the immediate protection of his fundamental rights',[18] and noted that children and minors can file lawsuits directly via this channel in Colombia.[19] The action was brought by 25 plaintiffs

[10] See section IV in ch 3 in this volume. See also commentary in section II in ch 5 in this volume on the Nigerian *Oil Pollution Watch* case: 'The passage of 12 years between the Trial Court's ruling and the Supreme Court's ruling is totally unacceptable in a grave environmental case of this kind, and if such delays are imported into serious climate cases in future it will prove detrimental to justice.'

[11] Villavicencio Calzadilla (n 3) 5.

[12] See also the temporal note on the judgment above at n 5.

[13] Political Constitution of Colombia 1991, art 86; Law 472 of 1998.

[14] A *tutela* action can be raised against public authorities and individuals where actions or omissions negatively impact or threaten an applicant's fundamental rights.

[15] Political Constitution of Colombia 1991, art 79.

[16] ibid arts 11, 1 and 2.

[17] ibid arts 44 and 49.

[18] Judgment (author), pt 2 para 3.

[19] ibid.

and some of these were minors, meaning that they enjoyed the same opportunity to request rights protection as the adults.

Part of the Supreme Court's judgment was given over to the issue of whether a *tutela* action could be employed to file a novel lawsuit of this kind. This was an important point, as the High Court had ruled against the action due to the collective rights at issue. 'Tutela' refers to 'guardianship' in English, and Castro has laid out the differences between the 'guardianship action' (ie, *tutela* action) brought in this case and the alternative 'popular action' channel that also exists in Colombian law.[20] In a 'Rights of Nature' case of this kind,[21] Castro writes that the latter channel is not geared towards initiating an action to protect the fundamental rights of the Amazon.[22] The lower court had taken the view that the claim was inadmissible, holding that *acción de tutela* could not rely on the protection of collective rights in this context;[23] however, the Supreme Court reversed this, ruling that the *tutela* could form a lawful basis for an action of this kind. Alvarado and Rivas-Ramírez summarise that 'this judgment creates a strong precedent regarding the scope and use of *acción de tutela* in Colombia. This is significant as it means that any Colombian court will have to consider judicial action on the basis of collective as well as individual rights'.[24]

The Supreme Court explained that:

> As a general rule, the tutela does not proceed for the protection of collective rights and interests, since it was conceived as a suitable mechanism for the protection of fundamental prerogatives, since those, as provided in Article 88 of the Political Constitution and Law 472 of 1998, are defended through popular actions. However, exceptionally, the constitutional jurisprudence has established that the protection of group interests is admissible.[25]

The Court held that a *tutela* involving collective rights rather than individual rights can only be filed where the lawsuit shows the connection between the violation of collective and fundamental or individual rights, demonstrates that the person filing the *tutela* is directly affected, proves the violation of a fundamental right, and seeks an order oriented towards restoration of individual rights rather than collective ones. The Supreme Court's determination is a positive development in terms of the *Colombian Amazon Case* itself, and cases like it.[26] In the context of climate

[20] See further Carla Judith Cetina Castro, 'Colombian Amazon as a Subject of Rights: Judgement of the Supreme Court of Justice of Colombia', in Luis Felipe Lacerda (ed), *Rights of Nature: Milestones for the Construction of a General Theory* (São Leopoldo, 2022), 73–75.

[21] See further section III below.

[22] See Castro (n 20) 74.

[23] See n 19 and the text to the note in Paola Andrea Acosta Alvarado and Daniel Rivas-Ramírez, 'A Milestone in Environmental and Future Generations' Rights Protection: Recent Legal Developments before the Colombian Supreme Court' (2018) 30(3) *Journal of Environmental Law* 519–26.

[24] ibid 526.

[25] Judgment (author), pt 2, para 1.

[26] The plaintiffs employed this channel because they deemed the *acción popular* an insufficient means of defence due to both 'fundamental' and 'collective' rights being affected; ibid pt 1 para 2.6.

litigation generally, it is a useful affirmation of the ability to undertake rights-based climate litigation in certain instances; however, taking the criteria for admission that has just been noted in isolation, it seems unhelpfully narrow.

The Nigerian case *Oil Pollution Watch*[27] examined in this volume, for example, appears to provide a generally superior channel to the courts for certain rights-sensitive climate litigation via the Supreme Court of Nigeria's willingness to hear justiciable environmental cases brought by NGOs and public-spirited individuals in the public interest.[28] In principle, this can include an instance where public spirited individuals (or NGOs) bring a rights-sensitive case in the public interest on behalf of parties impacted directly by alleged environmental harm, including climate change, who may be unable to afford the legal costs of bringing the case to court themselves and/or may lack the relevant expertise to do so, including knowledge of court procedures etc. *Tutela* applications in this vein appear to be fenced out robustly by the Colombian Supreme Court's criteria noted above, as the rights of the people bringing the lawsuit in this example are not directly affected by the alleged environmental harm over and above the parties in whose interest the case is being brought. The Colombian Supreme Court in its criteria for a *tutela* trial asserts that '[t]he plaintiff must be the person directly affected' and '[t]he infringement of the fundamental right must not be hypothetical, but fully proven in the course of time'.[29] Unlike *Oil Pollution Watch*, this channel does not lend itself to the type of climate litigation just outlined.

As the Nigerian experience indicates, availability of this form of climate litigation is necessary for a healthily functioning climate law system, and any obstacles such as may exist to its realisation in Colombia should be removed. The Colombian legal tradition has a significant history of thoughtfully developed contemporary environmental law. Writing in 1999, Ninio summarised that:

> The Colombian environmental legislation gives instruments to the people for claiming their environmental rights. There are eleven different procedures for the purposes that seek for the detention of environmental problems. The more used and debated actions are the Guardianship Claim Action (*Acción de Tutela*) or the Community Claim or *Acción Popular*. The 'Acción the [*sic*] Tutela' is a mechanism to protect fundamental rights of the individuals against abuse of state.[30]

Parties involved in the case have also indicated to the author over the course of discussions that the relatively fast pace at which *tutela* actions are processed by the Colombian courts also made the *tutela* channel extremely attractive.

[27] *Centre for Oil Pollution Watch v Nigerian National Petroleum Corporation* [2019] 5 NWLR (Pt 1666) 518.

[28] See ch 5 in this volume.

[29] Judgment (author), pt 2, para 1.

[30] Alberto Ninio, 'The Evolution of Environmental Law in Latin America: The Cases of Brazil, Colombia and Peru and the Effort to Protect Forest Resources' (1999) *OAS Digital Catalogue* 397, 414, https://www.oas.org/es/sla/ddi/docs/publicaciones_digital_XXVI_curso_derecho_internacional_1999_Alberto_Ninio_2.pdf.

The type of action described above, and actions similar to it, should be facilitated under the *acción popular*/popular action channel, or an equivalent avenue deemed appropriate in the domestic Colombian setting. Failing this, the *tutela* avenue should be developed further to accommodate such cases.

It appears that there may also be some logical contradiction underlying the technical framing of doctrinal law here where that framing is brought into contact with novel temporal problems raised by climate litigation. In some sense, everyone is impacted by climate change, insofar as it is a global problem shared by humanity. This problem is so pervasive that unborn 'future generations' can be understood to be a relevant consideration in relation to impacts, even though they do not exist yet,[31] and even though this term is highly generalist (ie, it is not typically predicated on an effort to distinguish *particular* impacted individuals who do not yet exist, but instead tends to recognise that individuals in some general sense who do not yet exist will be impacted). Of course, such unborn persons are not in a position to file a *tutela* themselves, but even if it were possible for an existing party to do so on their behalf, which in principle does not appear to be the case based on the Court's criteria above, it is not plain how it could be demonstrated that they are directly affected, nor how the violation of a fundamental right could be evidenced clearly. Making a case that an unborn party *is going to be* impacted differs significantly in law from making a case that one *is* or *has been* impacted (or indeed that a *living* person likely will be impacted).

It might be objected here that unborn future generations do not typically attract substantial weight in the context of doctrinal legal considerations; indeed, other major cases covered in this volume can exhibit sensitivity to future generations,[32] but it is fair to say that they do not typically incorporate the rights of unborn future generations as a heavy doctrinal determinative influence. However, this objection is more difficult to sustain in the context of the *Colombian Amazon Case* itself, because the Colombian Supreme Court is exemplary for the weight and importance that it accords to the safeguarding of future generations from negative climate impacts within the substance of the ruling itself (discussed below).[33]

[31] In legal discourse, the term 'future generations' has a tendency by logical implication to refer to generations as yet unborn; however, in principle courts are also at liberty to interpret *existing* generations as future generations if they choose to do so in reasonable terms. The Supreme Court of Colombia adopts this type of approach in the *Colombian Amazon Case*. Here, extant members of a young generation can amount to a 'future generation' in the sense that many members of that generation will likely be alive decades into the future. They will therefore experience climate impacts in decades to come, including in the 'second half of this century' period referenced as a key temporal phase in the Paris Agreement (art 4.1). Thus, the *Colombian Amazon Case* is sensitive to the unborn, but the plaintiffs also 'preach being pt of the future generation that will face the effects of climate change in the period 2041–2070 and 2071–2100': Judgment (author), pt 1, para 2.5.

[32] See, for example, the *Urgenda Case*, where the Supreme Court recognises the influence of the obligation at art 3(1) of the United Nations Framework Convention on Climate Change to safeguard 'present and future generations of humankind': *State of the Netherlands v Urgenda Foundation*, ECLI:NL:HR:2019:2006 (English translation ECLI:NL:HR:2019:2007), Judgment (Sup Ct Neth, 20 December 2019) (Neth), para [5.7.3].

[33] See further section IV.B below.

The Supreme Court seems to get around the problems raised here by construing the living plaintiffs as 'future generations' in their own right due to their young ages, such that the Court avoids engaging the concept of future generations purely in 'unborn' terms.[34] Although this case is a *tutela* action, it may be that the collective 'popular action' channel provides a richer seam for climate litigation that factors in unborn future generations strongly, given that an emphasis tends to fall logically on collective individuals who will constitute unborn future generations, rather than on individual persons who have not yet been born and thus cannot be specifically identified.

III. *Tierra Digna* and Environmental Rights in Colombia

The notion that citizens are imbued with environmental human rights is recognised and applied in the law in a direct and appealing way by the Supreme Court in the *Colombian Amazon Case*.[35] This is due in part to an emerging recognition in Latin American legal systems that a right to a healthy and functioning natural environment is an explicit constitutional entitlement. Indeed, this case was pioneered in some sense by Colombia's neighbour, Ecuador, as it was here that courts first applied the 'rights of nature' conception, in that instance to Ecuador's Vilcabamba River, doing so by drawing on Article 71 of the Constitution of Ecuador.[36] This explicitly recognises the intrinsic value of nature.[37] It will be discussed below that the Supreme Court in the *Colombian Amazon Case* recognises the intrinsic value of nature, interprets the Amazon Rainforest itself as being possessed of rights, and links this framing to human beings of both present *and* future generations: 'The environmental rights of future generations are based on the (i) ethical duty of the solidarity of the species and (ii) on the intrinsic value of nature.'[38] The Colombian Supreme Court opines that 'natural resources are shared by all inhabitants of

[34] See further Gómez-Betancur on how the plaintiffs 'asserted that they are living the same collective experience and would be the next generation that will face the harmful effects of climate change': Luisa Gómez-Betancur, 'The Rights of Nature in the Colombian Amazon: Examining Challenges and Opportunities in a Transitional Justice Setting' (2020) 25 *UCLA Journal of International Law and Foreign Affairs* 41–84, 67. See also section IV.B below; and the comments at n 31 above.

[35] Referring to judgments STC 7630 of 9 June 2016, STC 9813 of 19 July 2016, and STC 15985 of 3 October 2017, the Supreme Court opines that previous rulings clarify that 'the *tutela* action is admissible against the violation of the right to a healthy environment, when it is *prima facie* evident that its transgression inevitably produces "direct affectation of other fundamental prerogatives, including life, health and access to water of guardians and their family units"'. Judgment (author), pt 2, para 2.

[36] Natalia Greene, 'The First Successful Case on the Rights of Nature Implementation in Ecuador', *Global Alliance for the Rights of Nature* (21 May 2011), https://www.garn.org/first-ron-case-ecuador.

[37] See further Louis J Kotzé and Paola Villavicencio Calzadilla, 'Somewhere between Rhetoric and Reality: Environmental Constitutionalism and the Rights of Nature in Ecuador' (2017) 6(3) Transnational Environmental Law 401–33.

[38] Judgment (Dejusticia), pt 2 para 5.3.

Planet Earth, and by their descendants or future generations who do not yet have a physical hold of them, but who are tributaries, recipients' of those resources in times to come.[39]

The *Colombian Amazon Case* was preceded in Colombia by the pioneering case *Tierra Digna v Presidencia de la República and Others*, which is also of notable importance.[40] Here, in 2017 the Colombian Constitutional Court issued a major environmental judgment that departed from common legal conceptions of the environment by recognising the Atrato River as a legal subject imbued with rights that protect it. Prior to this, the Colombian Constitutional Court had indicated that nature was a subject of legal rights that must be guaranteed and protected,[41] and Villabona has discussed how Colombia's Political Constitution of 1991 helped to provide the foundations for the development of an environmental rule of law in the courts.[42] Against the backdrop of this green jurisprudence, the remarkable leap embodied by the *Tierra Digna* case is that the Constitutional Court took this framework to a next logical stage, applying it for the first time in a narrow, specific way to an identifiable ecosystem (the Atrato River). The facts of the case involved extensive illegal mining activities, which were giving rise to both substantial environmental damage, and to anthropocentric harm. In other words, the case engaged direct and serious negative impacts to both nature and people. These harms echo certain aspects of the Nigerian *Oil Pollution Watch* case, given that, among other things, negative environmental impact on water and health security, environmental cleanliness and similar was at issue. Here, Colombia's Constitutional Court moved beyond an anthropocentric perspective to recognise intrinsic rights of the environment, which the Nigerian courts neither did nor contemplated doing in the *Oil Pollution Watch* case.[43]

Villavicencio Calzadilla points out that the courts took the lead steps in developing this rights of nature approach, which was not set down in existing legislation

[39] ibid pt 2 para 5.3.

[40] *Tierra Digna v Presidencia de la República y otros*, del 10 de Noviembre del 2016, sentencia de la Corte Constitucional de Colombia, T-622 del 2016.

[41] Colombian Constitutional Court rulings: No C-595 of 27 July 2010 on a constitutional challenge filed by Juan Gabriel Rojas López, Expediente D-7977; C-632 of 24 August 2011 on a constitutional challenge filed by Luis Eduardo Montealegre Lynett, Expediente D-8379; and Protection Ruling (*Sentencia de Tutela*) T-080 of 20 February 2015 on an action of tutela (*Accíon de Tutela*) filed by Fundepúblico y otros v Sala Civil y de Familia del Tribunal Superior del Distrito Judicial de Cartagena, Expediente T-4.353.004. See further Villavicencio Calzadilla (n 3) at 3 fn 2 and the text to the note.

[42] Luis Armando Tolosa Villabona, 'Vanguardism and Environmental Justice Developments in Colombia' in Domenico Amirante and Silvia Bagni (eds), *Environmental Constitutionalism in the Anthropocene* (Routledge, 2022).

[43] But see also ch 5 in this volume, n 69 and text to the note concerning submissions made to the Supreme Court of Nigeria by the appellant. In Colombian jurisprudence, see also the 'Chucho' Bear case: case CSJ Civil. AHC4806–2017, *Habeas Corpus of the 'Chucho' Bear*, 26 July 2017; Case T-6.480.577 – Sentence SU-016/20 of 23 January 2020. Here, it was argued that habeas corpus should apply to an animal (an Andean bear), but Colombia's Constitutional Court ultimately rejected this. The case is considered in Villabona (n 42) s 5.2 (the electronic copy produced by the publisher that was provided to the author did not contain page numbering).

at that time.[44] In juxtaposing the *Tierra Digna* illegal mining at the Atrato River with deforestation at the Amazon in the *Colombian Amazon Case*, it is evident that both cases involve concrete, impactful activities engaging a major identifiable ecosystem that give rise to perceived environmental harm. Thus, it is perhaps unsurprising that the latter decision was informed by the *Tierra Digna* ruling, with Colombia's Amazon basin being recognised as the subject of rights.[45] The type of approach manifested in *Tierra Digna* and the *Colombian Amazon Case* has been described as 'ecocentric' and 'biocultural'.[46] Thus, the rainforest is a 'sujeto de derechos' (subject of rights) in the Atrato River case tradition.

Given that the *Tierra Digna* Atrato River case helped set the frame for thinking in the *Colombian Amazon Case*, it is notable that in the former case, the Colombian Constitutional Court recognised human beings as parts of the biosphere rather than as a species that fundamentally stands apart from it or that can be extricated.[47] This perspective points towards 'a deeply respectful and humble position toward nature',[48] and one where 'concepts limited to utilitarianism, the economy or efficiency'[49] are insufficient to capture and underpin that relationship. The environmental elements of the Atrato River case are framed by a rich constitutional backdrop. In its judgment, the Supreme Court opines that the Constitution of 1991 'updated our environmental order', highlighting a range of its provisions.[50] These include: 'the fundamental right to "a clean environment and the protection of the diversity and integrity of the environment" (art 79); … "to plan the management and use of natural resources, in order to guarantee their sustainable development" (art 80)'.[51] It also notes the role that the Constitutional Court has played in interpreting and fleshing out the environmental character of the state's Constitution:

> The Constitutional Court has … played an important role with its pronouncements, designing a line of jurisprudence based on the concepts and advances that have arisen on the subject in the international and academic scenario … [I]it has analyzed the constitutional postulates from a 'green' perspective, cataloguing the Political Charter as an 'Ecological Constitution' and elevating the 'environment' to the category of fundamental right.[52]

Castro explains that the Colombian Constitution of 1991 does not go as far as the Constitutions of Ecuador and Bolivia in recognising the intrinsic rights of nature;

[44] Villavicencio Calzadilla (n 3) 3.

[45] According to the Supreme Court: 'in order to protect this vital ecosystem for the global future, as the Constitutional Court declared the Atrato River, the Colombian Amazon is recognized as an entity, 'subject of rights', entitled to protection, conservation, maintenance and restoration by the State and the territorial entities that integrate it'. Judgment (author), pt 2, para 14.

[46] Villavicencio Calzadilla (n 3) 5.

[47] *Tierra Digna* (n 40).

[48] ibid Ground 9.27, cited by Villavicencio Calzadilla (n 3) 6 and fn 24.

[49] ibid.

[50] Judgment (author), pt 2, para 7.

[51] ibid.

[52] ibid.

instead, interpretation by the Constitutional Court and the Supreme Court has permitted the anthropocentric foundation laid by the Constitution to be viewed as a means of recognising that 'Nature' has a value per se.[53]

Discussing *Tierra Digna*, Villavicencio Calzadilla summarises that: 'For the Court, the way forward is an ecocentric and biocultural approach seeking to dissolve the human-nature binary interaction in order to reach "a new socio-legal understanding in which nature and her components are taken seriously and granted with full rights".'[54] In commentary that could have rich significance for climate litigation, the Constitutional Court states:

> [N]ow is the moment to take the first decisions to protect the planet and its resources efficiently before it is too late, or before the ecological damage became irreversible, not only for future generations, but for the human species.[55]

The Court notes that 'justice with and for nature has to be applied beyond the human interest and … must allow nature to be subject of rights'.[56] Villavicencio Calzadilla comments that: 'This interpretation, as the court highlights, is justified by the notion of the environment's superior interest as developed by … [Colombian] constitutional jurisprudence and included in various constitutional provisions revealing the transcendence of a healthy environment and the interdependency linkage with human beings.'[57]

Drawing the Atrato River and Amazon basin cases together, Villavicencio Calzadilla summarises that the jurisprudential paradigm shift that they embody, moving the overarching legal perspective from a human-centred to a non-anthropocentric worldview, 'establishes that nature and her non-human elements – here, the Atrato River and the Amazon basin – have an intrinsic value and can no longer be viewed as human property or useful senseless objects'.[58] Instead, they must be 'considered as subjects of rights deserving special protection'.[59] Thus, it can be seen that an emerging eco-jurisprudential heritage deriving from the Colombian Constitution, the green jurisprudence of the Constitutional Court, and the *Tierra Digna* ruling, helped to lay both a conceptual and a doctrinal legal path for the *Colombian Amazon Case*. One witnesses the emergence and application of the general legal notion that nature is imbued with rights (preceding constitutional jurisprudence),[60] the precisification of that concept through its

[53] Castro (n 20) 69, who also comments that '[t]he case of Colombia is a clear example of different fronts of struggle that can be built for the recognition of the Rights of Nature in the judiciary – and not in the legislature as happened in Bolivia and Ecuador' (at 78).

[54] Villavicencio Calzadilla (n 3) 6, drawing on Ground 9.27 of *Tierra Digna* (n 40).

[55] Villavicencio Calzadilla (n 3) 6, drawing on Ground 9.29 of *Tierra Digna* (n 40).

[56] Villavicencio Calzadilla (n 3) 6 fn 29, drawing on Ground 9.31 of *Tierra Digna* (n 40).

[57] Villavicencio Calzadilla (n 3) 6.

[58] ibid 3.

[59] ibid.

[60] For analysis of the Constitutional Court's green jurisprudence, see Iván Vargas Rodríguez Chaves, Alexandra Gloria Amparo Cumbe-Figueroa and Sandra-Estefanía Mora-Garzón, 'Recognizing the Rights of Nature in Colombia: The Atrato River Case' (2020) 17(1) *Jurídicas* 13–41.

narrow application to the Atrato River ecosystem (*Tierra Digna*, Constitutional Court), and the development of that approach through the incorporation of the Colombian Amazon rainforest by the Supreme Court (*Colombian Amazon Case*).

Viewed from a philosophical lawyerly perspective, this is surely a setting that can provide a potentially very comfortable home for meaningful and impactful climate litigation. This includes through the general weight accorded to environmental concerns and, within that, to doctrinal legal sensitivity to 'the environment' generally (per the earlier jurisprudence) and to *specific* 'environments' (per the later precisifying jurisprudence, linking natural rights doctrine to identifiable ecosystems including the Amazon basin). Bearing in mind that anthropogenic climate change is the most pressing environmental issue of our times, in a philosophical sense this setting weights the scales of justice towards assuming the importance of climate issues in law, and towards recognising the salience of associated rights protections. Indeed, the *Colombian Amazon Case* demonstrates this in practice. This is certainly far from the default tone set by many other courtrooms around the world. It also militates against providing a comfortable arena for judicial commentary that seems strongly resistant to climate issues, such as that advanced by Chief Justice Roberts and Justice Scalia in *Massachusetts v EPA*.[61]

IV. The Supreme Court Ruling

The case involved an action against the Colombian Government challenging its perceived failure to protect the Colombian Amazon rainforest and halt deforestation. As noted above, an application was lodged at the High Court of the Judicial District of Bogotá on 29 January 2018. The action was brought by 25 Colombian Amazonian children and young people, supported by the Colombian human rights NGO Dejusticia. The translation of excerpts of the judgment produced by Dejusticia places the plaintiffs at 'between 7 and 25 years of age';[62] Villavicencio Calzadilla writes that these plaintiffs were also 'representing the future generations which will have to face the major implications of climate change'.[63] They are described as 'living in cities that are part of the list of cities most at risk due to climate change'.[64] Interesting reference is made to their ages by the Supreme Court.

[61] See *Massachusetts v Environmental Protection Agency*, 549 US 497 (2007) (US Supreme Court).

[62] Judgment (Dejusticia), pt 1, para 2.1. Academic commentary has cited the bottom of the plaintiffs' age range as the considerably higher age of 15 at the time they initiated the case (see Alessandro Pelizzon, 'An Intergenerational Ecological Jurisprudence: The Supreme Court of Colombia and the Rights of the Amazon Rainforest' (2020) 2(1) *Law, Technology and Humans* 33–44, 33), but this is inaccurate as it conflicts with the information provided in the judgment. The author has also checked the case filing and this indicates seven as the bottom of the age range (the next oldest plaintiff is indicated as being eight years old).

[63] Villavicencio Calzadilla (n 3) 5.

[64] Judgment (Dejusticia), pt 1, para 2.1.

Given national life expectancy averages, it is noted that they have a statistical hope to live for 75 years for men and 80 years for women, and if one takes 78 years as a male-female average, according to the plaintiffs they can expect to develop their adult life between 2041 and 2070[65] and have old age from 2071 onwards.[66] The Court notes that according to climate change scenarios provided by IDEAM,[67] the average temperature in Colombia is expected to increase by 1.6°C and 2.14°C respectively over those periods.[68]

Rodríguez-Garavito summarises that the plaintiffs 'sued the Colombian Government for not fulfilling its own commitment to limit deforestation in the Amazon region, as part of the country's international pledge to reduce deforestation to net zero by 2020'.[69] Colombia had adopted the Paris Agreement via Law 1844 of 2017 and the national Law 1753 of 2015, with one of the Government's commitments including this 2020 deforestation reduction. In moral terms, it is important and valuable that the plaintiffs and their team pressed the importance of halting deforestation in the face of governmental inaction. In strict legal terms, their position seems quite weak insofar as the Government had not breached the obligation it was being held to – the date of 2020 was still two years away at this time. Nevertheless, in terms of practical reality, deforestation remained a serious and ongoing issue. Indeed, Villavicencio Calzadilla records that in this period deforestation was not only a continuing problem, but one that was getting worse: 'deforestation in the country's Amazon region had significantly increased recently … by 44% between 2015 and 2016'.[70] The judgment attributes this to land grabbing, illicit crops, illegal extraction of mineral deposits, infrastructure, agro-industrial crops and the illegal extraction of wood.[71]

The plaintiffs sought a number of outcomes, including that the state be ordered to produce and carry out a range of action plans, one of which should take the form of a national action plan to lower deforestation. They sought the Court to rule that deforestation must be halted, and to order that a plan should be instituted by the Government and civil society to protect the rainforest inter-generationally through deforestation reduction. They also sought adjustments to Territorial Management Plans[72] governing land use in order to strengthen deforestation protections, and desired deforestation-increasing activities identified by

[65] The Dejusticia translation of the judgment incorrectly translates these figures as 2041–2017 (Judgment (Dejusticia), pt 1, para 2.1).

[66] Judgment (author), pt 1, para 2.1.

[67] The National Institute of Hydrology, Meteorology and Environmental Studies, a governmental agency that collects and manages environmental data in Colombia, often referred to by its Spanish-language acronym, IDEAM.

[68] Judgment (Dejusticia), pt 1, para 2.1.

[69] César Rodríguez-Garavito, 'Human Rights: The Global South's Route to Climate Litigation' (2020) 114 *AJIL Unbound* 40–44, 42.

[70] Villavicencio Calzadilla (n 3) 5.

[71] Judgment (author), pt 1, para 2.3.

[72] See further Alvarado and Rivas-Ramírez (n 23) 521.

the Government agency IDEAM to be halted. The plaintiffs also wanted illegal mining and other illegal activities giving rise to deforestation to be investigated.[73]

A. The Ruling: Focusing in on Climate Issues

Judge Villabona delivered the judgment of the Court, as reporting judge. The judgment is marked as having been approved by the judges in session on 4 April 2018 and issued on 5 April 2018. The Dejusticia translation of the judgment[74] summarises that the appeal was taken against the Presidency of the Republic, the Ministries of Environment and Sustainable Development and Agriculture and Rural Development, the Special Administrative Unit of Natural National Parks, and the Governorships of the Amazon, Caquetá, Guainía, Guaviare, Putumayo and Vaupés.[75] At the heart of the case is the plaintiffs' challenge to the 'increase of deforestation in the Amazon'.[76] The plaintiffs note that under the Paris Agreement internationally and Law 1753 of 2015 domestically, the Government is required to achieve 'reduction of deforestation and the emission of greenhouse gases in a context of climate change', and that this includes an obligation to 'reduce the net rate of deforestation to zero in the Colombian Amazon by 2020'.[77] Forestry statistics are presented, including from the *Comprehensive Strategy for Controlling Deforestation and Management of Forests in Colombia*, which reported that the country lost 178,697 hectares in 2016, with deforestation increasing by 44 per cent compared to 2015 levels.[78]

Such dreadful figures highlight both the extent of the Government's neglect of its obligations in relation to deforestation management, and the importance of the case in raising the issue and endeavouring to remedy it. As noted earlier, some of the major reasons cited for the rise in deforestation include extensive land grabbing, illicit crops, illegal extraction of minerals and the illegal extraction of wood.[79] Negative impacts arising as a result are framed in relation to undermining climate change mitigation, where they contribute to 'global warming due to carbon dioxide emissions that in non-deforestation conditions are stored in forests'.[80] Negative impacts are also linked to particular localised harms, including negative alteration of water cycles and water supplies, and the decreased ability

[73] Alvarado and Rivas-Ramírez add that they also wanted 'to revise all public resources destined for the reduction of deforestation', although the authors' meaning seems somewhat unclear here: ibid. The authors may be referring to a budgetary review concerning resourcing functions indicated in the *acción de tutela* of 29 January 2018 at the end of para 7.

[74] See further n 1 above.

[75] Judgment (Dejusticia), headnote.

[76] Judgment (author), headnote.

[77] Judgment (Dejusticia), pt 1, para 2.2.

[78] ibid para 2.3.

[79] ibid.

[80] ibid para 2.4.

of soils to relieve against flooding by absorbing water.[81] In addition to posing self-evident problems in their own right, these localised impacts undermine climate change adaptation capacities at regional scales. All of this, the plaintiffs argued, has an injurious effect on their capacity to enjoy their right to a healthy environment.[82]

The climate harm at the heart of the case, then, is occasioned by deforestation, which 'leads to rampant emissions of carbon dioxide (CO_2) into the atmosphere, producing the greenhouse gas effect'.[83] The Amazon area is not the only area of Colombia to suffer from damaging deforestation, but Government statistics reveal it to be a site of extremely substantial activity; for example, it accounted for 66.2 per cent of deforestation over the first half of 2017.[84] Additional and associated harms arising from deforestation pointed to by the Court include the fragmentation of ecosystems, damage to individual species of flora and fauna native to the region, harm to water supplies, and land degradation. Ongoing damage to flora, fauna and ecosystemic integrity will be enough to amount to 'damage in ecological integrity' to the Amazon forest as a whole.[85] The Court also notes that IDEAM has found that ongoing extensive deforestation will lead to increases in undesirable rainfall and greater incidences of drought in parts of the country.[86]

The Court held that sufficient requirements were satisfied such that it could hear the claim on its merits and reach a decision.[87] An element it was required to determine was 'whether there is … a causal link between … climate change' and the progressive unlawful reduction of the Amazon, and 'whether the uncontrolled degradation of the jungle forests directly undermines the rights to life with dignity, to water and to food of the plaintiffs' that are connected to their right to a healthy environment.[88] The Court was satisfied in the affirmative on these points. It outlined a range of factors that 'directly generate the deforestation of the Amazon, causing in the short, medium and long term, an imminent and serious damage … for both present and future generations, because it uncontrollably unleashes the emission of carbon dioxide (CO_2) into the atmosphere, producing the greenhouse effect'.[89]

It is notable that a brief was provided to the Supreme Court 'on behalf of' James E Hansen,[90] the distinguished climate scientist. The brief argued that the

[81] ibid para 2.4.
[82] ibid para 2.5. Textual framing of the problem includes the construction that it 'cut[s] off the possibility of "enjoying a healthy environment"': ibid pt 1, para 2.5.
[83] Judgment (Dejusticia), pt 2, para 10.
[84] Judgment (author), pt 1, para 2.3.
[85] Judgment (Dejusticia), pt 2, para 11.
[86] ibid.
[87] Judgment (author) para 9.
[88] ibid para 11.
[89] ibid.
[90] ibid pt 1, para 14, filed by lawyer Daniel M Galpern.

precautionary principle 'counsels us to act now to avert calamitous climate change before every last detail is fully known (or fully appreciated)'.[91] This advocates for a correct application of the precautionary principle in the face of the climate challenge. In practice, however, the application of the precautionary principle in law tends to depend on two key factors: (a) the extent to which a given domestic legal order has incorporated provisions into law that manifest the principle actively; and (b) the extent to which such provisions are free from other legal (and political) constraints that restrict them from being applied meaningfully. The brief also notes that where the rights and interests of present generations can be said to be impacted and violated, the current understanding of the projected worsening condition of anthropogenic climate change over the rest of this century indicates that the rights and interests of future generations will be impacted and violated 'more severely still'.[92] This fusion of the violation of rights and interests (law) with scientific understanding (climate science), and the conclusions drawn from it, is logically sound. Thus, Hansen makes a good case that 'the principle of intergenerational equity' should compel the Court to reach a decision oriented towards the unburdening of both current and future generations.[93]

The brief also adds that '[c]onsidered interests … must not be limited to those within the specific region of this Court's usual jurisdiction'.[94] Presumably this comment is inspired by the global nature of anthropogenic climate change, which ideally requires the Court to bring a vision to its work that is sensitive to the problem's global character.[95] In addressing the need for 'the Colombian state to stop the causes of … GHG emissions from the abrupt forest reduction in the Amazon', the Supreme Court duly acknowledges the importance of this imperative to 'the plaintiffs' and to 'other people who inhabit and share the Amazonian territory'; however, it also goes beyond this to recognise its importance to 'nationals' and also 'foreigners, together with all inhabitants of the globe'.[96]

The Supreme Court is alert to the depth and seriousness of the problems posed by climate change: 'Day to day the news, articles and reports of different tiers presenting the gravity of the planetary conditions are abundant. There is a growing threat to the possibility of existence of human beings.'[97] It notes the negative environmental impacts arising,[98] and emphasises how 'an anthropocentric and selfish model' predicated on excessive demographic growth, rapid development and consumerism, and excessive exploitation of natural resources has helped to

[91] Judgment (Dejusticia), pt 1, para 14.
[92] ibid.
[93] ibid.
[94] ibid.
[95] On climate law's interaction with a problem that is global in scale and associated matters, see ch 1, section I in this volume.
[96] Judgment (Dejusticia), pt 2, para 11.3.
[97] ibid para 4.
[98] ibid.

generate and exacerbate the problem.[99] The Court stresses that '[h]umanity is the main actor responsible for this scenario'.[100]

In keeping with a common trend in major climate litigation rulings, statistics and targets are drawn upon in the judgment to gauge objectives, progress and shortfalls. The Court notes as follows in relation to the precautionary principle:

> Relative to the [precautionary principle], there is no doubt that there is a risk of damage, given that according to the IDEAM, the increase in GHG emissions resulting from deforestation in the Amazon forest would generate an increase in Colombia's temperature between '0.7 and 1.1. degrees Celsius between 2011 and 2040', while for the period 'between 2041 and 2070', the estimates indicate an increase between '1.4 and 1.7' degrees Celsius, to reach 2.7 degrees Celsius 'in the period between 2071 and 2100.[101]

Similarly, regarding the principle of intergenerational equity, the Court notes:

> In terms of intergenerational equity, the transgression is obvious, as the forecast of temperature increase is 1.6 degrees in 2041 and 2.14 in 2071; future generations, including children who brought this action, will be directly affected, unless we presently reduce the deforestation rate to zero.[102]

Thus, reference to targets and statistics, which tends to feature in landmark climate litigation, is very much present. This includes but is not limited to the 2020 net zero deforestation target marker.

The international arena is characterised by the Court as manifesting 'numerous regulations' composed of 'hard and soft law', which 'constitute a global ecological public order'.[103] The Court opines that this 'serves as guiding criteria for national legislation' and notes that the thrust of this ecological order is towards resolving complaints in favour of the protection of habitats and the associated rights of people.[104] The relevance of the rights of both present and future generations is underscored in this context,[105] and the 2015 Paris Agreement is emphasised within the global ecological public order as having particular importance in the present case. Among a range of references to distinct items of international environmental law,[106] the Paris Agreement stands in the foreground. The Court notes the broad socio-economic reach of the treaty's purpose, which is intended to mobilise 'vigorous and ambitious action to address the climate, by all parties and by non-parties, including civil society, the private sector, financial institutions,

[99] ibid.
[100] ibid.
[101] ibid para 11.1.
[102] ibid para 11.2.
[103] ibid para 11.3.
[104] ibid para 6.
[105] ibid.
[106] These include the Declaration of Stockholm, Declaration of Río, the Forest Principles, the Convention on Biological Diversity, the Amazon Cooperation Treaty, the International Covenant on Economic, Social and Cultural Rights, the Environmental Modification Convention and the first additional Protocol to the Geneva Conventions.

cities and other subnational authorities, local communities and indigenous peoples'.[107]

'Never before', the Court opines, 'has a tool of this type established binding measures to mitigate climate change, requiring countries to make concrete commitments to reduce pollution and the increase of global temperatures'.[108] While this statement catches the spirit of the Paris Agreement's importance, it could also have been helpful if the Court had reflected on the significance historically and at that time (2018) of the Kyoto Protocol.[109] The analysis of pertinent international law could also have benefitted from consideration of the United Nations Framework Convention on Climate Change 1992 (UNFCCC').[110] This seems like a relevant consideration, given the Court's national-international framing of the issues. If the Court had considered the UNFCCC, this could also have proven helpful to UNFCCC signatories around the world, providing an example to other jurisdictions of how UNFCCC principles might be concretised in a domestic legal order where the sorts of facts at issue in this type of climate case arise. Thus, in prefacing its consideration of the international legal order with the assertion that 'in the international sphere … [t]he most important legal instruments are the following',[111] inclusion of the UNFCCC could have enriched the Court's jurisprudence in a beneficial way. At any rate, the Court goes on to note that one of the responsibilities Colombia has agreed to within the Paris Agreement's parameters is 'reducing "deforestation in the Colombian Amazon"'.[112] The Court also draws on the Amazon Cooperation Treaty, and quotes its main objective: 'promotion of the harmonious development of the Amazon … which is fundamental for maintaining the balance between economic growth and environmental preservation'.[113] This has led to promotion of the 'Sustainable Colombia Initiative' and the 'Vision Amazon' fund to support implementation.[114]

It has been noted above that the Supreme Court reversed the decision of the lower court, which had held the claim to be inadmissible because in its view *acción de tutela* could not form a basis for this type of collective rights action. Additionally, the Supreme Court held that the right to a healthy environment is connected in law to a number of other rights, including rights to life, health, freedom and human dignity, and that this also facilitated the case's admissibility.[115] As noted above in the context of the discussion of *Tierra Digna* and

[107] Judgment (Dejusticia), pt 2, para 6.5.
[108] ibid.
[109] Colombia ratified the Kyoto Protocol in 2001, and approved it in Law 629 of 2000.
[110] See Judgment (author), pt 2, paras 6.1–6.5. Colombia ratified the UNFCCC in 1995.
[111] Judgment (author), pt 2, para 6.
[112] Judgment (Dejusticia), pt 2, para 10.
[113] ibid.
[114] ibid.
[115] Alvarado and Rivas-Ramírez comment that 'the Court relied on judgments [of] the Constitutional Court – T-362 and STC 7630 – that ruled that in some cases the violation of collective rights may have sever [*sic*] impact on human fundamental rights': Alvarado and Rivas-Ramírez (n 23) 522 fn 21.

Colombian environmental rights, Colombia's constitutional architecture includes a Constitutional Court.[116] This Court interprets the state's Constitution and produces jurisprudence that adds definition to its parameters. The Constitution itself includes a Bill of Rights and 'organic clauses'.[117] Alvarado and Rivas-Ramírez have discussed the implications of this framework:

> [T]he Constitution is based on both economic and ecological elements, the latter being developed by the Court, and which serve to connect the Colombian constitutional system with nature and the environment. In that sense, it imposes a general duty on the State to protect the environment as an individual right but also as a limit to the neoliberal economic model that the Colombian Constitution generally reflects.[118]

The plaintiffs argued that the Government was failing in its duty to safeguard their constitutional rights to a healthy environment, life, health, nutrition and water, while also failing to safeguard the rights of future generations. The Constitutional Court's 'green' jurisprudence, including its interpretation of the country's 'Ecological Constitution' and the 'elevat[ion of] the environment to the category of fundamental rights', was brought to bear on the Supreme Court's reasoning.[119]

César Rodríguez-Garavito, who worked with colleagues at Dejusticia to represent the 25 plaintiffs, has explained that 'the case was squarely based on human rights arguments'.[120] He elaborates:

> For each plaintiff, we documented how their constitutional rights – including the rights to life, physical integrity, health, housing, and a healthy environment – were directly violated or threatened by the climate emergency, which increasing deforestation made only worse. Both the Court and the plaintiffs invoked human rights norms enshrined in the Colombian Constitution and in international treaties, declarations, and soft-law norms. In choosing this framing and legal basis, we built on the advocacy experience and jurisprudence that Colombian and Latin American NGOs and courts have accumulated in the field of SER litigation.[121]

There is some sense of what might be described as a human rights 'layering up' method here. Multiple layers of human rights-based hard and soft legal material are combined with the rights-sensitive articulation of the plaintiffs' 'lives-as-lived' circumstances, presenting a cumulative picture to the Court that is persuasive and powerful.

The Supreme Court opines that: 'The conservation of the Amazon is a national and global obligation, as it is the main environmental axis of the planet, and as such has been called the "lung of the world"'.[122] A national-international perspective is brought to bear here ('national and global obligation'), with the Court recognising that climate change is an issue that transcends national borders and

[116] See section III above.
[117] See Alvarado and Rivas-Ramírez (n 23) 521.
[118] ibid.
[119] Judgment (Dejusticia), pt 2, para 7.
[120] Rodríguez-Garavito (n 69) 42.
[121] ibid. 'SER' litigation refers to 'socioeconomic rights' litigation (at 40).
[122] Judgment (Dejusticia), pt 2, para 10.

that the importance of the Amazon rainforest in this context does too. Here as elsewhere, the Supreme Court's recognition of complex national-international dimensions where appropriate should serve as a useful guide to courts around the world as they engage with the legally challenging multi-level character of climate change. The 'principle of solidarity' is also recognised by the Court. Pelizzon summarises that the principle pertains to 'solidarity with other humans, future generations and non-human beings'.[123] The Court understands the principle to impose 'the duty and co-responsibility on the Colombian state to stop the causes of the GHG emissions' from Amazon deforestation.[124]

The Supreme Court also identifies and emphasises a need for 'the preservation of this ecosystem due to its importance in regulating the global climate'.[125] It stresses concerns regarding 'the lack of scientific calculations of the release of tons of carbon through burning and the loss of biomass, which constitutes the vegetation cover',[126] the implication being that these practices may be making a significantly greater negative contribution to climate change than available statistics and analyses suggest. The Court opines that '[i]t is up to the authorities to respond effectively to … the problem', which includes a general need 'to confront climate change due to the destruction of the Amazon rainforest in the national territory'.[127] This direct language calls on state authorities to take ownership of the climate challenge by directly engaging and combating it robustly. Indeed, the Court is somewhat scathing in its denunciation of what it perceives as a 'serious ignorance of the obligations acquired by the State' under the Paris Agreement.[128] It continues:

> [Under] Paris 2015 … Colombia … undertook an agreement to reduce the 'deforestation in the Colombian Amazon', with the objective of reducing deforestation to zero in that region by 2020, as achieving it, according to the Ministry of Environment and Sustainable Development, would ensure that '… 44 megatons of greenhouse gases would not enter the atmosphere and 100,000 hectares of agriculture in areas of high deforestation would be more friendly to the environment'.[129]

The Supreme Court also makes an important socio-legal point. Referring to 'FARC [Fuerzas Armadas Revolucionarias de Colombia] and paramilitaries' that formerly operated significantly in the relevant area prior to the contemporary peace process,[130] the Court urges state authorities to seize the opportunity

[123] Pelizzon (n 62) 34.
[124] Judgment (Dejusticia), pt 2, para 11.3.
[125] ibid.
[126] ibid.
[127] ibid.
[128] ibid. Based on the Spanish wording in the judgment, the author would be inclined to translate this as a 'serious lack of knowledge', which results in a slightly less pejorative phrase in an English-language context than the Dejusticia translation quoted above.
[129] ibid.
[130] See further James Meernik, Jacqueline HR DeMeritt and Mauricio Uribe-López (eds), *As War Ends: What Colombia Can Tell Us About the Sustainability of Peace and Transitional Justice* (Cambridge University Press, 2019).

provided by the de-escalation of conflict to 'fill the void' that has been left with an active state presence geared towards environmental conservation.[131]

The state authorities' shortcomings are identified as broad and systemic, including their failure to fulfil their duty to evaluate, control and monitor natural resources, in addition to their failure to implement sanctions for deforestation.[132] Villavicencio Calzadilla summarises that the Court finds that 'the Amazon is ecologically important for the Planet's environmental balance and the regulation of the climate at world scale', highlighting this as one of the bases on which 'the court recognised the Amazon Basin as subject of rights'.[133] The Court criticises an anthropocentric perspective that, in its view, can substantially undermine environmental law and governance:

> [The human species'] hegemonic planetary position lead [*sic*] to the adoption of an anthropocentric and selfish model presenting various harmful features for the environmental balance, namely: i) a disproportionate demographic increase; ii) a dizzying development system guided by consumerism; and, iii) the limitless exploitation of natural resources.[134]

The Supreme Court embraces an emerging 'ecocentric-anthropogenic' framing of the issues, which endeavours to balance up environmental interests in concert with anthropocentric interests, interpreting the latter as frequently hyper-materialistic and therefore environmentally damaging.[135]

Though the author sees no benefit in applying the substantive philosophy of Hegel here, which is frequently obscurantist and would likely only introduce confusion – to the author's knowledge, nobody in the literature has attempted to do so – it does seem that the Hegelian *Thesis/Antithesis/Synthesis* paradigm might be referenced to some benefit in the form of a loose analogy (only).[136] Here, one can posit a ***thesis*** or status quo conception of environmental value, which will tend to be fundamentally *anthropocentric* in character, ie, human-centred. In direct relation to this, one can posit an ***antithesis***, or antithetical conception of environmental value, pertaining to *ecocentric* environmental value, namely a nature-centred sense of value that is typically neglected and

[131] Judgment (Dejusticia), pt 2, para 11.3. The plaintiffs' submission states that FARC's occupation, 'paradoxically', had assisted in maintaining the territories in 'a state of conservation'; see further Judgment (author), pt 1, para 2.6. For consideration of environmental law and policy in Colombia and its interaction with domestic conflict and the country's peace process, see further Gómez-Betancur (n 34).

[132] Judgment (Dejusticia), pt 2, para 13.

[133] Villavicencio Calzadilla (n 3) 7, who notes that she is referring to Ground 11 of the Supreme Court judgment.

[134] Villavicencio Calzadilla (n 3) 7.

[135] ibid, referring to Ground 5.3 of the Supreme Court judgment.

[136] See further Gustav Mueller, 'The Hegel Legend of "Synthesis-Antithesis-Thesis"' (1958) 19(3) *Journal of the History of Ideas* 411–14.

marginalised by the dominant *thesis* category. Thus, the following picture of the dominant *thesis* and marginalised *antithesis* emerges:

Thesis / *Antithesis* =

Anthropocentric conception(s) of environmental value [Thesis] /

Ecocentric conception(s) of environmental value [Antithesis]

The *thesis* position indicates the status quo viewpoint that tends to be widely assumed by dominant conceptions of environmental value within contemporary legal-political systems. In directly articulating the *antithesis* position in the above manner, one makes the suppressed notion of *ecocentric* environmental value explicit with reference to the dominant mode of thought, while simultaneously highlighting shortcomings in the *thesis* conception, by exposing its inherent marginalisation of *ecocentric* value.

Hegel's treatment of these categories – again, drawn on here as a loose-guide analogy only – allows that the inherent binary tension that has been posited might be resolved by achieving a ***Synthesis*** between the *thesis* and *antithesis* categories. This may be achieved by drawing the binary *thesis/antithesis* conceptions together into a new unified conception that can resolve the binary's inherent conflict. In the present case, this *thesis/antithesis* and outcome *synthesis* framing can be concretised in terms of the Colombian Supreme Court's ecocentric-anthropocentric interpretation of environmental value as follows:

Thesis / *Antithesis* =

Anthropocentric conception(s) of environmental value [Thesis] /

Ecocentric conception(s) of environmental value [Antithesis]

Synthesis =

Ecocentric-anthropocentric conception(s) of environmental value

Here, in the Supreme Court's *synthesis* form, humans and their interests remain central to the conception of environmental value, but ecological value is recognised simultaneously in its own right per se, in part due to the fact that the human species itself exists in nature and is part of nature. Ecocentric interests are recognised and integrated with anthropocentric interests in an inextricable manner, such that ecocentric value is no longer marginalised by anthropocentric fundamentalism (ie, the former dominant *thesis* category) and a new coherent conception of environmental value emerges.

Thus, commentary on the case has emphasised that 'the Court underlines the obligation of solidarity with the "other" … [including] nature, animal and plant species living on this planet (the others)'.[137] In addressing rights and the

[137] Villavicencio Calzadilla (n 3) 8, drawing on Ground 5.2 of the Supreme Court judgment.

environment, the Court opines that 'protection of fundamental rights not only involves the individual, but implicates the "other"'.[138] While the 'other' may include one's 'neighbour' and 'the other people that inhabit the planet', the Court asserts that it must be drawn to 'also include other animal and plant species'.[139] The Court identifies this neglected dimension of the 'other' – nature and its intrinsic value, and natural rights commensurate with that value – and 'balances it up' alongside anthropocentric notions of value in an integrated way. Put another way, the Court removes it from its position of marginalisation in relation to the dominant anthropocentric *thesis*, and integrates it into a *synthesis* that recognises a coherent ecocentric-anthropocentric construction of environmental value. Here, the Court asserts that 'all human beings have to stop thinking only in their own interest. We must realise how our daily activities and behaviour have an impact on society and nature'.[140] Villavicencio Calzadilla summarises that '[t]he court assures that this obligation of solidarity rests on the fact that humankind "is part of nature, 'being' itself nature"'.[141] Thus, the 'other' or 'antithesis' is synthesised into a new whole that resolves underlying conceptual tensions: 'a new 'ecocentric-anthropo[centric]' ideology has emerged'.[142] Natural value is absorbed into human value, and vice versa, as a part of the whole; human beings exist in nature, are part of it, and so cannot stand apart from it. The Supreme Court summarises that its vision 'transcends the anthropocentric perspective and focuses on 'ecocentric-anthropic' criteria, which places the human being on par with the environmental ecosystem'.[143]

Drawing on this rich conception of environmental value, in concert with the state's deforestation obligations in national and international law, and as interpreted in light of Colombian constitutional law and jurisprudence, the Supreme Court held that the Colombian Amazon rainforest is subject to environmental rights mandating its protection, conservation, sustenance and restoration,[144] and territorial entities of the Amazon region and the national Government therefore have an ability and indeed a duty where necessary to represent and realise those rights.[145]

B. Intergenerational Rights

One feature of the jurisprudential reasoning that stands out in this landmark climate case that distinguishes it from most other cases is the particular attention

[138] Judgment (Dejusticia), pt 2, para 5.2.
[139] ibid.
[140] Villavicencio Calzadilla (n 3) 8.
[141] ibid, referring to Ground 5.3 of the Supreme Court judgment.
[142] ibid 7, referring to Ground 5.3 of the Supreme Court judgment.
[143] Judgment (Dejusticia), pt 2, para 5.3.
[144] Villavicencio Calzadilla (n 3) 8, referring to Ground 14 of the Supreme Court judgment.
[145] Villavicencio Calzadilla (n 3) 8.

paid to the concept of future generations, and the bearing these generations have on the Court's reasoning. The Court refers to 'a binding legal relationship regarding the environmental rights of future generations', which can have an impact that 'translates into a limitation to the freedom of action of present generations' and that includes present generations 'tak[ing] on the care and stewardship of natural resources and the future world'.[146] Analysis by Pelizzon has explored the importance of this aspect of the case, with the author describing the ruling as 'the first successful climate change and future generations lawsuit in Latin America and, indeed, the world'.[147]

After a period of doctrinal and philosophical consideration of the nature of collective and individual rights, the duties that rights imply, and recognition of the principle of solidarity, which widens the scope of rights interests far beyond the self-interest of the atomised individual, the Court draws on the work of legal philosopher and politician Rodríguez Palop. This assists the judgment in rationalising the inclusion of future generations within this scope. Rodríguez Palop is quoted as follows:

> But who are these others to whom we must respond, who are those affected by our decisions? … It is interesting to note that when we speak of the inclusion of others, … the temporal dimension of the discourse cannot be avoided, a dimension that projects it in time. *Solidarity does not only make sense in our spatio-temporal coordinates, but also extends to future generations.* (Emphasis added)[148]

The Court summarises that '[t]he environmental rights of future generations are based on the (i) ethical duty of solidarity of the species and (ii) the intrinsic value of nature'.[149]

In its reasoning, the Supreme Court 'formulates a juridical relation' pertaining to the environmental rights of future generations, which calls for 'the performance of "not-doing"', ie, refraining from undertaking actions that will undermine the environment for future generations and the associated environmental rights of those generations.[150] The Court recognises that this 'effect is translated in a limitation of the present generations' freedom of choice' – that is to say, it imposes constraints and obligations on current generations regardless of the fact that an emphasis may fall on *not* doing something (as distinct from being compelled to actively do something).[151]

In ruling in favour of the plaintiffs, the Court has little difficulty in finding a violation of intergenerational equity:

> As for the criterion of intergenerational equity, its transgression is obvious, since the temperature increase forecast for the year 2041 will be 1.6°, and in 2071 up to 2.14°,

[146] Judgment (Dejusticia), pt 2, para 5.3.
[147] Pelizzon (n 62) 33.
[148] Judgment (author), pt 2, para 5.2.
[149] ibid para 5.3.
[150] ibid.
[151] ibid.

> with future generations, among them, the infants who interpose this safeguard, those who will be directly affected, unless the present ones reduce the rate of deforestation to zero.[152]

It is clear that the Court's conclusions are partly based on the notion that the young plaintiffs will classify as future generations in the decades to come. The ruling thus also affords protection to the unborn by this channel. Unlike the plaintiffs, the unborn are unable to bring a case of this kind directly on their own behalf. It is uncertain whether the Court would have found that a clear breach of intergenerational equity had occurred if it was limited to considering unborn generations *only*, as it would be, for example, if all of the plaintiffs were very elderly. This element of the reasoning might benefit from greater clarity, first because it is possible to choose to conceptualise 'future generations' purely in terms of the unborn in climate litigation, and second because the Supreme Court in this case states that it is concerned to protect 'the unborn, who deserve to enjoy the same environmental rights as we do'.[153] Thus, in going forward, where courts choose to identify and apply a distinction between 'living' and 'unborn' future generations, doctrine might benefit from greater clarity as to whether an application of the law seeks to treat these categories homogenously or heterogeneously, and what if any consequences might arise from such an approach in law.

Alvarado and Rivas-Ramírez summarise that:

> The ruling is significant in at least two respects. First, the Court's [*sic*] relies on future generations to press the government to take action on climate change, including in dealing with deforestation, which represents unusual legal reasoning for this Court. Second, the Court's use of international law as part of the founding argument of its judgment is also remarkable.[154]

It will be seen below that the plans that the Supreme Court ordered the Government and others to produce include the creation, agreement and implementation of an *Intergenerational Pact for the Life of the Colombian Amazon*, which must be sensitive to future generations as well as current ones.

C. Outcome

The Supreme Court ordered the presidency and relevant ministries, 'in coordination with the sectors of the National Environmental System, and the participation of the plaintiffs, the affected communities and the population in general', to formulate a short, medium and long-term action plan within four months of notification of the decision, to counteract the rate of deforestation in the Amazon and its associated climate change impact.[155] Within five months,

[152] ibid para 11.2.
[153] ibid para 5.2.
[154] Alvarado and Rivas-Ramírez (n 23) 522.
[155] Judgment (author), pt 3, first order.

these governmental actors, 'with the active participation of the plaintiffs, the affected communities, scientific organizations or environmental research groups, and the interested population in general', were ordered to produce an *Intergenerational Pact for the Life of the Colombian Amazon*.[156] This should include 'measures … adopted to reduce deforestation and greenhouse gas emissions to zero, which must have national, regional and local implementation strategies, of a preventive, mandatory, corrective and pedagogical type, aimed at adapting to climate change'.[157]

Colombian Amazon municipalities were given a maximum of five months to update and implement their Territorial Management Plans, including the incorporation of an action plan for zero deforestation in their territory, and strategies aimed at improving climate change adaptation.[158] Relevant bodies were also directed to implement an action plan to counteract deforestation problems reported by IDEAM through police, judicial and administrative measures as appropriate.[159] Relevant respondent agencies were given 48 hours to commence an increase in actions to mitigate deforestation while the above orders were being carried out,[160] including where necessary via 'urgently file[d] complaints and lawsuits with the corresponding administrative and judicial entities'.[161]

It is notable that in ordering the *Intergenerational Pact*, the Court required this to incorporate both mitigation and adaptation elements. As noted above, in addition to formulating measures aimed at bringing down greenhouse gas emissions levels and reducing deforestation to zero (*mitigation*), the plan should incorporate 'national, regional and local implementation strategies, of a preventive, mandatory, corrective and pedagogical type, aimed at adapting to climate change' (*adaptation*).[162] In updating municipal Land Management Plans in the interest of bringing deforestation in their territories to zero, local authorities are also required to incorporate 'preventative, mandatory, corrective, and pedagogical measurable strategies, oriented towards climate change adaptation'.[163] In some sense, the Supreme Court uses the deforestation case's primary *mitigation* focus as a lever to expand *adaptation* obligations on state authorities, based on the implied recognition that climate change involves interactive and co-connected mitigative and adaptive strands of law and policy.[164] Efforts on the part of the plaintiffs to expand outcomes to the adaptation sphere were incorporated into their argumentation, including in their request for the Court to order the creation of 'an intergenerational agreement on

[156] ibid second order.
[157] ibid.
[158] ibid third order.
[159] ibid fourth order.
[160] ibid.
[161] ibid fourth order/conclusion of the four orders section.
[162] ibid second order.
[163] Judgment (Dejusticia), Decision.
[164] On mitigation and adaptation as fundamental strands of climate law, see ch 1, section I in this volume.

the measures to be adopted to reduce deforestation and greenhouse gas emissions, including the strategy for adaptation and mitigation of climate change in each of the country's vulnerable cities and municipalities'.[165] This legal approach was clearly effective.

In summarising the Court orders, Rodríguez-Garavito writes that the Court 'order[ed] the Colombian government to issue an effective plan of action against deforestation in the Amazon, declaring the Colombian Amazon a subject of rights, and mandating the government to sign an "intergenerational pact" against climate change'.[166] This emphasises how these orders engage an ecosystem that is now held explicitly to be a *subject of rights* in law.

V. Concluding Thoughts

It is clear that the Constitutional Court in *Tierra Digna* and the Colombian Supreme Court in the *Colombian Amazon Case* have unfolded a strand of law in a mutually complementary and interconnected way, establishing a very particular environmental framework that creates an increasingly friendly context for climate litigation in Colombia. Villavicencio Calzadilla summarises the recognised legal rights of the river and rainforest at issue in these two cases as 'including the rights to protection, conservation, maintenance and restoration', which in principle can be enforced by local communities and individuals in the courts.[167] As a logical consequence, she notes that the guardians and representatives of those ecosystems can also be sued in principle for failing to fulfil their responsibilities.[168] Research and analysis of climate litigation in Latin America indicates that the *Colombian Amazon Case* has made a leading-edge contribution to a new typology of climate litigation that appears to be starting to emerge in the region, which recognises the intrinsic value and interests of all life forms.[169]

It is notable that the Supreme Court interprets the Amazon rainforest as having international as well as national significance, given that it is 'a pivotal environmental area on Earth' functioning as 'the lungs of the planet'.[170] It is imbued with rights of nature. The intergenerational aspects of the case are also of major significance, and they have a capacity to serve as a useful point of reference for courts around the world in cases where courts are compelled by climate litigation to engage with

[165] Judgment (author), pt 1, para 2.6, quoting submissions to the Court by the plaintiffs.
[166] Rodríguez-Garavito (n 69) 42.
[167] Villavicencio Calzadilla (n 3) 9.
[168] ibid.
[169] Fernanda de Salles Cavedon-Capdeville, Maria Valeria Berros, Humberto Filpi and Paola Villavicencio Calzadilla, 'An Ecocentric Perspective on Climate Litigation: Lessons from Latin America' (2024) 16(1) *Journal of Human Rights Practice* 89–106. For an ongoing case (at the time of writing) that takes inspiration from the *Colombian Amazon Case* to challenge deforestation of the Amazon rainforest in Peru, see *Álvarez et al v Perú*, Corte Superior de Justicia de Lima (16 December 2019).
[170] Villavicencio Calzadilla (n 3) 8.

the issue of future generations. Further, regarding domestic Colombian law, the ruling adjusts the *acción de tutela* channel to the Colombian courts, such that courts will have to look beyond individual rights applications to consider a wider field of potential admission for climate and environmental lawsuits based in part on collective rights in certain circumstances. Alvarado and Rivas-Ramirez also comment that the ruling clarifies that 'international environmental law, and the Paris Agreement in particular' can assist in serving directly as a legal basis for such action and 'for the interpretation of constitutional rights, such as the right to life, health and a healthy environment, as well as rights of future generations'.[171] Thus, the case has created scope for ambitious and creative lawyers and applicants to leverage environmental law in general, and the Paris Agreement in particular, to bolster climate litigation in the Colombian courts.

Work from Peel and Lin has highlighted a tendency in mainstream climate litigation scholarship to focus most particularly on the Global North, which can serve in the process to neglect important developments and learnings that can be derived from the increasingly rich emerging tradition of climate litigation in the Global South.[172] Serious consideration of the Global South can reveal 'new avenues and strategies for climate litigation that have not been the focus of attention in the Global North'.[173] There is a mutual learning process that becomes visible where the *Colombian Amazon Case* is juxtaposed with *Climate Case Ireland*.[174] In the Colombian case, the Colombian Supreme Court developed a rich legal conception of the environment that embeds its intrinsic value in law, whereas in the Irish case, the Irish Supreme Court negated a constitutional environmental right that had previously been interpreted into the Irish Constitution by the lower courts in *Friends of the Irish Environment* (2017).[175] Here, the Irish courts can benefit from reflection on the Colombian approach: the juxtaposition of the two cases suggests that the Irish Supreme Court's jurisprudence is comparatively insensitive and unresponsive to the overt recognition of important environmental constitutional rights. Indeed, the Irish Supreme Court appears actively retrograde, insofar as *Climate Case Ireland* actively reversed the lower courts' environmental jurisprudence.[176] The Irish Supreme Court might learn valuable lessons from reflection on the Colombian Supreme Court's jurisprudential approach to environmental value and rights.

Conversely, in the domain of enforcement, the Irish Supreme Court may provide a positive example for the Colombian setting. It has been pointed out

[171] Alvarado and Rivas-Ramírez (n 23) 526.

[172] Jacqueline Peel and Jolene Lin, 'Transnational Climate Litigation: The Contribution of the Global South' (2019) 113(4) *American Journal of International Law* 679–726.

[173] ibid 686.

[174] *Friends of the Irish Environment v Government of Ireland* [2020] IESC 49.

[175] *Friends of the Irish Environment v Fingal County Council* [2017] IEHC 695.

[176] Technically this can be interpreted as obiter dicta, but nevertheless it directs the lower courts to interpret the 'unenumerated' constitutional environmental right engaged in *Friends of the Irish Environment* (n 174) as erroneous. See further ch 7 in this volume.

that the *Tierra Digna* case and cases like it are difficult to enforce, albeit that some progress has been made.[177] Such progress, tentative as it may be at present, differentiates this from a case like *Gbemre v Shell* (2005) in Nigeria, an important precursor to *Oil Pollution Watch*, where the Nigerian courts found against fossil fuel gas flaring, but no meaningful enforcement action was taken.[178] In *Climate Case Ireland*, the Irish Supreme Court did definitively and unequivocally quash the Irish Government's inadequate *National Mitigation Plan*. Although doing so in an effective way poses significantly less practical difficulty than ordering the prevention of rainforest deforestation occurring on a broad geographical front, this is a very important governmental policy document, and its quashing provides a robust example of a climate litigation enforcement outcome in practice. The *Plan* was quashed, a new *Plan* was ordered, the Government was required to produce this, and it did so.

This might provide some degree of good-practice inspiration for outcomes enforcement in Colombia, demonstrating a standard of what should be expected when the highest court in the land orders the Government to achieve climate litigation outcomes. A postgraduate at the Norwegian University of Life Sciences has investigated the implementation of the *Colombian Amazon Case* as part of a Master's Degree thesis (published in 2023), finding that some significant progress has been made, but that much still remains to be done.[179] Research from Richardson and Bustos on implementation, including detailed data analysis and interviews, exposes a picture of partial but currently inadequate compliance in the face of a complex socio-political environment where entrenched problems remain.[180] These problems include a tendency for vulnerable local groups to receive apparently unjust and unreasonable treatment as part of the official anti-deforestation drive, rather than being integrated as a constituent and participant part of the process in a humane and respectful way.[181] Richardson and Bustos also record as follows: after the ruling, Dejusticia filed a subsequent non-compliance complaint in April 2019, leading to the District Court of Cundinamarca hosting a 10-day public hearing in an effort to move implementation forward; in December 2020, the Superior Court of Bogotá acknowledged that progress on implementation remained insufficient, ordering the creation of a Technical Committee to progress implementation and a Monitoring Committee to monitor the implementation of the Court's orders.[182]

[177] Villavicencio Calzadilla (n 3) 10.

[178] *Gbemre v Shell Petroleum Development Company Nigeria Limited*, Suit No FHC/B/C/153/05. See further ch 5 in this volume.

[179] Geovanna Esperanza Guerrero Ascuntar, 'Exploring the Ruling on the Rights of the Colombian Amazon: Taking Stock of the Implementation of Ruling 4360 of 2018' (MS thesis, Norwegian University of Life Sciences, 2023), in particular 77–91.

[180] Whitney Richardson and Camila Bustos, 'Implementing Nature's Rights in Colombia: The Atrato and Amazon Experiences' (2023) 54 *Revista Derecho del Estado* 227–75. It should be noted that the plaintiffs were not amongst the interviewee cohort as the authors were unable to reach them.

[181] ibid.

[182] ibid. See also this note concerning problematic aspects of participation in relation to affected indigenous communities: Dayana Castro, 'Press Release: The People of the Centre are Opening a Path of

Writing with other colleagues, Bustos and her co-authors have emphasised that some progress on implementation has been made, but that significant hindrances remain.[183] They have also noted that the 'media continuously monitors the issue' in Colombia now,[184] which highlights the useful level of consciousness-raising that major climate litigation can contribute to. Further, they have drawn attention to the following:

> Traditionally, human rights studies and practice have been more occupied with litigation than on monitoring the implementation of a judicial decision. The same has happened around the world in the emerging field of climate change litigation. To counteract this trend, the plaintiffs and stakeholders in the Colombian case have pushed for compliance with the court ruling.[185]

While implementation is still inadequate, this sustained pressure placed on governmental actors by the plaintiffs, stakeholders and, indeed, the courts holds a general lesson for climate litigation. In best-practice public interest cases, a focus on sustained implementation pressure should follow on the heels of a landmark climate ruling wherever possible. In this sense, a landmark climate law ruling does not conclude a case, but rather heralds a new implementation-oriented phase of endeavour.

Understanding with the Colombian Government to Jointly Safeguard the Future of Life in the Amazon', Forest Peoples Programme, 27 October 2023.

[183] Camila Bustos, Valentina Rozo-Ángel and Gabriela Eslava-Bejarano, 'Protecting the Rights of Future Generations through Climate Litigation: Lessons from the Struggle against Deforestation in the Colombian Amazon' (2020) *Standing up for a Sustainable World* 163.

[184] ibid 167.

[185] ibid 166.

5

Nigeria

The Centre for Oil Pollution Watch Case

> [T]here is increasing concern about climate change, depletion of the ozone layer, waste management, flooding, global warming … The plaintiff/appellant being in the vanguard of protecting the environment should be encouraged to ensure that actions or omissions by Government agencies or Multi-national oil companies that tend to pollute the environment are checked.
>
> *Oil Pollution Watch*, Supreme Court of Nigeria, p 580

I. Why is this Case of Interest to Climate Lawyers?

In comparison to the other chapters providing deep-dive studies into breakthrough climate law rulings in this volume, this important Nigerian case is something of a joker in the pack. It is a highly important case, and one that has major legal significance in the sphere of environmental protection in Nigeria in particular. It widens avenues to public interest climate litigation that would otherwise have been narrow. It is not, however, a landmark climate law case in the sense that the other cases covered in the case-study chapters in this volume are. Those cases have been selected on the basis of being the first major breakthrough climate law cases in their jurisdictions to both (a) reach the highest courts in the land, and (b) deal explicitly and substantially with climate-specific issues.[1] *Centre for Oil Pollution Watch v Nigerian National Petroleum Corporation* (2018)[2] (hereafter '*Oil Pollution Watch*')

[1] Chapter 6 in this book covers *Gloucester Resources Limited v Minister for Planning* [2019] NSWLEC 7, a decision of the New South Wales Land and Environment Court. Regarding point (a), the highest court in Australia itself is the High Court of Australia; however, in the jurisdiction of New South Wales in the context of the *Gloucester Resources Case*, the Land and Environment Court is a powerful court equivalent to a Supreme Court in the New South Wales court hierarchy.

[2] *Centre for Oil Pollution Watch v Nigerian National Petroleum Corporation* [2019] 5 NWLR (Pt 1666) 518; 20 July 2018, hereinafter cited as 'Judgment'. The official judgment contains a range of typographical and grammatical slips, which the author has rarely but occasionally adjusted in quotations in the interest of clarity. The case year is cited in the main body of this chapter as 2018 and in the report citation in this footnote as 2019 because the case was decided in 2018 and published in the official Nigerian law reports in 2019.

satisfies element (a), being as it is an important Supreme Court of Nigeria ruling; however, it does not fully satisfy element (b).

Although climate-specific issues are raised in the judgment,[3] climate change and the associated overt themes and concerns engaged typically by landmark climate cases do not receive substantial attention. Instead, the case can be understood as a door that has been pushed open by the Supreme Court of Nigeria, expanding the capacity for public interest climate litigation to be initiated in the country (and public interest environmental litigation more generally).[4] Ekhator and Okumagba find that 'there are no explicit climate change cases in Nigeria' yet to arise; however, they can conceptualise *Oil Pollution Watch* as 'climate litigation caselaw or jurisprudence' due both to its significance for climate and environmental justice issues, and to the recognition it has received internationally for its importance to climate law.[5] Etemire notes that climate litigation in Nigeria is still 'in its infancy', but that the case represents a 'paradigm shift' that can serve to 'clear the way' for richer developments.[6] In this respect, the broader implications of *Oil Pollution Watch* for climate law are as important as the case's narrower facts and issues – indeed, more so.[7]

Oamen and Erhagbe describe the ruling as an outcome that has 'clearly heralded a robust climate change litigation opportunity in Nigeria',[8] such that 'the future of climate change litigation looks bright'.[9] In addition to its inclusion in this

[3] Judgment, 580 (Aka'ahs, JSC).

[4] Note: after a successful ruling from the Supreme Court on the matter of locus standi in favour of the NGO bringing this environmental damage lawsuit (discussed below), the Supreme Court referred the case back to the Trial Court. The author cannot find evidence that a ruling was then delivered by the Trial Court leading to compensation and environmental remediation for the affected communities and their environs. So far as the author can see, the academic literature is also silent on this point. This is highly unsatisfactory, as the environmental damage and serious negative impacts on people and place arising may remain unredressed.

[5] Eghosa Ekhator and Edward Okumagba, 'Climate Change, Multinationals and Human Rights in Nigeria: A Case for Climate Justice', page 18 of the 2023 working paper for the then forthcoming book: Kim Etemire Bouwer, Tracy-Lynn Uzuazo Field and Ademola Oluborode Jegede (eds), *In Pursuit of Climate Justice in Africa* (subsequently published as *Climate Litigation and Justice in Africa* (Bristol University Press, 2024)). The authors also suggest that the case *Gbemre v Shell Petroleum Development Company Nigeria Limited* (Suit No FHC/B/C/153/05 Judgment delivered on 14/11/2005 at Federal High Court, Benin Judicial Division) can be interpreted as a climate case on the grounds noted above. This is a Federal High Court ruling of 2005, where the court found in favour of a plaintiff seeking to compel Shell to end harmful gas flaring in the vicinity of his community.

[6] Uzuazo Etemire, 'The Future of Climate Change Litigation in Nigeria: COPW v NNPC in the Spotlight.' (2021) 15 *CCLR*, 158, 158.

[7] The case also has wider regional significance, given that the Supreme Court of Nigeria draws significantly on the African Charter on Human and Peoples' Rights in its reasoning. At the time of writing, the African Commission on Human and Peoples' Rights reports that this important African human rights agreement has been ratified by 54 African Union Member States. See African Commission on Human and Peoples' Rights, 'State Parties to the African Charter', https://achpr.au.int/en/states.

[8] Philip E Oamen and Eunice O Erhagbe, 'The Impact of Climate Change on Economic and Social Rights Realisation in Nigeria: International Cooperation and Assistance to the Rescue?' (2021) 21(2) *African Human Rights Law Journal* 1080–1111, 1089.

[9] ibid 1090.

volume due to the importance of its subject matter, the broader issues it raises and its wider implications for climate law, consideration of *Oil Pollution Watch* also helps to shine a light on the African Global South, the rich legal culture that exists there, and lessons that might be learned from it by other jurisdictions around the world.[10]

II. *Oil Pollution Watch*: Journey Through the Courts

This case concerns extensive and prolonged spillage from a ruptured oil pipeline that discharged its contents into streams and the surrounding environment in an area of Abia State, Nigeria, resulting in widespread environmental damage and negative impacts to human life and health for communities residing in the area and visiting it. Litigation was initiated seeking reinstatement, restoration and remediation of the contaminated environment, provision of a fresh water supply to substitute for contaminated water, and medical facilities for the examination and treatment of people suffering negative health consequences. The case raises fundamental questions around which parties should have direct access to the courts in situations concerning public nuisance injurious to human life, public health and the environment. The issue of access to the courts is very important in its own right, but it is rendered all the more important given that research has identified a lack of political will amongst governmental actors to enforce adequate environmental laws to regulate the environmental consequences of crude oil exploitation in Nigeria.[11]

Oil Pollution Watch commenced at the Federal High Court, Lagos Judicial Division (hereinafter the 'Trial Court'),[12] then proceeded to the Court of Appeal, Lagos Division, before reaching the Supreme Court of Nigeria. The Supreme Court's decision overturned the decisions of the lower courts. The Trial Court issued its ruling on 31 October 2006, where the plaintiff's standing to sue was successfully challenged by the respondent and the case was struck out.[13] Here, 'standing' refers to locus standi, namely the plaintiff's ability to bring its lawsuit. This decision was appealed to the Court of Appeal, which upheld the finding of the lower court.[14] This decision was appealed in turn to the Supreme Court,

[10] See further the section entitled 'Climate Litigation in Africa – An Analysis' in Jovan Ivan Mugga, Joyeeta Gupta and René Lefeber, 'Shaping Africa's Climate Action through Climate Litigation: An Impact Assessment' (2023) 26(1) *RiA Recht in Afrika| Law in Africa| Droit en Afrique* 26–54, 40–45.

[11] Abosede Omowumi Babatunde, 'Oil Pollution and Water Conflicts in the Riverine Communities in Nigeria's Niger Delta Region: Challenges for and Elements of Problem-solving Strategies' (2020) 38(2) *Journal of Contemporary African Studies* 274–93, 286.

[12] The shortening to 'Trial Court' here follows Nweze, JSC's approach in his leading judgment; Judgment, 548.

[13] ibid 582.

[14] *Centre for Oil Pollution Watch v NNPC* [2013] 15 NWLR 556.

where that Court overturned the previous decisions and found in favour of the appellant.[15] The Supreme Court decision was issued by a bench of seven Justices on 20 July 2018.[16] The passage of 12 years between the Trial Court's ruling and the Supreme Court's ruling is wholly unacceptable in a grave environmental case of this kind, and if such delays are imported into serious climate cases in future, this will prove detrimental to justice. The Supreme Court's ruling was decisive and unanimous. The leading judgment was provided by Nweze, JSC (with JSC indicating 'Justice of the Supreme Court').[17] The other Justices were in agreement with this, and each offered remarks and points of emphasis of their own in support.

The Trial Court had struck out the lawsuit in *limine*,[18] meaning that it had heard the respondent's application for an order to strike out the case and found that the plaintiff lacked the standing to bring the action in the first place, prior to a trial proper on the full facts and issues having taken place. When the Trial Court ruling was appealed to the Court of Appeal, it was the task of the higher court to adjudicate on the Trial Court's decision on the issue of standing. As noted above, it affirmed the lower court's ruling.[19] Research finds that oil spills have been a persistent problem in Nigeria and that environmental frameworks have been ineffective in providing a comprehensive, robust and suitably enforceable regulatory environment in the face of environmental damage arising.[20] Restrictive rules on standing can assist in perpetuating and entrenching these problems unacceptably.

Given the court process just noted and the respondent's success in pressing the standing point at the Trial Court and the Court of Appeal, the detailed facts and issues underlying the case did not get an airing in a trial context prior to the Supreme Court stage, due to the plaintiff's perceived lack of standing to proceed to trial in the first place. These circumstances applied substantial constraints to the Supreme Court phase in turn, which took place in the absence of a trial on the facts and issues having occurred, and where the Court was tasked with the relatively narrow technical issue of determining whether the decision on standing was correct or not, and no more than this. Oluduro has found that technical rules of standing have been actively exploited by energy corporations to restrict the ability of victims to access environmental justice in contemporary Nigeria, leaving

[15] Judgment.

[16] The Justices were: Chima Centus Nweze, JSC, reading the leading judgment; Walter Samuel Nkanu Onnoghen, CJN (Chief Justice); Musa Dattijo Muhammad, JSC; Kumai Bayang Aka'ahs, JSC; Kudirat Motonmori Olatokunbo Kekere-Ekun, JSC; John Inyang Okoro, JSC; and Ejembi Eko, JSC.

[17] Judgment, 548–71 (Nweze, JSC).

[18] ibid 525.

[19] *Centre for Oil Pollution Watch* (n 14).

[20] BE Ewulum, Ejike Okaphor and Nnedimma Ezenwa-Ohaeto Okoli, 'An Appraisal of the Impact of the National Oil Spill Detection and Response Agency on Environmental Pollution in Nigeria' (2020) 2 *IJOCLLEP* 58–65.

climate litigation vulnerable to this practice in the process.[21] This highlights the crucial importance of the standing point at issue.

At the Supreme Court, Onnoghen, CJN summarised the background to the case in the lower courts and the legal issue for resolution as follows:

> An appeal to the lower court was dismissed resulting in the instant further appeal, the issue for the determination of which is: 'Whether the learned Justices of the Court of Appeal were right in dismissing the appellant's appeal for want of *locus standi* to maintain the suit?'[22]

Supreme Court judge Kekere-Ekun, JSC emphasised that '[a]t this stage, all that is being determined is whether the appellant has the *locus standi* to sue. Whether the suit will ultimately succeed is not for consideration at this stage'.[23] It has been noted that the Supreme Court reversed the decision of the lower courts, finding that the appellant did have standing to bring the lawsuit. At first glance, one might assume that the parameters of the question being resolved would lead to a judgment articulating a narrow, dry statement of the doctrinal technicalities of locus standi; however, the outcome judgment is much richer, offering interesting and detailed consideration of broader facts and elements over the course of its reasoning. This is driven in part by the character of locus standi itself, where the cause of action and facts at issue become actively relevant to the calculation of standing in this context.[24] As noted in *Fawehinmi v Akilu* (1987), 'one has to look at the cause of action and the facts of the case to ascertain whether there is disclosed a *locus standi* or standing to sue'.[25]

III. The Parties: Centre for Oil Pollution Watch and the Nigerian National Petroleum Corporation

The appellant is described in the Supreme Court judgment as an NGO with a focus on issues including 'the function of ensuring reinstatement, restoration and remediation of environments impaired by oil spillage/pollution'.[26] Its name is the Centre for Oil Pollution Watch (COPW). Its remit includes a focus on 'the environment that belongs to no-one in particular'.[27] This is an appealing characterisation of aspects of the communal natural environment that arises in Nigerian legal discourse.

[21] Olubisi F Oluduro, 'Combating Climate Change in Nigeria: An Appraisal of Constitutional and Legal Frameworks.' (2020) 38 *Wisconson International Law Journal* 269–300, 289.

[22] Judgment, 571 (Onnoghen, CJN). See also Nweze, JSC, 550; Okoro, JSC, 590.

[23] ibid 586 (Kekere-Ekun, JSC).

[24] *Adesanya v The President of Nigeria* (1981) 2 NCLR 358, 392.

[25] *Fawehinmi v Akilu* (1987) 4 NWLR (Pt. 67) 797, 80. See also *Owodunni v Reg Trustees, CCC* (2000) 10 NWLR (Pt 675) 315.

[26] Judgment, 548 (Nweze, JSC, quoting an amended statement of claim filed at the Trial Court stage).

[27] ibid 524.

It appears to recognise an underlying sense of environmental value common to humanity that can often get lost in certain legal perspectives, particularly in fundamentalist private property conceptions and narratives rooted in private ownership rights, which arguably tend to predominate in a very pronounced manner in Western law in particular.[28] This 'environment that belongs to no-one in particular' concept is referred to at a number of points throughout the Supreme Court's judgment,[29] due both to the type of environmental lands at issue and to the NGO's focus on the matter in its activities, serving to emphasise the strong public interest dimension undergirding the NGO's claim. The judgment also notes that the environmental remit that the NGO seeks to assist in protecting 'includes but [is] not limited to Rivers/Sea Birds/Ecosystems and Aquatic lives'.[30] The organisation 'ensures that the environments that belong to no one are kept clean and safe for human and aquatic lives/consumption',[31] and includes over 2,000 members from across Nigeria and outside of it.[32] The Supreme Court records that '[s]ome of her members are indigenes of and/or live at Acha community and use the water from Ineh and Aku Streams/Rivers'.[33] In other words, they are part of the communities impacted by the environmental damage at issue.

The respondent is the Nigerian National Petroleum Corporation (NNPC). This is a corporation that was established by an Act of Parliament, which 'carries on business of prospecting, mining, producing, exploring and storing persistent hydrocarbon mineral oil'.[34] It operates offices, oil installations and infrastructure across Nigeria. Etemire has highlighted tensions underlying climate governance and fossil fuel policy in Nigeria: 'The Nigerian oil and gas industry is the nation's major source of greenhouse gas (GHG) emissions through its massive gas flares, but is also the backbone of its economy.'[35] Since the Supreme Court's ruling in *Oil Pollution Watch*, the Petroleum Industry Act has been signed into law in 2021, restructuring NNPC from a state-owned corporation to a limited liability company that can now sell shares.[36] *African Business* has summarised the practical consequences of this development as follows: 'The former state-owned company, known for its relatively poor leadership and lack of profits for some 45 years, will now be independent of government and operate without state funding, with the new goal of delivering value to its shareholders.'[37]

[28] Sean Coyle and Karen Morrow, *The Philosophical Foundations of Environmental Law: Property, Rights and Nature* (Hart Publishing, 2004).
[29] See, eg, Judgment, 553 (Nweze, JSC).
[30] ibid 524.
[31] ibid.
[32] ibid.
[33] ibid 548 (Nweze, JSC, drawing on an amended Statement of Claim, filed 9 February 2006).
[34] ibid 525.
[35] Etemire (n 6) 158.
[36] Leo Komminoth, 'Nigeria's NNPC becomes private company', *African Business* (22 July 2022), https://african.business/2022/07/energy-resources/nigerias-nnpc-becomes-private-company.
[37] ibid.

Legal argumentation from counsel for the appellant COPW took care to draw out the importance of underlying proximity between NNPC and the Government.[38] Pointing to the relevance of provisions of the Federal Environmental Protection Agency Act (in force at the time the action arose) and to the National Oil Spill Detection and Response Agency (Establishment) Act 2006,[39] counsel emphasised the structure of NNPC:

> [T]he respondent is a statutory corporation; its Board Members are members of the Federal Executive and/or appointed by the President of the Federal Republic of Nigeria. Its chairman is a Minister in the Government of the Federation.[40]

Counsel elaborated that under law 'it is the Federal Environmental [Protection] Agency that has the duty of protection and development of the environment as well as punishment or prosecution of offenders or polluters of the environment in conjunction with the Nigerian Police';[41] however, he also noted that 'the said agency is an integral part of the Presidency'.[42] He argued that it would be 'absurd and contrary to the provisions' of the Federal Environmental Protection Agency Act and the National Oil Spill Detection and Response Agency (Establishment) Act 2006 'to suggest that [the Federal Environmental Protection Agency] or the National Oil Spill Detection and Response or the Attorney General of the Federation will sue a fellow Federal Government Agency or corporation/parastatal',[43] as to 'do that would amount to the Federal Government suing itself'.[44] Indeed, he argued that 'there is no provision in any law empowering the Government to sue itself'.[45] In her judicial opinion in support of Nweze, JSC's leading judgment, Kekere-Ekun, JSC found that 'where a government agency fails to carry out its statutory function in circumstances such as this, it is highly unlikely that the government, Federal or State, would institute an action against its own agency. The public would be left without a remedy'.[46]

Given NNPC's proximity to Government, certain perceived constraints on state agency litigation and a capacity for conflicting interests, this provides an overwhelming argument for standing to be recognised so that a facility for public interest litigation can be accessed in the interest of environmental protection, in this environmental context and in contexts like it, including where climate litigation is at issue. Thus, NNPC's structure and governmental proximity in the period when the case arose had an influential bearing on the Supreme Court's resolution of the locus standi issue.

[38] NNPC appears to have been quite defensive about how its structure was to be characterised in law, with Eko, JSC noting that: 'While the respondent, as the defendant, denied the objects ascribed to it as a public corporation by the plaintiff, it however admitted its status as a "statutory corporation established by the Act of Parliament"'. Judgment, 592.

[39] ibid 552.

[40] ibid 553.

[41] ibid.

[42] ibid.

[43] ibid.

[44] ibid.

[45] ibid.

[46] ibid 587.

IV. Background, Facts and Issues

It is recorded that NNPC had constructed and laid oil pipelines in the vicinity of the Ineh and Aku streams/river in Acha autonomous community in Isukwuato Local Government Area of Abia State over 25 years before the commencement of the lawsuit[47] and that on 13 May 2003, the appellant noticed oil on top of the streams.[48] The oil began to increase in the days ahead 'to the point where it overflowed from the streams and surged into the adjoining lands, estuaries, creeks and mangroves'.[49] It transpired that an oil pipeline in need of maintenance had ruptured and was feeding vast oil emissions into the streams and river of Ineh and Aku.

The appellant, COPW, argued that the respondent NNPC was negligent in allowing the spillage to arise and in failing to contain it appropriately. COPW pointed out to the Supreme Court that 'two pre-action notices were served on the respondent; and that up till the time of filing the suit, no steps had been taken to remedy, reinstate or restore the damaged environment in the Acha community',[50] in spite of substantial environmental damage arising. At the Trial Court application stage, COPW contended that '[t]he defendant only stopped the leakage/spillage but never cleaned-up and/or adequately cleaned up or remedied the … Ineh/Aku Streams'.[51] This environmental damage, it was alleged, included amongst other things the contamination of the local community's water supply and negative health effects warranting medical treatment.

In its defence, the respondent NNPC argued that the pipeline had been sabotaged, implicating 'unscrupulous persons within the affected community'.[52] It is notable that evidence for the proposition that members of the community undertook sabotage detrimental to their own water supply and surrounding environment does not appear to have been provided.[53] It is also notable that NNPC did not to the author's knowledge initiate any litigation in relation to its claim, and indeed endeavoured to halt matters proceeding to trial – where its accusation would have had a substantive airing in a legal setting – via contesting COPW's standing. Further, while it is true that the respondent NNPC would be shielded from the charge of negligence in relation to the leak if the pipeline had been sabotaged by another party, NNPC's alleged failure to adequately inspect, surveil, contain and remediate the spillage would appear to pose additional problems in negligence in its own right.

[47] ibid 525.
[48] ibid.
[49] ibid.
[50] ibid.
[51] ibid 549, quoting para 11.c of the amended statement of claim filed on 9 February 2006 by COPW at the Trial Court stage.
[52] ibid 525.
[53] Albeit that substantive considerations were at a standstill due to the issue of standing preventing matters from proceeding to full trial.

The environmental and human impacts of the spillage appear to be extremely severe. COPW informed the courts that local inhabitants had no alternative water supply,[54] and so people were forced to draw on contaminated water that could cause severe negative health impacts. The long-term nature of these problems was also stressed by COPW:

> [E]ven after 10 years of the incident that oil still remains on the affected streams/lives causing skin diseases, cancer, damaging the reproductive system and respiratory system of users of the affected streams. It also leads to major social and psychologicale [*sic*] impact like depression and post-traumatic stress disorder.[55]

Indeed, the actual spillage discharge process had something of a long-term character in its own right, insofar as the discharge apparently continued not just for days – which would likely have been very damaging in its own right – but for weeks. The judgment records that '[t]his spillage and drifting of the respondent's crude hydrocarbon oil into Ineh and Aku streams/rivers … started on May 13, 2003 till June 21, 2003'.[56]

Thus, the central issue confronting the Supreme Court was an important one. As discussed, this concerns locus standi, namely the NGO's 'standing' or ability to bring a lawsuit of this kind in the first place.[57] Scholars summarise that: 'Locus standi is the technical word for standing. It simply refers to the right of the litigant to institute a claim.'[58] If the Supreme Court is to find that there is no standing to bring the case, the NGO has fallen at the first fence and the case collapses. If this hurdle is surmountable, the case can be returned to the lower courts, where the facts and associated elements of law at issue can be engaged by trying the case. The point is therefore crucial. More generally, if an environmental NGO is fenced out from undertaking litigation in this way, the case simultaneously shuts down environmental NGOs from taking public interest climate litigation via this same type of channel. The consequences of the ruling are therefore far-reaching.

[54] See para 13 of the amended statement of claim filed on 9 February 2006 by COPW at the Trial Court stage; see also Judgment, 550.

[55] Judgment, 549, quoting para 11.e of the amended statement of claim filed on 9 February 2006 by COPW at the Trial Court stage. The Supreme Court summarised points raised by counsel for the appellant Joseph N Mbadugha in the following terms: 'The devastating effect of oil splits [*sic*] on the ecosystem, marine life and the forest system persist for several decades except when properly and constantly cleaned for several years (minimum of 5 years) and even after ten years of the incident that oil still remains on the affected streams/rivers causing skin diseases, cancer, damaging the reproductive system and respiratory system of users of the affected streams' (at 551).

[56] ibid 552.

[57] '[G]oing by settled judicial authorities of this court and elsewhere, the term *locus standi* denotes legal capacity to institute proceedings in a court of law.' ibid 590 (Okoro, JSC).

[58] Miriam Chinyere Anozie and Emmanuel Onyedi Wingate, 'NGO Standing in Petroleum Pollution Litigation in Nigeria: Centre for Oil Pollution Watch v Nigerian National Petroleum Corporation' (2020) 13(5–6) *Journal of World Energy Law & Business* 490–97, 491.

V. The Supreme Court's Judgment

A. Some Initial Points

Nweze, JSC provided the leading judgment.[59] Each of the other Justices was in agreement, and each also offered comments and points of emphasis in support. Before proceeding to outline and explore the Supreme Court's reasoning, conclusions and the implications of the Court's determination, a few observations will be helpful.

There is no dispute that the respondent, NNPC, constructed and laid its oil pipelines at the Ineh and Aku streams/river area in Acha Autonomous Community in Isukwuato Local Government Area, Abia State, over 25 years before the institution of the initial lawsuit.[60] It would seem reasonable on common sense grounds that one could anticipate potential trouble with pipelines over such a time span, emphasising the reasonable expectation that the respondent would suitably monitor the infrastructure for safety purposes. Furthermore, it is noted that NNPC appears to have contained the spillage after some time and provided some relief materials to the affected communities,[61] but failed to adequately clean up and reinstate the Ineh/Aku streams, thus extending and compounding the problem.[62] Okoro, JSC summarises the apparent environmental consequences arising as a result:

> The oil spillage left the Ineh/Aku Stream impure, soiled and contaminated and they could no longer be put to their ordinary and natural use. They became unfit for human consumption and aquatic lives, sea birds, fauna and flora no longer abound in them.[63]

Importantly, it was argued that containment on the surface of the water masked the existence of excessive crude oil in the bottom sediments of the streams/river.[64] As noted above, it is also recorded that although two pre-action notices were served on the respondent prior to the filing of the lawsuit, no steps were taken to remedy, reinstate or restore the damaged environment in response.[65] It is also notable that the Court recognised that the appellant COPW 'does not seek any personal benefit from the litigation', but rather seeks the enforcement of existing legislation in the interest of those affected and those likely to be affected by the impacts of the oil spillage.[66] Thus, the facility to undertake public interest environmental litigation is

[59] Judgment, 548–71 (Nweze, JSC).
[60] See, eg, ibid 581.
[61] Described in the judgment as follows: 'The respondent provided relief materials … includ[ing] but not limited to bottle/sachet water to the community.' ibid 588, per Okoro, JSC. Eko, JSC also notes: 'The defendant, allegedly, provided relief materials, including bottled/sachet pure drinking water to the community.' ibid 593.
[62] ibid 581.
[63] ibid 588 (Okoro, JSC).
[64] ibid 581.
[65] ibid 582.
[66] ibid 586 (Kekere-Ekun, JSC).

at issue, which in turn has a crucial bearing on the capacity for NGOs and public spirited individuals to initiate climate litigation.

B. Interesting Points Raised by Counsel for COPW

Counsel for the appellant COPW, Joseph N Mbadugha, raised a variety of important points in arguing before the Supreme Court that the appellant should be understood to have standing. One problem he faced in Nigerian law was the fact that an impersonal NGO taking this sort of case is not in a position comparable to a distinguishable *person(s)* who has *directly* suffered injury and thus has clear standing to bring a lawsuit. In tackling this, he distinguished the rights at issue from private rights, and argued that a plaintiff seeking to establish the maintenance of a law for the public interest has locus standi regardless of whether he has any sufficient interest in the matter or has suffered any injury above every other member of the society in respect of it.[67] He emphasised that COPW is a registered NGO with a function to ensure that the reinstatement, restoration and remediation of environments impaired by oil spillage/pollution is achieved, and particularly in instances where the 'un-owned environment or the environment that belongs to no one in particular' is at issue.[68] Its role and activities place an emphasis on both protection for humans in relation to the environment and, slightly echoing themes that arise in a more pronounced way in the *Colombian Amazon Case*, protections for the environment itself.[69]

Mbadugha stressed that the inhabitants of Acha Community, and indeed visitors and travellers, have since continued to use the impacted waters 'for all purposes that water is used' in the wake of the incident because there is no alternative water supply available to them.[70] He also emphasised that 'the appellant's action is purely for public interest without any private interest; the action is very important',[71] and noted that 'the appellant has sincere concern for the environment, particularly, but not limited to the one in issue'.[72] Further, he argued that the dominant objective of the rule of law is to ensure that the law is observed, and that this can best be achieved by allowing NGOs and public citizens to bring public interest actions.[73]

These elements speak to the theme of climate change, where climate litigation is proceeding in a direction that sees increasing litigation being taken by environmental NGOs and public-spirited individuals in the general public interest

[67] ibid 550. See also *Adesanya v The President of Nigeria* (1981) 2 NCLR 358.

[68] Judgment, 551.

[69] For example: 'It … ensures that the environments that belong to no one are kept clean and safe for human consumptions *and aquatic live* [*sic*].' ibid (emphasis added). See further the study of the *Colombian Amazon Case* in ch 4 of this volume, where intrinsic rights of nature arise.

[70] Judgment, 551.

[71] ibid.

[72] ibid 552.

[73] ibid. See also *Fawehinmi v President, FRN* (2007) 14 NWLR (Pt 1054) 275, 334–35, G-D.

around the world.[74] A restrictive interpretation of locus standi adopted by the Supreme Court would serve to constrain such litigation in Nigeria unhelpfully. Counsel for the appellant also argued that this type of public action should be afforded on the grounds that it falls within the maintenance of appropriate 'civil rights' protections.[75] Overall, although primary technical considerations are limited in *Oil Pollution Watch* to the matter of standing, counsel for the appellant's general emphasis on the civil rights of citizens, advancement of the rule of law, the necessary role of public interest litigation in assisting in the protection of the environment, and similar, provides a rational and appealing way of underscoring the value afforded by a capacity to bring public interest litigation in the interest of redressing climate change.

C. The Amici Curiae

A number of individuals provided advisory views and argumentation to the Supreme Court in the capacity of amicus curiae, and these views were incorporated by the Court into its reasoning. Amicus curiae is a Latin legal term meaning a 'friend of the Court'.[76] It pertains to a person who is not a party to a lawsuit directly, but who has petitioned the Supreme Court or been requested by the Court to file a brief on the issues. In Nigeria this will usually be a member of the Bar, and the country's law officers may also be called upon or permitted on their own request to contribute argumentation to a case even though they are not instructed by the formal parties.[77] Where more than one individual is referred to, the term 'amicus curiae' is normally pluralised to 'amici curiae'. In *Oil Pollution Watch*, these parties included Dayo Apata, Solicitor-General of the Federation, Wole Olanipekun, SAN, Asiwaju Adegboyega Awomolo, SAN, Abubakar B Mahmoud, SAN, and Lucius E Nwosu, SAN ('SAN' indicates 'Senior Advocate of Nigeria').

Dayo Apata, Solicitor-General of the Federation,[78] took the view that the current condition of the law in Nigeria, including the Supreme Court's extant decisions, indicated that 'the court should not extend *locus standi* to private citizens and NGOs in matters of environmental degradation'.[79] This provided support to NNPC. Wole Olanipekun, SAN, also inclined towards NNPC's position. Amongst a range of points raised, he was of the view that 'there is no nexus between the

[74] Aka'ahs, JSC summarises that 'public interest litigation … is instituted in the interest of the general public'. Judgment, 579, Aka'ahs, JSC, discussing the submissions of the amici curiae (see further below).

[75] See 'Civil Rights and Obligation', Judgment, 552–53.

[76] 'Amicus Curiae' in Daniel Greenberg (ed), *Jowitt's Dictionary of English Law*, 5th edn (Sweet & Maxwell, 2019).

[77] *Atake v Afejuku* [1994] 9 NWLR (Pt 368) 379, 410.

[78] Dayo Apata, Solicitor-General of the Federation, representing the Hon Attorney-General of the Federation.

[79] Judgment, 556.

reliefs being sought and the appellant',[80] opining that the NGO's 'membership is abstract, inchoate and opaque'.[81] Although the fundamental matter at issue is whether an environmental NGO has standing to bring a case in the public interest, it is notable that this characterisation of the NGO sidesteps the inter-related matter of some of its members being recorded as belonging to the impacted community.[82] In principle, such persons would presumably evince a nexus between the reliefs sought and the impact upon those members as individuals. In this respect, interesting cross-reference can be made to a separate contribution from another amicus curiae, Asiwaju Adegboyega Awomolo, SAN, whose argumentation was sympathetic to COPW. Over the course of his submission, the Supreme Court summarised that he:

> [R]eferred to the averment that some of the appellant's members are indigenes of and/or live in Acha Community and use the water from Inet and Akis [*sic*] streams/rivers. In his submission, that was a sufficient link to a territorial actor and upon which public interest litigation and broad interpretation of legal standing can rest.[83]

He also advanced existing English jurisprudence as persuasive legal authority, where an NGO has been held to have standing to make an application to the English courts,[84] and contended that the type of standing sought in the present case 'has become inevitable', given the diverse context in which public interest litigation now operates in the face of oil spillages and associated environmental damage in Nigeria.[85]

Abubakar B Mahmoud, SAN, also provided a view sympathetic to the appellant COPW. In addition to basing his reasoning on learned doctrinal legal argumentation, the position he advanced had something of a persuasive 'natural law' character – that is to say, he stressed the apparent injustice that would arise by prohibiting an NGO from bringing this type of environmental action, summarised by the Supreme Court as follows:

> He submitted that it is a matter of grave constitutional principle of justice that if a private oil prospecting company for profit transgressed the law in a way which affects, offends and injures several thousands of Nigerians, any of those injured or any person with genuine and public-spirited intention should be permitted to approach the court for restitution, restoration with a view to getting the law enforced. The court, in his submission, should relax the rule of *locus standi* because the suit seeks to expose illegality and bring immeasurable environmental benefits, which would have gone unredressed.[86]

[80] ibid 557.
[81] ibid.
[82] See, eg, ibid 548 (Nweze, JSC).
[83] ibid 558.
[84] *R v Secretary of State for Foreign and Commonwealth Affairs ex parte World Development Movement Ltd.* (1995) 1 All ER 611, 620.
[85] Judgment, 558.
[86] ibid 559.

This account has a human rights flavour, and the learned senior advocate drew a direct link between 'environmental rights as human rights',[87] thus prefiguring the perspective on climate damage adopted subsequently by the Dutch Supreme Court in the *Urgenda Case*.[88] He bolstered this rights-based emphasis by highlighting the African Charter on Human and Peoples' Rights, which he stressed 'has been domesticated in Nigeria' under the African Charter on Human and Peoples' Rights (Ratification and Enforcement) Act.[89] (The African Charter is discussed further below.)

Oil was first discovered in commercial quantities in Nigeria in 1956,[90] and research has found that the Nigerian legal tradition has a history in which 'litigation against oil companies faces severe obstacles'.[91] These obstacles diminished to some extent over the 1990s, establishing a slightly more favourable context for litigation than had existed previously.[92] Nevertheless, litigation has remained subject to substantial constraints, negatively impacting the capacity for citizens to realise their rights effectively. This has not been helped by historic underdevelopment of the branch of Nigerian law catering to the environment, which according to Popoola did not begin to receive overt focused development until the late 1980s.[93] Thus, AB Mahmoud, SAN's framing of *Oil Pollution Watch* as an opportunity to improve access to justice and the realisation of environmental and human rights is both helpful and appropriate.

A further underlying tension implicit in AB Mahmoud's argumentation, which also arose as a major feature of the *Urgenda* litigation, concerns the *separation of powers* between the judicial, parliamentary and executive branches of the state.[94] Drawing on the Oil Pipelines Act,[95] he noted that the Act provides for compensation for those who have suffered injury as a result of a pipeline holder's activities, arguing that the legislature had 'more than satisfied its obligation to protect the environment' pursuant to sections 13 and 20 of the Constitution.[96] Given this groundwork laid by the legislature,[97] this 'leav[es] the judiciary to determine the rest',[98] namely by the Supreme Court giving effect to sections 13 and 20 of the Constitution to protect the environment via the application of the

[87] 'He devoted paragraphs 4.17–4.21, pages 13–14 of the brief to the subject of environmental rights as human rights.' ibid 560.

[88] *State of the Netherlands (Ministry of Economic Affairs and Climate Policy) v Urgenda Foundation*, Supreme Court of the Netherlands, 20 December 2019, ECLI:NL:HR:2019:2006.

[89] Judgment, 559.

[90] Oluduro (n 21) 288.

[91] Jedrzej George Frynas, *Oil in Nigeria: Conflict and Litigation between Oil Companies and Village Communities* (LIT Verlag, 2000), 7.

[92] See ibid ch 6, 'Compensation Claims in Oil Related Litigation', 182–224.

[93] Ebunoluwa Popoola, 'An Examination of Factors Militating against Effective Enforcement of Environmental Law in Nigeria' (2019) 19 *University of Maiduguri Law Journal* 20–44.

[94] See section III.D in ch 3 in this volume.

[95] Oil Pipelines Act, ss 11(5), 19–22.

[96] Judgment, 560.

[97] Nigeria's Parliament is called the National Assembly.

[98] Judgment, 560.

Oil Pipelines Act.[99] After initially summarising AB Mahmoud's position at an earlier stage of his leading judgment, Nweze, JSC would return to this point, and points associated with it, finding that 'there is considerable merit in the above submission'.[100] This became influential in the Court's determination that section 6 of the Constitution should not be held to place definitive constraints upon the Court in articulating the scope of locus standi.[101]

The Court's approach here has important implications for the issue of climate change. Oluduro writes that where one considers 'provisions of the Constitution in relation to combating climate change in Nigeria', there are 'no express provisions' explicitly engaging the matter.[102] This means that the Nigerian courts' interpretation of the Constitution in light of the climate change challenge becomes particularly important. In *Oil Pollution Watch*, potential avenues for public interest climate litigation are enabled by the Supreme Court's finding that the Constitution supports environmental rights in a context where section 6 does not prevent the courts from according standing to NGOs and public-spirited individuals.

AB Mahmoud, SAN, also engaged with the relationship between COPW as a registered NGO and the environmental harm arising. Here, he advised that 'the court should make a finding to determine *locus standi* on the basis of the corporate interests of some of the appellant's 2000 members said to be affected by the pollution of the water courses'.[103] This view on standing was bolstered by a further amicus curiae, Lucius E Nwosu, SAN, who appeared to argue that locus standi should be cast in broad terms in such environmental cases: 'any interest whatsoever shown to enure in favour of the plaintiff on the subject matter, no matter howsoever trivial, is sufficient to support his *locus standi* in other words, whether he has shown any interest deserving of protection in the subject matter of litigation'.[104]

Muhammad, JSC summarises that amongst the amicus curiae, Wole Olanipekun, SAN and the Solicitor-General, representing the Federal Attorney General, associate themselves with the respondent's position.[105] Conversely, in summarising support for COPW, Aka'ahs, JSC notes that the 'amici curiae who are sympathetic to this stance were Asiwaju Adegboyega Awomolo SAN; Abubakar Mahmoud SAN, President of the Nigeria Bar Association and Lucius E. Nwosu SAN'.[106] It is perhaps unsurprising that the Federal Attorney General's representative, Dayo Apata, opposed the appellant, given in principle that the Attorney General's office

[99] ibid.
[100] ibid 568.
[101] See the discussion under the heading '*Locus Standi* of Non-governmental Organizations (NGOs) in Environmental Protection: Perspectives from the Constitution' commencing ibid 568, particularly 568–70.
[102] Oluduro (n 21) 270.
[103] Judgment, 560.
[104] ibid.
[105] ibid 576.
[106] ibid 578.

surely should have taken some form of action already if a clearly arguable breach of the law arising from the environmental damage at issue had occurred/was ongoing. An expansion of locus standi also represents some degree of dispersal in the power and influence of the office, insofar as a field of litigation significantly within its purview is potentially being opened up by the courts to a much wider set of litigants. In summarising the overall position of the Court, Onnoghen, CJN states that '[t]his is a public interest litigation in which the chambers of the Honourable Attorney-General of the Federation traditionally holds sway but the law on *locus standi* in that regard has grown beyond that and now encompasses public spirited individuals and NGOs'.[107] It is possible that this perceived dispersal of authority might have seemed unpalatable to the Attorney General's office; however, this in itself does not provide a valid reason for advocating for constraints on the development of environmental law where such development appears necessary.

D. Resolution of Standing: The Leading Judgment

The Supreme Court bench provided a learned and detailed consideration of the relevant facts, issues and law, with Nweze, JSC delivering the leading judgment. It has been seen that the central issue for resolution is summarised thus:

> Whether the Court of Appeal was right in dismissing the appellant's appeal for want of *locus standi* to maintain the suit.[108]

It has been clarified that the resolution of this problem is of importance not only to the environmental damage at issue in the case, but in setting a broader precedent determining who or what entity can bring a public interest environmental case. This includes in relation to public interest climate litigation.

In addressing the problem, the Supreme Court took particular cognisance of Article 24 of the African Charter on Human and Peoples' Rights (Ratification and Enforcement) Act (hereinafter the 'African Charter Act'),[109] and sections 20 and 33(1) of the Constitution.[110] Article 24 of the African Charter Act asserts that: 'All peoples shall have the right to a general satisfactory environment favourable to their development.'[111] Section 20 of the Constitution of the Federal Republic of Nigeria 1999 (as amended) asserts that '[t]he State shall protect and improve the environment and safeguard the water, air and land, forest and wildlife of the country',[112] and section 33(1) states that '[e]very person has a right to life, and no one shall be deprived intentionally of his life, save in execution of the sentence of a court

[107] ibid 575.
[108] ibid 524.
[109] African Charter on Human and Peoples' Rights (Ratification and Enforcement) Act, Cap A9, LFN, 2004.
[110] 1999 Nigerian Constitution, ss 20, 33(1).
[111] African Charter Act, art 24.
[112] 1999 Nigerian Constitution, s 20.

in respect of a criminal offence of which he has been found guilty in Nigeria'.[113] Careful consideration was also given to the Oil Pipelines Act, which includes the assertion that: 'Every licence shall be subject to the provisions contained in this Act as in force at the date of its grant and to such regulations concerning public safety … and the prevention of pollution of such land or any waters as may from time to time be in force.'[114] The Oil and Gas Pipeline Regulations place obligations on oil pipeline licence holders to take steps to prevent accidents and to control and remedy accidents that may arise.[115] The National Policy on the Environment (revised 2016) also recognises the role NGOs play in the protection of the environment.[116]

English common law on the origins and development of standing is cited fairly early on in Nweze, JSC's reasoning,[117] including the statement by Lord Diplock that standing rules were made by judges rather than sourced in statute.[118] This leads on to extensive consideration of the matter in a section headed 'English Courts: Expanding the Frontiers of *Locus Standi*'.[119] It is clarified that locus standi is not something that has been set in stone in the British courts, but rather that it has been developed by judges over time. Nweze, JSC explains:

> The truth of the matter, as [Lord Diplock] held[120] … is that the rules as to standing could not be found in any statute for they were made by Judges of the Realm; 'by Judges they can be changed; and so they have been over the years to meet the need to preserve the integrity of the rule of law … *Any judicial statements on matters of public law if made before 1950 are likely to be misleading guide to what the law is today*'. (Emphasis in original)[121]

Nweze, JSC cites a range of cases that developed standing in England, including *R v Secretary of State for Foreign and Commonwealth Affairs, ex parte World Development Movement Ltd* (1995),[122] where an NGO was held to have standing.[123]

Taking the view that section 6 of the Constitution does not impede the judiciary from interpreting the scope of locus standi[124] – indeed, finding in a sense that it requires judicial interpretation of standing via this constitutional standard when

[113] ibid s 33(1).
[114] Oil Pipelines Act, s 17(4).
[115] Oil and Gas Pipeline Regulations, reg 9(a)(ii), (b)(ii).
[116] National Policy on the Environment, paras [8.1] and [8.2].
[117] Judgment, 561.
[118] *R v Inland Revenue Commissioners, ex parte National Federation of Self-Employed and Small Business Ltd* (1982) AC 617, 641; Judgment, 561.
[119] Judgment, 567–68.
[120] *R v Inland Revenue Commissioners* (n 118) 640–41.
[121] Judgment, 568.
[122] *R v Secretary of State for Foreign and Commonwealth Affairs, ex parte World Development Movement Ltd* (1995) 1 All ER 611, 620.
[123] Judgment, 568.
[124] See s 6(6)(b) of the 1979 Nigerian Constitution, re-enacted in s 6(6)(b) of the 1999 Nigerian Constitution. See also its interpretation in *Adesanya v The President of Nigeria* (1981) 2 NCLR 358. In *Oil Pollution Watch* the Supreme Court clarified that s 6 delineates the exercise of judicial power, rather than establishing standing rules.

read in the context of other constitutional provisions[125] – Nweze, JSC reaches the following overall conclusion:

> [S]ince the Interpretation Act[126] … defines 'person' to include 'anybody' or 'persons corporate' or [']incorporated', I take the view that … as determinant of the appellant's *locus standi*, the reliefs sought, I am on safe grounds by making a finding in favour of the appellants' *locus standi*.[127]

This paves the way to the conclusion that '[b]eyond this fact, what is obvious, from the appellants' pleadings is that the respondent, a public authority, has by these acts complained of, acted in violation' of both its 'constitutional obligation' under section 20 of the Constitution and 'its statutory obligations' under section 17 of the Oil Pipelines Act.[128]

Nweze, JSC thus summarises as follows: 'In all, then, I take the humble view that, in environmental matters, such as the instant one, NGOs, such as the plaintiff in this case, have the requisite *standi* to sue.'[129] This means that the decisions of the lower courts are reversed, the appeal is allowed and the matter is to be remitted back to the Trial Court for a re-assigned hearing and determination.[130] Academic work by Ogowewo,[131] which is drawn upon significantly in the judgment, has distinguished between *personal standing*, involving parties seeking to establish standing on the basis of their own personal interests, and *representative standing*, involving parties seeking standing on the basis that they represent the interests of other identifiable individuals or the 'public interest'.[132] Ogowewo found that the Nigerian standing rules had a very narrow concept of personal standing that focused on private legal rights and that fenced out representative standing.[133] This constrained the law from being enforced in certain instances of illegality, and the *Oil Pollution Watch* ruling has helped to correct for this.[134]

It is notable that the leading judgment and the supporting opinions of other Justices make considerable reference to the jurisprudence of other common law jurisdictions. The influence of English law has been noted above. In supporting Nweze, JSC's leading judgment, Muhammad, JSC[135] emphasises that in the view

[125] See *Olafisoye v FRN* (2004) 4 NWLR (Pt.864) 580, 659 (per Tobi, JSC). See also Judgment, 569 (Newze, JSC).
[126] Interpretation Act, Cap 123 Vol 7 LFN.
[127] Judgment, 570.
[128] ibid.
[129] ibid 571 (Nweze, JSC).
[130] ibid (Nweze, JSC).
[131] Tunde I Ogowewo, 'Wrecking the Law: How Article III of the Constitution of the United States Led to the Discovery of a Law on Standing to Sue in Nigeria' (2000) 26(2) *Brooklyn Journal of International Law* 527–89.
[132] ibid 542–43.
[133] ibid.
[134] Anozie and Wingate point out that certain developments have occurred since the time of Ogowewo's work permitting public interest litigation and class actions in certain cases, but they are too narrow to be of assistance to an NGO in a case like this. Anozie and Wingate (n 58) 492–93.
[135] Judgment, 575–77 (Muhammad, JSC).

of the Court, the notion of legal influence from non-Nigerian jurisdictions is an important consideration: 'The issue the appeal raises is whether in the light of developments in similar jurisdictions elsewhere, courts in this country need to liberalize its approach on the principle of *locus standi*.'[136] As noted above, the fact that the English courts have liberalised their approach to standing affords the Nigerian Supreme Court a persuasive point of reference. The jurisprudence of other common law jurisdictions is also factored into the Court's thinking. For example, the jurisprudence of the High Court of Ghana[137] is drawn upon significantly by Eko, JSC.[138] The courts of India, Australia, Canada and the US are also referenced at a number of points.[139] Amongst the amici curaie, Abubakar B. Mahmoud, SAN is noted in particular by the Supreme Court as having 'explored the developments in other common law jurisdictions … [in his] brief',[140] and Asiwaju Adegboyega Awomolo, SAN makes an influential reference in support of the applicant's case to a ruling by the Supreme Court of the Philippines,[141] concerning remediation of environmental damage at Manila Bay.[142]

The intellectual drivers behind such references are summarised by Kekere-Ekun, JSC in the following terms:

> [T]he English courts and the courts in other commonwealth countries, which have similar legal systems as Nigeria, as well as the United States of America, have begun to adopt a more liberal approach to the issue of *locus standi* in public interest litigation. Where there is a dearth of precedents in our jurisprudence on a particular issue, it is permissible to look to other climes where similar issues have arisen for guidance.[143]

Nweze, JSC notes that India's Supreme Court is cited by the appellant in relation to the maintenance of a clean environment.[144] He returns to this jurisprudence later in his judgment to highlight the fact that, without any statutory enactment, India's Supreme Court determined that an overall need to do justice in relation to environmental degradation required a liberalisation of the traditional rules on *locus standi*.[145] He summarises that this was because, 'in the court's view, maintaining a clean environment is the responsibility of all persons in the country'.[146] This example thus influenced the Supreme Court of Nigeria in its decision to rule in a similar direction.

[136] ibid 575 (Muhammad, JSC).
[137] *Public Interest Law and Another v Tema Oil Refinery* – unreported suit No E 12/91/07.
[138] Judgment, 598–99 (Eko, JSC).
[139] See, eg, ibid 563, 567.
[140] ibid 560.
[141] See ibid 558–59, 586.
[142] *Metropolitan Manila Development Authority v Concerned Residents of Manila Bay* Nos 171947–48, 574 SCRA 665 of 18 December 2008.
[143] Judgment, 584.
[144] ibid 560–61.
[145] *Maharaj Singh v State of UP*, AIR (1976) SC 2607; *Municipal Council, Ratlam v Vardhichard*, AIR (1980) SC 1622; *SP Gupta v President of India*, AIR (1982) SS 149; Judgment, 568.
[146] Judgment, 568, referencing the cases in n 145.

Given that judges and the courts play a primary role in determining the scope of environmental standing for parties including NGOs, commentators have suggested that the positive implications of this case for environmental protection may indicate a 'greening of the judiciary' in Nigeria, where a greater judicial sensitivity to the importance of environmental matters can be seen coming to the fore.[147] In considering climate litigation and locus standi in Nigeria, Ngwoke and Oguguo conclude that it is right for the courts to place 'best practices and legal sentiments on care for the environment and peoples above legal technicalities', ie, above an unduly restrictive interpretation of standing.[148] The Supreme Court has followed this approach in *Oil Pollution Watch*, and it is beneficial that it has done so.

E. Resolution of Standing: The Supporting Judgments

A separate and shorter judgment provided by the Chief Justice of Nigeria agrees with the reasoning and conclusions set out in the leading judgment, and adds some additional emphases and points of its own.[149] Onnoghen, CJN takes note of the expansion of *locus standi* by Lord Diplock and the English courts,[150] and like Nweze, JSC, emphasises a range of environmental cases on the basis of this expansion[151] 'to cloth even NGOs with standing'.[152] He also emphasises the centrality of the Constitution and Oil Pipelines Act, providing additional validity to Nweze, JSC's interpretation. It has been noted above that section 20 of the Constitution provides that the 'State shall protect and improve the environment and safeguard the water, air and land, forest and wildlife of the country'.[153] The Oil Pipelines Act has also been noted above and Onnoghen, CJN draws on section 17(4):

> Every licence shall be subject to the provisions contained in this Act … and to such regulations concerning public safety, the avoidance of interference with works of public utility in, over and under the land … and the prevention of pollution of such land or any waters.[154]

[147] Emeka Polycarp Amechi and Agent Ihua-Maduenyi, '"Greening the Judiciary" in Nigeria: Centre For Oil Pollution Watch v NNPC in Perspectives' (2022) 1(2) *African Journal of Law and Justice System* 39–60.

[148] Rita A Ngwoke and Rita Oguguo, 'Application of the Rule of *Locus Standi* in Climate Change Litigations in Nigeria' (2020) 101 *Journal of Law Policy & Globalization* 49–55, 55. Strangely, the authors do not comment on *Oil Pollution Watch* itself.

[149] Judgment, 571–75 (Onnoghen, CJN).

[150] *R v Inland Revenue Commissioners* (n 118) 640–41.

[151] ibid 639; *R v Foreign Secretary of State for Foreign and Commonwealth Affairs, ex parte World Development Movement Ltd* (1995) 1 WLR 386; *R v Somerset County Counsel ARC Southern Ltd, ex parte Dixon* (1998) Env LR 111; *Secretary of State for Foreign and Commonwealth Affairs, ex parte World Development Movement Ltd* (1995) 1 All ER 611, 620.

[152] Judgment, 572 (Onnoghen, CJN).

[153] 1999 Nigerian Constitution, s 20.

[154] Oil Pipelines Act, s 17(4); Judgment, 572 (Onnoghen, CJN).

In following Nweze, JSC, Onnoghen, CJN finds that these provisions, interpreted in concert with the environmental damage at issue and the capacity in principle for locus standi to evolve, entitle the NGO to be heard. He also introduces the UK case *Rylands v Fletcher* (1868)[155] into his thinking, finding that the law of nuisance as articulated in that case suggests the imposition of a duty of care on the respondent NNPC.[156] Here again, the shared tradition and legal influence between English and Nigerian law can clearly be seen.

The other Justices are also in full support of Nweze, JSC's leading judgment, and add various remarks of their own by way of emphasis and elaboration. This includes Muhammad, JSC,[157] who sees the Court's decision as assisting in the necessary application of environmental rights generally and, in this particular instance, requisite oil pipeline standards:

> Courts in this country … are by virtue of sections 16(2), 17(2)(d) (3), and 20 of the 1999 Constitution, section 17(4) of the Oil Pipelines Act … and the Oil and Gas Pipeline Regulations under duty to protect the environment and would fail in that duty if in the instant case they do not facilitate the protection these laws have put in place.[158]

He stresses that the case is stepping into new terrain, insofar as 'the peculiar facts of the instant suit distinguishes it from the previous cases pronounced upon by this court'.[159] This catches the spirit of the door opened by *Oil Pollution Watch* in going forward, affirming that NGOs and public-spirited citizens are not prevented automatically from bringing such litigation in the interest of environmental protection in Nigeria. Commensurate with this, standing for NGOs and public spirited individuals to undertake climate-specific environmental litigation in the public interest in Nigeria is broadened.

Aka'ahs, JSC's opinion, offered in support of the leading judgment, links the major environmental problems posed by climate change to this legal imperative to recognise the entitlement of environmental NGOs like COPW to bring public interest environmental cases.[160] He notes that there is 'increasing concern about climate change, depletion of the ozone layer … global warming'[161] and that 'nationally and internationally, countries and organizations are adopting stronger measures to protect and safe guard the environment for the benefit of the present and future generations'.[162] Thus, the 'issue of environmental protection against degradation has become a contemporary issue',[163] and given that COPW is 'in the vanguard of protecting the environment', it 'should be encouraged to ensure that

[155] *Rylands v Fletcher* (1868) LR 3 HL 330.
[156] Judgment, 575.
[157] ibid 575–77.
[158] ibid 577.
[159] ibid 576.
[160] ibid 577–81 (Aka'ahs, JSC).
[161] ibid 580 (Aka'ahs, JSC).
[162] ibid (Aka'ahs, JSC).
[163] ibid (Aka'ahs, JSC).

actions or omissions by Government agencies or Multi-national oil companies that tend to pollute the environment are checked'.[164] A judicial colleague, Kekere-Ekun, JSC, also points out that the harms raised by the pollution in this case – including 'skin diseases, lung damage, cancer damage to reproductive systems, to name a few'[165] – are factors that could 'affect generations yet unborn'.[166] This is evocative of the environmental theme of intergenerational equity and associated concerns arising in the sphere of climate law, where the interests of future generations as well as present generations are recognised, given the long-term nature of the climate change challenge and its current and projected environmental impacts.[167] Prior to *Oil Pollution Watch*, major climate litigation had yet to break through in the Nigerian courts, albeit that *Gbemre v Shell Petroleum Development Company Nigeria Ltd and Others* (2005)[168] had helped to concentrate some attention on the matter due to reference being made to climate change in the context of a challenge to gas flaring practices by a fossil fuel company.[169] Given the lack of overt and substantial climate litigation,[170] it is especially significant that Aka'ahs, JSC stresses climate change as an issue of prominent relevance at the Supreme Court level in this setting.

Aka'ahs, JSC's reasoning also displays a sensitivity to human rights issues. In providing his opinion on what he describes as 'the vexed issue' of whether the

[164] ibid (Aka'ahs, JSC).

[165] ibid 586 (Kekere-Ekun, JSC).

[166] ibid (Kekere-Ekun, JSC).

[167] Lydia Slobodian, 'Defending the Future: Intergenerational Equity in Climate Litigation' (2019) 32 *Georgetown Environmental Law Review*, 569–89; Petra Minnerop, 'Intergenerational Preparedness: Climate Change, Community Interest Obligations, and the Environmental Rule of Law' (2023) *Global Policy*. See further the consideration of intergenerational equity and the unborn in section IV.B in ch 4 of this volume.

[168] *Gbemre v Shell Petroleum Development Company Nigeria Limited* (Suit No FHC/B/C/153/05, Judgment delivered on 14 November 2005 at the Federal High Court, Benin Judicial Division).

[169] Louis Kotzé and Anél du Plessis, 'Putting Africa on the Stand' (2019) 50(3) *Environmental Law* 615–63.

[170] Some commentators consider the *Gbemre* litigation to amount to substantial climate litigation, but in the author's view, this tends to overstate its significance in this context. This is for reasons including but not limited to the following: it is a ruling of the High Court that does not bind on the courts above it; explicit climate issues were not at the heart of the case; climate change was mentioned by the court briefly, and in obiter; the ruling was not adequately enforced.

In terms of enforcement, the *Gbemre* outcome is completely unacceptable. Faturoti et al write that: '*Gbemre* has been turned into a pyrrhic victory by the Nigerian Federal Government when it failed to implement the decision of the court' (Bukola Faturoti, Godswill Agbaitoro and Obinna Onya, 'Environmental Protection in the Nigerian Oil and Gas Industry and Jonah Gbemre v Shell PDC Nigeria Limited: Let the Plunder Continue?' (2019) 27(2) *African Journal of International and Comparative Law* 225–45, 235), namely the decision that harmful gas flaring negatively impacting a community was to be halted. After the relevant applicant filed for contempt of court in response, the Federal High Court of Nigeria ordered Shell and NNPC to submit a detailed scheme aimed at reducing gas flaring to zero over a court-specified time period. Faturoti et al continue that: 'This order was not obeyed by either party. This was further complicated by the sudden transfer of the judge to another judicial division and the mysterious disappearance of the case file … More than ten years after *Gbemre* was decided, no cogent action has been undertaken either by the executive or legislative arm of the government in actualising its spirit' (at 235). Thus, 'it may be argued that the so-called landmark case has shrunk into oblivion' (at 235).

appellant has legitimate standing or is 'merely a busybody who is perambulating all over Nigeria in order to sue and prosecute',[171] the influence of amicus curiae AB Mahmoud, SAN and the emphasis he placed on human rights in his submission to the Court is evident.[172] Aka'ahs, JSC notes that AB Mahmoud, SAN equated environmental rights with human rights in rationalising his support for COPW's standing to sue.[173] This is linked to the section 33 right to life provided by the Constitution, and acts or omissions that threaten the health of the people of the community can amount to threats to life that trigger a constitutional breach.[174] Section 33 of the Constitution is complimented in this context by section 20, which requires the State to protect and improve the environment, and to safeguard the country's water, air, land, forests and wildlife.[175] This line of reasoning is in concert with the thrust of the *Urgenda Case*, including the section 33 right to life element in particular, insofar as the Dutch courts in *Urgenda* understood climate harm to have a capacity to breach the right to life under the European Convention on Human Rights, based on interpretation of that Convention in the particular context of the Dutch legal order.[176] It is notable that in Sub-Saharan Africa, where Nigeria is located, scholars have described climate litigation as being 'relatively more recent when compared with the countries of the Global North',[177] and have speculated that an emphasis on human rights that is tending to emerge in cases in the Global North might exert a useful influence in encouraging the continued emergence of rights-based perspectives in the Global South.[178] *Oil Pollution Watch* clarifies that the Supreme Court of Nigeria already possesses a sophisticated sensitivity to rights-based issues in the context of environmental damage. This leaves Nigerian lawyers well placed to link that framing to climate issues in the context of climate litigation in order to test its scope and application going forward.

[171] Judgment, 577.

[172] See the consideration of elements of AB Mahmoud, SAN's argumentation by Aka'ahs, JSC at ibid 580.

[173] ibid.

[174] ibid.

[175] 1999 Nigerian Constitution, s 20; Judgment, 587.

[176] See ch 3 in this volume. The European Court of Human Rights has also produced jurisprudence while this book has been prepared for publication that is somewhat in concert with this position – see *Verein Klimaseniorinnen Schweiz and Others v Switzerland*, Grand Chamber, European Court of Human Rights (Application No 53600/20), 9 April 2024; *Duarte Agostinho and Others v Portugal and 32 Others*, Grand Chamber, European Court of Human Rights (Application No 39371/20), 9 April 2024; *Carême v France*, Grand Chamber, European Court of Human Rights (Application No 7189/21), 9 April 2024.

[177] Muyiwa Adigun and Ademola Oluborode Jegede, 'A Human Rights Approach to Climate Litigation in Nigeria: Potentialities and Agamben's State of Exception Theory' (2022) 16(3) *Carbon and Climate Law Review* 179–91, 179.

[178] *ibid*. Note also that Obani has suggested that a broad consideration of domestic cases involving the environmental impact of hydrocarbon exploration and production across Africa, including in Nigeria, could conceivably expand the volume of climate change cases across the continent. See further Pedi Obani, 'Climate Litigation in South Africa and Nigeria: Legal Opportunities and Gender Perspectives' in Bouwer et al (n 5).

Kekere-Ekun, JSC emphasises in her judgment that Nigeria is a signatory to the African Charter on Human and Peoples' Rights, such that rights-based protections are further bolstered by Article 24 of the African Charter Act.[179] This provision states that: 'All people shall have the right to a general satisfactory environment favourable to their development.'[180] Thus, she notes that constitutional, legislative and African Charter provisions cohere to 'recognize the fundamental rights of the citizenry to a clean and healthy environment to sustain life'.[181] Drawing on the case *Molokwu v COP* (1972),[182] Eko, JSC summarises in his supporting opinion that:

> The African Charter … an international treaty, having been domesticated, forms part of our *corpus juris*. For as long as Nigeria remains signatory to the African Charter … and other international treaties on environment and other global issues for so long also would the Nigerian courts protect and vindicate human rights entrenched therein.[183]

Thus, Eko, JSC quotes Article 24 of the Charter directly to find that '[t]he Acha Community and all people living around and beside Ineh and Aku Streams … "have a right to a general environment favourable to their development"' and they also 'have the right to life guaranteed by the Constitution'.[184] Commenting in scholarly print, advocate Joseph N Mbadugha, SAN, finds that in interpreting the Constitution, legislation (via the Oil Pipelines Act) and the African Charter to manifest the fundamental right of the citizenry to a clean and healthy environment to sustain life, the *Oil Pollution Watch* ruling plays an important role in establishing that the right to a healthy environment is 'a variant of human right in Nigeria'.[185] He describes the elevation of the concept of an environmental right to a human right as a welcome development,[186] commenting as follows: 'by raising maintaining a healthy environment to the status of a human right, the Supreme Court has ensured that everybody will have access to the court in environmental matters affecting life provided the action is framed as a Fundamental Right and as the main claim'.[187] Since the ruling, Babalola has set out an analysis elaborating the technical legal options that he understands to be open to applicants seeking to enforce the right to a clean environment as a fundamental right in the Nigerian courts, based on this case and the broader condition of relevant Nigerian law and procedure.[188]

[179] Judgment, 587 (Kekere-Ekun, JSC).
[180] African Charter Act, art 24.
[181] Judgment, 587 (Kekere-Ekun, JSC).
[182] *Molokwu v COP* (1972) 2 ECSLR 979 at 801; see also *Adewole v Jakande* (1981) 1 NCLR 262.
[183] Judgment, 598 (Eko, JSC).
[184] ibid (Eko, JSC).
[185] Joseph N Mbadugha, 'Environmental Public Interest Litigation in Nigeria: A Case Comment on Centre for Oil Pollution Watch v Nigerian National Petroleum Corporation' (2021) 11 *Nnamdi Azikiwe University, Awka Journal of Public and Private Law* 53–66, 61. See generally at 61–62.
[186] ibid 62.
[187] ibid.
[188] See further Ayodele Babalola, 'The Right to a Clean Environment in Nigeria: A Fundamental Right' (2020) 26(1) *Hastings Environmental Law Journal* 3–14.

These are elements that should be linked to climate issues by forward-thinking Nigerian lawyers, so that their scope and applicability can be tested in the courts in the context of public interest climate litigation.

Aka'ahs, JSC's judgment also subtly exposes a contextual fallacy underlying the judgment of the Court of Appeal. Referring to the local communities impacted detrimentally by the oil spill, the lower court had opined that 'the members of the community itself are better placed positioned and armed with the standing to sue the respondent for any damage caused. The decision of the [Trial Court] that it had no *locus standi* cannot be faulted'.[189] This neglects the matter of whether economically challenged communities have the requisite funds to mount a large case like this against an affluent energy institution in the first place. In this respect, it is worth bearing in mind that in his judgment, Eko, JSC emphasised the submissions of two of the amici curiae who maintained that 'the Acha community comprised mostly 'natives (who) are uneducated peasant farmers who have no means, capacity or courage to access the court' to seek redress for the environmental injustice'.[190] By the time of the Supreme Court judgment, it will be recalled that the case has already proceeded through two major court levels prior to reaching this third one,[191] duly increasing procedural complexity, resourcing demands and costs burdens on the parties in the process.

The Court of Appeal's perspective also neglects both the issue of whether the local community has adequate knowledge of the law and legal pathways for recourse that are open to it, and the issue of whether it can adequately organise itself to engage the legal system to its advantage. The support of COPW is crucial in these respects, assisting the community in areas that at best would likely prove intimidating, and at worst could prove entirely prohibitive of legal action. Indeed, there is also a question mark over what would constitute the relevant local 'community', given that the impacts of the oil spill allegedly ranged relatively far and wide.[192] Further, in the legal literature, Oluduro has addressed the future of climate litigation in Nigeria; Oluduro emphasises that Nigerian court requirements in environmental cases for injured litigants to retain experts to carry out scientific studies of environmental damage in order to prove damage place financial burdens on members of the public that can deny them access to justice,[193] with the case *Ogiale and Others v Shell* (1997) highlighting the problem.[194] Given these factors, Aka'ahs, JSC provides a humane and sensible contextual interpretation of the law

[189] Judgment, 579, quoting Amina Augie, JCA (as he then was).

[190] Judgment, 598 (Eko, JSC).

[191] See section II above.

[192] Thus, one of the Justices notes that 'in this case, damage to the environment is alleged to have spread or to have the capability of spreading over a very wide expanse of water, covering several communities, where it would be impracticable for every member of the community to sue or would be impossible to identify every person affected.' Judgment, 583 (Kekere-Ekun, JSC).

[193] Oluduro (n 21) 290.

[194] *Ogiale and Others v Shell* [1997] 1 NWLR 180 (Nigeria).

when he flags the danger that '[t]he communities affected by the spillage leading to the environmental degradation may not muster the financial muscle to sue and if good spirited organizations such as the plaintiff is denied access to sue, it is the affected communities that stand to lose'.[195] A related but additional matter, which is highlighted by Kekere-Ekun, JSC with reference to English common law,[196] is that regular communities may be unlikely to command the expertise, experience in environmental matters, and access to relevant scientific and other experts (including lawyers) that a specialist NGO will be able to muster.[197] As Anozie and Wingate summarise, 'NGOs active in the environmental space are best equipped to provide such speedy and competent response to protect the environment'.[198] For all of these reasons, it is clear that the Supreme Court's corrective to the lower courts here is appropriate.

Insightfully, Kekere-Ekun, JSC[199] highlights a further objection to COPW's case, which receives little overt attention in the judgment, but that does not stand up to scrutiny at any rate. She notes that it has been argued that allowing the appeal 'would open the floodgates to frivolous litigation and overwhelm the already overburdened court dockets'.[200] This objection is unconvincing, in no small part because locus standi in Nigerian law in this type of case requires a plaintiff to have a sufficient justiciable interest based on the pertinent facts and issues.[201] Widening standing for NGOs and public spirited persons expands the range of parties that can bring a case, but it does not simultaneously widen the standard that fences out frivolous or otherwise unacceptable claims from proceeding. Such claims continue to depend on evincing a sufficient justiciable interest contingent on the facts and circumstances of the case in question.[202] Thus, in relation to this and all other objections arising, Kekere-Ekun, JSC concludes that 'I am in full agreement with [Nweze, JSC's] sound reasoning and conclusions'.[203]

Eko, JSC's comments in support of the leading judgment,[204] which have been referred to above, are preceded in the judgment by those of Okoro, JSC,[205] who is also in strong agreement with the leading judgment. In addition to the learned judge's doctrinal legal reasoning, in the author's view, his remarks are notable for a humane sense of empathy that they seem to demonstrate towards the impacted communities, which appears to assist in informing the contextual

[195] Judgment, 581 (Aka'ahs, JSC).
[196] *R. v Inspectorate of Pollution and Another, ex parte Greenpeace Ltd (No 2)* (1994) 4 All ER 329, 350.
[197] Judgment, 584–85 (Kekere-Ekun, JSC).
[198] Anozie and Wingate (n 58) 491.
[199] Judgment, 581–88 (Kekere-Ekun, JSC).
[200] Judgment, 584.
[201] *Inakoju v Adeleke* (2007) 4 NWLR (Pt 1025) 423, 601–02 H-B; *Thomas and Others v Olufosoye* (1986) 1 NWLR (Pt 18) 669; *Adesanya v The President of Nigeria* (1981) 2 NCLR 358; *Iteogu v LPDC* (2009) 17 NWLR (Pt 1171) 614.
[202] See also Judgment, 584.
[203] ibid 583.
[204] ibid 592–601 (Eko, JSC).
[205] ibid 588–92 (Okoro, JSC).

interpretation of the issues that are to be brought to bear on the matter of locus standi. He opines:

> It is the duty of Government to protect the environment for the good of all and where government agencies desecrate such environments and other relevant government agencies fail, refuse and/or neglect to take necessary steps to enforce compliance, non-governmental organizations, which do not necessarily seek their personal interest, can, in my opinion bring an action in court to demand compliance and ensure the restoration, remediation and protection of the environment.[206]

Thus, in a hypothetical instance where the Supreme Court was to reject this appeal, he poses the following rhetorical question: 'Are [these communities] to be sentenced to [a] perpetual life of servitude in an environment where the observance of law amongst government institutions is observed more in the breach than in observance?'[207]

In the opinion of the Dean of the Faculty of Law at the University of Ibadan, Nigeria, and one of his colleagues, the Supreme Court 'expressed judicial activism in this judgment'.[208] They define judicial activism as 'judicial interpretative creativity as opposed to unnecessary restraint in the act of judicial practice' that 'enjoins judges to depart from strict adherence to judicial precedents and literal interpretation of statutes where the need so arises'.[209] They opine that the Court adopted this approach in spite of the fact that 'the defendant is the highest revenue-generating agency of the Nigerian government',[210] finding that in their opinion this 'is opposed to earlier passivism and the paternalistic approach of the Nigerian judiciary to environmental litigations'.[211] Their particular perspective serves to highlight the importance of the ruling. That said, the scope of its environmental implications in practice should not be overstated. Scholars at Delta State University, Nigeria, for example, have suggested that the procedures for prosecuting environmental claims in Nigeria remain much too restricted and the law continues to require substantial liberalisation going forward in the interest of justice.[212] Indeed, it has been argued that an environmental court with bespoke standing practices and procedures tailored to the environmental sphere could provide the Nigerian court system with a useful vehicle for improvement[213] (and it has been suggested that

[206] ibid 591–92 (Okoro, JSC).

[207] ibid 591 (Okoro, JSC).

[208] Adeniyi I Olatunbosun and Kingsley Osinachi N Onu, 'The Liberalisation of *Locus Standi* in Environmental Cases in Nigeria: An Appraisal of the Supreme Court's Decision in Centre for Oil Pollution Watch v NNPC' (2020) 11(2) *Gravitas Review of Business & Property Law* 1–11, 9.

[209] ibid 9, fn 47.

[210] ibid 9.

[211] ibid.

[212] Brown Etareri Umukoro and Moses Ogorugba Omozue, 'Prosecuting Environmental Pollution Cases in Nigeria: The Head of a Carmel Passing through the Eye of a Niddle' (2022) 15(2) *Baltic Journal of Law & Politics* 2232–43. The curious title ('Carmel', 'Niddle'), appears to be inspired by a remark made by Jesus in the Gospel of Matthew – it is easier for a camel to go through the eye of a needle than for a rich man to enter the kingdom of God.

[213] SA Fagbemi and AR Akpanke, 'Environmental Litigation in Nigeria: The Role of the Judiciary' (2019) 10(2) *Nnamdi Azikiwe University Journal of International Law and Jurisprudence* 26–34, 34.

the Land and Environment Court of New South Wales engaged in the Australian case study in this book might serve as an inspiration).[214] Alatise has praised the *Oil Pollution Watch* decision as boding well for climate litigation going forward, but suggests entrenching its development of the standing rules in binding parliamentary legislation, in part because this can mitigate the risk of lower courts narrowing standing by distinguishing the facts of the case from particular climate cases.[215]

VI. Concluding Thoughts

It has been noted in the opening section of this chapter that in comparison to the other deep-dive studies of major climate law rulings in this book, *Oil Pollution Watch* is something of a joker in the pack. It is a highly significant case that has widened the scope of locus standi in the Nigerian courts in relation to environmental harm where actions are brought in the public interest, incorporating parties that might not have suffered any injury either directly or at all. This is important to the development of environmental litigation generally in Nigeria, including in cases where negative environmental impacts arise from oil company activities (notably in the Niger Delta Region),[216] but not limited to such cases. *Oil Pollution Watch* also has clear relevance for climate change, as the world's most pressing environmental problem. It means in principle that climate litigation can be brought by NGOs and others acting in the public interest in Nigeria. Aka'ahs, JSC emphasised the subtlety of the distinction between parties bringing a lawsuit 'purely for public interest' who may not have suffered 'any injury above every other member of the society from the subject matter of the suit', and parties who 'may not have suffered any injury at all'.[217] The former category in particular has a facility to lend itself broadly to public interest climate litigation, given that, for example, all citizens are negatively impacted in principle by a state's failure to adequately mitigate greenhouse gas emissions over time, and an NGO or public-spirited person might seek to initiate mitigation-specific litigation to address some aspect of that problem where some particular breach may be perceived to arise in law. In their latest work, Ekhator and Okumagba comment that '[i]n Nigeria, there is yet to be an explicit climate litigation case' at the time of writing, but they note that *Oil Pollution Watch* has helped to pave the way for things to come.[218]

[214] Taofeeq N Alatise, 'Jurisdictional Problem in Environmental Litigation in Nigeria: Lessons from New South Wales' (2022) 30(1) *International Islamic University Malaysia Law Journal* 75–103, 75. *Gloucester Resources* is discussed at 98.

[215] Taofeeq N Alatise, 'The Future of "Standing to Sue" in Environment and Climate Change Litigations in Nigeria' (2022) 13(1) *Nnamdi Azikiwe University Journal of International Law and Jurisprudence* 28–39, 37.

[216] John Oluwole A Akintayo and David Tarh-Akong Eyongndi, 'Promoting the Right to Environmental Justice through the Supreme Court's Liberalisation of *Locus Standi* in Nigeria' (2019) 25(1) *South African Journal of Environmental Law and Policy* 201–31.

[217] Judgment, 578 (Aka'ahs, JSC).

[218] Ekhator and Okumagba (n 5) 26.

Where a particular climate-related environmental lawsuit is justiciable in the public interest, this should enable an NGO or other party that does not appear to have been harmed by climate impacts directly above and beyond others to bring a climate case in the general interest. Given the long-term impacts of climate change, and given the sensitivity exhibited in this case to long-term harm,[219] there is a possibility that this might be drawn to include lawsuits incorporating the interests of unborn future generations as well as current generations (who in being unborn as yet have not suffered any direct injury in their own right above and beyond anyone else). Furthermore, in a justiciable climate case where an NGO or public-spirited individual endeavouring to bring a lawsuit has suffered neither any injury above every other member of society forming the subject matter of the action, nor any discernible injury at all, *Oil Pollution Watch* suggests the existence of a capacity for the NGO or individual to bring a lawsuit in the interest of parties who may have suffered *particular* harm. To take a hypothetical example for the purposes of illustration, this could mean that, for example, where an identifiable community has suffered significant damage due to intensive and prolonged climate-driven flooding, and where some form of requisite climate adaptation assistance has not been provided by authorities over a prolonged period, a case might be initiated in principle on the community's behalf by an environmental NGO, even though the community has suffered the identifiable climate damage, and the party bringing the lawsuit in the community's interest has not been the subject of that damage.

Etemire has provided an overview of the climate change regulatory framework in Nigeria in the context of climate litigation considerations, revealing that only a relatively weak regulatory regime engaging climate issues is in place.[220] However, in spite of 'the fact that the regulatory framework for climate change in Nigeria is weak in several aspects and requires considerable improvement',[221] he notes that a Climate Change Bill – passed since the time of his analysis later that year as the Climate Change Act 2021[222] – may provide an opportunity to 'foster the rapid growth of climate litigation in Nigeria'.[223] Such developments, in concert with the *Oil Pollution Watch* ruling, suggest that Nigeria is moving into a new era that can enable significant climate litigation instead of unduly constraining it.[224] Alatise has considered these matters and also sees cause for optimism, though he has highlighted that the Kenya Climate Change Act, which influenced the Nigerian Act,

[219] See, eg, n 167 above and the text to the note.

[220] Etemire (n 6) 158; see also 160–62, 'II. An Overview of the Climate Change Regulatory Framework in Nigeria'.

[221] ibid 162.

[222] The content of the Act is helpfully overviewed (and linked to the concept of climate litigation) in Muhammed Ladan, 'Nigeria's Climate Change Act and Policy 2021 and the Future of Climate Litigation' (2022), https://papers.ssrn.com/sol3/papers.cfm?abstract_id=4019698.

[223] Etemire (n 6) 160.

[224] Aaron Olaniyi Salau, 'The Future of Climate Change Litigation in Pursuit of Environmental Sustainability in Africa: A Review of Nigeria's 2021 Climate Change Act' in, Jean-Claude N Ashukem and Semie M Sama (eds), *Domestic and Regional Environmental Laws and Policies in Africa: A Research Companion* (Routledge, 2024).

provides that: 'For the purpose of this section [concerning an application to the courts in relation to climate change impacts], an applicant does not have to demonstrate that a person has incurred loss or suffered injury.'[225] Alatise comments that '[t]his has clearly removed any form of standing hurdle for prospective litigants', but notes that 'the recently passed Nigerian Climate Change Act, 2021, does not have a similar provision for open standing regime even though the law is substantially modelled after the Kenyan Climate Change Act.'[226] He suggests that this appears to indicate that the Nigerian Government has not fully committed to a level of open access to justice appropriate to the needs of climate litigation.[227]

While *Oil Pollution Watch* is not a landmark climate case in the direct way that the other major cases covered in this volume's case study chapters are, it has major legal importance in the sphere of environmental protection in Nigeria, and thus major importance in the climate sphere, opening up vital channels to public interest climate litigation in Nigeria for the first time. The Supreme Court itself is also explicitly sensitive to climate-specific issues in its ruling, and factors them into its thinking.[228] The case has importance for climate litigation in Nigeria going forward, but it also holds importance for other jurisdictions around the world that might be grappling with similar issues concerning standing.

'Environmental justice', in a legal sense, is partly predicated on access to the courts, insofar as without access to justice the broader notion of environmental justice itself is undermined.[229] Put another way, it is possible in legal terms to distinguish procedural rights and substantive rights in the context of Nigerian environmental law (and environmental law in general), and where procedural rights are constrained, including via standing constraints, this can choke off access to what may otherwise be robust substantive rights.[230] It has been seen that the Nigerian courts looked in part to rulings from the English courts and other courts around the world for guidance on this matter, and *Oil Pollution Watch* can be recommended to courts in other jurisdictions around the world in its own right, providing a distinctly Nigerian point of reference illustrative of the need to permit adequate access to the courts on public interest grounds where perceived climate and other environmental harms arise. Indeed, this internationalist process of transnational reference and reflection is an ongoing two-way street, and Okumagba has observed that Nigeria itself currently seems to be well positioned to consider the

[225] Climate Change Act 2016, s 23(3) (Kenya).

[226] Alatise (n 215) 38.

[227] ibid. Ekhator and Okumagba seem to take a more optimistic view; see their discussion of s 34 of the Act at n 5, 20.

[228] See the discussion of Aka'ahs, JSC's judgment in section V.E above.

[229] Eloamaka Carol Okonkwo, 'Assessing the Role of the Courts in Enhancing Access to Environmental Justice in Oil Pollution Matters in Nigeria' (2020) 28(2) *African Journal of International and Comparative Law* 195–218.

[230] Ibrahim Obadina, 'Nigerian Supreme Court's Stealth Relaxation of *Locus Standi* in Environmental litigation: Redirecting Judicial Approach to Public Interest Litigation' (2021) 2(2) *Journal of Private and Business Law* 200.

absorption of various approaches to climate litigation from around the world into its own domestic legal order.[231]

Etemire has summarised the practical legal implications of *Oil Pollution Watch* in the following terms:

> [O]ver the years climate change litigation in Nigeria has been impeded by a weak climate change regime, an unduly restrictive standing rule, and a judicial attitude that has privileged the economy over the environment … However, the COPW case marks a sea change in Nigerian environmental and climate litigation: Firstly, it liberalizes the agelong restrictive standing rule by introducing environmental public interest litigation; secondly, it clearly indicates a major shift in the attitude of the court, from a pro-economy to a 'greener' approach to climate matters; and thirdly, it freshly and firmly establishes alternative constitutional and human rights grounds for addressing environmental and climate issues.[232]

Umukoro and Omozue comment that the 'issue before the apex court was only on the *locus standi* of NGOs on public interest litigation on environmental matters' and so the 'pronouncements on the right to clean environment are obiter dicta';[233] however, the Supreme Court's guidance has 'given judicial impetus' to Nigeria's Fundamental Rights (Enforcement Procedure) Rules and has put the Government on notice that courts will likely expect to see the implementation of appropriate environmental laws and policies on this type of basis.[234]

In moving the law away from a confining conception of locus standi that catered to a person who has suffered a specific legal injury by an actual or threatened violation of his or her protected interests, to instead embrace a broader remit including NGOs and public-spirited persons seeking to right environmental wrongs in the public interest, *Oil Pollution Watch* has moved Nigerian law in a positive direction. COPW included members who were part of the impacted community/communities, and this helped the NGO to accrue standing, but even without the existence of such members, the Supreme Court ruling suggests that the NGO could have brought its case successfully. Thus, Eko, JSC opines that:

> [E]very *person, including NGO's* [sic], who bona fide seek in the law court the due performance of statutory functions or enforcement of statutory provisions or public laws, especially laws designed to protect human lives, public health and environment, should be regarded as proper persons clothed with standing in law to request adjudication on such issues of public nuisance that are injurious to human lives, public health and environment. (Emphasis added)[235]

[231] Edward Okumagba, 'Examining Global Court Practices in Reducing Climate Change Impacts through Litigation: Lessons for Nigeria' in Eghosa O Ekhator, Servel Miller and Etinosa Igbinosa (eds), *Implementing the Sustainable Development Goals in Nigeria: Barriers, Prospects and Strategies* (Routledge, 2021).

[232] Etemire (n 6) 158, 160.

[233] Brown Etareri Umukoro and Moses Ogorugba Omozue, 'Environmental Protection and the Role of National Policy and Guidelines in Nigeria' (2022) 15(1) *Baltic Journal of Law & Politics* 2016–29, 2027.

[234] ibid 2027.

[235] Judgment, 595, per Eko, JSC, referring to *Fawehinmi v Akilu* (1987) 4 NWLR (Pt 67) 797.

Roy and Woerdman have noted what they describe as 'diffusion' in relation to the *Urgenda Case*,[236] and the notion of inter-referentiality between various climate judgments across differing jurisdictions arises at many points throughout this book. It is interesting that in *Oil Pollution Watch*, counsel for COPW referred to 'the common law, which Nigeria inherited from the United Kingdom'.[237] Citing a modern English case,[238] he highlighted that the English courts have extended the meaning of locus standi, the point of the reference being that in the appellant's view, the Supreme Court should consider this case as a persuasive ruling illustrative of the appropriateness of an expansion to the Nigerian rules of locus standi.[239] In response, NNPC's lawyer cited a range of Nigerian cases that were in his view 'all to the effect that as the law stands there is no room for the adoption of the modern views on locus standi in England and Australia'.[240] It is notable that the respondent lawyer endeavoured to close off the influence of both English *and* Australian law via extant Nigerian law. It has been seen that the Supreme Court found against the respondent NNPC. In terms of climate litigation, which engages with a shared, global problem common to humanity, the identifiable internationalist, multi-jurisdictional influence that is present here underscores a potential capacity amongst common law countries through their legal similitude and shared common law traditions to learn from one another over the course of climate rulings. It may be that in future cases in Nigeria, England, Australia and beyond, common law climate law rulings might come to exert a similar or indeed even greater degree of persuasive cross-jurisdictional influence than the substantial influence exerted by transnational locus standi jurisprudence in *Oil Pollution Watch*. Time will tell.

[236] Suryapratim Roy and Edwin Woerdman, 'Situating Urgenda v The Netherlands within Comparative Climate Change Litigation' (2016) 34(2) *Journal of Energy & Natural Resources Law* 165–89, 167.

[237] Judgment, 554.

[238] *R v Inland Revenue Commissioners* (n 118) 639.

[239] Judgment, 554.

[240] *SPDC v Nwawka* (2001) 10 NWLR (Pt 720) 64; *Busari v Oseni* (1992) 4 NWLR (Pt 237) 557; *Fawehinmi v Akilu* (1987) 4 NWLR (Pt 67) 797; *Thomas and Others v Olufosoye* (1986) 1 NWLR (Pt 18) 669. See further Judgment, 555.

6

Australia

The Gloucester Resources Case

> There is a causal link between the Project's cumulative GHG emissions and climate change and its consequences. The Project's cumulative GHG emissions will contribute to the global total of GHG concentrations in the atmosphere. The global total of GHG concentrations will affect the climate system and cause climate change impacts. The Project's cumulative GHG emissions are therefore likely to contribute to the future changes to the climate system and the impacts of climate change.
>
> *Gloucester Resources*, Land and Environment Court, paragraph 525

I. Background, Circumstances and Outcomes

The Australian case *Gloucester Resources Limited v Minister for Planning* (2019)[1] is to be numbered among the world's initial landmark climate law rulings. It is a significant ruling in terms of its practical consequences, and an interesting ruling in terms of the legal issues and facts arising. It will be referred to here as the *Gloucester Resources Case*, or simply *Gloucester Resources*; in print, the case is sometimes referred to in Australia as the *Rocky Hill* case,[2] but this is less helpful given that 'Rocky Hill' does not appear in the title of the official case reports.

Australia contains six states. This case arose in the Australian state of New South Wales, where it came before the New South Wales Land and Environment Court (hereafter 'Land and Environment Court' or 'the Court'). Court hearings took place in August, November and December 2018, and the Court's decision was issued on 8 February 2019. It was heard by Justice Preston (hereafter 'Preston CJ'), Chief Judge of the Land and Environment Court. The applicant was Gloucester Resources Limited (GRL), the first respondent was the Minister for Planning, and the second respondent, who joined the first respondent in opposing the applicant, was Groundswell Gloucester Inc.

[1] *Gloucester Resources Limited v Minister for Planning* [2019] NSWLEC 7; (2019) 234 LGERA 257 (hereafter cited as 'Judgment').

[2] See, eg, Margaret Gleeson, 'Rocky Hill Decision Rocks Mining Lobby' (2019) 1221 *Green Left Weekly* 10–20.

The Minister for Planning, by his delegate the Planning and Assessment Commission (hereafter 'the Commission'), had refused GRL permission to construct an open cut coal mine in New South Wales, known as the Rocky Hill Coal Project, determining that the proposal was incompatible with the State Environmental Planning Policy (Mining, Petroleum Production and Extraction Industries) 2009.[3] The Land and Environment Court upheld the Minister's development refusal, building on it in interesting ways in relation to climate considerations. The proposed development was expected to result in the production of 21 million tonnes of coal over a period of 16 years. While the extensive production and subsequent use of coal is damaging to the climate, the proposal had merits too, including the anticipated provision of support for 'up to 110 jobs during operation and 60 jobs during construction'.[4]

The case tested the extent to which the Government could refuse or permit a coal mine project based on its projected climate change impacts and a range of other environmental and socio-economic factors.[5] White and others have commented on its landmark character as follows:

> When the Chief Judge of the New South Wales Land and Environment Court delivered judgment in 'Gloucester Resources Limited v Minister for Planning' ... on 8 February, it drew attention around the world. Why? Because it was the first time an Australian court had refused a coal mine (or any development) on the basis of its climate change impacts.[6]

Elsewhere, White has added that the case is:

> [S]ignificant across a number of dimensions, not the least of which because it is the first of its kind to refer to carbon emissions and climate change as one of the reasons for ruling against the mine proposal.[7]

The Land and Environment Court itself is the 'oldest specialist court of its kind in Australia (one of only three in Australia dealing specially with environmental matters)', and the first specialist superior environmental court globally, having been created by the Land and Environment Court Act in 1979 in order to deal with

[3] This type of development is a 'State significant development' under the terms of s 4.36(1) of the Environmental Planning and Assessment Act 1979 (NSW).

[4] Peter Briggs and Tom Dougherty, 'Climate Change Impacts used to Reject new NSW Coal Mine', 15 February 2019, Australia, Herbert Smith Freehills, 1–8, 1.

[5] These elements are discussed below.

[6] Robert White, Jemilah Hallinan and Belinda Rayment, 'Environmental Law: Climate Change Takes Centre Stage in Land and Environment Court' (2019) *LSJ: Law Society Journal* 54. According to Gleeson, it was the 'first time in legal history [that] the impact of a new coalmine on climate change was a determining factor in refusing consent'. Margaret Gleeson, 'NSW Land Court Rules against New Coalmine' (2019) 1209 *Green Left Weekly* 8. In writing for an Australian publication, the inference here may be that Gleeson is referring to the history of Australia only. In relation to this case as an Australian 'first', see also John Watts, Ken Eveleigh, Michael Manikas and Jeff Kite, 'What You Didn't Know about the Landmark Rocky Hill Judgment' (2019) 57 *Law Society Journal* 72–73.

[7] Robert White, 'Eco-justice and Destructive Mining in Australia: Lessons from the New South Wales Land and Environmental Court' in Yuliya Zabyelina and Daan van Uhm (eds), *Illegal Mining: Organized Crime, Corruption, and Ecocide in a Resource-Scarce World* (Springer Nature, 2020) 530.

environmental and related issues within a single specialised court.[8] The highest court in Australia is the High Court of Australia, and the Land and Environment Court is a powerful court within the New South Wales court system, equivalent to the Supreme Court in the hierarchy of New South Wales courts in a case of this kind.[9]

Gloucester itself is a relatively small town with 'a population of fewer than 3,000 people' that 'derives most of its income from tourism, timber, beef and dairy'.[10] Hughes, however, outlines that resistance to the mine proposal, which was first lodged by GRL in December 2012 as a Development Application for consent to undertake the proposed project, was anything but small:

> There was an immediate outcry against the proposed mine. A total of 1,700 submissions on the proposal were received by the NSW Planning Assessment Commission … including 13 from government agencies, 18 from special interest groups, and approximately 570 from individuals in the Gloucester area. Many of the submissions were coordinated by Groundswell Gloucester,[11] a community action group previously formed to oppose expansion of coal mining in the valley.[12]

GRL amended the Development Application and produced a new Environmental Impact Statement[13] in 2016, but this 'elicited an even greater number of submissions than the original 2013 submission – 2,570 in total, of which 2,308 were from individuals opposing the development'.[14] The Commission noted objections it received from Mid-Coast Council[15] and the public, and ultimately refused development consent for the mine in 2017. Hughes has rightly emphasised the important point that the 'Commission's judgment made no mention of GHGs or climate impacts'.[16]

The Minister, by his delegate, the Commission, refused the application in December 2017 for a variety of reasons, including incompatibility with local land use zone objectives, visual impacts and the project not being sufficiently in the public interest. GRL then lodged a merits appeal against the decision with the Court.[17] At this stage, local community action group Groundswell Gloucester Inc

[8] ibid 534–35.

[9] ibid 535. On the Australian court system, see further John Carvan, *Understanding the Australian Legal System*, 8th edn (Lawbook Co Australia, 2022).

[10] Lesley Hughes, 'The Rocky Hill Decision: A Watershed for Climate Change Action?' (2019) 37(3) *Journal of Energy & Natural Resources Law* 341–51, 341.

[11] Note that Groundswell Gloucester is sometimes referred to or known as 'Gloucester Groundswell'.

[12] Hughes (n 10) 343.

[13] Under the Environmental Planning and Assessment Act 1979 (NSW), an Environmental Impact Statement must be submitted with a development application where it is deemed likely that a development will significantly impact the environment. These technical planning statements are discussed further below.

[14] Hughes (n 10) 343.

[15] The Council representing the local government area in New South Wales in which Gloucester is situated.

[16] Hughes (n 10) 343.

[17] It is notable that when the appeal against the Minister for Planning's refusal to grant consent was lodged with the Land and Environment Court in December 2017, this was not made public until some

joined proceedings, opposing the appeal. As such, this case is to some extent in the tradition of an emerging strand of climate law cases that are (at least) partly and overtly driven by robust community and grassroots-level action in the courts. In this instance – in contrast to *Climate Case Ireland*, for example[18] – it is notable that the Government and community-aligned group are on the same side, arguing together against a major private sector actor that its development application should be denied.

As noted above, the Land and Environment Court upheld the Government's denial of the application. GRL had until 8 May 2019 to lodge an appeal and did not do so.[19] Lawyers acting for Groundswell Gloucester called it a 'once in a generation case'.[20] It has gone on to exert a significant influence on Australian jurisprudential thinking, with the decision being considered by the courts in a range of subsequent cases.[21] It has also been referred to in climate litigation by major courts around the world, including the Supreme Court of Canada[22] and the Court of Appeal of England and Wales.[23] Peel has interpreted the case's sensitivity to jurisprudence from Australia and other jurisdictions, climate science and legal scholarship as cohering to embody a contribution to the 'transnationalisation of law', where 'the mainstream binary division of law into either national law or international law is challenged by the generation of transcendental norms'.[24] Briggs and Dougherty have summarised a main legal takeaway from the case as follows:

> Proponents seeking consent for new projects, or modifications of existing projects, with 'material' greenhouse gas emissions across all industries in NSW should carefully assess climate change impacts, particularly if the proposal is not 'carbon neutral'.[25]

time later, and there was upset at the facility to appeal the decision in this way when imbalances in the Australian system meant that 'such an opportunity was routinely denied to opponents of Mining'; see further Hughes (n 10) 343–44.

[18] See ch 7.

[19] Although Gloucester Resources lodged a Notice of Intention to Appeal, it did not formally appeal. See Peter Hannam, 'Coal Miner Lodges Plan to Appeal against Landmark NSW Climate Verdict', *Sydney Morning Herald*, 8 March 2019, https://www.smh.com.au/environment/climate-change/coal-miner-lodges-plan-to-appeal-against-landmark-nsw-climate-verdict-20190308-p512sc.html.

[20] Peter Hannam, '"We Won": Landmark Climate Ruling as NSW Court Rejects Coal Mine', *Sydney Morning Herald*, 8 February 2019, www.smh.com.au/environment/climate-change/we-won-landmark-climate-ruling-as-nsw-court-rejects-coal-mine-20190207-p50wer.html.

[21] *Waratah Coal Pty Ltd v Youth Verdict Ltd and Others (No 6)* [2022] QLC 21; *Mullaley Gas and Pipeline Accord Inc v Santos NSW (Eastern) Pty Ltd* [2021] NSWLEC 110; *Bushfire Survivors for Climate Action Inc v Environment Protection Authority* [2021] NSWLEC 92; *KEPCO Bylong Australia Pty Ltd v Independent Planning Commission (No 2)* [2020] NSWLEC 179; *KEPCO Bylong Australia Pty Ltd v Bylong Valley Protection Alliance Inc* [2021] NSWCA 216; *Statewide Planning Pty Ltd v Blacktown City Council* [2019] NSWLEC 1397; *Visionary Investment Group Pty Ltd v Wollongong City Council* [2019] NSWLEC 1234; *Australian Coal Alliance Inc v Wyong Coal Pty Ltd* [2019] NSWLEC 31.

[22] *References re Greenhouse Gas Pollution Pricing Act* [2021] SCC 11 (Canada).

[23] *R (on the Application of Finch) v Surrey County Council* [2022] EWCA Civ 187 (17 February 2022, under appeal to the Supreme Court at the time of writing). In the UK, see also the High Court decision *R (Friends of the Earth) v Secretary of State for International Trade* [2022] EWHC 568 (Admin).

[24] Jacqueline Peel, 'The Land and Environment Court of New South Wales and the Transnationalisation of Climate Law: The Case of *Gloucester Resources v Minister for Planning*' in Elizabeth Fisher and Brian J Preston (eds), *An Environmental Court in Action* (Hart Publishing, 2022), 73, 74.

[25] Briggs and Dougherty (n 4) 1.

As will be seen below, there are a range of important elements underlying this ruling from a climate law perspective.

II. The Case: Issues, Facts, Law

A. Key Lines of Reasoning Advanced by Gloucester Resources Limited, and the Court's Response

The *Gloucester Resources* judgment as reported in its standard neutral citation edition ([2019] NSWLEC 7) spans an enormous 205 pages.[26] In terms of the Court's approach to assessing greenhouse gas emissions, taken at its highest level, it is important that the Court chose to recognise both the 'effects of carbon in the atmosphere arising from activities in the Project site' *and* 'the burning of the coal extracted from the mine'[27] (this aspect is considered in detail in section II.B below). While there are a number of legal strands to this case in addition to its overt climate change considerations, the climate strand is the most novel, and it is prominent and richly developed. It is also of particular importance in the early history of landmark climate litigation, due in part to the extent to which the Court *builds climate law considerations into* the relevant issues, whereas in the decision prior to the appeal, such considerations had not featured.

GRL advanced four major lines of reasoning that it argued should lead the Court to find in favour of the application, even though the project would lead to emissions increases:

- greenhouse gas emissions from the project would be balanced out by emissions reductions in other sectors (for example, transportation, electricity generation);[28]
- emissions reductions must be achieved at the least possible cost;[29]
- coal will be mined and exploited by other producers to meet global demand because of market substitution and carbon leakage;[30]
- there is unique demand for coking coal for steel production that justifies the project's greenhouse gas emissions.[31]

[26] A table of contents breaks the Judgment down into digestible headings, including a major section entitled 'The Impacts of the Mine on Climate Change' (commencing Judgment, para [422]) replete with 11 climate-focused subheadings; see further 'Table of Contents' in the [2019] NSWLEC 7 report. The prominence given to climate change in the structure of the reported Judgment attests to its treatment as a major issue.

[27] Judgment, para [422]. The Court here is summarising an approach to greenhouse gas appraisal advocated by Groundswell Gloucester, which the Court ultimately accepted.

[28] ibid paras [529]–[530].

[29] ibid paras [531]–[533].

[30] ibid paras [534]–[545].

[31] ibid paras [546]–[549].

The Court was unpersuaded by these points.[32]

On the first point, concerning the balancing out of emissions reductions in other sectors, the Court noted that no plans to balance out the emissions through other projects had been put forward by GRL (or anyone else).[33] On the second point, concerning reductions at least possible cost, the Court found that it is not sensible or rational for the decision maker to speculate on broad issues of cost-effectiveness in reductions in the context of its narrow decision-making functions in a case like this.[34] In the author's view, GRL also appears to have missed (or avoided) the nuance that emissions are not being reduced. Emissions are sitting at a current level, and the proposal is to institute a project that will *add to them* significantly. Prevention of the project itself does not actively reduce emissions by shutting a current project down; it merely maintains current circumstances. Thus, the concept of reducing emissions at least possible cost is at best rather tenuously applicable to the concrete circumstances of the proposed coal mine itself. On the fourth point (the third point is addressed below), namely the argument that the project would produce coking coal that is needed to maintain steel production, this refers to the intended primary use of the mined coal for the production of steel. The production process involves coking coal and iron ore being used in a 'basic oxygen furnace' process,[35] and it was argued that the unique demand for coking coal in steel production provided justification for the development. This did not convince the Court;[36] indeed, the Court noted that evidence suggested that existing and approved coking coal mines in Australia could likely meet current and projected demand as things stood.[37]

As noted above, a third strand of argument contended that coal will be mined and exploited by other producers to meet global demand in place of this project if it is refused. This element received particularly significant attention from the Court. GRL contended that *carbon leakage* and *market substitution* would arise if the project was refused, and therefore it was pointless to refuse it on climate grounds. *Carbon leakage* in this context pertains to coal mining of this kind moving from Australia to countries with less stringent climate standards if Australian project developments are curtailed, leading to greater greenhouse

[32] Conversely, the main arguments presented as to why the planning appeal should fail can be summarised as follows: (1) the proposed mine was incompatible with the existing, approved and likely preferred uses of nearby land; (2) the mine would occasion adverse visual impacts; (3) the mine would occasion adverse social impacts; (4) uncertainty surrounded the economic and public benefits of the mine, which were not shown to be greater than the public costs of the mine; (5) the matters in (1)–(4) place the development outside the public interest, and the development is contrary to the concept of *ecologically sustainable development* because direct and indirect greenhouse gas emissions occasioned by the mine will contribute to climate change (author's summary drawn from ibid para [24]).

[33] ibid para [530].

[34] ibid paras [532]–[533].

[35] ibid paras [464], [466].

[36] ibid para [549].

[37] See ibid para [536].

gas emissions.[38] The Court was unconvinced, and although the case was not a binding authority, it pointed out that its reasoning was echoed in a comparable way by the *Urgenda* ruling in the Netherlands.[39] Similar to *carbon leakage*, *market substitution* in this context pertains to new mines being developed in other countries in the event of these sorts of projects being refused in Australia, in order to fill a gap in demand that would otherwise be filled by coal mines like GRL's. Bell-James and Collins summarise the *market substitution* principle in relation to coal mining as 'the assertion that, if a particular mine is rejected, another mine will be developed elsewhere in its stead – therefore approving the mine has no consequences for the environment'.[40]

As with the related issue of *carbon leakage*, the Court was unpersuaded by the *market substitution* argument, and in dismissing it made interesting reference to the United Nations Framework Convention on Climate Change (UNFCCC), leaning on the international treaty and international agreements that have flowed from it (the Kyoto Protocol, the Paris Agreement) to support and emphasise its points.[41] Over the course of dispensing with the argument, the Court stated that: 'If a development will cause an environmental impact that is found to be unacceptable, the environmental impact does not become acceptable because a hypothetical and uncertain alternative development might also cause the same unacceptable environmental impact.'[42] In other words, the 'environmental impact remains unacceptable regardless of where it is caused'.[43] This means that the 'potential for a hypothetical but uncertain alternative development to cause the same unacceptable environmental impact is not a reason … for approving the Project and its unacceptable GHG emissions and climate change impacts'.[44] It is submitted that the Court's cogent line of reasoning in relation to *market substitution* and *carbon leakage* can be drawn on usefully by other courts around the world that might be compelled by climate litigation to address these issues. McGinness and Raff have situated the Court's dismissal of the *market substitution* argument in the broader context of contemporary Australian litigation, finding that the judgment marks something of a turning point in court interpretation of the issue.[45] Formerly, this

[38] See further 'What is Carbon Leakage?' in Helge Næss-Schmidt et al, *Carbon Leakage in the Nordic Countries: What are the Risks and how to Design Effective Preventative Policies* (Nordic Council of Ministers, 2019), 17–18.

[39] Judgment, para [537]; *State of the Netherlands v Urgenda Foundation*, ECLI:NL:GHDHA:2018:2591 (English translation ECLI:NL:GHDHA:2018:2610), Judgment (Ct App, The Hague, 9 October 2018) (Neth).

[40] Justine Bell-James, and Briana Collins, '"If We Don't Mine Coal, Someone Else Will": Debunking the "Market Substitution Assumption" in Queensland Climate Change Litigation' (2020) 37(2) *Environmental and Planning Law Journal* 167–85, 167.

[41] Judgment, para [539].

[42] ibid para [545].

[43] ibid.

[44] ibid.

[45] See Victoria McGinness, and Murray Raff, 'Coal and Climate Change: A Study of Contemporary Climate Litigation in Australia' (2020) 37(1) *Environmental and Planning Law Journal* 87–127.

fundamentally weak line of argument had carried significant weight in Australian court reasoning, but Preston CJ's lucid and rational treatment of the issue has exposed and clarified its weakness in the context of a clear climate ruling that can assist other judges in their approach to the matter.[46]

It is noteworthy that the Court looked to a US Court of Appeals case, *WildEarth Guardians v US Bureau of Land Management* (2017),[47] for a degree of guidance. Here, the US court rejected a decision from the US Bureau of Land Management that had approved coal leases that would expand coal mines partially within national grassland.[48] The Bureau of Land Management had concluded that the open market would result in the same amount of coal being sourced from elsewhere if the leases were not issued. The US Court of Appeals pointed out that the Bureau ignored key issues such as the nation's stores of coal, whether a deficit could be filled from elsewhere, whether it could be filled at a comparable price etc, meaning that it incorrectly projected a picture of certainty onto an area that was fundamentally uncertain.[49] Relatedly, the Court of Appeals found that the overall market 'assumption itself is irrational', being 'contrary to basic supply and demand principles';[50] thus, its application in this type of context 'was an abuse of discretion to rely on an economic assumption, which contradicted basic economic principles, as the basis for distinguishing between the no action alternative and the preferred alternative'.[51]

The Land and Environment Court also rejected the *market substitution* and *carbon leakage* arguments by reference to the norm inherent in the UNFCCC and the Paris Agreement that every signatory has a responsibility to take mitigation measures to reduce greenhouse gas emissions in their country.[52] Whilst the extent of action to be taken is self-determined, and subject to the principle of common but differentiated responsibilities and respective capabilities, every party has committed to taking ambitious efforts to achieve both the temperature target in Article 2 and the time target in Article 4 of the Paris Agreement.[53] Developed countries, such as Australia, are to take the lead in climate change mitigation, including by refusing new sources of greenhouse gas emissions such as new coal mines, and developing countries may be encouraged by such action to do likewise. Hence, there is no certainty that a refusal of a new coal mine in Australia will lead to another country, including developing countries such as India or Indonesia, approving a substitute coal mine.[54] *Market substitution* or *carbon leakage* is not inevitable. Thus, White has emphasised that: 'Among other reasons, this was

[46] See ibid.
[47] *WildEarth Guardians v US Bureau of Land Management* 870 F 3d 1222 (10th Cir, 2017).
[48] Judgment, para [542].
[49] See ibid para [453]; and *WildEarth Guardians* (n 47).
[50] *WildEarth Guardians* (n 47) 1236.
[51] ibid 1237–38.
[52] For additional consideration of the international regime, see sections II.B and II.C below.
[53] Judgment, para [539].
[54] ibid para [540].

rejected in the light of increasing global momentum to tackle climate change and therefore reject future coalmine proposals.'[55]

Furthermore, in the author's view, it is notable that shifting national and international fossil fuel markets, including coal markets, are complex and can be subject to substantial unanticipated market alterations, such that (for example) market contractions that can be difficult to predict may occur, reducing the need for coal and thus the need for project approvals of this kind.[56] Dehm has commented in relation to the concept of *market substitution* as follows: 'Underpinning this ... is the notion that the market for coal is 'demand-driven' (rather than 'supply-driven')';[57] such markets, taken internationally, are unstable, fluctuate and are difficult to predict with a degree of certainty. The Court acknowledged the impossible task of calculating such markets with absolute certainty, and it is important that it did so.[58] At any rate, as noted above, on a point of general principle, Australia and other developed countries have a responsibility to lead in taking mitigation measures, as asserted under the international treaties through the principle of common but differentiated responsibilities.[59]

B. The Court's Treatment of Greenhouse Gas Emissions

Where the Court turned to assess directly whether the application should be refused on climate change grounds, it took as a main focal point the estimated increase in greenhouse gas emissions that would likely arise from the project. Against the backdrop sketched out above, the Court considered the relationship between the problem of climate change and the contribution that the project's cumulative emissions could make to it. Here, the Court recognised the existence of a *causal link* between the greenhouse gas emissions that would arise from the project and climate change, noting that the development would result in an increase to the total emissions concentration in the climate system, thus establishing a causal link to negative climate impacts.[60] Relatedly, but slightly distinct in terms of nuance, GRL had advanced the position that the emissions resulting

[55] White (n 7) 551.

[56] This could happen for any number of reasons. Consider, for instance, the slowdown in fossil fuel consumption as a result of international lockdowns occasioned by the COVID-19 crisis: Zhu Deng Liu et al, 'Global Patterns of Daily CO_2 Emissions Reductions in the First Year of COVID-19' (2022) 15(8) *Nature Geoscience* 615–20.

[57] Julia Dehm, 'Coal Mines, Carbon Budgets and Human Rights in Australian Climate Litigation: Reflections on Gloucester Resources Limited v Minister for Planning and Environment' (2020) 26(2) *Australian Journal of Human Rights* 244–73, 256.

[58] Judgment, para [451].

[59] See ibid para [539]. See also Paris Agreement, art 4(3); *Urgenda Foundation v The State of the Netherlands*, ECLI:NL:RBDHA:2015:7145 (English translation ECLI:NL:RBDHA:2015:7196), Judgment (Dist Ct, The Hague, 24 June 2015) (Neth), para [4.79].

[60] Judgment, para [525].

from the mine would be so small in a global context as to be irrelevant to the Court's decision.

This latter argument is sometimes put forward in climate litigation,[61] but it is devoid of logic. In a sense, lawyers making this case endeavour to have their cake and eat it. In effect, on the one hand, it is accepted implicitly or explicitly that there *is* a causal link between project emissions and climate change due to contributions from a project to impactful emissions in the atmosphere; at the same time, on the other hand, it is accepted that there is *no* causal link insofar as a project's emissions are so small in the grand scheme of global emissions as to render a causal link legally non-existent. At its core, such sophistry attempts to accept a causal link and reject it in the same breath. In clearly and concisely rejecting this position, *Gloucester Resources* stands as a helpful example to other courts.[62] The Court recognised that projects like the proposed mine contribute in a *cumulative* way all over the world to the stock of greenhouse gases in the earth's atmosphere, which in turn contributes to climate change, and so the emissions such projects produce both individually and collectively (ie, in concert with other installations around the world) are directly connected to climate change. Preston CJ asserted that 'climate change is caused by cumulative emissions from a myriad of individual sources, each proportionally small relative to the global total of GHG emissions, and will be solved by abatement of the GHG emissions from these myriad of individual sources'.[63] It is notable that court jurisprudence in New South Wales had previously acknowledged that the cumulative character of emissions can be relevant where a particular coal mine project is at issue, even if it is difficult or impossible to project or measure the climate impact that those emissions might have in very accurate terms.[64] This ruling in essence refined and cemented that position.

The Court was measured and reasonable in its assessment of the causal connection between the project's projected emissions and climate impact, neither overblowing it nor creating any pretence that this individual project taken in isolation would be a substantial driver of climate change; it correctly and accurately asserted that a causal link could be identified clearly between a project like this and anthropogenic climate change, and that the project would make a contribution

[61] *Massachusetts v Environmental Protection Agency* (2007) 127S Ct 1438 (US Supreme Court), [523]–[524]; *Waratah Coal Pty Ltd v Youth Verdict Ltd and Others (No 6)* [2022] QLC 21 (Land Court of Queensland, Australia), para [955]; *Greenpeace Nordic Association v Ministry of Petroleum and Energy (People v Arctic Oil)* HR-2020-2472-P (case no 20-051052SIV-HRET) (Norwegian Supreme Court), para [42].

[62] Kierra Parker, 'Litigating at the Source: Attributing Climate Change Impacts to Coal Mines' (2020) 37 *Environmental and Planning Law Journal* 67.

[63] Judgment, para [516]. Professor Will Steffen, providing evidence for Groundswell Gloucester, summarised the issue as follows: 'global greenhouse gas emissions are made up of millions, and probably hundreds of millions of individual emissions around the globe. All emissions are important because cumulatively they constitute the global total of greenhouse gas emissions'. Steffen, quoted in ibid para [450].

[64] *Gray v Minister for Planning* [2006] NSWLEC 720, para [98].

to the problem. Preston CJ opined that: 'It matters not that this aggregate of the Project's GHG emissions may represent a small fraction of the global total of GHG emissions. The global problem of climate change needs to be addressed by multiple local actions to mitigate emissions by sources and remove GHGs by sinks.'[65] Professor Will Steffen summed the matter up concisely in his evidence as follows: 'Just as many emitters are contributing to the problem, so many emission reduction activities are required to solve the problem.'[66] The straightforward and lucid application of logic by the Court in addressing these issues can serve as a model to other courts in other jurisdictions where such matters arise in the context of climate litigation.[67]

The Dutch case *Urgenda*[68] and the influential Supreme Court of the United States case *Massachusetts v Environmental Protection Agency* (2007)[69] were both acknowledged by the Court.[70] The US courts' broader treatment of projects and decisions in the context of environmental impacts was also considered in some detail.[71] This US case law, which is sensitive to downstream and upstream emissions and impacts, appears to have had a degree of persuasive influence on the Court.[72] This underscores an increasing global sensitivity within internal national court systems to prominent climate law judgments arising externally in other countries. Courts in one country looking to those of another for some degree of reference, or even a degree of guidance, is nothing new in itself, but it appears to be a particularly prevalent feature of climate law. Given the global and shared nature of the climate change challenge, it seems likely that the character of the problem itself is shaping the law in this regard, encouraging courts towards a more pronounced degree of inter-referentiality.[73]

It is also notable that the judgment integrated influential consideration of the notion of *ecologically sustainable development* (ESD). Although this

[65] Judgment, para [515].

[66] ibid.

[67] Elsewhere, Preston CJ has noted in relation to this form of argument as follows: 'While courts have been mixed in their response to this argument, both before and after the Paris Agreement came into force, it will become increasingly difficult for courts to accept that the individual emissions of an entity are inconsequential when the Paris Agreement recognises that climate change mitigation is a global responsibility requiring "the engagements of all levels of government and various actors". See Brian J Preston, 'The Influence of the Paris Agreement on Climate Litigation: Legal obligations and Norms (Part I)' (2021) 33(1) *Journal of Environmental Law* 1–32, 15.

[68] See, eg, Judgment, para [539].

[69] *Massachusetts v Environmental Protection Agency* (2007) 127S Ct 1438.

[70] Judgment, para [519].

[71] See ibid paras [504]–[512].

[72] See ibid.

[73] See further the consideration in scholarly print of interjurisdictional judicial dialogue by Preston CJ, the judge who ruled on this case: Brian J Preston, 'The Influence of the Paris Agreement on Climate Litigation: Causation, Corporate Governance and Catalyst (Part II)' (2021) 33(2) *Journal of Environmental Law* 227; Brian J Preston, 'Changing Climate Law and Governance: A Multi-level Perspective' (2023) *Global Policy* 1. See also the analysis of the characteristics of climate law in ch 1 of this volume.

term is constructed as a singular compound noun, it is applied linguistically in the case as a plural: 'the *principles* of ecologically sustainable development (ESD)' (emphasis added).[74] The Court noted the presence and relevance of ESD within the applicable State Environmental Planning Policy (Mining, Petroleum Production and Extractive Industries) 2009 and the Gloucester Local Environmental Plan 2010. ESD is connected directly in the ruling to climate change concerns. The planning application to undertake a state significant development of the kind at issue requires the consideration and approval of the consent authority,[75] and a developer is required to submit an Environmental Impact Statement with the application.[76] This statement must address a range of matters, including those required by the consent covering the development's likely impact on the environment and reasons justifying the development, with regard being had to biophysical, economic and social considerations.[77] These include 'the principles of ecologically sustainable development (ESD)'.[78] The Court summarises ESD as follows:

> The principles of ESD are defined to be the precautionary principle, inter-generational equity, conservation of biological diversity and ecological integrity, and improved valuation, pricing and incentive mechanisms … [C]onsideration of the principles of ESD can involve consideration of climate change.[79]

This affirmed that ESD fell to be considered, and that this can incorporate climate change issues, underscoring in the Court's view the pertinence of taking upstream and downstream emissions into account.

A tendency to discuss and treat 'greenhouse gas emissions' as one composite or uniform entity often predominates in legal discourse, but these gases are certainly not always conceived of in this way within climate law. For example, legal reasoning or assessment may hone in on one particular gas, such as carbon dioxide (CO_2), the most abundant greenhouse gas being tackled under the major international climate frameworks, or methane (CH_4),[80] another particularly prominent and problematic gas. Another way to conceptualise greenhouse gas emissions that has become prevalent, which has been driven by the categorisation of emissions for businesses and organisations, pertains to the 'scope' of emissions. Here, emissions are typically divided into Scope 1, Scope 2 and Scope 3 emissions. The World Economic Forum summarises that 'Scope 1 emissions … are "direct"

[74] Judgment, para [488].

[75] Environmental Planning and Assessment Act 1979 (NSW), s 4.38(1).

[76] Environmental Planning and Assessment Act 1979 (NSW), s 4.12(1) and 4.39(1)(a); Environmental Planning and Assessment Regulation 2000 (NSW), cl 50(1)(a), sch 1, cl 2(1)(e).

[77] Judgment, para [488]; Environmental Planning and Assessment Regulation 2000 (NSW) sch 1, cl 7.

[78] Judgment, para [488].

[79] ibid.

[80] See, eg, Northern Ireland's Climate Change Act, which regulates methane, but treats it differently from other regulated greenhouse gases: Climate Change Act (Northern Ireland) 2022, s 1(3).

emissions – those that a company causes by operating the things that it owns or controls'.[81] Scope 2 emissions are 'indirect' emissions created by the production of the energy that an organisation buys.[82] Scope 3 emissions are also indirect emissions – meaning emissions not produced by the company itself – but they differ from Scope 2 as they cover emissions produced by customers using the company's products and emissions produced by suppliers making products that the company uses.[83] This is of significance in this case because Scope 1–3 emissions were raised and addressed by the Court.

As the World Economic Forum summary that has just been quoted makes clear, Scope 1–3 emissions are also construed as 'direct' and 'indirect' emissions. Scope 1 emissions are direct emissions, and Scope 2 and 3 emissions are indirect emissions. In summary, the Court's understanding of direct/indirect and Scope emissions is as follows:

> Direct Emissions: Scope 1
>
> 'Direct GHG emissions are emissions that occur from sources that are owned or controlled by the reporting entity.'[84]
>
> Indirect Emissions: Scope 2
>
> 'Indirect GHG emissions are emissions from the generation of purchased energy products (principally electricity) by the entity (referred to as Scope 2 emissions) … Scope 2 emissions physically occur outside the boundary of the coal mine, such as at the power station that generates the electricity that is purchased. These are "upstream" indirect emissions.'[85]
>
> Indirect Emissions: Scope 3
>
> 'Other indirect GHG emissions are emissions that are a consequence of the activities of an entity, but which arise from sources not owned or controlled by that entity (referred to as Scope 3 emissions).'[86] This includes, amongst other things, the 'combustion of product coals'.[87] Such emissions are '"downstream" emissions as they physically occur at the power stations or steel mills combusting product coal from the mine.'[88]

In the amended Environmental Impact Statement, GRL had provided a greenhouse gas assessment that included Scope 1 and Scope 2 emissions, but that did not provide complete coverage for Scope 3.[89] The Court highlighted the incomplete treatment of Scope 3, while acknowledging some degree of rationale for the omission: 'emissions from the shipping of product coal were not included due to

[81] World Economic Forum, 'What is the Difference between Scope 1, 2 and 3 Emissions, and What are Companies Doing to Cut All Three?', 20 September 2022, https://www.weforum.org/agenda/2022/09/scope-emissions-climate-greenhouse-business.
[82] ibid.
[83] ibid.
[84] Judgment, para [425].
[85] ibid para [427].
[86] ibid para [428].
[87] ibid.
[88] ibid.
[89] ibid para [486].

the uncertainties in emission estimates, including in future export destinations and limited data on emission factors and/or fuel consumption for ocean going vessels'.[90] GRL argued that the Court should not consider Scope 3 emissions in determining the application. In doing so, it advanced an interesting argument based on the UNFCCC and the Paris Agreement. Here, it submitted that the terms of these international agreements made it clear that signatory states were required to account for emissions in their own countries and not in other countries, whereas the effect of Scope 3 emissions in this application would be to compel emissions in other countries to be accounted for.[91]

The Court was not persuaded by this, which is unsurprising given that relevant Australian law and policy required decision makers to take account of both direct and indirect emissions in considering consent applications.[92] Here, one finds testament to the characteristic weakness of international climate law, with comparative strength resting with the relevant national/domestic legal order at issue. Interestingly, if one accepts GRL's argument (which, like the Court, the author does not),[93] in this instance domestic planning law and policy has been used to correct a point of international climate law that would weaken climate governance in practice rather than strengthen it. The Court reinforced its view on the basis that a consent authority was required to consider the public interest, which has been held in New South Wales to incorporate the principles inherent in ESD.[94] As noted above, these principles include the precautionary principle and principle of intergenerational equity, which have been 'held to require consideration of the impact of a development on climate change and the impact of climate change on a development'.[95] Thus, the Court determined that indirect downstream emissions were a relevant consideration in relation to this type of application, where fossil fuel is at issue, and held that Scope 3 as well as Scope 1 and 2 emissions justified consideration.[96]

[90] ibid para [430].

[91] ibid para [453].

[92] Dehm has summed up the previous treatment of this issue in the Australian case law as follows: 'litigation in various jurisdictions prior to Rocky Hill had already succeeded in demonstrating that Scope 3 emissions are a relevant consideration under environmental and planning laws. However, the key challenge remained showing that the environmental impact of the project was so significant that the grant of approval for the project should be affected'. See Dehm (n 57) 255.

[93] The argument should be rejected, given that the international regime does not expressly prohibit a signatory from calculating Scope 3 emissions and factoring those calculations into some aspect of domestic law or policy should it choose to do so.

[94] Judgment, para [498].

[95] ibid.

[96] Following *Gloucester Resources*, the Court has provided further helpful consideration of the meaning and conceptualisation of 'greenhouse gases' in the context of climate litigation; see *Mullaley Gas and Pipeline Accord Inc v Santos NSW (Eastern) Pty Ltd* [2021] NSWLEC 110. This includes consideration of Scope 1–3 emissions (see further the discussion of 'greenhouse gases' at ibid paras [98]–[101]). The jurisprudence suggests that where conditions are imposed on a development project consent application by the relevant decision maker, those conditions may potentially include the imposition of a requirement for emissions offsets where exceedances of acceptable Scope 1 and Scope 2 emissions arise

C. The International Climate Law Regime

Elements of the international climate law regime have been considered above, but further points of note remain. Upon introducing the importance of the Paris Agreement and quoting Article 4.1 at some length,[97] the judgment stresses the interconnection between the Agreement and the UNFCCC, emphasising Australia's Nationally Determined Contributions (NDCs) commitments under the international regime:

> Australia is a party to both the Climate Change Convention and the Paris Agreement. Under the Paris Agreement, each party commits to make its contribution to keeping the global average temperature rise to the 1.5–2°C range by reducing their GHG emissions through their Nationally Determined Contributions (NDC). Australia's NDC is to reduce GHG emissions by 26–28% below 2005 levels by 2030. The NSW Government has endorsed the Paris Agreement and has set a more ambitious objective to achieve net zero emissions by 2050 (see NSW Climate Change Policy Framework, October 2016, pp 4, 5).[98]

In returning to the *Climate Change Policy Framework*[99] referred to in this quotation later on in the judgment and acknowledging its Net Zero commitment, Preston CJ notes that: 'It is true that the Paris Agreement, Australia's NDC of reducing GHG emissions in Australia by 26 to 28% below 2005 levels by 2030 or NSW's Climate Change Policy Framework do not prescribe the mechanisms by which these reductions in GHG emissions to achieve zero net emissions by 2050 are to occur.'[100] This includes 'no proscription on approval of new sources of GHG emissions, such as new coal mines'.[101] In essence, this renders the Paris Agreement a treaty that assists in framing the issues, and that, in the Court's view, indicates that an unavoidable downward pressure on fossil fuel emissions is required to an extent that means the Court can bring the Agreement to bear on the issues as an influential consideration.[102] All of this is important, but it also highlights the sharp limits in legal terms to the Paris Agreement's influence on the narrow decision to approve the specific coal mine or not.

from the project. It also suggests that it will not be unreasonable to *exclude* the imposition of equivalent Scope 3 emissions offsets where such indirect downstream emissions are wholly outside the direct control of the development project. Here, the Court opined that: 'This question of the degree of control of the proponent over the indirect emissions is an evaluative one to be answered by the consent authority on the particular facts and circumstances of the development, the proponent of the development, and the suppliers or end users concerned'; ibid para [107].

[97] Judgment, para [439].

[98] ibid para [440]. Note that in 2022, Australia submitted a strengthened NDC that commits to reducing GHG emissions by 43 per cent below 2005 levels by 2030: Australian Government Department of Industry, Science, Energy and Resources, *Australia's Nationally Determined Contribution Communication 2022*.

[99] Office of Environment and Heritage, *NSW Climate Change Policy Framework* (Australia, 2016).

[100] Judgment, para [526].

[101] ibid para [527].

[102] See, eg, ibid.

Nonetheless, and as noted, the Paris Agreement and the UNFCCC do appear in the judgment as overt legal influences. The Court draws on Article 4(4) of the Paris Agreement to emphasise that '[d]eveloped countries such as Australia have a responsibility, including under the Climate Change Convention, the Kyoto Protocol and the Paris Agreement, to take the lead in taking mitigation measures to reduce GHG emissions'.[103] Article 4(1) and Article 2 of the Paris Agreement are referenced to stress the need to balance anthropogenic emissions by sources and removal by sinks in the second half of this century in order to hold the increase in global average temperature to well below 2°C above pre-industrial levels.[104] Article 4(3) is also drawn on to stress that each State's successive NDCs framework is to reflect its highest possible ambition.[105] Parties to the Agreement are required to produce NDCs 'that they intend to achieve and [are required] to pursue domestic mitigation measures with the aim of achieving the objectives of such contributions',[106] and successive NDCs should reflect the country's 'highest possible ambition, reflecting its common but differentiated responsibilities and respective capabilities, in the light of different national circumstances'.[107] Given, then, that Australia has subscribed to the Paris Agreement, the Court found it significant that the type of coal mining project at issue is 'likely to run counter to the actions that are required' to bring down global emissions under the treaty.[108]

D. The 'Global Carbon Budget'

It is also notable that the Court displayed a sensitivity to the notion of a *global carbon budget*. The judgment elaborates on this concept that: 'The approach is based on the approximately linear relationship between the cumulative amount of CO_2 emitted from all human sources since the beginning of industrialisation (often taken as 1870) and the increase in global average surface temperature'.[109] It continues: 'Once the carbon budget has been spent (emitted), emissions need to become "net zero" to avoid exceeding the temperature target'.[110] Here, and in relation to the global carbon budget concept generally, the Court relied significantly on the evidence of Professor Will Steffen, a distinguished earth systems scientist and Emeritus Professor at the Australian National University, who recommended the global carbon budget perspective to the Court upon being invited to give evidence by Groundswell Gloucester.[111] The concept underscores the sense

[103] ibid para [539]; Paris Agreement, art 4(4).
[104] Judgment, para [539]; Paris Agreement, arts 4(1), 2.
[105] Judgment, para [539]; Paris Agreement, art 4(3).
[106] Paris Agreement, art 4.2; Judgment, para [539].
[107] Paris Agreement, art 4.3. Judgment, para [539].
[108] Judgment, para [526].
[109] Judgment, para [441].
[110] ibid.
[111] See ibid paras [440]–[450].

of causality between the greenhouse gas increases that would arise from the mine project and negative climate impacts. It also highlights how leaving less fossil fuel in the ground (ie, approving the application) militates against remaining within the global carbon budget and achieving the long-term goal of keeping average global temperatures between 1.5°C and 2°C above pre-industrial levels.[112]

As noted earlier, the Court found that every new source of greenhouse gas emissions contributes to climate change, which reduces the available carbon budget. Unless there is a ban on any new source of greenhouse gas emissions, such as new fossil fuel mining or extraction, a decision will need to be made as to which new fossil fuel project can be approved and still stay within the available carbon budget. In *Gloucester Resources*, the Court needed to decide whether the particular new coal mine could and should be approved. To assist in deciding this, the Court proposed an approach of considering the greenhouse gas emissions of the project in absolute and relative terms.[113] It explained this approach as follows:

> I consider the better approach is to evaluate the merits of the particular fossil fuel development that is the subject of the development application to be determined. Should this fossil fuel development be approved or refused? Answering this question involves consideration of the GHG emissions of the development and their likely contribution to climate change and its consequences, as well as the other impacts of the development. The consideration can be in absolute terms or relative terms.
>
> In absolute terms, a particular fossil fuel development may itself be a sufficiently large source of GHG emissions that refusal of the development could be seen to make a meaningful contribution to remaining within the carbon budget and achieving the long term temperature goal. In short, refusing larger fossil fuel developments prevents greater increases in GHG emissions than refusing smaller fossil fuel developments.
>
> In relative terms, similar size fossil fuel developments, with similar GHG emissions, may have different environmental, social and economic impacts.[114]

In the case of this project, the Court considered the climate and environmental impacts of the project in relative terms.[115]

Dehm has linked the incorporation of the global carbon budget perspective to human rights considerations and has advanced the following:

> I suggest that by endorsing the concept of a global 'carbon budget' – alongside the rejection of the 'market substitution' defense – this judgment arguably provides an important building block that might support the eventual acceptance of further legal arguments that new fossil fuel developments should be refused due to the human rights impacts of climate change.[116]

[112] See, eg, ibid para [550].
[113] ibid para [553].
[114] ibid paras [553]–[555].
[115] ibid para [556].
[116] Dehm (n 57) 248.

This vision has ethical appeal, but it seems speculative in terms of technical law in the absence of Dehm pointing carefully to legal authority that bridges the notion of a global carbon budget and human rights law in the domestic Australian legal order.[117] Regardless, Dehm persuasively notes in relation to Preston CJ's rejection of *market substitution* and associated matters that 'the take up of his reasoning by other courts and other jurisdictions could have a transformative effect on climate litigation around coal developments in Australia'.[118]

Hughes, a climate scientist, has commented on the Court's recognition of a global carbon budget as follows:

> By placing an understanding of the rapidly dwindling carbon budget at the core of the argument against the mine, it would seem that the law, at least in this case, has caught up with the scientific understanding of global climate change. Emissions from fossil fuels, and the impacts they cause, do not respect country or jurisdictional boundaries – a notion that would be obvious to anyone with the [*sic*] only the barest understanding of this global issue. As such, it seems extraordinary that this is the first case in Australia, and one of only a handful in the world, in which this simple fact has been at the core of a legal judgment.[119]

It is not in fact uncommon for landmark climate law judgments to acknowledge the global nature of the problem, and other cases do acknowledge carbon budgets,[120] but the particular global carbon budget discussion in this case may offer a useful frame for other courts to draw on in going forward.

E. Additional Issues

This book is focused on, and interested in, climate law. However, in addition to the climate-focused points arising above, which comprise a major component of the judgment, the court also dealt with other issues and points of law. These elements will be discussed briefly in this section. It is possible to view these components as being to a significant extent distinct from the climate-focused elements above, but certain features overlap or intersect with climate issues in a clear way (eg, the notion of 'social impact', discussed below); therefore, they can also be viewed as co-connected. More broadly, the totality of the case's legal elements form the cumulative substance of *Gloucester Resources*, and it is probably unwise to excise the issue of 'climate change' from the broader context it is enmeshed in, as if it is a

[117] Dehm notes that 'the Rocky Hill decision did not develop a human rights analysis of the proposed coal mine or draw a direct connection between the climate change implications of the project and human rights impacts' in law; ibid. For an ultimately unsuccessful attempt to link human rights and climate change at the Federal Court of Australia, see *Minister for the Environment v Sharma* [2022] FCAFC 35.

[118] Dehm (n 57) 265.

[119] Hughes (n 10) 351.

[120] For example, see paras [6], [45]–[47] etc in *R (on the Application of Friends of the Earth Ltd and Others) v Heathrow Airport Ltd* [2020] UKSC 52. See also ch 3 in this volume.

matter that can purely stand alone. Where a climate lawyer does this, it can seem much like a doctor excising the heart from the human body to observe how it functions in isolation; the heart must be interconnected with the broader human form, or else it stops beating. So too when major elements of climate law sit at the heart of a landmark court judgment like this one.

It has been seen that the Court found against authorisation of the coal mine development due to its projected climate impacts. In addition, it also found against the application due to the broader environmental and social costs of establishing the mine in the proposed area. In working towards these conclusions, the concept of *public interest* received prominent consideration. The Environmental Planning and Assessment Act 1979[121] requires the public interest to be taken into account as part of the planning consent decision process. This was a significant feature in the Court's reasoning across a range of social and environmental issues, and including climate change. The Court found that the project would not be in the public interest, in part because, in weighing the costs and benefits, the Court allowed for consideration of the projected impact of direct and indirect greenhouse gas emissions on climate change. Taking this element broadly, Preston CJ found that:

> [T]he negative impacts of the Project, including the planning impacts on the existing, approved and likely preferred land uses, the visual impacts, the amenity impacts of noise and dust that cause social impacts, other social impacts, and climate change impacts, outweigh the economic and other public benefits of the Project.[122]

In following the state's social impact assessment guideline for large-scale petroleum and extractive industry projects, the Court addressed the proposed project's impact across a number of socio-cultural indicators:

- way of life;
- community;
- access to and use of infrastructure, services and facilities;
- culture;
- health and well-being;
- surroundings;
- personal and property rights;
- decision making systems;
- fears and aspirations.[123]

In addition to being discrete categories, the Court acknowledged that these fields can be subject to overlap and interconnection.[124] It found the mining company's

[121] Environmental Planning and Assessment Act 1979 (NSW), s 5.15(1).
[122] Judgment, para [688].
[123] ibid para [270].
[124] ibid para [271].

social impact assessment to be a relatively poor piece of work,[125] and therefore a somewhat misleading one.

Australia has an Aboriginal population with a very rich culture and history, and it is notable that the Court found that the mining company had failed to engage adequately with the project's potential impacts on Aboriginal people.[126] It was clear to the Court that the project would impact identified Aboriginal sites, and that it would probably impact unidentified sites that had not been caught by an incomplete survey process.[127] Submissions to the Court also made interesting reference to so-called 'solastalgia', a concept emerging from environmental philosophy that was established in 2005, pertaining to a sense of place-based distress that people can experience as a consequence of environmental change.[128] The Court's recognition of this concept has been explored by Brown et al,[129] and it stands as an interesting example of a court judgment exhibiting sensitivity to emerging eco-philosophical thinking.[130]

The Court also found that '[p]eople who value living, working and playing in a clean and green environment may leave the Gloucester area, adversely affecting the local community and economy'[131] due to physical and mental health impacts arising from particulate, noise and light pollution if the project was undertaken. In its reasoning, the Court placed some significant emphasis on 'people's way of life, community' and factors representing local scales of concern that environmental public participation theory suggests should be a necessary feature of adequate decision-making processes.[132]

It is also notable that the Court accorded a significant focus in its social impacts reasoning to *distributive inequity*, a notion prevalent in legal social scientific research and scholarship.[133] The Court summarised that '[d]istributive justice concerns the just distribution of environmental benefits and environmental burdens of economic activity'.[134] It also drew on the established principles of intragenerational equity and intergenerational equity in this setting.[135]

[125] ibid para [323].

[126] White has emphasised that 'the Project group (Rio Tinto Warkworth), when undertaking the Social Impact Assessment as part of the Environmental Impact Assessment, did not appear to have included specific consultations with Aboriginal people or Aboriginal organizations'. White (n 7) 548.

[127] Judgment, para [345].

[128] Glenn Albrecht, '"Solastalgia": A New Concept in Health and Identity' (2005) 3 *PAN: Philosophy Activism Nature* 41–55.

[129] Jasper Brown et al, 'Solastalgia: Recognition by the Land and Environment Court of the Social Impacts of Fossil Fuel Developments' (2021) 38(4) *Environmental and Planning Law Journal* 295–314.

[130] For a very prominent example of eco-philosophical thinking, see the jurisprudence of the Supreme Court of Justice of Colombia discussed in ch 4 in this volume.

[131] Judgment, para [367].

[132] Benjamin J Richardson and Jona Razzaque, 'Public Participation in Environmental Decision-Making' in Benjamin J Richardson and Stepan Wood (eds), *Environmental Law for Sustainability* (Hart Publishing, 2006), 165–94.

[133] Judgment, 'Distributive Inequity of the Project', paras [398]–[416].

[134] ibid para [398].

[135] See ibid paras [389]–[416].

On intragenerational equity, which concerns fairness and justice across people, communities and actors within a generation, the Court's consideration of the proposed development in this context clarified that '[t]he people who benefit are likely to live sufficiently geographically distant from the Project so as not to be affected, or to be less affected, by the physical impacts of the Project'.[136] On intergenerational equity, concerning inequity in the distribution between current and future generations, the Court reasoned that:

> The economic and social benefits of the Project will last only for the life of the Project (less than two decades), but the environmental, social and economic burdens of the Project will endure not only for the life of the Project but some will continue for long after.[137]

This includes the fact that 'the Project will emit greenhouse gases and contribute to climate change, the consequences of which will burden future generations'.[138] Therefore: 'The benefits of the Project are … distributed to the current generation but the burdens are distributed to the current as well as future generations (intergenerational inequity).'[139]

Over the course of his considerations concerning the projected social impacts of the mine, Preston CJ reached a range of important conclusions on the evidence, including as follows: 'I find that the Project will affect adversely the social composition of the community and the current rural town atmosphere';[140] 'I have explored, and have found substantiated, the residents' concerns about the Project's impacts on people's way of life, community, culture, and health and wellbeing'.[141] Thus, after a thorough consideration of the evidence before the Court relating to the categories noted above and interpreted in concert with relevant guidelines, Preston CJ held that: 'The Rocky Hill Coal Project will cause a variety of negative social impacts, many of which are likely to have a high or extreme social risk rating.'[142]

The Court concluded that the 'significant net negative social impacts are a justification for refusing consent to the Project'.[143] It is clear that even if the climate change impacts of the proposed development were not factored in, the mining company would have remained unsuccessful in its appeal. It is notable, however, that in an instance where a similar case might arise involving an application that *does not* seem to be prohibitive on explicit grounds of social impact (bearing in mind that the Minister for Planning did not incorporate climate issues into his

[136] ibid para [413].
[137] ibid para [415].
[138] ibid. See further the consideration of this issue section IV.B in ch 4 of this volume.
[139] Judgment, para [416]. For a helpful consideration of the Court's approach to intergenerational issues in the context of other coal mine approval decisions that are also sensitive to the issue, see Edward Cleary, 'Judicial Consideration of Intergenerational Equity in Australian Coal Mine Approval Litigation' (2021) 38(3) *Environmental and Planning Law Journal* 3.
[140] Judgment, para [309].
[141] ibid para [371].
[142] ibid paras [557–[685].
[143] ibid para [421].

rejection of this application prior to the appeal), where this circumstance is interpreted in the light of *Gloucester Resources*, it does not necessarily mean that the consent would be permissible. *Gloucester Resources* indicates that the application would also need to be tested on climate change grounds, in conjunction with all other salient issues, and satisfy the decision maker that negative climate impacts do not create conditions prohibitive of the consent being granted.[144]

In a related but distinct line of reasoning, the Court also addressed the 'economic and public benefits' of the mine.[145] This included consideration of anticipated public benefits of the proposed project in relation to whether the project's benefits outweigh its costs to the members of the relevant community and whether the project's public benefits outweigh the public benefits of other land uses.[146] The notion of *distributive inequity* discussed above was also returned to in the context of the Court's economic considerations, in order to assist in conceptualising the balance of costs and benefits.[147] In relation to public benefits of the proposed project and the existing, approved and likely future uses of land in the vicinity, the Court noted that at present, '[t]hese uses undoubtedly yield public benefits, including economic benefits. The Project will impact on these uses'.[148] It found that 'the Project will have a significant impact on the likely preferred uses and will be incompatible with the existing, approved and likely preferred uses'.[149] Thus, the project would 'adversely affect the public benefits' of these uses.[150] Beyond this, '[t]here was no other economic assessment of other uses of land in the vicinity of the Project in order to quantify the public benefits of the other land uses'.[151] Therefore, 'it is not possible on the evidence to evaluate and compare quantitatively the respective public benefits of the Project and the other land uses'.[152]

The Court also considered a Cost Benefit Analysis and a Local Effects Analysis that had been provided by GRL as part of its Environmental Impact Statement submission. It found that the Cost Benefit Analysis significantly overstated the project's benefits while appearing to significantly understate '[e]nvironmental, social and transport related costs',[153] and that the second analysis was similarly 'unreliable and unhelpful'.[154] Relatedly, Preston CJ found that the 'economic benefits of the Project' presented in key information to the Court were 'uncertain and

[144] For further consideration of the social impacts dimension of the case, see the section entitled 'The Court's Unprecedented Decision on Social Impacts of the Mine' in Elena Aydos et al, 'Rocky Hill: A Legal Breakthrough in the Consideration of Climate Change and Social Impacts of Coal Mines' (2020) 98 *Climate and Carbon Law Review* 98–106, 103–05.
[145] Judgment, para [417].
[146] ibid para [557].
[147] See further ibid para [669].
[148] ibid para [685].
[149] ibid.
[150] ibid.
[151] Judgment, para [684].
[152] ibid.
[153] ibid para [655].
[154] ibid para [681].

in any event substantially overstated'.[155] He opined that: 'Environmental, social and transport related costs are likely to be greater than the low values assigned … but these cannot be quantified on the evidence.'[156] Overall, the Court determined on the evidence that direct and indirect benefits were relatively small, while indirect costs were relatively high, thus undercutting the economic benefit of the project: 'The consequence of the significantly smaller direct and indirect benefits and the greater indirect costs will be a significantly reduced net economic benefit of the Project.'[157]

III. Concluding Thoughts

This case centred on an attempt to introduce a new open cut coal mine that was projected to produce 21 million tonnes of coal over 16 years, which is no small issue given that the Intergovernmental Panel on Climate Change's scientific work has long been evidencing that a rapid phase-out of coal is necessary to keep the global community within the parameters of the Paris Agreement.[158] The Court was required to determine the planning application on its merits. In being required to rule on the substantive aspects of the application, the Court is quite far from a *Heathrow Runway Case*-type scenario, where the UK Supreme Court was required to consider procedural rather than substantive issues.[159] The question of the UK Government's substantive support for the expansion of runway capacity at Heathrow Airport was a matter for the UK Government itself, and thus was not at issue in that case, with the UK Supreme Court addressing matters of procedure instead. More generally, *Gloucester Resources* is rather nuanced when read against the other cases in this volume, insofar as the Court was exercising a consent review capacity in the context of an appeal against the Minister for Planning's consent refusal, which was in some respects analogous to the Minister's own initial consent powers. Again, this imbues the case with a very particular character.

In terms of climate change itself, the State Environmental Planning Policy (Mining, Petroleum Production and Extractive Industries) 2009 and the Gloucester Local Environmental Plan 2010 were applicable. It is notable that the former framework does require consideration of Scope 3 emissions,[160] and the latter requires recognition of the 'cumulative impacts' of climate change,[161]

[155] ibid para [664].
[156] ibid para [665].
[157] ibid para [666].
[158] Paola A Yanguas Parra, Gaurav Ganti, Robert Brecha, Bill Hare, Michiel Schaeffer, Ursula Fuentes and Andreas Geiges, *Global and Regional Coal Phase out Requirements of the Paris Agreement: Insights from the IPCC Special Report on 1.5°C* (Climate Analytics, 2019).
[159] See ch 2 in this volume.
[160] State Environmental Planning Policy (Mining, Petroleum Production and Extractive Industries) 2009, cl 14(2); Judgment, para [492].
[161] Gloucester Local Environmental Plan 2010, cl 1.2(2)(d).

to which direct and indirect project emissions contribute. Australian case law has clarified that 'impact' includes both direct and indirect effects of a relevant action.[162] The Court as the consent authority also needed to consider the public interest,[163] which the New South Wales courts have held to include ESD;[164] the courts have held that this concept incorporates consideration of climate change impacts in the context of development applications.[165] Thus, on general reflection, it seems to make perfect legal sense that climate change *would* be at the heart of a case like this.

Viewed in the light of applicable law and policy, then, the judgment is sensible and logical. Moreover, it appears to offer something of a corrective to the decision that was initially issued by the Minister for Planning, by his delegate, the Commission, which was under appeal before the Court. The Minister had neglected to factor climate change considerations into his decision, and the Court's approach served to correct for this by building these neglected considerations into the decision-making process on appeal after they were raised by Groundswell Gloucester. Thus, climate change has been injected as a crucial consideration at the appeal stage, providing an example of a court actively assisting in integrating and expanding climate change considerations in a rational and impactful manner. Indeed, it is also notable that the Court went beyond merely integrating climate change as a consideration; it determined that it was a *very important* consideration. It was not a light-touch feature introduced as a background issue. Given the applicable legal and policy considerations, in combination with the current condition of scientific knowledge concerning the scale of the problem, climate change formed a major component of the judgment.

A notable point that should not be lost due to the complexity of the case and the important influence of climate issues on the Court's reasoning is as follows: the Court did *not* apply a stand-alone refusal to the project on climate grounds. If the Court had done so, this could amount to a policy-style ruling, potentially signalling that all applications to develop state significant installations that would increase fossil fuel emissions significantly should be refused. This was not the case. Thus, Preston CJ asserted as follows:

> Refusal of consent to the Project would prevent a meaningful amount of GHG emissions, although not the greater GHG emissions that would come from refusal of a larger coal mine. However, the better reason for refusal is the Project's poor environmental and social performance in relative terms. As I have found elsewhere in the judgment, the Project will have significant and unacceptable planning, visual and social

[162] *Minister for Environment and Heritage v Queensland Conservation Council* (2004) 139 FCR 24.
[163] Environmental Planning and Assessment Act 1979 (NSW), s 4.15(1)(e).
[164] *Telstra v Hornsby Shire Council* (2006) 67 NSWLR 256; *Minister for Planning v Walker* (2008) 161 LGERA 423.
[165] *Gray v Minister for Planning* (2006) 152 LGERA 258; *Taralga Landscape Guardians Inc v Minister for Planning and RES Southern Cross Pty Ltd* (2007) 161 LGERA 1; *Aldous v Greater Taree City Council* (2009) 167 LGERA 13; *Hunter Environment Lobby Inc v Minister for Planning* [2011] NSWLEC 221.

> impacts, which cannot be satisfactorily mitigated. *The Project should be refused for these reasons alone. The GHG emissions of the Project and their likely contribution to adverse impacts on the climate system, environment and people adds a further reason for refusal.* (Emphasis added)[166]

Thus, climate change is one determinative factor amongst a range of factors. It is a very important factor – receiving more detailed treatment in the judgment than any other individual issue – but it is clear that the Court would have refused the application even if climate change considerations had not been deemed relevant.

The judgment is certainly a landmark case in climate law, but is the ruling actually radical? The UK Supreme Court *Heathrow Runway Case*[167] may appear radical on the face of it, but careful analysis of the law at issue indicates that it was not in fact a radical ruling.[168] The same can be said for this case.[169] White and others have commented that:

> [T]he judgment is not radical, being firmly grounded in established principles of planning and environmental law. Preston CJ's finding that the climate change impacts justified the refusal of the proposed mine was part of a broader consideration of the environmental impacts of the mine, a factor his Honour was legally bound to consider.[170]

In addition, measurement of the impact of the case, and cases like it, must also be kept in perspective. For example, a previous important and environmentally oriented judgment delivered by the Court in the *Bulga Mine* case involved an application for a mining permit extension by a large mining company.[171] Here, the relevant Minister had approved the extension. The matter was appealed on grounds relating to negative ecological and social impact and the appeal was upheld, but the Government ultimately managed to facilitate the extension anyway.[172] It is notable that the decisions of the Minister and the Court were at odds in the *Bulga Mine* case (approval-rejection), whereas in *Gloucester Resources* they both refused the development (rejection-rejection).

In terms of the broader weight to be accorded to the ruling itself in technical law, academic lawyer Bell-James has commented that 'Preston's reasoning … should

[166] Judgment, para [556].

[167] *R (on the Application of Friends of the Earth Ltd and Others) v Heathrow Airport Ltd* [2020] UKSC 52.

[168] See ch 2 in this volume.

[169] While the Court's technical application of the law might not be radical, one might seek to distinguish the application of law from the case's broader implications and suggest that the implications themselves are radical, as evoked by Aravind's title in her blog discussion: Sakshi Aravind, 'Gloucester Resources and its Radical Implications for Indigenous Environmental Justice', *Oxford Human Rights Blog*, 18 March 2019, https://ohrh.law.ox.ac.uk/gloucester-resources-and-its-radical-implications-for-indigenous-environmental-justice.

[170] White et al (n 6).

[171] *Bulga Milbrodale Progress Association Inc v Minister for Planning and Infrastructure and Warkworth Mining Limited* [2013] NSWLEC 48.

[172] See further, Amanda Kennedy, 'The Bulga Case Study' in *Environmental Justice and Land Use Conflict: The Governance of Mineral and Gas Resource Development* (Routledge, 2017).

be a highly persuasive precedent',[173] but one must be careful here, as the case does not form a precedent in the technical legal sense, ie, as a ruling binding on subsequent decisions of the courts. The ruling does not preclude mining projects in general. As a spokesman for NSW Minister for Planning Anthony Roberts noted, this type of decision is made 'on a case-by-case basis',[174] and taken narrowly the case, which is a merits appeal, does not form a precedent in the conventional common law sense of the term. However, speaking to the *Sunday Morning Herald*, lawyer Rosemary Lyster has also pointed out the following:

> 'If other cases come before the same tribunal to challenge a decision to allow or not allow a coal mine by way of a merits appeal, the reasoning could go the same way', she said. It could also influence other tribunals or courts in the future, Lyster added.[175]

Similarly, Don C Smith, the editor of the *Journal of Energy and Natural Resources Law*, reminded readers in a lead editorial shortly after the ruling that:

> [T]he groundbreaking – indeed revolutionary – consequence of Preston's decision should not be downplayed. Emeritus Professor Ben Boer of the University of Sydney pointed out that Preston's court is 'a superior court of record on the same level as the Supreme Court of [New South Wales]' [*sic*]. In addition, Boer suggested that perhaps the most important aspect of the decision is that: 'It sets out a whole new line of legal reasoning in this area, which will be studied by climate change litigators around the world.'[176]

Indeed, there is no doubt that *Gloucester Resources* has exerted some positive influence in encouraging greater environmental sensitivity and weighting in particular planning decisions.[177]

Beyond the narrow realm of technical law, Hasler suggests that the case can be understood as one that 'highlights the importance of leaving coal in the ground'.[178] Similarly, White has observed that a particular merit of the judgment that transcends the technical parameters of the narrow case is that it has 'provided a detailed rationale as to why climate change and carbon emissions ought to be included as significant factors in judgments concerning proposed coal mining operations'.[179] Indeed, White has also taken a broader view of the Court itself,

[173] Justine Bell-James, 'Landmark Rocky Hill Ruling Could Pave the Way for More Courts to Choose Climate over Coal', *The Conversation*, 11 February 2019, https://theconversation.com/landmark-rocky-hill-rulingcould-pave-the-way-for-more-courts-to-choose-climate-over-coal-111533.

[174] Hannam (n 20).

[175] James Thornhill, 'Coal's Perfect Storm Hits $70 Billion Australian Projects', *Sydney Morning Herald*, 27 February 2019, www.smh.com.au/business/the-economy/coal-s-perfect-storm-hits-70-billionaustralian-projects-20190227-p510ha.html?cspt=1551349884|970e862223715421d735822af6b975e8.

[176] Don C Smith, 'Editorial: Landmark Climate Change-Related Judicial Decisions Handed Down in the Netherlands and Australia: A Preview of What's to Come?' (2019) 37(2) *Journal of Energy & Natural Resources Law* 145–47, 146.

[177] Aydos et al (n 144) 105–06.

[178] Olivia Hasler, 'Mining as Ecocide: The Case of Adani and the Carmichael Mine in Australia' in Zabyelina and Daan van Uhm (n 7) 497–527, 521.

[179] White (n 7) 554.

suggesting favourably that 'this Court exemplifies ... an ecocentric approach to dealing with environmental matters'.[180] Assessing the detail of general trends in the Court's approach to cases over time is beyond the scope of this chapter,[181] but it is interesting to note that one can endeavour to read a landmark climate law case within the cultural continuum of this type of court tradition. Further study in this area (targeted at this Court or any other court of interest) could usefully form the basis of Doctoral projects or other scholarly work in the field of climate law, namely the investigation of potentially distinguishable persistent court trends that might permit one to identify, for example, embedded ecocentric approaches, which might in turn inform analysis of the emergence of landmark climate litigation rulings within specific court settings in enlightening ways.

White has highlighted that '[r]esource extraction here [in Australia] has a long history and extensive geographical reach. It is also tied to who has the power to do what, where, how cost effectively, and for whose benefit'.[182] Perhaps unsurprisingly, and unfortunately, this environmentally sensitive judgment received substantial public criticism by sections of the political-industrial complex and the right-wing press,[183] in a country where entrenched interests have proven particularly resistant to progressive environmental action in the context of mining.[184] Indeed, White describes a 'Right-Wing Backlash' to the ruling arising in the press, which is unfortunate given that anthropogenic climate change is rooted in objective science, thus transcending the superficialities of right and left-wing politics as an overarching problem relevant to humanity in general.[185] Fankhauser and others have conducted initial empirical research which suggests that legislative responses to climate change from left-wing and right-wing governments have been relatively comparable around the world, with the exception of 'Anglo-Saxon' countries, where left-right politics appear to drive a divergence.[186] If this is the case, care must be taken in going forward where possible to ensure that climate litigation outcomes are not misunderstood in some jurisdictions due to an artificial left-right distortion of an issue (climate change) that is in fact rooted in objective science that transcends such perceived ideological boundaries.

[180] ibid 530.

[181] For rich coverage of the New South Wales Land and Environment Court that includes reference to *Gloucester Resources*, see Ben Boer, 'Transnational Dimensions of the Land and Environment Court of New South Wales' in Elizabeth Fisher and Brian Preston (eds), *An Environmental Court in Action* (Hart Publishing, 2022) 93; Megan Davies, 'The Land and Environment Court of New South Wales and the Recognition of Indigenous Peoples' Environmental Rights' in Fisher and Preston (eds), ibid 175; Jeff Smith, and Sue Higginson, '"Please Come in": Access to Justice and the Development of Jurisprudence in the Land and Environment Court of New South Wales' in Fisher and Preston (eds), ibid 253.

[182] White (n 7) 531.

[183] See further White (ibid) in particular on the 'media mobilizations and political donations that are associated with these powerful economic actors'.

[184] See further Paul Cleary, *Mine-Field: The Dark Side of Australia's Resources Rush* (Black Inc, 2012).

[185] White (n 7) 551–53.

[186] Sam Fankhauser, Caterina Gennaioli and Murray Collins, 'The Political Economy of Passing Climate Change Legislation: Evidence from a Survey' (2015) 35 *Global Environmental Change* 52–61.

In relation to human rights law as an emerging consideration in climate litigation, it is notable that this case 'does not explicitly engage with human rights arguments'.[187] Additionally, this book has a particular focus on climate issues and so it has emphasised climate matters. While these are central to this landmark ruling, it has been noted above that the Court's rejection of the appeal also involves a number of other considerations, and Watts et al emphasise that care should be taken not to lose sight of this fact:

> Preston CJ dismissed the appeal partly on the basis of the likely contribution of the coal mine to climate change-causing greenhouse gas emissions ... However, what has been often overlooked is that Preston CJ's decision was also based on the likely significant social impacts of the mine, including a failure by GRL to properly assess the impacts of the mine on Aboriginal people.[188]

Further, in commenting on the Court's rejection of the planning application in its summary of the case, it is submitted that the Sabin Center for Climate Change Law employs an interesting turn of phrase. It summarises that: 'The court ... remain[ed] unpersuaded by petitioner's arguments ... related to ... the inefficiency of *this denial as a mechanism for global abatement of emissions*' (emphasis added).[189] Here an interesting perspective arises, namely that a court's denial of such an application might be perceived potentially as a practical abatement mechanism in its own right. Whether or not this type of perspective applies to climate litigation in some general sense comes down to how one chooses to view a climate litigation ruling where climate mitigation is involved as a live practical issue. Such a perspective suggests that climate litigation might conceivably be interpreted as a practical tool in the toolbox of emissions abatement.

Viewed in relation to the climate change challenge as a whole, Australia certainly benefits from a judgment like *Gloucester Resources*. During the case, an energy economist called by Groundswell Gloucester to provide evidence pointed out that 'there are a number of new coking coal mines already in operation, or approved and under development, across Australia, such that the Rocky Hill Coal Project is not required'.[190] This is concerning at a time where the global community needs to mitigate fossil fuel use substantially, and where the developed world has a requirement to lead the way under the burden-sharing approach adopted by the UNFCCC and the Paris Agreement. Returning to the phrase from the Sabin Center noted above, it seems likely that climate litigation will be mobilised increasingly as a mechanism to assist in driving the global abatement of emissions in Australia and beyond in going forward.

[187] Dehm (n 57) 245.
[188] Watts et al (n 6) 72.
[189] Sabin Center for Climate Change Law, 'Climate Case Chart: *Gloucester Resources Limited v Minister for Planning*', http://climatecasechart.com/non-us-case/gloucester-resources-limited-v-minister-for-planning.
[190] Judgment, para [479] (quoting Mr Tim Buckley).

7

Ireland

Climate Case Ireland

> Clearly one of the principal aspects of the factual background to these proceedings concerns the current scientific understanding of climate change itself, the consequences of a continuation of current trends and of the type of measures which may need to be put in place to minimise the extent of the rise in temperatures.
>
> *Climate Case Ireland*, Supreme Court of Ireland, paragraph 3.1

I. *Climate Case Ireland*

In 2017, the non-profit activist group Friends of the Irish Environment (FIE) brought a case against the Government of Ireland,[1] alleging that the Government's approval of Ireland's first iteration of a *National Mitigation Plan* (hereafter 'the *Plan*'), published on 18 July 2017, was invalid.[2] This was a statutory plan adopted under Ireland's national Climate Change Act,[3] entitled the Climate Action and Low Carbon Development Act 2015 (hereafter 'Irish Climate Change Act' or 'the 2015 Act'[4]). The Supreme Court summarised the grounds of the case as follows:

> The applicants/appellants ('FIE') contend that the Government, in the plan in question, has failed adequately to vindicate rights which are said to be guaranteed by either or both of the [Irish] Constitution and the European Convention on Human Rights … It is also said that the Plan is *ultra vires*[5] the relevant legislation.[6]

[1] *Friends of the Irish Environment v Government of Ireland* [2020] IESC 49 (Supreme Court of Ireland). Hereafter cited as 'Judgment'.

[2] Department of the Environment, Climate and Communications, *National Mitigation Plan* (Ireland, 2017).

[3] Andrew Jackson, 'Ireland's Climate Action and Low Carbon Development Act 2015: Symbolic Legislation, Trojan Horse, Stepping Stone?' in Thomas L Muinzer (ed), *National Climate Change Acts: The Emergence, Form and Nature of National Framework Climate Legislation* (Hart Publishing, 2021), ch 6, 129–52.

[4] The 2015 Act has been subject to amendment. Unless otherwise stated, references are to the 2015 Act as it stood at the time of the Supreme Court case.

[5] From Latin, meaning 'beyond the powers'.

[6] Judgment, para [1.2].

The case was initially filed in 2017, argued before the High Court in January 2019, and on 19 September 2019 the High Court ruled in favour of the Government.[7] FIE then lodged an appeal.

Given the time-sensitive nature of climate change itself, and bearing in mind that time-sensitive emissions reduction targets[8] and similar temporal legal drivers[9] can often be a key consideration within climate law, it is fitting that the Irish court service then expedited the case through its court system. On 22 November 2019, when FIE appealed the High Court ruling, it also applied to 'leapfrog' what would typically be the next phase in a conventional Irish appeal process, namely appeal to the Court of Appeal; instead, FIE requested to move the case on a fast track to the Supreme Court. On 13 February 2020, the Supreme Court decided that the uncommon circumstances at issue did warrant a direct appeal, due to factors including the 'urgency' and 'gravity' of the matters arising, and the 'issues of general and public legal importance' raised by the case.[10] The recognition accorded by the Irish courts to temporal earnestness amounts to an example of good court practice that other jurisdictions might learn from: the temporal urgency of the climate change challenge and the frequent time-sensitivity arising within climate law doctrine and procedure (here, involving a five-year *National Mitigation Plan* cycle) indicates that it is poor practice to subject non-frivolous, serious lawsuits to extensive procedural delays.

The *Plan* was adopted under the provisions of the Irish Climate Change Act. The relevant Government Minister[11] is required to prepare and submit the *Plan* for approval to the Government of Ireland[12] under section 3(1) of the 2015 Act, '[f]or the purpose of enabling the State to pursue, and achieve, the transition to a low carbon, climate resilient and environmentally sustainable economy by the end of the year 2050',[13] an obligation summarised in the legislation as the 'National Transition Objective' (NTO).[14] Within every subsequent five-year period, the Minister must submit a new iteration of the *Plan* to the Government for approval.[15] This keeps the planning process moving forward towards 2050. The Supreme Court mistakenly cites the NTO as involving the enabling of an '*environmental*

[7] *Friends of the Irish Environment v The Government of Ireland* [2019] IEHC 747.

[8] *State of the Netherlands v Urgenda Foundation*, ECLI:NL:HR:2019:2006 (English translation ECLI:NL:HR:2019:2007), Judgment (Sup Ct Neth, 20 December 2019) (Neth).

[9] In this particular case, the relevant Government Minister had a maximum of five years in which to submit each subsequent *National Mitigation Plan* iteration to the Irish Government for approval: Climate Action and Low Carbon Development Act 2015, s 4(1)(b). Thus, time constraints are an important issue that render broad delays in court process highly undesirable.

[10] *Friends of the Environment v The Government of Ireland & The Attorney General* [2020] IESCDET 13, paras [8], [10].

[11] At the time of the case, this was the Minister for the Environment, Community and Local Government.

[12] On the Government's approval procedures, see Climate Action and Low Carbon Development Act 2015, s 4(1), 4(4).

[13] ibid s 3(1).

[14] ibid.

[15] ibid s 4(1)(b).

sustainable economy' (emphasis added)[16] rather than an '*environmentally* sustainable economy', but the slip appears to have no discernible impact on the Court's decision.

It should be noted that after the Irish Climate Change Act was passed in 2015, it became understood that the framework was unfit for purpose in a range of crucial areas (including in part because of the successful challenge to aspects of the regime embodied by this case).[17] As a consequence, the 2015 Act was substantially amended in 2021.[18] Over the course of the amendments, the NTO was removed, and a 'National Climate Objective' replaced it at section 3(1). *National Mitigation Plans* were also pruned out in favour of carbon budgets and 'Climate Action Plans'. Thus, the landmark ruling of the Irish Supreme Court currently under examination concerns the 2015 Act *prior to* these amendments. References in this discussion are to the 2015 Act as at the time of the case (unless otherwise stated). It should be noted that the amended version of the 2015 Act is very similar in spirit and substance to the original 2015 Act, and that the Supreme Court judgment assists one in interpreting how the Irish courts view aspects of the present framework, notwithstanding the fact that the case itself preceded the 2021 amendments.

Appropriately, given that the Irish Supreme Court is a legal body rather than a scientific body, the Court noted from the outset of its judgment that it accepted the scientific consensus on climate change, as did the parties to the case. The Court also chose to set out a summary of the scientific understanding of climate change and its consequences for the purposes of clarity, under the heading 'A Brief Overview of the Science'.[19] Against the backdrop of consensus scientific concerns, FIE had pointed out that the Government's *Plan* actually envisaged a significant *increase* in greenhouse gas emissions. The Supreme Court noted as follows:

> A key argument advanced by FIE suggests that … it is the total amount of emissions which drive climate change and that an initial increase in emissions, even if the ultimate target of zero net emissions by 2050 is achieved, will inevitably lead to a greater total volume of emissions in the period to 2050 thus it is said, not contributing sufficiently to the aim of reducing warming. There is a dispute between the parties as to whether any, or any sufficient, basis is given in the Plan for adopting this initial target which allows for an increase in emissions.[20]

This element raises a significant point of principle relevant to climate litigation more broadly. It is quite possible for a state to apply, eg, a legally binding Net Zero emissions reduction target for 2050, but if the law does not simultaneously incorporate a trajectory that ratchets emissions downward consistently over time, it is also possible in principle for a state to *increase* its emissions substantially for many

[16] Judgment, para [4.1].
[17] Jackson (n 3).
[18] Climate Action and Low Carbon Development (Amendment) Act 2021 (32/2021).
[19] Judgment, section 3, paras [3.1]–[3.8].
[20] ibid para [4.3]. Thus, FIE contended that in adopting a *Plan* that allowed for an increase in emissions in this manner, the Government had acted unlawfully: para [4.5].

years before steeply reducing them towards the end of the approach to 2050 in order to reach Net Zero. In this type of hypothetical case, the legal obligation to achieve Net Zero has been secured, but substantial environmental harm has been done through a pronounced increase in the stock of greenhouse gases in the earth's atmosphere, which will remain in the atmosphere for many years exerting a cumulative negative climate impact.[21] The fact that the Irish Government's intention was to facilitate an initial significant increase in emissions in its *Plan* instead of clearly sketching out some means by which the Net Zero NTO reductions would be achieved steadily militated against the Government succeeding in the case, and played a role in the Supreme Court finding for FIE.[22]

II. The Plan and the Irish Climate Change Act

The unanimous judgment of the Court was written and delivered by Mr Justice Clarke, Chief Justice of Ireland.[23] Over the course of summarising key background issues, he noted in his judgment that:

> [T]he case as originally pleaded focused much more substantially on an allegation that the Plan was *ultra vires* the 2015 Act. As the case evolved, the rights based elements of the argument took greater prominence … If FIE are correct in saying that the Plan did not comply with the 2015 Act then it would follow that the Plan would have to be quashed and that the Government would have to adopt a new Plan … I, therefore, propose to turn first to the question of whether the Plan complied with the 2015 Act.[24]

A range of general questions relating to the significance of a statute being engaged in this way (ie, the 2015 Act) are outlined in paragraphs [6.1]–[6.6].[25] Prior to addressing the interpretation of the 2015 Act in this context, the Court first considered and clarified technical aspects of the range of issues that it was deemed appropriate for the Court to engage with, after the relevant range of issues was queried by the Government late on in the process at oral hearing for the first time.[26] It was concluded that the established range of issues that were canvassed

[21] Jeffrey S Gaffney and Nancy A Marley, *Chemistry of Environmental Systems*, (Wiley, 2020), 355–89.

[22] This perspective has some commonality with the *Colombian Amazon Case*, insofar as in that case the plaintiffs sought to challenge extensive ongoing deforestation of the Amazon rainforest in the face of a commitment from the Colombian Government to reduce the deforestation net rate to zero by 2020. The case was ruled on in 2018, prior to 2020, meaning that technically speaking the Government had not yet breached this 2020 objective. Just as the Supreme Court of Ireland did not look favourably on proposed *increases* in emissions in the context of an ongoing emissions reduction drive, the Supreme Court of Justice of Colombia looked unfavourably on extensive ongoing deforestation in the context of an overall process where deforestation should be rapidly declining. See further ch 4 in this volume.

[23] The other judges in the case were Mr Justice Irvine, Mr Justice O'Donnell, Mr Justice MacMenamin, Ms Justice Dunne, Ms Justice O'Malley and Ms Justice Baker.

[24] Judgment, para [5.60].

[25] ibid paras [6.1]–[6.6].

[26] ibid para [6.10].

previously before the High Court, included in written submissions to the Supreme Court from FIE, responded to by the Government's legal team in the current Supreme Court appeal, and included in the Statement of Case[27] pertaining to the Supreme Court appeal, did establish the range of issues that it was proper for the Supreme Court to consider.[28]

Section 4 of the 2015 Act creates an obligation for the relevant Government Minister to produce a 'national mitigation plan' draft no later than 18 months after the initial passing of the Act,[29] and subsequently no less than once in every five-year period,[30] and submit it to the Government for approval. This *Plan* must 'specify the manner in which it is proposed to achieve the national transition objective'.[31] As Mr Justice Clarke characterises it, 'the legislation contemplates a series of rolling plans each of which must be designed to specify, both in general terms and on a sectoral basis, how it is proposed that the NTO is to be achieved'.[32] Section 1, 'Interpretation', states that '"national transition objective' has the meaning assigned to it by section 3(1)'.[33] At section 3(1), the NTO is defined in a slight syntactical tangle, as follows:

> 3(1) For the purpose of enabling the State to pursue, and achieve, the transition to a low carbon, climate resilient and environmentally sustainable economy by the end of the year 2050 (in this Act referred to as the 'national transition objective') the Minister shall make and submit to the Government for approval [etc].[34]

In other words, the NTO is *the pursuit and achievement by the Irish State of a low carbon, climate resilient and environmentally sustainable economy by the end of 2050.*

Section 4(2) of the 2015 Act requires *Plans* to specify the policy measures that the Government considers necessary to achieve the NTO,[35] and to specify the mitigation policy measures that Ministers will adopt in relation to individual economic sectors.[36] Concerning justiciability, the Government contended that the *Plan* involves the adoption of policy, and such matters of policy are not justiciable in the Irish courts.[37] The Government did accept that judicial review was

[27] The Statement of Case was issued by the Supreme Court prior to the oral hearing. In Irish court practice, a Statement of Case is a document that can be issued in advance of hearings to these ends: 'The statement of case will set out the Court's understanding as to the following matters … The issues which appear to the Court to require determination on the appeal having regard to the determination granting leave to appeal, any refinement of the issues determined by the case management judge and the submissions of the parties; and … The position of the parties on those issues'. *Supreme Court Practice Directions: Conduct of Proceedings in Supreme Court*, SC19, s 20(b),(c)–(d).

[28] See Judgment, paras [6.7]–[6.16].

[29] Climate Action and Low Carbon Development Act 2015, s 4(1)(a).

[30] ibid s 4(1)(b).

[31] ibid s 4(2)(a).

[32] Judgment, para [6.20].

[33] Climate Action and Low Carbon Development Act 2015, s 1.

[34] ibid s 3(1).

[35] ibid s 4(2)(b).

[36] ibid s 4(2)(d), 4(3)(a).

[37] Judgment, para [6.23].

available in relation to the 2015 Act process, but argued that it could extend only to 'process or procedural matters and not to the substantive content' of the *Plan*.[38] Quite correctly, the Supreme Court did not accept this view. Although it properly acknowledged that '[i]t is possible … that there may be elements of a compliant Plan under the 2015 Act which may not truly be justiciable',[39] Mr Justice Clarke opined that the following appears to be 'absolutely clear':

> [W]here the legislation requires that a plan formulated under its provisions does certain things, then the law requires that a plan complies with those obligations and the question of whether a plan actually does comply with the statute in such regard is a matter of law rather than a matter of policy. It becomes a matter of law because the Oireachtas [ie, the Irish Parliament] has chosen to legislate for at least some aspects of a compliant plan while leaving other elements up to policy decisions by the government of the day.[40]

These elements and associated passages of the judgment – notably paragraphs [6.23]–[6.27] – can be read by courts in other jurisdictions and other members of the legal community engaged in climate law matters to usefully inform general consideration of the relationship between policy and law in this type of context. These considerations can also be cross-referenced to other salient instances of judicial thinking in major cases, notably the UK Supreme Court's consideration in the landmark *Heathrow Runway Case* of whether or not the Paris Agreement amounted to 'Government policy' within the meaning of a statutory requirement set out in section 5(8) of the UK's Planning Act 2008.[41] In that case, the UK Supreme Court found that it did not.[42] The outcome of the *Urgenda Case* also renders the boundary between law/policy a focal issue.[43] Here, the Dutch courts crystallised a minimum 25% greenhouse gas emissions reduction target for the Netherlands for 2020, deriving the target from a number of sources including international law and standards, and human rights law. In ordering the Dutch Government to implement this minimum target, the courts imposed a form of climate objective that had typically emerged in the policy sphere prior to the ruling, and some have therefore interpreted this as a possible over-reach of the courts' discretion.[44]

In the present case, the Irish Supreme Court opined that:

> [T]he requirements of s.4, as to what a plan must specify, come within a category of statutory obligation which is clearly law rather than policy. Whether a plan complies, for example, with the obligation that it be specific as to how the NTO is to be achieved is, in my view, clearly a matter of law.[45]

[38] ibid para [6.26].

[39] ibid para [6.27].

[40] ibid.

[41] *R (on the Application of Friends of the Earth Ltd and Others) v Heathrow Airport Ltd* [2020] UKSC 52; see further ch 2 in this volume.

[42] *R (on the Application of Friends of the Earth Ltd and Others)* (n 41).

[43] *State of the Netherlands v Urgenda Foundation* (n 8).

[44] See ch 3 in this volume.

[45] Judgment, para [6.27].

This finding highlights that climate law may well lead to instances where statutory requirements compel courts to address certain substantive aspects of governmental policy documents (within reasonable limits and as confined by relevant statutory parameters). This is a significant point, given that substantive policy is typically the primary domain of the Government rather than of the courts. Here, then, the Supreme Court moved beyond purely procedural considerations. While the 'choices as to how the NTO might be achieved may well be policy choices and real questions might arise as to the extent to which those choices might be justiciable', the Court found that 'whether the Plan does what it says on the statutory tin is a matter of law and clearly justiciable'.[46]

Relatedly, the Court also carefully considered the relationship between the type of *Plan* at issue and the type of statute (the 2015 Act) that enabled its creation with reference to rights:

> If it is possible to have a lawful plan under the statute but if, equally, it might be possible to have a plan which, while in technical compliance with the statute, breached rights in some way so that it too was invalid, a challenge mounted on such grounds would clearly not, in my view, amount to a collateral attack [on the statute]. It would simply amount to an assertion that the plan chosen was invalid but that other plans could have been chosen which were valid.[47]

In other words, in principle there might be certain cases where a *Plan* of this sort is in accord with the relevant statute but is still invalid, even though the statute that created it is not invalid, eg, where the *Plan* might breach the Irish Constitution in some clear way, but the statute itself does not.[48] Indeed, the fundamentals of this case bear out the underlying point, namely that an attack on the *Plan* is not necessarily an attack on the statute. The matter of whether the *Plan* in this case was sufficiently specific to meet the mandatory requirements of section 4 of the 2015 Act was considered to be a justiciable issue that did not amount to a collateral attack on the statute itself.[49] It turned, therefore, on the merits of the *Plan*.

Coming, then, to the crucial matter of the level of specificity required by the 2015 Act to deliver the first 2017 *Plan* at issue adequately, here the Court addressed and underscored a range of factors. These included the importance of public participation and the public consultation process at section 4(8) of the 2015 Act,[50] and associated issues of transparency. It was emphasised that the statutory need for the *Plan* to be specific on how the NTO will be achieved by 2050 allows

[46] ibid.

[47] ibid para [6.30].

[48] Commenting on the High Court outcome prior to the Supreme Court appeal, Forde underscored the difference between directly challenging a *Plan* with reference to an Act, as in this case, and 'an interest group challenging the 2015 Act [directly] in relation to its inadequacy in dealing with the climate crisis'. See further Eoin Forde, 'The Future of Climate Litigation in Ireland: An Appraisal of Climate Case Ireland' (2019) *Trinity College Law Review Online*, https://trinitycollegelawreview.org/the-future-of-climate-litigation-in-ireland-an-appraisal-of-climate-case-ireland.

[49] Judgment, para [6.32].

[50] Climate Action and Low Carbon Development Act 2015, s 4(8).

'the reasonable and interested member of the public' to consider the matters and form a view as to whether the Government's approach appears to be effective and appropriate.[51] The Court's overall view here is summarised as follows:

> [T]he level of specificity required of a compliant plan is that it is sufficient to allow a reasonable and interested member of the public to know how the government of the day intends to meet the NTO so as, in turn, to allow such members of the public as may be interested to act in whatever way, political or otherwise, that they consider appropriate in the light of that policy.[52]

The Court found that a sufficient level of specific detail as to how the Government intended to meet the NTO was absent from the *Plan*. This was an important shortcoming in legal as well as policy terms, with the Court emphasising the existence of 'a clear present statutory obligation on the Government, in formulating a plan, to at least give some realistic level of detail about how it is intended to meet the NTO. Some general indication of the sort of specific measures which will or may be required needs to be given'.[53] It added that '[t]he legislation does, after all, require that a plan "specify" how the NTO is to be met'.[54]

In other words, the Court found that the *Plan* fell short of the requisite level of specificity, meaning in turn that the reasonable and interested observer would be unable to know how the present Government intended to achieve the NTO by 2050.[55] Due to the fact that the *Plan* did not comply with its legislative remit under the 2015 Act, the Court ruled that it was ultra vires.[56] Thus, it held that the *Plan* did not comply with section 4 of the 2015 Act, and quashed it.[57] Renglet has emphasised the just character of this aspect of the decision, noting that 'by its clear condemnation of vague and aspirational policies, the decision of the Irish Supreme Court … constitutes a great step towards government accountability for climate change'.[58]

One interesting argument made by the Government was that the Government had published a Climate Action Plan in 2019 that arguably attended to such perceived inadequacies to a significant extent by building on the 'policy, framework,

[51] Judgment, para [6.37].

[52] ibid para [6.38].

[53] ibid para [6.45].

[54] ibid.

[55] ibid para [6.46].

[56] ibid para [9.1].

[57] ibid para [6.48]. Roy has characterised the line between specificity and actual policy as follows: 'What the Supreme Court does in effect is introduce a "reasonable specificity test" – the Plan should be specific enough for members of the public to appreciate how NTO may be achieved. This line of reasoning does not amount to substituting policy; rather, it sets out a condition that any policy should be intelligible, and a marker of intelligibility is specificity. This *intelligibility – specificity property* does not amount to substitution of policy by the judiciary.' Suryapratim Roy, 'The Domestic Life of Climate Law: *Friends of the Irish Environment v Ireland*' (2021) 3 *Irish Supreme Court Review* 141–60, 151.

[58] Charlotte Renglet, 'The Decision of the Irish Supreme Court in *Friends of the Irish Environment v Ireland*: A Significant Step towards Government Accountability for Climate Change?' (2020) 3 *Carbon and Climate Law Review* 163–76, 176.

measures and actions' of the official 2017 *Plan*.[59] The Supreme Court found this unpersuasive, pointing out that 'it is not a plan in the sense in which that term is used in the 2015 Act. It has not been, for example, through the public consultation process which the 2015 Act mandates',[60] and it does not provide the same level of transparency about the Government's thinking as of 2019 'in the very formal way which the 2015 Act mandates'.[61] In critiquing Climate Change Acts,[62] analysts have noted that this type of legislation can be interpreted as comprising distinct *substantive* and *procedural* duties.[63] Thus, a further point of interest concerns the sense in which the Supreme Court asserted that the *Plan* was being 'quashed on grounds which are substantive rather than purely procedural'.[64] This meant that the Government was not permitted to resubmit the current *Plan* with a mild variation(s) applied to it; rather, it had to produce a new *Plan*. Thus, Mr Justice Clarke stated that 'this plan will never fall to be assessed again, for any new plan adopted under the 2015 Act will need to be different so as to meet the deficiencies which have been identified'.[65]

The Court also had a good deal to say in relation to temporal aspects of climate *Plans*. Regarding the procedural creation of the *Plans* over the five-year timeframes laid down by the 2015 Act, Mr Justice Clarke opined that:

> [I]t would be wrong, in my view, to suggest that the legislation contemplates a series of five year plans. Rather, the legislation contemplates a series of rolling plans … Given that the Plan was adopted in 2017, it was required to be a 33-year plan albeit one which the legislation understood was likely to be adjusted within five years to take into account further developments.[66]

It might be noted that this could appear to be somewhat contradictory. On the one hand, it appears to be suggested that the 2017 *Plan* is a *33-year Plan that would be adjusted on a rolling basis* every five years or less until 2050 (ie, over 33 years).[67] On the other hand, it might be suggested that the 2017 *Plan* appears to be conveyed as the first articulation of a more distinct set of individual rolling plans, arguably implied by the construction '*the legislation contemplates a series* of rolling plans' (emphasis added).[68] Setting this possible internal contradiction aside, the

[59] Judgment, para [6.34].
[60] ibid para [6.35].
[61] ibid.
[62] Thomas L Muinzer 'What are National "Climate Change Acts"?' (2021) 39(4) *Journal of Energy & Natural Resources Law* 419–38.
[63] See further Richard Macrory and Thomas L Muinzer, 'The UK's Climate Change Act' in Thomas L Muinzer (ed), *National Climate Change Acts: The Emergence, Form and Nature of National Framework Climate Legislation* (Hart Publishing, 2021) 70.
[64] Judgment, para [6.49].
[65] ibid.
[66] ibid para [6.20].
[67] Implied by the construction 'it was required to be a 33-year plan albeit one which … was likely to be adjusted within five years' (quoting ibid), meaning that the subsequent version(s) amounts to an adjustment of the existing *Plan*.
[68] ibid para [6.20].

legislation itself stipulates that: 'The Minister shall not later than 18 months after the passing of this Act and not less than once in every period of 5 years, make, and submit to the Government for approval, a plan, which shall be known as a national … mitigation plan.'[69] This textual construction – concerning the making and submitting of a plan not less than '*once in every*' five-year period – appears to envisage a succession of distinct *Plans*, namely the conception rejected by the Supreme Court.[70]

Regardless of how the initial and subsequent five-year *Plans* are conceptualised, the Court was both firm and persuasive in its treatment of temporal issues where it asserted that it 'seems clear that s.4 requires that the measures necessary to achieve the NTO *must be specified not only for the first five years but for the full length of the period then unexpired up to 2050*' (emphasis added).[71] Given the length of time at issue and the difficulties in predicting suitable policy responses and outcomes so far into the future, the Court stated that:

> The level of specificity for the latter years may legitimately be less but there must be, nonetheless, a policy identified which does specify in some reasonable detail the kind of measures that will be required up to 2050.[72]

Although the measures 'may come to be adjusted over time' as knowledge, data and technology develop, this 'does not alter the fact that a best current estimate as to how the NTO is going to be achieved needs to be made and not left to sometime in the future'.[73] Thus, in the case of the 2017 *Plan*, it is summarised that 'this is not a five-year plan but rather ought to have been a 33-year plan'.[74]

The significance of temporal issues in relation to statutory climate plans should not be under-estimated. Note, for instance, that plans oriented at a relatively distant target/date (here, the NTO/2050) that are produced a number of decades in advance (here, in 2017) might be more inclined to be vague in their content about the attainment of the target/date in earlier iterations. This could be due to it being harder to address the more distant future than the nearer future in concrete political terms, but also due potentially to such an approach more easily facilitating governmental inclinations to defer harder climate policy choices away from the immediate present in favour of more distant dates. In principle, a conception of a distinct five-year *Plan*, in contrast to a conception of a 33 (or similar) year *Plan* that is updated on a rolling basis, may compel more immediate, focused and

[69] Climate Action and Low Carbon Development Act 2015, s 4(1)(b).

[70] '[I]t would be wrong, in my view, to suggest that the legislation contemplates a series of five year plans': Judgment, para [6.20].

[71] ibid para [6.45]. Similarly, given that the NTO is pegged to the date of 2050, the Court emphasised the following: 'While the detail of what is intended to happen in later years may understandably be less complete, a compliant plan must be sufficiently specific as to policy over the whole period to 2050' (para [9.2]).

[72] ibid para [6.45].

[73] ibid.

[74] ibid.

short-term progressive action if significant action is required to occur in demonstrable terms within those five years. In this Irish case, Mr Justice Clarke correctly notes that it 'would be wrong to suggest that the legislation envisages that details be provided for only the first five years'[75] – this is self-evident from section 4(2)(a), which requires the *Plan* to specify how it proposes to achieve the 2050 NTO.[76] The broader underlying tension evoked here concerns a need to ensure emissions reductions are suitably ratcheted down gradually over successive short-term periods that add up to an articulated longer term. Thus, it is notable that five-year legally binding carbon budgets, which are absent in the Irish Climate Change Act here,[77] are applied in the UK under the terms of the UK Climate Change Act.[78] This reduces these sorts of temporal problems by compelling an ongoing sharp five-year oriented reduction focus in the short term,[79] but within the broader context of a legally binding target date of Net Zero for 2050.[80]

It is also notable that the views of Ireland's Climate Change Advisory Council (CCAC), which was established under section 8 of the 2015 Act, are factored into considerations. The CCAC advises and makes recommendations to the Government in relation to the *Plans*,[81] in addition to discharging other functions including providing annual reports[82] and other periodic review reports[83] to the Government. Its appraisals of progress towards the NTO had not been positive. In its 2018 annual report, the judgment highlights that the CCAC stated: 'Ireland's greenhouse gas emissions for 2016, and projections of emissions to 2035, are disturbing. Ireland's greenhouse gas emissions increased again in 2016 … Ireland is completely off course in terms of its commitments to addressing the challenges of climate change.'[84] In its 2017 periodic review, the CCAC found that: 'Ireland is not projected to meet 2020 emissions reduction targets and is not on the right trajectory to meet longer term EU and national emission reduction commitments.'[85]

The Supreme Court notes in relation to the CCAC that:

> Under s.12(2) of the 2015 Act, the annual report of the Advisory Council is required to include recommendations in relation to the most cost-effective manner of achieving reductions in GHG emissions in order to enable the achievement of the NTO and such other recommendations or advice as the Advisory Council considers necessary or appropriate in order to enable the achievement of the NTO. Section 13(7) provides that a periodic review report should contain a consideration of the NTO and any matter

[75] ibid para [6.20].
[76] ibid; Climate Action and Low Carbon Development Act 2015, s 4(2)(a).
[77] The Irish Climate Change Act has since been revised to include carbon budgets in 2021.
[78] Climate Change Act 2008 (UK), ss 4–10.
[79] Thomas L Muinzer, *Climate and Energy Governance for the UK Low Carbon Transition: The Climate Change Act 2008* (Palgrave Macmillan, 2019), 48–63.
[80] Climate Change Act 2008, s 1(1).
[81] Climate Action and Low Carbon Development Act 2015, s 11.
[82] ibid s 12.
[83] ibid s 13.
[84] Judgment, para [6.42], quoting the CCAC's 2018 annual report.
[85] Judgment, para [6.42], quoting the CCAC's 2017 periodic review.

> relating to that objective as the Advisory Council considers appropriate … together with such advice or recommendations as the Advisory Council considers appropriate in relation to the Plan.[86]

Thus, while the CCAC is established by the statute in part to advise on how the Government can achieve the NTO, it is notable that it is a reporting and advisory body only insofar as it does not set policy and its recommendations do not bind the Government.

While the parameters and limits of the CCAC's remit are both set out in the statute and reflected in the judgment, the Supreme Court itself, of course, is not a constrained advisory and reporting body. It can and does strike down the *Plan* in its ruling. In doing so, the CCAC's partially negative account of progress towards the NTO exerted some influence on the Court's reasoning. 'It is of some relevance to consider what the Climate Change Advisory Council says', Mr Justice Clarke states, before doing so and concluding that '[h]aving considered what the Plan says it does seem to me to be reasonable to characterise significant parts of the policies as being excessively vague or aspirational'.[87] Thus, the judgment is in some sense indicative of how aspects of both the limits and influence of such statutory Advisory Councils might crystallise in the context of court reasoning.

III. Constitutional and Human Rights Issues

In determining that the *Plan* was to be quashed, the Supreme Court resolved the heart of the dispute. However, other important points of law also arose in the case within the sphere of constitutional and human rights. It had not been disputed that FIE had standing to argue that the *Plan* was *ultra vires* the 2015 Act, and although this strand of argument was successful, it was less clear whether FIE could also rely on a variety of additional rights in the way that it sought to. The rights at issue fell into two separate but related strands: constitutional rights and human rights. In relation to FIE's constitutional arguments, it was argued that the right to life in the Irish Constitution was engaged, including 'what is said to be the obligation of the State to seek to protect persons against a future threat to life arising from climate change'.[88] It was also argued that the constitutional right to bodily integrity was engaged, where it was advanced that the consequences of climate change will significantly impact the health and bodily integrity of persons.[89] Reliance was also placed on Articles 2 and 8 of the European Convention on Human Rights (ECHR). The ECHR is applied in Ireland via the European Convention on Human Rights

[86] ibid para [6.40].
[87] ibid para [6.43].
[88] ibid para [5.3].
[89] ibid.

Act 2003. Article 2 ECHR and Article 8 ECHR pertain to the 'Right to Life' and the 'Right to Respect for Private and Family Life' respectively.[90]

The Government objected that all of these rights – both the constitutional rights to life and bodily integrity, and the Article 2 and 8 ECHR rights – were personal rights that FIE was not entitled to rely on. FIE conceded that as a corporate entity it did not enjoy the rights it relied on itself,[91] but noted that entities have been permitted to bring cases in a similar fashion before in Ireland.[92] The Government also highlighted that Irish constitutional law places constraints on *actio popularis*, namely actions brought on behalf of the public as a whole.[93] Further, it flagged up constraints in relation to *jus tertii*, namely the capacity to rely on rights enjoyed by others in bringing a case.[94] Over the course of standing considerations, some interesting links were made in the context of existing Irish law between the rights of an unborn child that might rely on another party to enforce its rights[95] and a Penal Reform Trust bringing a case in the interest of prisoners.[96] In the field of climate law, the extent to which private citizens/NGOs/other parties may have the legal entitlement to initiate a lawsuit is a frequently contested matter that landmark cases in the area have often been compelled to grapple with and clarify.[97]

Under Irish law, the typical norm is that a claimant needs to show that an allegedly unconstitutional measure has potentially interfered with rights that he or she enjoys, or that there is a danger that such interference is going to occur: *Cahill v Sutton*.[98] However, there is also a degree of flexibility. Per Henchy J in *Cahill v Sutton*, 'the stated rule of personal standing may be waived or relaxed if, in the particular circumstances of a case, the court finds that there are weighty countervailing considerations justifying a departure from the rule'.[99] In addressing the issue of 'why a corporate entity has chosen to bring these proceedings relying, as FIE does, on personal rights which it does not enjoy',[100] the Supreme Court was not persuaded that FIE should be afforded an exceptional right to standing. It found

[90] European Convention on Human Rights, arts 2 and 8; European Convention on Human Rights Act 2003, sch 1.

[91] Judgment, para [7.3].

[92] ibid.

[93] See ibid para [7.4].

[94] ibid.

[95] *SPUC Ltd v Coogan (No 1)* [1989] I.R. 734, per Finlay CJ, at 742: 'In this case that right is the right to life of an unborn child in its mother's womb. The threat to that constitutional right which it is sought to avoid is the death of the child.' See also Judgment, para [7.13]. The rights of unborn future generations in the context of climate litigation are discussed in ch 4 in this volume.

[96] *Irish Penal Reform Trust v Minister for Justice* [2005] IEHC 305. See Judgment, paras [7.15]–[7.18]. See also *Digital Rights Ireland v Minister for Communications* [2010] 3 IR 151, discussed at Judgment, paras [7.19]–[7.20] and [5.36]–[5.37], which inter alia addressed the scope of the capacity for body corporates to be accorded personal standing by the Irish courts.

[97] See further the *Oil Pollution Watch* case examined in ch 5 in this volume, which is focused on the issue of standing.

[98] *Cahill v Sutton* [1980] IR 269, 285.

[99] ibid 285.

[100] Judgment, para [7.22].

that 'no real explanation was given as to why an individual or individuals could not have brought these proceedings instead of FIE'[101] and that '[t]o hold that FIE had standing in the circumstances of this case would … involve a move to a situation where standing was greatly expanded and the absence of standing would largely be confined to cases involving persons who simply maintain proceedings on a meddlesome basis'.[102] In addition to the technical legal problems it was thought that this might create, it was also underscored that avenues for people to bring such proceedings already existed: 'FIE have [not] put forward any adequate basis to explain why these proceedings could not have been brought in the ordinary way by persons who would undoubtedly enjoy the right to life and the right to bodily integrity on which reliance is placed'.[103] In sum, it was held that FIE did not have standing to rely on the constitutional rights that it sought to.

As to the ECHR, the Court was prepared to consider FIE's attempted reliance on human rights law. It found that although FIE would not have standing to bring this sort of complaint before the European Court of Human Rights, this did not necessarily mean it could not bring such a claim before the Irish courts, in spite of the fact that reliance on Ireland's European Convention on Human Rights Act 2003 was at issue.[104] It is notable that FIE evoked the *Urgenda Case*, highlighting that the Dutch Supreme Court was influenced by Articles 2 and 8 ECHR in issuing its landmark ruling:[105]

> FIE placed significant reliance in its submissions on *Urgenda* and suggested that this Court should consider the reasoning of the Supreme Court of the Netherlands as being persuasive as to the proper application of the ECHR to climate change. It was argued by FIE that, if the relevant interpretation of the Convention as determined by the Dutch Supreme Court is correct, then it would follow, on the facts, that Ireland is also in breach of its obligations under the Convention.[106]

The Supreme Court was not persuaded by this. This is unsurprising, given that *Urgenda* was a foreign ruling that was not legally binding on Ireland, that was issued in the context of a differing legal system and that was engaging with a distinct set of issues.[107] The Court also noted the close proximity and equivalence in character between the constitutional rights FIE sought to rely on unsuccessfully and the human rights it sought to rely on, finding that it did not make rational

[101] ibid.
[102] ibid.
[103] ibid.
[104] ibid para [7.6].
[105] *State of the Netherlands v Urgenda Foundation* (n 8); Judgment, para [5.12].
[106] Judgment, para [5.13].
[107] See ch 3 in this volume. Ireland's Supreme Court had no landmark climate ruling from the European Court of Human Rights engaging the ECHR rights at issue to draw on for guidance at this point in time. For relevant jurisprudence produced by the European Court subsequently, see *Verein Klimaseniorinnen Schweiz and Others v Switzerland*, Grand Chamber, European Court of Human Rights (Application No 53600/20), 9 April 2024; *Duarte Agostinho and Others v Portugal and 32 Others*, Grand Chamber, European Court of Human Rights (Application No 39371/20), 9 April 2024; *Carême v France*, Grand Chamber, European Court of Human Rights (Application No 7189/21), 9 April 2024.

sense to facilitate reliance on human rights that were so 'analogous' to the constitutional rights at issue in this context, given that reliance on those constitutional rights had been rejected. Thus, the human rights arguments were similarly rejected.[108] Jackson wrote in the wake of the case that the Supreme Court's treatment of standing was disappointing, and set out arguments suggesting it could have facilitated standing for personal constitutional and ECHR rights on a credible doctrinal basis.[109]

IV. The Reversal of Ireland's Constitutional Environmental Right

A further key point was also raised, one that is both novel and, in the context of Irish constitutional law, important. In *Friends of the Irish Environment v Fingal County Council* (2017),[110] Ireland's High Court had recognised for the first time that a right to an environment consistent with human dignity could be legitimately interpreted into the Irish Constitution, in spite of the fact that an environmental right was not explicitly stated in the Constitution itself.[111] Initially, FIE had endeavoured to rely on this right in *Climate Case Ireland* in order to bolster its case. In the 2017 High Court ruling that has just been noted, this environmental right had been interpreted as an 'unenumerated right'.[112] In the present ruling, the Supreme Court expressed dissatisfaction with this characterisation, preferring the construction 'derived right': 'The term "unenumerated rights" is not accurate for it describes rights which are not expressly referred to in the text of the Constitution itself.'[113] Prior to *Climate Case Ireland* reaching the Supreme Court, when the case was being heard at the High Court, this lower court did accept the existence of the unenumerated constitutional right to an environment consistent with human dignity that had been acknowledged in 2017. The Supreme Court saw fit to undo this.[114]

One particularly notable feature of the Supreme Court's decision to provide a detailed statement on the issue of whether or not a derived constitutional right to

[108] Judgment, paras [7.23]–[7.24].

[109] See further Andrew Jackson, 'Systemic Climate Litigation in Europe: Transnational Networks and the Impacts of *Climate Case Ireland*' in Joana Setzer, Catherine Higham, Andrew Jackson and Javier Solana, 'Climate Change Litigation and Central Banks' (2021) *European Central Bank Legal Working Paper Series* 21, 37–39. See also the comments on the 'margin of appreciation' afforded to national courts under European human rights law in Suryapratim Roy, 'Is Climate Change an Issue of Human Rights?', *Irish Times*, 15 October 2019.

[110] *Friends of the Irish Environment v Fingal County Council* [2017] IEHC 695.

[111] Constitution of Ireland – Bunreacht na hEireann.

[112] For further consideration of unenumerated rights in relation to this ruling, see Orla Kelleher, 'The Revival of the Unenumerated Rights Doctrine: A Right to an Environment and its Implications for Future Climate Change Litigation in Ireland' (2018) 25(3) *Irish Planning and Environmental Law* 97.

[113] Judgment, para [5.4].

[114] Note that McLoughlin has considered the constitutional elements of *Climate Case Ireland* in detail, arguing persuasively that in spite of the ruling's rejection of the position that the Irish Constitution

a healthy environment could be said to exist in Ireland[115] is that it was *unnecessary* in this case to do so. It was unnecessary for two main reasons: first, it was accepted at the Supreme Court that the limits of pertinent 'environmental' issues arising in the case were encompassed by the rights to life and bodily integrity; and, second, the Supreme Court had determined that FIE did not have standing to rely on personal constitutional rights anyhow.

On the first point, concerning pertinent issues in the case being encompassed by the rights to life and bodily integrity, Mr Justice Clarke opined as follows:

> [A]t the oral hearing, counsel for FIE accepted that, in the context of these proceedings, there was no material difference, insofar as this case was concerned, between the established constitutional rights relied on, being the right to life and the right to bodily integrity, and any right to a healthy environment, should one exist.[116]

He found that:

> [N]o such issues arose in this case so that any right to a healthy environment which might be held to exist for the purposes of these proceedings would not extend beyond the boundaries of the right to life and the right to bodily integrity. *In those circumstances, it does not seem to me that it is either necessary or appropriate to give any additional consideration to the question of identifying those persons or bodies as might have standing to maintain a claim based on the asserted right to a healthy environment said to derive from those quintessentially personal rights.* (Emphasis added)[117]

In spite of these limitations to the relevance of an asserted right to a healthy environment and it not being 'necessary or appropriate' to probe aspects of its outworking in the current context, later on in his judgment, Mr Justice Clarke returned to the matter and proceeded to interrogate, deconstruct and negate the 2017 acknowledgement of the right.

The unenumerated or derived right at issue had been identified by Barrett J in the landmark *Fingal Co Council* ruling noted above,[118] in the following terms:

> A right to an environment that is consistent with the human dignity and well-being of citizens at large is an essential condition for the fulfilment of all human rights. It is an

overtly protects a right to a healthy environment (discussed further below), extant provisions in the Irish Constitution and constitutional commentary in *Climate Case Ireland* itself appear to provide a basis for identifying environmental rights protections that might in turn be linked credibly to a State obligation to redress climate change in future litigation: Jamie McLoughlin, 'Whither Constitutional Environmental (Rights) Protection in Ireland after "Climate Case Ireland"?' (2021) 5(2) *Irish Judicial Studies Journal* 26–47.

[115] This was phrased variously as a 'right to a healthy environment' and a 'right to an environment consistent with human dignity'; see further *Friends of the Irish Environment v Fingal County Council* (n 110); Judgment, paras [7.7], [8.2].

[116] Judgment, para [7.7].

[117] ibid.

[118] *Friends of the Irish Environment v Fingal County Council* (n 110). The court's approach had been slightly prefigured by *Brownfield Restoration Ireland Ltd v Wicklow County Council* [2017] UEHC 456, where Humphreys J had made reference to 'effective protection of the environment' in terms of 'an implied constitutional obligation' (para [307]), although Barrett J's latter Judgment did not refer to this.

> indispensable existential right that is enjoyed universally, yet which is vested personally as a right that presents and can be seen always to have presented, and to enjoy protection, under Art. 40.3.1° of the Constitution.[119]
>
> … Concrete duties and responsibilities will fall in time to be defined and demarcated. But to start down that path of definition and demarcation, one first has to recognise that there is a personal constitutional right to an environment that is consistent with the human dignity and well-being of citizens at large and upon which those duties and responsibilities will be constructed. This the court does.[120]

In the present case, MacGrath J in the High Court '[a]ccept[ed] for the purposes of this case, that there is an unenumerated right to an environment consistent with human dignity'.[121] In the closing stages of the Supreme Court's judgment, after it had been concluded that the *Plan* was to be quashed and the pertinent rights-based points had been disposed of, Mr Justice Clarke stated that 'I feel it is necessary to go on to make at least some observations on that issue' of the environmental right.[122] These observations in effect amounted to a rejection and therefore a closing down of the right. Jackson has thus commented that it 'might better be considered Schrödinger's right to an environment: it both existed (briefly via the High Court, never applied in an applicant's favour) yet never existed (according to the Supreme Court)'.[123]

Irish constitutional law has a capacity to crystallise certain rights that are not directly stated in the Constitution but that can be discerned as existing within its parameters. The right to privacy has been discerned in this way: *McGee v The Attorney General*.[124] So has the right to work: *NVH v Minister for Justice and Equality*.[125] This flexibility tends to be understood as both useful and necessary in Ireland, in part because, as the courts have noted, the 'infinite variety in the relationships between the citizen and his fellows and between the citizen and the State makes an exhaustive enumeration of the guaranteed rights difficult, if not impossible'.[126] Mr Justice Clarke pointed out that the environmental right at issue, could it be said to exist, is most aptly to be understood as a 'derived' right, meaning that it is derived from the Irish Constitution or some part of it.[127] This adjustment of Barrett J's use of the term 'unenumerated' is appropriate on technical legal grounds, in particular because, as Mr Justice Clarke emphasised, it is less ideal to construe such a right as 'unenumerated' because there may be a danger that the use of that term could incorrectly convey the impression that 'judges simply identify rights of which they approve and deem them to be part of the Constitution'.[128]

[119] ibid para [264].
[120] ibid.
[121] *Friends of the Irish Environment v The Government of Ireland* [2019] IEHC 747, para [133].
[122] Judgment, para [7.25].
[123] Jackson (n 109) 41.
[124] *McGee v The Attorney General* [1974] IR 284.
[125] *NVH v Minister for Justice and Equality* [2018] 1 IR 246.
[126] *McGee* (n 124) 235.
[127] Judgment, paras [8.4]–[8.6].
[128] ibid para [8.5].

The Supreme Court opined that the derived environmental right pointed to by Barrett J was 'very vague in nature',[129] could not legitimately be said to exist and thus should be set aside. In the Supreme Court's view, it was not clear that the parameters of this 'impermissibly vague' right[130] went beyond overt rights such as those to life and bodily integrity (as illustrated by this case, where it was deemed not to go beyond them). If it did go beyond such rights, it was not clear what its parameters were and what sort of general definition might encompass it.[131] Thus, the Chief Justice found 'the asserted right to a healthy environment to be an either unnecessary addition (if it does not go beyond the right to life and the right to bodily integrity) or to be impermissibly vague (if it does)'.[132]

It is concluded that '[f]or present purposes, I think it is sufficient to indicate that the ill-defined right to a healthy environment sought to be relied on is either superfluous or lacking in precision and I would not suggest that a right as so described can be derived from the Constitution'.[133] It remains unclear how this was sufficient 'for present purposes' insofar as it was unnecessary for the Court to endeavour to dispose of Barrett J's assumed right in this context, given that it had been agreed that the relevant issues were encompassed by the rights to life and bodily integrity, and given that constitutional (and ECHR) rights-based arguments attaching to FIE had already been rejected by the Court. Technically, then, the comments appear to be obiter dicta,[134] but they clearly provide guidance to the lower courts to reject the derived environmental right. This interpretation and its practical impact have been confirmed at the High Court in *Coyne v An Bord Pleanála*.[135] Here, Holland J dismissed a claim arguing that a decision to grant planning permission for a data centre breached rights including the applicants' right to a healthy environment.[136] Kelleher has summarised as follows: 'Holland J observed that because the dicta of Barrett J in [the *Fingal Co Council* ruling] and of Clarke CJ in *Climate Case Ireland* could be considered obiter, it remained open to him to identify such a right.'[137] However, as the Supreme Court's observations in *Climate Case Ireland* were '"of the highest possible authority (a unanimous court of seven)", Holland J saw no reason not to follow the Supreme Court's conclusions'.[138]

[129] ibid para [8.11].
[130] ibid.
[131] ibid.
[132] ibid para [8.14].
[133] ibid para [8.17].
[134] In other words, the comments are judicial guidance from the Supreme Court that are not part of the ruling's binding precedent.
[135] *Coyne v An Bord Pleanála* [2023] IEHC 412.
[136] One line of argumentation – rejected by the court – was that electricity generation for the data centre would produce carbon dioxide emissions, exacerbate climate change and thus compromise the applicants' rights; see further ibid; and Orla Kelleher, 'Environmental Constitutionalism: A Transformative Legal Discourse?' (2023) 7(3) *Irish Judicial Studies Journal* 47–78, 57–58.
[137] Kelleher (n 136) 57; *Coyne* (n 135) para [304].
[138] Kelleher (n 136) 57; *Coyne* (n 135) para [304].

It does not necessarily seem self-evident that an environmental constitutional right would be bounded sharply by the rights to life and bodily integrity to the extent that the environmental right would be rendered superfluous.[139] Adelmant et al, who also raise this issue,[140] suggest that the right might interact with some appropriate degree of breadth inhering in Irish law:

> [A] great deal depends on how broadly or narrowly the rights to life and bodily integrity are construed in assessing how much the recognition of a third right would add. Given the narrowness of the Irish Supreme Court's approach in that regard, it seems inconceivable that interpreting them in light of an additional right to a healthy environment would not have significantly extended their scope … [T]here is a significant literature on the ways in which such a right has effects that go far beyond existing rights to life and bodily integrity. It would be odd for over a hundred countries to have recognized this right if doing so was entirely superfluous, as the Irish Supreme Court suggested.[141]

Further consideration of the Supreme Court's approach to the environmental right issue can be found in the next section.

V. Concluding Thoughts

Climate Case Ireland is one of the world's early landmark climate law rulings. Writing in 2020, O'Neill and Alblas provided an insightful comparative analysis of *Climate Case Ireland* and the Dutch *Urgenda* ruling, including consideration of the shaping influence that this type of litigation can exert on broader spheres of 'politics and policy change'.[142] They observe as follows:

> *Climate Case Ireland* is now only one of the two global cases in which the highest national court of law has required a Government to increase the ambition of the national climate policy, together with the Dutch '*Urgenda*' case that is often described as a model and inspiration of a successful climate litigation action.[143]

Roy notes that *Climate Case Ireland* was generally well received in the media in Ireland.[144] This may be unsurprising: significant public concern regarding climate change exists in Ireland, in spite of the fact that the country has had

[139] For a broad interpretation of environmental rights in the context of climate litigation that ranges far beyond such limited parameters, see the approach adopted by the Supreme Court of Justice of Colombia in ch 4 of this volume.

[140] Victoria Adelmant, Philip Alston and Matthew Blainey, 'Human Rights and Climate Change Litigation: One Step Forward, Two Steps Backwards in the Irish Supreme Court' (2021) 13(1) *Journal of Human Rights Practice* 1–23.

[141] ibid 18.

[142] Sadhbh O'Neill, and Edwin Alblas, 'Climate Litigation, Politics and Policy Change: Lessons from Urgenda and Climate Case Ireland' in David Robbins, Diarmuid Torney and Pat Brereton (eds), *Ireland and the Climate Crisis* (Palgrave Macmillan, 2020), 57–72.

[143] ibid 58.

[144] Roy (n 57) 142.

the third-highest per capita emissions in the EU, and there have been 'lapses on compliance with EU targets'.[145]

More narrowly, in addition to the overt matter of the Supreme Court quashing the 2017 *Plan* for lack of specificity, it is notable that the Court recognised and integrated into its reasons for doing so the fact that 'both public participation in the process leading to the adoption of a plan' and 'transparency as to the formal government policy' were undermined by this lack of specificity.[146] In other words, it can be seen that legal requirements in relation to specificity, public participation and transparency cannot be substantially extricated in this particular type of context. By throwing these intertwined features into relief in its doctrinal reasoning, the Supreme Court's perspective might usefully assist courts in other jurisdictions to clearly perceive and address the extent to which such matters can be crucially bound up with one another in these sorts of climate cases. It is also notable that the Supreme Court not only quashed the *Plan*, but in doing so asserted that 'it follows that an identical plan cannot be made in the future',[147] meaning that the Government can neither repeat its mistake nor merely endeavour to recycle the same *Plan* in some sort of light-touch way.

It is also significant that it was clarified that FIE as a corporate entity, which does not in itself enjoy the right to life or the right to bodily integrity in the context of Irish law, was found by the Court not to have standing to rely on the rights-based arguments that it tried to advance under the Irish Constitution and the ECHR. Given the structure of Irish law, and with the case arising prior to any landmark climate ruling emerging from the European Court of Human Rights in relation to the ECHR, this was not particularly surprising (in the author's opinion); however, this novel type of climate case had never come before the Supreme Court in Ireland before, and so the clarification was important.

In 'Climate Case Brings Good News and Bad', the author has criticised the Supreme Court's rejection of Ireland's environmental constitutional right in this case. There, I noted as follows:

> It is stated [by Chief Justice Clarke] that [the Supreme Court's] position is arrived at for two reasons:
>
> 1) '[The environmental right] either does not bring matters beyond the right to life or the right to bodily integrity, in which case there is no need for it'; or
> 2) 'If it does go beyond those rights, then there is not a sufficient general definition … about the sort of parameters within which it is to operate.'[148]

[145] ibid 143.

[146] Judgment, para [9.2].

[147] ibid para [9.4].

[148] Thomas L Muinzer, 'Climate Case Brings Good News and Bad', *Irish Legal News*, 13 August 2020, https://www.irishlegal.com/articles/dr-thomas-muinzer-climate-case-brings-good-news-and-bad, quoting para [8.11] of the Judgment.

I describe this as 'unsatisfactory'.[149] In relation to point 1, I note that there is a case to be made based on the law and Barrett J's 2017 judgment that the environmental right may not necessarily need to be 'trenchantly confine[d]' to the parameters of the constitutional rights to life and to bodily integrity.[150] Professor Owen McIntyre, a leading authority on Irish environmental law, has been similarly critical, observing that 'the Court's view that a right to environment might add no additional protection over and above the established rights to life and bodily integrity is clearly disappointing', especially where 'one considers that practically no environmental jurisprudence has emerged in connection with these constitutional rights, despite the fact that the right to bodily integrity was first recognised in 1965 and that Ireland has in recent years experienced extensive public interest environmental litigation'.[151] He finds that this 'suggests that these established rights have tended to lack an "environmental orientation"'.[152]

Regarding point 2 above, my commentary finds that the Supreme Court also deals with this point in an unsatisfactory way, because it 'chooses to pass up its opportunity in this actual judgement to flesh out aspects of the environmental right in a useful way for lawyers'.[153] This could have been done via obiter dicta, in place of the commentary that reverses the right.[154] Indeed, I note, 'the Court uses its opportunity, instead, to row back on that right, notwithstanding that this goes against the grain of the thrust of Barrett J's delineation, the approach of the trial judge in this case, and the essence of points 1 and 2 as established by the Supreme Court itself'.[155] Again, McIntyre is similarly critical, noting that '[e]laboration and enforcement of such an inferred right would align neatly with developing constitutional practice globally and with Ireland's international commitments on addressing climate change'.[156] I further suggest that the Court's position that 'either' of the two points above might be applicable betrays its own underlying ambivalence.[157] In sum, in the author's view, Alston et al strike an erudite balance in their work in hailing the case as a landmark victory for public interest climate litigation, while also underscoring problematic elements attaching to the Court's treatment of rights issues.[158]

[149] ibid.
[150] ibid.
[151] Owen McIntyre, 'The Irish Supreme Court Judgement in Climate Case Ireland: One Step Forward and Two Steps Back', *IUCN*, 28 August 2020, https://iucn.org/news/world-commission-environmental-law/202008/irish-supreme-court-judgment-climate-case-ireland-one-step-forward-and-two-steps-back.
[152] ibid.
[153] Muinzer (n 148).
[154] See n 134 above and the text to the note.
[155] Muinzer (n 148).
[156] McIntyre (n 151).
[157] Muinzer (n 148).
[158] See further Philip Alston, Victoria Adelmant, and Matthew Blainey, 'Courts, Climate Action and Human Rights: Lessons from the Friends of the Irish Environment v Ireland Case' in César Rodríguez-Garavito (ed), *Litigating the Climate Emergency: How Human Rights, Courts, and Legal Mobilization Can Bolster Climate Action* (Cambridge University Press, 2022), 305–18.

8

Conclusions

The *Heathrow Runway Case*, which it has been seen involved a dispute regarding the development of additional runway capacity at Heathrow Airport in England, provides an illustration of the extent to which major policy documents of national strategic importance can sit at the heart of landmark climate litigation. Similarly, in *Climate Case Ireland*, the Government of Ireland's *National Mitigation Plan* was in dispute. In the UK case, the Government's *Airports National Policy Statement* was at issue. The UK Government had been unsuccessful in the Court of Appeal – indeed, fairly emphatically so, given the robust judgment delivered against it. Yet the Government's position went on to succeed at the Supreme Court, as the Law Lords delivered a unanimous decision in favour of Heathrow Runway Limited's appeal in support of the Government's policy statement. This strong reversal of the Court of Appeal's decision serves to demonstrate just how difficult it can be to anticipate outcomes in advance in complex climate cases, as both major courts differed significantly here. In the Irish case, it has been seen that the Government of Ireland's *National Mitigation Plan* was quashed by the Supreme Court of Ireland. Read together, the UK and Irish judgments afford insight into ways in which major national policy plans and statements can be approached by the courts in landmark climate litigation, while also providing an interesting juxtaposition of a successful (UK) and unsuccessful (Ireland) ruling towards each respective Government.

While the Supreme Court of Ireland's ruling in *Climate Case Ireland* amounts to a major 'climate-aligned' or 'positive' environmental outcome,[1] this aspect of the case pales in comparison to the *Urgenda* decision, where it has been seen that the Supreme Court of the Netherlands ordered the Dutch Government to reduce national greenhouse gas emissions by a minimum of 25 per cent below 1990 levels by 2020. The Irish courts did not approach anything close to the calculation and imposition of a national emissions reduction target on the executive branch of the state (and nor of course did the UK courts in the *Heathrow Runway Case*, which was even more narrowly confined to procedural issues concerning the relevant national policy statement). The power of NGOs to drive change is exemplified here, as embodied most robustly by the *Urgenda Case*, but also by *Climate Case Ireland*.

[1] See ch 1, section II in this volume. See also Joana Setzer and Catherine Higham, *Global Trends in Climate Change Litigation: 2022 Snapshot* (London: Grantham Research Institute on Climate Change and the Environment and Centre for Climate Change Economics and Policy, London School of Economics and Political Science, 2022), 7.

While the environmental NGOs Plan B Earth and Friends of the Earth were ultimately unsuccessful in the *Heathrow Runway Case*, the Dutch and Irish NGOs the Urgenda Foundation and Friends of the Irish Environment did achieve major success, employing climate litigation to drive substantial change that would otherwise not have occurred.

These elements in turn underscore the importance of the Supreme Court of Nigeria's ruling in *Oil Pollution Watch*. Here, it has been seen that the Nigerian Court expanded the scope of locus standi, so that NGOs and public-spirited individuals would now be in a strengthened position to undertake public interest litigation in relation to environmental damage. This opens a capacity for climate cases to be brought to court by NGOs in the public interest that otherwise would have been fenced out automatically. Nigerian NGOs can now look to *Urgenda*, *Climate Case Ireland* and cases like them for inspiration and guidance in practice in terms of going forward. Similarly, jurisdictions with overly restrictive standing rules can look to *Oil Pollution Watch* itself for guidance. It has also been seen that the enablement of climate litigation via an *acción de tutela* for the first time in the *Colombian Amazon Case* has pushed the boundaries of the traditional parameters of Colombian guardianship actions, albeit that in this case the NGO involved (Dejusticia) was supporting the plaintiffs across the court process, but was not bringing the case itself. Taken together, such cases demonstrate and emphasise the important role that NGOs can play in successfully driving the implementation of climate law (*Climate Case Ireland*) and in expanding climate law (*Urgenda*), which in turn relies on appropriate standing rules (*Oil Pollution Watch*). All this being said, the foregoing chapters have also clarified that climate litigation is diverse and various, and not all environmentally successful landmark climate cases will involve NGOs directly. The *Colombian Amazon Case* has just been noted, and this is further demonstrated by *Gloucester Resources*, which involved an appeal by Gloucester Resources Limited against a planning consent decision by the Minister for Planning in New South Wales.[2]

Juxtaposition of the *Gloucester Resources* ruling and the *Heathrow Runway Case* also affords insight into instances of courts engaging with substantively focused and procedurally focused climate litigation. The focus in the *Heathrow Runway Case* is very much on procedure; the UK Supreme Court is not concerned with the issue of whether the UK Government should or should not pursue support for additional runway capacity at Heathrow Airport, as this is a policy decision. In *Gloucester Resources*, by contrast, the Land and Environment Court is required to rule on the substance of an open cut coal mine development application. A case like *Climate Case Ireland*, while more in the tradition of *Heathrow Runway*, occupies a hinterland between both of these cases to some extent, insofar as the Irish case does have a procedural emphasis, but the Supreme Court is also required to

[2] Though note also the significance to this case of community action group Groundswell Gloucester; see further ch 6 in this volume.

judge whether the content of the Irish Government's mitigation plan meets certain statutory requirements (finding that it does not, due to a lack of policy specificity).

While narrow technical elements arising in the field of climate law are discussed throughout all of the judgments spotlighted in this book, the *Gloucester Resources* judgment can be distinguished for the breadth of technical matters that it engages with in a meaningful way. As has been seen, these elements include, but are not limited to, the *global carbon budget*, *carbon leakage*, *market substitution*, *causal linkage* (between development projects and climate change), and the doctrinal conceptualisation of 'greenhouse gas emissions' (including recognition of *Scope 1*, *2* and *3* emissions). Further principles and concepts of particular note engaged in the Australian judgment include *ecologically sustainable development*, the relationship between 'public interest' and climate change, *solastalgia* and *distributive inequity*. These and other technical components engaged by the studies and cases in this book can be usefully looked to by courts, lawyers and others around the world as a point of reference in climate litigation in going forward.

The helpful points of reference or active guidance that these cases and analyses can provide where a complex climate issue or legal problem arises in a climate case extend to both directly construed doctrinal/black letter law and broader general principles.[3] In relation to doctrinal law, for example, where some aspect of the interpretation or application of the international Paris Agreement is at issue, it is notable that the Paris Agreement forms both a central part of the UK Supreme Court's jurisprudence in the *Heathrow Runway Case* and arises as an important feature of the Land and Environment Court's reasoning in *Gloucester Resources*. Thus, these cases and pertinent commentaries on their jurisprudence can be consulted as a useful point of reference on aspects of the Paris Agreement's application. In relation to principles, where (for example) the principle of intergenerational equity and the associated rights of present and future generations arise as an important live issue in a climate case, the *Colombian Amazon Case* affords a useful reference point, where the principle forms a central element.

Taken generally, the studies in this volume serve to highlight that a necessity for climate litigation to drive robust climate outcomes in the domestic sphere becomes all the more imperative where the weakness of international climate law is recognised. Such weakness has been witnessed at many points in this book. One indication is nested within the facts of *Climate Case Ireland*, insofar as the *National Mitigation Plan* at issue in that case actively envisaged an *increase* in Irish emissions over the immediate term at a time where international legal standards were directing Ireland to work towards emissions reductions. The Irish Supreme Court took important note of the issue of governmentally facilitated national emissions increases, but did not engage deeply with it (nor with the irony that it was provided for in a *mitigation* plan), as this was understood to fall most directly within the purview of governmental policy rather than law. This is in contrast to the more

[3] On doctrinal law and characteristics of 'climate law', see ch 1, section I in this volume.

radical stance adopted by the Dutch Supreme Court in *Urgenda*, which intervened to impose a stricter mitigation target on the Dutch Government based directly in part on international legal standards. The *Heathrow Runway Case* affords a more explicit example of the weakness of international law in doctrinal terms, where it has been seen that the Paris Agreement does not apply directly in the UK's domestic legal order and, at any rate, the UK Government would have been free to take whatever decision it wished in terms of supporting or precluding the runway expansion at issue regardless of the Paris Agreement's application. The compliance issue that was raised merely hinged on consideration of whether the Paris Agreement had been taken into account procedurally. The *Colombian Amazon Case* may provide some better cause for environmental optimism here. It has been seen that the Supreme Court of Justice of Colombia construed the international arena as manifesting 'numerous regulations' composed of 'hard and soft law', which constitutes 'a global ecological public order'.[4] This 'serves as guiding criteria for national legislation',[5] and in the view of the Colombian Court, the thrust of this ecological order is towards resolving climate and other complaints in favour of the protection of the environment and the associated rights of people.

As noted above, the cases examined and the studies undertaken in this book help to elucidate a variety of complex points arising in climate law. Thus, *carbon leakage*, *market substitution* and the *waterbed effect*, which are often proffered as counter-arguments to climate-aligned litigation, are engaged in a manner that exposes their general lack of doctrinal credibility. In the *Urgenda Case*, where the *waterbed effect* was raised, the Court of Appeal had rejected this argument in advance of the Supreme Court stage. Similarly, it had disposed of the *carbon leakage* argument put forward by the Government. In *Gloucester Resources*, it has been seen that *carbon leakage* and *market substitution* arguments were advanced by Gloucester Resources Limited. These arguments were rejected lucidly and persuasively by Preston CJ. Such jurisprudence highlights the characteristic weakness in this line of argumentation, and provides guidance for courts and lawyers in general where such issues arise.

Another important point elucidated over the course of this study that can be subject to misunderstanding or neglect within climate litigation pertains to recognition of the fact that *climate harm is occurring now*. A fundamentalist tendency to focus on climate harm that will arise in the future in landmark climate cases is unhelpful to the extent that it neglects or appears to disavow the fact that harm is occurring in the present as well. This issue is dealt with in Chapter 3, where it is noted that 'on a point of general principle, this quasi-legal norm [ie, acknowledgement of anticipated future negative climate impacts only] is founded on inaccuracy – demonstrable harm is occurring on a gradual

[4] See ch 4 in this volume (quoting *Colombian Amazon Case*, Supreme Court judgment, part 2, para 11.3, Dejusticia translation).

[5] *Colombian Amazon Case*, Supreme Court judgment, part 2, para 6.

basis continually, including at the present (and in the past)'.[6] It is noted that Wewerinke-Singh and McCoach's work is important in picking up on this frequently neglected point.[7] They opine that the Dutch Supreme Court's 'assumption that dangerous climate change is exclusively a future concern remains problematic'.[8] The author supports this point, but adds that in addition to being problematic, it is incorrect.

The issue of 'time' and 'timing' has also arisen as an important element across this work. This has been engaged in relation to temporal climate targets and policy plans in particular. It is possible for a state to apply, eg, a legally binding Net Zero emissions reduction target for 2050 that is devoid of a legally binding trajectory that ratchets emissions downward consistently over time across the years in advance of 2050. In the period of the *Heathrow Runway Case*, the UK's Climate Change Act contained a Net Zero 2050 target and legally binding carbon budgets designed to ratchet emissions downwards progressively.[9] When *Climate Case Ireland* occurred, Ireland's Climate Change Act contained a national transition objective for 2050 that was roughly equivalent to the UK 2050 target, but the Irish Act was devoid of binding carbon budgets or equivalent legally embedded downward ratcheting mechanisms.[10] In this latter type of scenario, it is possible in principle for a state to *increase* its national emissions very substantially for many years, before steeply reducing them as 2050 begins to come close, ultimately meeting the 2050 obligation. Where a state has a legal obligation to achieve Net Zero by 2050, it can be achieved lawfully in such a circumstance in spite of the substantial environmental harm arising through the pronounced increase of greenhouse gases into the earth's atmosphere prior to a relatively short, sharp reduction period in the immediate lead-up to 2050. Such underlying tensions can be seen across a number of cases in this book, notably *Climate Case Ireland*, where the *National Mitigation Plan* at issue facilitated an increase in emissions in the immediate term (although this was intended to be temporary). In the *Urgenda Case*, contention over the pace of the pre-2050 national emissions reduction process also underlay the dispute. Both the Urgenda Foundation and the Dutch Government agreed on reduction ambitions for 2030 and 2050, but the NGO sought to replace the Dutch Government's weaker level of ambition for 2020 with a stronger minimum mitigation target. This served to place timing – the pace of mitigation from the present to 2050 – at the heart of the dispute.

A further time-related aspect engaged in the case studies concerns the pace at which a court process itself moves. This can be a critical factor in climate litigation.

[6] See ch 3, p 63 in this volume.

[7] Margaretha Wewerinke-Singh and Ashleigh McCoach, 'The State of the Netherlands v Urgenda Foundation: Distilling Best Practice and Lessons Learnt for Future Rights-Based Climate Litigation' (2021) 30(2) *Review of European, Comparative & International Environmental Law* 275–83, 280–82.

[8] ibid 280.

[9] Climate Change Act 2008, ss 1, 4–10.

[10] See further ch 7 in this volume.

The *Urgenda Case* involved a disputed 2020 emissions reduction target. It has been seen that the slow pace at which the Dutch courts service moved the time-sensitive case along was inappropriate. The District Court had produced its ruling in June 2015, years in advance of 2020, whereas the final Supreme Court ruling appeared in late December 2019, unhelpfully close to the conclusion of the target date.[11] The length of time between the Trial Court ruling (October 2006) and the Supreme Court ruling (July 2018) in *Oil Pollution Watch* was even more inappropriate, given the serious and pressing issues involved. Such a timespan alone could prove wholly detrimental to a climate case involving time-sensitive emissions reduction targets or similar temporal climate law components (eg, carbon budgets, or the statutorily time-limited production of policy plans). By contrast, the swift priority treatment accorded by the Colombian court system via its *tutela* channel to the time-sensitive *Colombian Amazon Case*, which was filed in 2018 and involved deforestation goals for 2020, provides an example of best practice. *Climate Case Ireland* also provides a positive example, where a 'leapfrog' process allowed the case to be fast-tracked directly to the Supreme Court on appeal from the High Court. This was due in part to the 'urgency' and 'gravity' of the case and the 'issues of general and public legal importance' raised.[12] As summarised in Chapter 7, 'the temporal urgency of the climate change challenge and the frequent time-sensitivity arising within climate law doctrine and procedure (here, involving a five-year *National Mitigation Plan* cycle) indicates that it is poor practice to subject non-frivolous, serious lawsuits to extensive procedural delays'.[13]

The unhelpfulness of conflating mitigation and adaptation in technical legal discourse and doctrine has also been identified in the foregoing chapters.[14] *Mitigating* the release or presence of the greenhouse gases driving anthropogenic climate change is distinguishable from *adapting* to the impacts of anthropogenic climate change. Thus, the Dutch Supreme Court's rhetorical assertion that 'it is correct that the consequences of climate change can be mitigated by taking adaptation measures'[15] has been found to be unhelpful. In the *Urgenda Case*, it also risked affording unintended support to the Government's unconvincing argument that adaptation measures can absolve a need to meet distinct mitigation objectives (an argument that both the Court of Appeal and the Supreme Court correctly rejected). As noted in the analysis of the case, '[t]o talk of climate impacts being "*mitigated* by *adaptation*" in a technical legal judgment … is unhelpful rhetorically, because mitigation and adaptation are technical terms with distinct meanings'.[16]

[11] As discussed in ch 3 in this volume, the target was required to be achieved by the end of 2020.

[12] *Friends of the Environment v The Government of Ireland & the Attorney General* [2020] IESCDET 13, paras [8], [10].

[13] See ch 7, p 176 in this volume.

[14] On *mitigation* and *adaptation* as distinctive *strands/components* of climate law, see ch 1 in this volume.

[15] *Urgenda Case*, Supreme Court judgment, para [7.5.2] (English translation provided by the Dutch courts service).

[16] See ch 3, p 79 in this volume.

Again as clarified in that chapter, '[i]t is not sensible to argue in legal terms that adaptation measures in effect cover mitigation measures, because adaptation and mitigation are related and mutually complimentary yet fundamentally distinct features of climate law'.[17]

The importance of maintaining suitable distinctions between treaties, statutes, policies and similar in climate litigation has also been identified. Conceptual issues arise in this line in the *Heathrow Runway Case* in particular. Here, the chapter analysis has suggested that the distinction between *treaties* and *policies*, which are distinct things by definition, could be drawn more clearly by the UK Supreme Court, as could the distinction between statute law (in this case, the Climate Change Act 2008) and 'policy'. It has been seen that a doctrinal principle that appears to suggest itself from a careful reading of the *Heathrow Runway Case* is that *policy is to be in accordance with the policy direction represented by the statute*.[18] If distinctions between law and policy are unhelpfully blurred as a matter of course in climate litigation, in addition to introducing unnecessary confusion into the field, a further risk is that this will assist in compounding a potential lack of clarity that can arise in relation to the *separation of powers* between the courts, the executive and parliament. It has been seen that the *Urgenda Case* provides an example where such tensions and complexities are to the fore. Here, some have suggested that the Dutch courts may have overstepped the bounds of their traditional role, concerning the interpretation and application of *law*, and strayed into the executive's domain by establishing *policy*. It should be recalled that the Dutch courts ordered the Dutch Government to implement a minimum 25 per cent greenhouse gas emissions reduction target for the Netherlands for 2020, a type of climate objective that had typically emerged in the policy sphere prior to the ruling.

A useful example of a carefully drawn distinction between broad-brush *law/policy* considerations is provided by *Climate Case Ireland*. This sort of case is to be differentiated from a climate case like *Gloucester Resources*, in which the New South Wales Land and Environment Court was required to assess a planning application on its merits in a relatively clear-cut way. In the Irish case, Ireland's Climate Change Act required the creation of mitigation plans specifying the policy measures deemed necessary by the Government to achieve the state's 2050 national transition objective, including specification of policy measures that Government Ministers would adopt in relation to individual economic sectors. The Government argued before the Supreme Court of Ireland that such plans concern the adoption of policy and that matters of policy are not justiciable in the Irish courts, such that the Supreme Court must limit itself to procedural considerations. Had this argument been accepted, the Government in likelihood would have succeeded in the case. The Irish Supreme Court, however, correctly held that the relevant legislation required the content of such plans to comply

[17] See ch 3, p 78 in this volume.
[18] See ch 2, p 39 in this volume.

with certain statutory requirements, meaning that assessment of aspects of the policy content could be legitimately undertaken *as a matter of law* (rather than as a matter of policy intrusion). The Court opined that: 'It becomes a matter of law because the [Irish Parliament] has chosen to legislate for at least some aspects of a compliant plan while leaving other elements up to policy decisions by the government of the day.'[19] Thus, the Court held that 'the requirements of s.4, as to what a plan must specify, come within a category of statutory obligation which is clearly law rather than policy'.[20] If the Court's assessment of the level of policy specificity in the mitigation plan *had* amounted to a matter of policy intrusion, or if the Court had dealt with this point incorrectly, the outcome of the case would have likely swung in favour of the Government, which went on to lose. Far from such *law/policy* distinctions amounting to a pedantic point of casual consequence, this case emphasises the benefit and importance of drawing these distinctions clearly and carefully in climate litigation.

The case study investigations have also found that the *Colombian Amazon Case* is particularly instructive for its treatment of *environmental rights* in the context of climate litigation. The recognition by Colombia's Supreme Court of the 'rights of nature' forms an important component of the judgment, with the Court applying an 'ecocentric-anthropocentric' frame that balances up environment-centred interests with human-centred interests. This judgment can help to inform – and perhaps inspire – a richer degree of environment-oriented doctrinal sensitivity where climate litigation arises in other jurisdictions. It has been seen in the chapter analysis that an emerging eco-jurisprudential heritage has been knitted together across the Colombian Constitution and the jurisprudence of the Colombian Constitutional and Supreme Courts. This provides a context for climate litigation in which nature is imbued with rights, and where this rights framework can crystallise onto specified ecosystems, as with the Atrato river ecosystem in the *Tierra Digna* case and the Colombian Amazon rainforest in the *Colombian Amazon Case* itself. The associated notion that citizens are imbued with *environmental human rights* is also recognised and applied. This is bolstered by the legal understanding that a right to a healthy and functioning natural environment is a fundamental constitutional entitlement. Were it to be responded to in the spirit of this jurisprudence, the question of whether the European Convention on Human Rights is to be interpreted as manifesting meaningful climate-relevant environmental protections at Articles 2 and 8 would be answered roundly in the affirmative.[21] It has

[19] *Climate Case Ireland*, Supreme Court judgment, para [6.27].

[20] ibid.

[21] While this book has been prepared for publication, the European Court of Human Rights has held that art 8 does incorporate a human right to protection by the state from the serious adverse effects of climate change; see further *Verein Klimaseniorinnen Schweiz and Others v. Switzerland*, Grand Chamber, European Court of Human Rights (Application No 53600/20), 9 April 2024. Note that applicants in other climate cases adjudicated by the European Court of Human Rights in the same period have been less successful: *Duarte Agostinho and Others v Portugal and 32 Others*, Grand Chamber,

also been seen that the Irish Supreme Court in *Climate Case Ireland* rolled back an environmental right that had previously been identified in the Irish Constitution. This element of the decision has received some criticism in this volume. Juxtaposed with the *Colombian Amazon Case*, this feature of *Climate Case Ireland* seems comparatively insensitive and unresponsive to the overt recognition of important environmental constitutional elements.

The relevance of 'the environment that belongs to no-one in particular' in *Oil Pollution Watch* speaks to a similar theme, bringing an underlying sense of environmental value common to humanity to the fore in that case's expansion of Nigeria's locus standi rules. This legal concept is referred to at a number of points throughout the Supreme Court's judgment, is relevant to the facts at issue and is one of the focal points of the day-to-day work of the NGO that brought the case. Further, it has been seen over the course of the *Oil Pollution Watch* analysis that the Supreme Court of Nigeria possesses a sophisticated sensitivity to rights-based issues in the context of environmental damage. This is driven in part by the African Charter on Human and Peoples' Rights, where protections are applied domestically by Article 24 of the African Charter Act. Here, '[a]ll people shall have the right to a general satisfactory environment favourable to their development'.[22] The case analysis has determined that Nigerian lawyers are well placed to link environmental rights framing in Nigeria to climate issues going forward as they test the scope of climate litigation.

The plaintiffs also argued in the *Colombian Amazon Case* that the Government was failing in its duty to safeguard the constitutional rights of *future generations*, including in relation to a healthy environment. The Court identifies 'a binding legal relationship regarding the environmental rights of future generations', which in practice can translate in part 'into a limitation to the freedom of action of present generations', due to the necessity of 'tak[ing] on the care and stewardship of natural resources and the future world'.[23] The Court finds that '[t]he environmental rights of future generations are based on the (i) ethical duty of solidarity of the species and (ii) the intrinsic value of nature'.[24] This case stands as an important point of reference for lawyers and courts in climate cases where *intergenerational equity* and associated matters arise significantly. The chapter analysis has highlighted some lack of clarity in the doctrinal position on *unborn* future generations; however, the extent to which the ruling affords protection to 'living' and unborn future generations, and the rationale provided by the Court for doing so in the context of climate litigation, positions this as a leading case on the matter. Relatedly, the court-ordered production and implementation of an

European Court of Human Rights (Application No 39371/20), 9 April 2024; *Carême v France*, Grand Chamber, European Court of Human Rights (Application No 7189/21), 9 April 2024.

[22] African Charter on Human and Peoples' Rights (Ratification and Enforcement) Act (Nigeria), art 24.

[23] *Colombian Amazon Case*, Supreme Court judgment, part 2, para 5.3 (Dejusticia translation).

[24] *Colombian Amazon Case*, Supreme Court judgment, part 2, para 5.3 (author's translation).

Intergenerational Pact for the Life of the Colombian Amazon, which must be sensitive to current and future generations, also renders the orders issued by the Court as a useful point of reference.

As to the issue of access to the courts, it has been seen that *Oil Pollution Watch* underscores the value and necessity of the following position: where a particular climate-related environmental lawsuit is justiciable in the public interest, an NGO or public-spirited individual should have a broad facility to bring a climate case in the general interest, even though that party may not have been harmed directly above and beyond others. The case clarifies that restrictive rules on standing can assist in perpetuating and entrenching environmental damage unacceptably. It also emphasises the importance of the availability of public interest litigation where proximity to government, actual or purported constraints on state agency litigation, and possible conflicting interests are at issue; such matters were raised by the structure and governmental proximity of the respondent in the case. Further, *Oil Pollution Watch* highlights the importance of community access to courts. *Gloucester Resources* also provides a useful demonstration of the importance of community participation in practice, through the activity of local community action group Groundswell Gloucester, which joined proceedings at the Land and Environment Court to successfully oppose Gloucester Resources Limited's appeal.

Each of the major court judgments explored in detail in this volume are underpinned by generally cogent and sophisticated doctrinal legal reasoning and application. Yet, it has also been seen at various stages that certain elements of judicial reasoning or jurisprudential accuracy may (at best) be open to question. For example, it has been discussed that the UK Supreme Court arguably provides an unhelpful interpretation when it opines that 'the UK's obligations under the Paris Agreement are given effect in domestic law, in … the existing carbon target under section 1 of the Climate Change Act 2008' (etc).[25] The Climate Change Act 2008 preceded the Paris Agreement 2015 by years and was not designed in any way to give effect to the Agreement, which was unforeseen at that time. It is true that the Paris Agreement was an influential consideration when the UK's original 80 per cent greenhouse gas emissions reduction for 2050, measured from 1990 levels, was later amended upward to 100 per cent (ie, Net Zero); however, a range of other important considerations were also taken into account at this time. The UK operates a dualist legal system, where international law is not automatically binding in the UK without being incorporated directly into the legal order by domestic legislation. The shaky line of reasoning advanced by the Supreme Court to reach the conclusion above was not a small point in the case, given the centrality of the relationship between the Paris Agreement and the Climate Change Act 2008 to the issues. Similarly, inaccuracy of a less interpretive doctrinal nature can also arise, as where the Supreme Court in *Urgenda* makes important reference to

[25] *Heathrow Runway Case*, Supreme Court judgment, para [122].

paragraphs in the Court of Appeal judgment that do not exist.[26] The lesson here is that climate litigation and the judgments arising from it should be approached with some reasonable degree of critical caution.

It is also the case that the literature and commentary on climate litigation often have a strong tendency to focus on human rights law, in part no doubt because of the importance of human rights and in part, perhaps, because of the powerful influence exerted by the human rights-based *Urgenda* litigation. Cases like *Climate Case Ireland*, however, where Friends of the Irish Environment succeeded in spite of rights issues being set aside actively by the Irish Supreme Court, and *Gloucester Resources*, where the court was not directly concerned with human rights law, show that human rights law is not the only game in town – far from it. Research and analysis, and the practical construction of climate cases themselves in the courts, need to take important account of human rights law where appropriate, but must also recognise that human rights do not represent an outer limit of climate litigation. If human rights avenues cannot assist in a case, there may well be other avenues that can.

Analysis in this volume has also identified that the implementation of court rulings can be highly inadequate, as clarified in Chapter 4 and as witnessed in the Nigerian experience in particular.[27] This indicates that in best-practice public interest climate cases – and any other form of climate case as relevant – a focus on sustained implementation pressure should follow in the wake of a major climate ruling where possible. Viewed in this way, a landmark climate litigation ruling does not conclude a case, but rather heralds a new implementation phase, which may require sustained pressure to be placed on governmental actors or other accountable stakeholders.

In closing, it is of benefit to be mindful of the Colombian Supreme Court's recognition in the *Colombian Amazon Case* of the notion of *citizens of the world*. This is raised to an extent that can usefully inspire other major courts around the world to recognise that climate litigation is an unusual area of law that engages a fundamentally global problem (climate change). The Court acknowledges the importance of interests arising in the case to 'the plaintiffs', to 'other people who inhabit and share the Amazonian territory', and to 'nationals' and 'foreigners, together with all inhabitants of the globe'.[28] It opines that '[t]he conservation of the Amazon is a national and global obligation, as it is the main environmental axis of the planet, and as such has been called the "lung of the world"'.[29] The Court's national-international perspective, which recognises that climate change is

[26] See ch 3, section III.A in this volume.

[27] See the comments on *Gbemre v Shell Petroleum Development Company Nigeria Ltd and Others* (2005) in ch 5 in this volume at n 170. Note also that the *Oil Pollution Watch* case was remitted back to the lower courts after Nigeria's Supreme Court dealt with the issue of locus standi, so this ruling itself did not result in the implementation of remediation (etc) of the environmental damage at issue.

[28] *Colombian Amazon Case*, Supreme Court judgment, part 2, para 11.3 (Dejusticia translation).

[29] ibid part 2, para 10.

an issue that transcends national borders, and that the importance of the Amazon rainforest at issue in the case therefore does too, should inform and inspire climate judges and lawyers around the world to keep this notion of *citizens of the world* in mind, and to incorporate it as a legally influential perspective where necessary. The related 'principle of solidarity' that informs the Colombian Court's thinking in this line is also a principle that climate lawyers can usefully keep to mind. In facing down the climate challenge, we are all in this together.

BIBLIOGRAPHY

Acosta, Alvarado, Paola, Andrea and Rivas-Ramírez, Daniel, 'A Milestone in Environmental and Future Generations' Rights Protection: Recent Legal Developments before the Colombian Supreme Court' (2018) *Journal of Environmental Law* 30(3), 519–26.

Adelmant, Victoria, Alston, Philip and Blainey, Matthew, 'Human Rights and Climate Change Litigation: One Step Forward, Two Steps Backwards in the Irish Supreme Court' (2021) *Journal of Human Rights Practice* 13(1), 1–23.

Adigun, Muyiwa and Jegede, Ademola Oluborode, 'A Human Rights Approach to Climate Litigation in Nigeria: Potentialities and Agamben's State of Exception Theory' (2022) *Carbon and Climate Law Review* 16(3), 179–91.

Akintayo, John Oluwole A and Eyongndi, David Tarh-Akong, 'Promoting the Right to Environmental Justice through the Supreme Court's Liberalisation of *Locus Standi* in Nigeria' (2019) *South African Journal of Environmental Law and Policy* 25(1), 201–31.

Alatise, Taofeeq N, 'Jurisdictional Problem in Environmental Litigation in Nigeria: Lessons from New South Wales' (2022) *International Islamic University Malaysia Law Journal* 30(1), 75–103.

Alatise, Taofeeq N, 'The Future of "Standing to Sue" in Environment and Climate Change Litigations in Nigeria' (2022) *Nnamdi Azikiwe University Journal of International Law and Jurisprudence* 13(1), 28–39.

Albi, Anneli and Bardutzky, Samo, *National Constitutions in European and Global Governance: Democracy, Rights, the Rule of Law: National Reports* (Springer Nature, 2019).

Albrecht, Glenn, '"Solastalgia": A New Concept in Health and Identity' (2005) *PAN: Philosophy Activism Nature* 3, 41–55.

Alogna, Ivano, Bakker, Christine and Gauci, Jean-Pierre (eds), *Climate Change Litigation: Global Perspectives* (Brill, 2021).

Alston, Philip, Adelmant, Victoria and Blainey, Matthew, 'Courts, Climate Action and Human Rights: Lessons from the Friends of the Irish Environment v Ireland Case', in César Rodríguez-Garavito (ed), *Litigating the Climate Emergency: How Human Rights, Courts and Legal Mobilization Can Bolster Climate Action* (Cambridge University Press, 2022), 305–18.

Amechi, Emeka Polycarp and Ihua-Maduenyi, Agent, '"Greening the Judiciary" in Nigeria: Centre for Oil Pollution Watch v NNPC in Perspectives' (2022) *African Journal of Law and Justice System* 1(2), 39–60.

Anozie, Miriam Chinyere and Wingate, Emmanuel Onyedi, 'NGO Standing in Petroleum Pollution Litigation in Nigeria: Centre for Oil Pollution Watch v Nigerian National Petroleum Corporation' (2020) *Journal of World Energy Law & Business* 13(5–6), 490–97.

Antonopoulos, Irene, 'The Future of Climate Policymaking in Light of Urgenda Foundation v the Netherlands' (2020) *Environmental Law Review* 22(2), 119–24.

Aydos, Elena, et al, 'Rocky Hill: A Legal Breakthrough in the Consideration of Climate Change and Social Impacts of Coal Mines' (2020) *Climate and Carbon Law Review*, 98, Part V, 103–05.

Babalola, Ayodele, 'The Right to a Clean Environment in Nigeria: A Fundamental Right' (2020) *Hastings Environmental Law Journal* 26(1), 3–14.

Babatunde, Abosede Omowumi, 'Oil Pollution and Water Conflicts in the Riverine Communities in Nigeria's Niger Delta Region: Challenges for and Elements of Problem-Solving Strategies' (2020) *Journal of Contemporary African Studies* 38(2), 274–93.

Backes, Chris W and van der Veen, Gerrit A, 'Urgenda: The Final Judgment of the Dutch Supreme Court' (2020) *Journal for European Environmental & Planning Law* 17(3), 307–21.

Banda, Maria L and Fulton, Scott. 'Litigating Climate Change in National Courts: Recent Trends and Developments in Global Climate Law' (2017) *Environmental Law Report News & Analysis* 47, 10121–34.

Barritt, Emily, 'Consciously Transnational: Urgenda and the Shape of Climate Change Litigation: The State of the Netherlands (Ministry of Economic Affairs and Climate Policy) v Urgenda Foundation' (2020) *Environmental Law Review* 22(4), 296–305.

Barritt, Emily M and Sediti, Boitumelo, 'The Symbolic Value of Leghari v Federation of Pakistan: Climate Change Adjudication in the Global South' (2019) *King's Law Journal*, 30(2), 203–10.

Bell, Joanna, Bogojević, Sanja and Hamlyn, Olivia, 'Friends of the Earth & Legal Interdisciplinarity: Introduction by the Analysis Editors' (2021) *Journal of Environmental Law* 33(2), 437–40.

Bell, Joanna and Fisher, Elizabeth, 'The Heathrow Case in the Supreme Court: Climate Change Legislation and Administrative Adjudication' (2023) *Modern Law Review* 86(1), 226–37.

Bell, Joanna and Fisher, Elizabeth, 'The "Heathrow" Case: Polycentricity, Legislation and the Standard of Review' (2020) *Modern Law Review* 83(5), 1072–85.

Bell-James, Justine and Collins, Briana, '"If We Don't Mine Coal, Someone Else Will": Debunking the "Market Substitution Assumption" in Queensland Climate Change Litigation' (2020) *Environmental and Planning Law Journal* 37(2), 167–85.

Bergkamp, Lucas, 'A Dutch Court's Revolutionary Climate Policy Judgment: The Perversion of Judicial Power, the State's Duties of Care and Science' (2015) *Journal of European Environmental and Planning Law* 12, 241–63.

Bodansky, Daniel, Brunnée, Jutta and Rajamani, Lavanya, 'Introduction', Section IV, in *International Climate Change Law* (Oxford University Press, 2017).

Boer, Ben, 'Transnational Dimensions of the Land and Environment Court of New South Wales' in Elizabeth Fisher and Brian Preston (eds), *An Environmental Court in Action* (Hart Publishing, 2022), 93–112.

Bouwer, Kim, 'The Unsexy Future of Climate Change Litigation' (2018) *Journal of Environmental Law* 30(3), 483–506.

Brown, Jasper et al, 'Solastalgia: Recognition by the Land and Environment Court of the Social Impacts of Fossil Fuel Developments' (2021) *Environmental and Planning Law Journal* 38(4), 295–314.

Burgers, Laura and Staal, Tim, 'Climate Action as Positive Human Rights Obligation: The Appeals Judgment in Urgenda v The Netherlands' in *Netherlands Yearbook of International Law*, vol 49 (TMC Asser Press, 2019), 223–44.

Burnett-Hall, Richard and Jones, Brian, *Burnett-Hall on Environmental Law*, 3rd edn (Sweet & Maxwell, 2012).

Bustos, Camila, Rozo-Ángel, Valentina and Eslava-Bejarano, Gabriela, 'Protecting the Rights of Future Generations through Climate Litigation: Lessons from the Struggle against Deforestation in the Colombian Amazon' (2020) *Standing up for a Sustainable World* 163–70.

Campbell, David, 'Temperature Tantrum' (2021) *Law Quarterly Review* 137, 380–84.

Carvan, John, *Understanding the Australian Legal System*, 8th edn (Lawbook Co, 2022).

Castro, Bianca, 'Barrister Who Flouted Supreme Court Embargo Disbarred', *Law Society Gazette*, 21 January 2023.

Castro, Carla Judith Cetina, 'Colombian Amazon as a Subject of Rights: Judgement of the Supreme Court of Justice of Colombia', in Luis Felipe Lacerda (ed), *Rights of Nature: Milestones for the Construction of a General Theory* (São Leopoldo, 2022), 67–79.

Castro, Dayana, 'Press Release: The People of the Centre are Opening a Path of Understanding with the Colombian Government to Jointly Safeguard the Future of Life in the Amazon', Forest Peoples Programme, 27 October 2023.

Chaves, Iván Vargas, Rodríguez, Gloria Amparo, Cumbe-Figueroa, Alexandra and Mora-Garzón, Sandra-Estefanía, 'Recognizing the Rights of Nature in Colombia: The Atrato River Case' (2020) *Jurídicas* 17(1), 13–41.

Cleary, Edward, 'Judicial Consideration of Intergenerational Equity in Australian Coal Mine Approval Litigation' (2021) *Environmental and Planning Law Journal* 38(3), 3–21.

Cleary, Paul, *Mine-Field: The Dark Side of Australia's Resources Rush* (Black Inc, 2012).
Committee on Climate Change, *Net Zero: The UK's Contribution to Stopping Global Warming* (2019).
Cox, Roger, 'A Climate Change Litigation Precedent: Urgenda Foundation v The State of the Netherlands' (2016) *Journal of Energy & Natural Resources Law* 34(2), 143–63.
Coyle, Sean and Morrow, Karen, *The Philosophical Foundations of Environmental Law: Property, Rights and Nature* (Hart Publishing, 2004).
Davies, Megan, 'The Land and Environment Court of New South Wales and the Recognition of Indigenous Peoples' Environmental Rights' in Elizabeth Fisher, and Brian Preston (eds), *An Environmental Court in Action* (Hart Publishing, 2022), 175–94.
de Graaf, Kars J and Jans, Jan H, 'The Urgenda Decision: Netherlands Liable for Role in Causing Dangerous Global Climate Change' (2015) *Journal of Environmental Law*, 27(3), 517–27.
de Montesquieu, Charles, *Montesquieu: The Spirit of the Laws* (Cambridge University Press, 1989).
Dehm, Julia, 'Coal Mines, Carbon Budgets and Human Rights in Australian Climate Litigation: Reflections on Gloucester Resources Limited v Minister for Planning and Environment' (2020) *Australian Journal of Human Rights* 26(2), 244–73.
Department for Transport, *Appraisal of Sustainability: Airports National Policy Statement* (UK Government, 2018).
Department for Transport, *Airports National Policy Statement* (UK Government, 2018).
Department for Transport, *The Future of Air Transport* (UK Government, 2003).
Department of the Environment, Climate and Communications, *National Mitigation Plan* (Ireland, 2017).
Eckes, Christina, 'The Urgenda Case is Separation of Powers at Work' in N de Boer et al (eds), *Liber Amicorum Besselink (Amsterdam, 2021), Amsterdam Law School Research Paper* 2021–39 (2021).
Editorial, 'Climate Legislation Amended following SCELN's Seventh Gas Campaign', *Scottish Legal News*, 13 March 2023.
Ekhator, Eghosa and Okumagba, Edward, 'Climate Change, Multinationals and Human Rights in Nigeria: A Case for Climate Justice' in Kim Bouwer, Uzuazo Etemire, Tracy-Lynn Field and Ademola Oluborode Jegede (eds), *In Pursuit of Climate Justice in Africa* (Bristol University Press, 2024).
Ellemers, Naomi and de Gilder, Dick, *The Moral Organization: Key Issues, Analyses and Solutions* (Springer Nature, 2022).
Environmental Rights Recognition Project, *The Right to a Healthy Environment in the United Kingdom: Supporting the Proposal for a New Protocol to the European Convention on Human Rights* (King's College London, 2022).
Etemire, Uzuazo, 'The Future of Climate Change Litigation in Nigeria: COPW v NNPC in the Spotlight' (2021) *CCLR* 158–70.
Ewulum, BE, Okaphor, Ejike and Okoli, Nnedimma Ezenwa-Ohaeto, 'An Appraisal of the Impact of the National Oil Spill Detection and Response Agency on Environmental Pollution in Nigeria' (2020) *International Journal of Comparative Law and Legal Philosophy* 2, 58–65.
Fagbemi, SA and Akpanke, AR, 'Environmental Litigation in Nigeria: The Role of the Judiciary' (2019) *Nnamdi Azikiwe University Journal of International Law and Jurisprudence* 10(2), 26–34.
Fankhauser, Sam, Gennaioli, Caterina and Collins, Murray, 'The Political Economy of Passing Climate Change Legislation: Evidence from a Survey' (2015) *Global Environmental Change* 35, 52–61.
Faturoti, Bukola, Agbaitoro, Godswill and Onya, Obinna, 'Environmental Protection in the Nigerian Oil and Gas Industry and Jonah Gbemre v Shell PDC Nigeria Limited: Let the Plunder Continue?' (2019) *African Journal of International and Comparative Law* 27(2), 225–245.
Fisher, Elizabeth, Scotford, Eloise and Barritt, Emily, 'The Legally Disruptive Nature of Climate Change' (2017) *The Modern Law Review* 80(2), 173–201.
Frynas, Jedrzej George, *Oil in Nigeria: Conflict and Litigation between Oil Companies and Village Communities* (LIT Verlag, 2000).
Fuller, Lon, 'The Forms and Limitations of Adjudication' (1978) *Harvard Law Review* 92(2), 353–409.
Gaffney, Jeffrey S and Marley, Nancy A, *Chemistry of Environmental Systems* (Wiley, 2020).
Ghaleigh, Navraj Singh, 'Climate Constitutionalism of the UK Supreme Court' (2021) *Journal of Environmental Law* 33(2), 441–47.

Gleeson, Margaret, 'NSW Land Court Rules against New Coalmine' (2019) *Green Left Weekly* 1209, 8.
Gleeson, Margaret, 'Rocky Hill Decision Rocks Mining Lobby' (2019) *Green Left Weekly* 1221, 10.
Gómez-Betancur, Luisa, 'The Rights of Nature in the Colombian Amazon: Examining Challenges and Opportunities in a Transitional Justice Setting' (2020) *UCLA Journal of International Law and Foreign Affairs* 25, 41–84.
Gordhan, Sonam, 'Plan B Earth v Secretary of State for Transport: Airport Expansion, the Paris Agreement and the Planning Act 2008' (2020) *Journal of Environmental Law* 32(3), 559–575.
Greenberg, Daniel (ed), *Jowitt's Dictionary of English Law*, 5th edn (Sweet & Maxwell, 2019).
Guerrero Ascuntar, Geovanna Esperanza, 'Exploring the Ruling on the Rights of the Colombian Amazon: Taking Stock of the Implementation of Ruling 4360 of 2018' MS thesis (Norwegian University of Life Sciences, 2023).
Haddon, Catherine, Hogarth, Raphael and Nice, Alex, 'Judicial Review and Policy Making: The Role of Legal Advice in Government' (Institute for Government, 2021).
Hart KC, David, 'Climate Change Human Rights Claim Wins in the Dutch Courts', *UK Human Rights Blog*, 14 October 2018.
Hasler, Olivia, 'Mining as Ecocide: The case of Adani and the Carmichael mine in Australia' in Yuliya Zabyelina and Daan van Uhm (eds), *Illegal Mining: Organized Crime, Corruption and Ecocide in a Resource-Scarce World* (Springer Nature, 2020) 497–527.
Hawkins, Joanne, 'A Lesson in Un-creativity: (R (on the Application of Friends of the Earth Ltd and Others) v Heathrow Airport Ltd [2020] UKSC 52' (2021) *Environmental Law Review* 23(4), 344–49.
Hicks, Celeste, *Expansion Rebellion* (Manchester University Press, 2022).
Hilson, Christopher J, 'Climate Change Litigation: An Explanatory Approach (or Bringing Grievance Back in)' in F Fracchia and M Occhiena (eds), *Climate change: la riposta del diritto* (Editoriale Scientifica, 2010), 421–36.
Hughes, Lesley, 'The Rocky Hill Decision: A Watershed for Climate Change Action?' (2019) *Journal of Energy & Natural Resources Law* 37(3), 341–51.
Hughes-Gerber, Laura, 'A Third Runway for Heathrow? To Build or Not to Build? A Brief Review of the Supreme Court's Recent Judgment' (2021) *Air and Space Law* 46(2), 309–14.
IPCC, *Global Warming of 1.5^o: An IPCC Special Report* (IPCC, 2018).
Jackson Andrew, 'Ireland's Climate Action and Low Carbon Development Act 2015: Symbolic Legislation, Trojan Horse, Stepping Stone?' in Thomas L Muinzer (ed), *National Climate Change Acts: The Emergence, Form and Nature of National Framework Climate Legislation* (Hart Publishing, 2021), 129–52.
Jäger, Jill and O'Riordan, Tim, 'The History of Climate Change Science and Politics' in *The Politics of Climate Change* (Routledge, 2019), 1–31.
Kahl, Wolfgang and Weller, Marc-Philippe (eds), *Climate Change Litigation* (Beck, 2021).
Kelleher, Orla, 'The Revival of the Unenumerated Rights Doctrine: A Right to an Environment and its Implications for Future Climate Change Litigation in Ireland' (2018) *Irish Planning and Environmental Law* 25(3), 97.
Kelleher, Orla, 'Environmental Constitutionalism: A Transformative Legal Discourse?' (2023) *Irish Judicial Studies Journal*, 7(3), 47–77.
Kennedy, Amanda, *Environmental Justice and Land Use conflict: The Governance of Mineral and Gas Resource Development* (Routledge, 2017).
Kotzé, Louis and du Plessis, Anél, 'Putting Africa on the Stand' (2019) *Environmental Law* 50(3), 615–63.
Kotzé, Louis J and Villavicencio Calzadilla, Paola, 'Somewhere between Rhetoric and Reality: Environmental Constitutionalism and the Rights of Nature in Ecuador' (2017) *Transnational Environmental Law* 6(3), 401–33.
Krommendijk, Jasper, 'Beyond Urgenda: The Role of the ECHR and Judgments of the ECtHR in Dutch Environmental and Climate Litigation' (2022) *Review of European, Comparative & International Environmental Law* 31(1), 60–74.
Kulovesi, Kati, 'Exploring the Landscape of Climate Law and Scholarship: Two Emerging Trends' in Erkki J Hollo, Kati Kulovesi and Michael Mehling (eds), *Climate Change and the Law* (Springer, 2013), 31–62.

Kysar, Douglas A, 'What Climate Change Can Do about Tort Law' (2011) *Environmental Law* 41, 1–72.
Lee, David S, *The Current State of Scientific Understanding of the Non-CO_2 Effects of Aviation on Climate* (Department for Transport, 2018).
Leijten, Ingrid, 'Human Rights v Insufficient Climate Action: The Urgenda Case' (2019) *Netherlands Quarterly of Human Rights* 37(2), 112–18.
Lin, Jolene, 'The First Successful Climate Negligence Case: A Comment on Urgenda Foundation v The State of the Netherlands (Ministry of Infrastructure and the Environment)' (2015) *Climate Law* 5(1), 65–81.
Liu, Zhu et al, 'Global Patterns of Daily CO_2 Emissions Reductions in the First Year of COVID-19' (2022) *Nature Geoscience* 15(8), 615–20.
Macrory, Richard and Muinzer, Thomas L, 'The UK's Climate Change Act', in Thomas L Muinzer (ed), *National Climate Change Acts: The Emergence, Form and Nature of National Framework Climate Legislation* (Hart Publishing, 2021), 69–92.
Martin, Stevie, 'Friends of the Earth: "Government Policy", Relevant Considerations and Human Rights' (2021) *Journal of Environmental Law* 33(2), 449–54.
Mathis, Charles-François, 'King Coal Rules: Accepting or Refusing Coal Dependency in Victorian Britain' (2018) *Revue Française de Civilisation Britannique. French Journal of British Studies* 23.XXIII-3.
Maxwell, Lucy, Mead, Sarah and van Berkel, Dennis, 'Standards for Adjudicating the Next Generation of Urgenda-Style Climate Cases' (2022) *Journal of Human Rights and the Environment* 13(1), 35–63.
Mayer, Benoit, 'The Contribution of Urgenda to the Mitigation of Climate Change' (2023) *Journal of Environmental Law* 35(2), 167–84.
Mayer, Benoit, 'Climate Change Mitigation as an Obligation under Human Rights Treaties?' (2021) 115 *American Journal of International Law* 409–51.
Mayer, Benoît and Zahar, Alexander (eds), *Debating Climate Law* (Cambridge University Press, 2021).
Mbadugha, Joseph N, 'Environmental Public Interest Litigation in Nigeria: A Case Comment on Centre for Oil Pollution Watch v Nigerian National Petroleum Corporation' (2021) *Nnamdi Azikiwe University, Awka Journal of Public and Private Law* 11, 53–66.
McConville, Mike and Chui, Wing Hong, 'Introduction and Overview', in Mike McConville and Wing Hong Chui (eds), *Research Methods for Law* (Edinburgh University Press, 2017).
McDonald, Jan, 'The Role of Law in Adapting to Climate Change' (2011) *Wiley Interdisciplinary Reviews: Climate Change* 2(2), 283–95.
McGinness, Victoria and Raff, Murray, 'Coal and Climate Change: A Study of Contemporary Climate Litigation in Australia' (2020) *Environmental and Planning Law Journal* 37(1), 87–127.
McLoughlin, Jamie, 'Whither Constitutional Environmental (Rights) Protection in Ireland after "Climate Case Ireland"?' (2021) *Irish Judicial Studies Journal* 5(2), 26–46.
Meernik, James, DeMeritt, Jacqueline HR and Uribe-López, Mauricio (eds), *As War Ends: What Colombia Can Tell Us about the Sustainability of Peace and Transitional Justice* (Cambridge University Press, 2019).
Meguro, Maiko, 'State of the Netherlands v Urgenda Foundation' (2020) *American Journal of International Law* 114(4), 729–35.
Ministry of Housing, Communities and Local Government, *National Planning Policy Framework* (UK, July 2018).
Minnerop, Petra, 'Intergenerational Preparedness: Climate Change, Community Interest Obligations and the Environmental Rule of Law' (2023) *Global Policy*, 1–22.
Mitchell, Edward, 'Climate Change and Nationally Significant Infrastructure Projects: R (on the Application of Plan B Earth) v Secretary of State for Transport' (2020) *Environmental Law Review* 22(2), 125–32.
Mueller, Gustav, 'The Hegel Legend of "Synthesis-Antithesis-Thesis"' (1958) *Journal of the History of Ideas*, 19(3), 411–14.
Mugga, Jovan Ivan, Gupta, Joyeeta and Lefeber, René, 'Shaping Africa's Climate Action through Climate Litigation: An Impact Assessment' (2023) *RiA Recht in Afrika/Law in Africa/Droit en Afrique* 26(1), 26–54.

Muinzer, Thomas L,'The 20-20-20 Climate and Energy Package', in 'An Evaluation of the Implications of EU Climate and Energy Governance for the UK in Light of Brexit' (2017) 23(2) *European Journal of Current Legal Issues*, s 4.2.

Muinzer, Thomas L, *Climate and Energy Governance for the UK Low Carbon Transition: The Climate Change Act 2008* (Springer, 2018).

Muinzer, Thomas L, 'What are National "Climate Change Acts"?' (2021) *Journal of Energy & Natural Resources Law* 39(4), 419–38.

Muinzer, Thomas L (ed), *National Climate Change Acts: The Emergence, Form and Nature of National Framework Climate Legislation* (Hart Publishing, 2021).

Muinzer, Thomas L and Paterson, John B, 'La Ley de Cambio Climático y Energía en Reino Unido' ('The Law of Climate Change and Energy in the United Kingdom') in José Francisco Alenza García and Lorenzo Mellado Ruiz (eds), *Estudios Sobre Cambio Climático y Transición Energética* (*Studies on Climate Change and Energy Transition*) (Marcial Pons, 2022), 743–60.

Murad, Cesar Augusto and Pearse, Jillian, 'Landsat Study of Deforestation in the Amazon Region of Colombia: Departments of Caquetá and Putumayo' (2018) *Remote Sensing Applications: Society and Environment* 11, 161–71.

Næss-Schmidt, Helge Sigurd, Hansen, Martin Bo Westh, Holm, Sixten Rygner and Lumby, Bjarke Modvig, 'What is Carbon Leakage?' in *Carbon Leakage in the Nordic Countries: What are the Risks and How to Design Effective Preventative Policies* (Nordic Council of Ministers, 2019).

Ngwoke, Rita A and Oguguo, Rita, 'Application of the Rule of *Locus Standi* in Climate Change Litigations in Nigeria' (2020) *Journal of Law Policy & Globalization* 101, 49–55.

Nussberger, Angelika, *The European Court of Human Rights* (Oxford University Press, 2020).

O'Neill, Sadhbh and Alblas, Edwin, 'Climate Litigation, Politics and Policy Change: Lessons from Urgenda and Climate Case Ireland', in David Robbins, Diarmuid Torney and Pat Brereton (eds), *Ireland and the Climate Crisis* (Palgrave Macmillan, 2020), 57–72.

Oamen, Philip E and Erhagbe, Eunice O, 'The Impact of Climate Change on Economic and Social Rights Realisation in Nigeria: International Cooperation and Assistance to the Rescue?' (2021) *African Human Rights Law Journal* 21(2), 1080–1111.

Obadina, Ibrahim, 'Nigerian Supreme Court's Stealth Relaxation of *Locus Standi* in Environmental Litigation: Redirecting Judicial Approach to Public Interest Litigation' (2021) *Journal of Private and Business Law* 2(2), 200–18.

Obani, Pedi, 'Climate Litigation in South Africa and Nigeria: Legal Opportunities and Gender Perspectives', in Kim Bouwer, Uzuazo Etemire, Tracy-Lynn Field and Ademola Oluborode Jegede (eds), *In Pursuit of Climate Justice in Africa* (Bristol University Press, 2024).

Office of Environment and Heritage, *NSW Climate Change Policy Framework* (Australia, 2016).

Ogowewo, Tunde I, 'Wrecking the Law: How Article III of the Constitution of the United States Led to the Discovery of a Law on Standing to Sue in Nigeria' (2000) *Brooklyn Journal of International Law* 26(2), 527–90.

Okonkwo, Eloamaka Carol, 'Assessing the Role of the Courts in Enhancing Access to Environmental Justice in Oil Pollution Matters in Nigeria' (2020) *African Journal of International and Comparative Law* 28(2), 195–218.

Okumagba, Edward, 'Examining Global Court Practices in Reducing Climate Change Impacts through Litigation: Lessons for Nigeria' in Eghosa O Ekhator, Servel Miller and Etinosa Igbinosa (eds), *Implementing the Sustainable Development Goals in Nigeria: Barriers, Prospects and Strategies* (Routledge, 2021).

Olatunbosun, Adeniyi I and Onu, Kingsley Osinachi N, 'The Liberalisation of *Locus Standi* in Environmental Cases in Nigeria: An Appraisal of the Supreme Court's Decision in Centre for Oil Pollution Watch v NNPC' (2020) *Gravitas Review of Business & Property Law* 11(2), 1–11.

Oluduro, Olubisi F, 'Combating Climate Change in Nigeria: An Appraisal of Constitutional and Legal Frameworks' (2020) *Wisconson International Law Journal* 38, 269–300.

Osofsky, Hari M, 'The Continuing Importance of Climate Change Litigation' (2010) *Climate Law* 1(1), 3–29.

Parpworth, Neil, 'Breaching an Embargo on the Publication of a Judgment: A Criminal Contempt of Court? Her Majesty's Attorney General v Crosland [2021] UKSC 15' (2021) *Journal of Criminal Law* 85(6), 466–70.

Parker, Kierra, 'Litigating at the Source: Attributing Climate Change Impacts to Coal Mines' (2020) 37 *Environmental and Planning Law Journal* 67–86.

Pedersen, Ole W, 'The Networks of Human Rights and Climate Change: The State of the Netherlands v Stichting Urgenda, Supreme Court of the Netherlands, 20 December 2019 (19/00135)' (2020) *Environmental Law Review*, 22(3), 227–34.

Peel, Jacqueline, 'Climate Change Law: The Emergence of a New Legal Discipline' (2008) *Melbourne University Law Review* 32(3), 922–79.

Peel, Jacqueline, 'The Land and Environment Court of New South Wales and the Transnationalisation of Climate Law: The Case of *Gloucester Resources v Minister for Planning*' in Elizabeth Fisher and Brian Preston (eds), *An Environmental Court in Action* (Hart Publishing, 2022).

Peel, Jacqueline and Lin, Jolene, 'Transnational Climate Litigation: The Contribution of the Global South' (2019) *American Journal of International Law* 113(4), 679–726.

Peel, Jacqueline and Osofsky, Hari M, *Climate Change Litigation* (Cambridge University Press, 2015).

Peel, Jacqueline and Osofsky, Hari M, 'Climate Change Litigation' (2020) *Annual Review of Law and Social Science* 16, 21–38.

Peeters, Marjan, 'Urgenda Foundation and 886 Individuals v The State of the Netherlands: The Dilemma of More Ambitious Greenhouse Gas Reduction Action by EU Member States' (2016) *Review of European, Comparative & International Environmental Law* 25(1), 123–29.

Pelizzon, Alessandro, 'An Intergenerational Ecological Jurisprudence: The Supreme Court of Colombia and the Rights of the Amazon Rainforest' (2020) *Law, Technology and Humans* 2(1), 33–44.

Popoola, Ebunoluwa, 'An Examination of Factors Militating against Effective Enforcement of Environmental Law in Nigeria' (2019) *University of Maiduguri Law Journal* 19, 20–44.

Preston, Brian J, 'The Influence of the Paris Agreement on Climate Litigation: Legal Obligations and Norms (Part I)' (2021) *Journal of Environmental Law* 33(1), 1–32.

Preston, Brian J, 'The Influence of the Paris Agreement on Climate Litigation: Causation, Corporate Governance and Catalyst (Part II)' (2021) *Journal of Environmental Law* 33(2), 227–56.

Preston, Brian J, 'Changing Climate Law and Governance: A Multi-level Perspective' (2023) *Global Policy* 1–12.

Rainey, Bernadette, McCormick, Pamela and Ovey, Clare, *Jacobs, White and Ovey: The European Convention on Human Rights* (Oxford University Press, 2021).

Renglet, Charlotte, 'The Decision of the Irish Supreme Court in Friends of the Irish Environment v Ireland: A Significant Step towards Government Accountability for Climate Change?' (2020) 3 *Carbon and Climate Law Review* 163–176.

Report of the Office of the UN High Commissioner for Human Rights [OHCHR] on the Relationship Between Human Rights and Climate Change, UN Doc A/HRC/10/61 (15 January 2009).

Richardson, Benjamin J and Razzaque, Jona, 'Public Participation in Environmental Decision-making', in Benjamin J Richardson and Stepan Wood (eds), *Environmental Law for Sustainability* (Hart Publishing, 2006), 165–94.

Richardson, Whitney and Bustos, Camila, 'Implementing Nature's Rights in Colombia: The Atrato and Amazon Experiences' (2023) *Revista Derecho del Estado* 54, 227–75.

Robiou du Pont, Yann and Meinshausen, Malte, 'Warming Assessment of the Bottom-up Paris Agreement Emissions Pledges' (2018) *Climate Change Nature* 9(4810), 1–10.

Rodríguez-Garavito, César, 'Human Rights: The Global South's Route to Climate Litigation' (2020) *AJIL Unbound* 40–44.

Romppanen, Seita and Huhta, Kaisa, 'The Interface between EU Climate and Energy Law' (2023) *Maastricht Journal of European and Comparative Law* 30(1), 45–62.

Roy, Suryapratim, 'Is Climate Change an Issue of Human Rights?', *The Irish Times*, 15 October 2019.

Roy, Suryapratim, 'The Domestic Life of Climate Law: Friends of the Irish Environment v Ireland' (2021) 3 *Irish Supreme Court Review* 141–60.

Roy, Suryapratim and Woerdman, Edwin, 'Situating Urgenda v the Netherlands within Comparative Climate Change Litigation' (2016) *Journal of Energy & Natural Resources Law* 34(2), 165–89.

Roy, Suryapratim, 'Distributive Choices in Urgenda and EU Climate Law' in *European Energy Law Report XI* (Intersentia, 2017), 47–68.

Roy, Suryapratim, 'Urgenda II and its Discontents' (2019) *Carbon & Climate Law Review* 13(2), 130–41.

Salau, Aaron Olaniyi, 'The Future of Climate Change Litigation in Pursuit of Environmental Sustainability in Africa: A Review of Nigeria's 2021 Climate Change Act' in Jean-Claude N Ashukem and Semie M Sama (eds), *Domestic and Regional Environmental Laws and Policies in Africa: A Research Companion* (Routledge, 2024).

de Salles Cavedon-Capdeville, Fernanda, Valeria Berros, Maria, Filpi, Humberto and Villavicencio Calzadilla, Paola, 'An Ecocentric Perspective on Climate Litigation: Lessons from Latin America' (2024) *Journal of Human Rights Practice* 16(1), 89–106.

Savaresi, Annalisa and Setzer, Joana, 'Rights-Based Litigation in the Climate Emergency: Mapping the Landscape and New Knowledge Frontiers' (2022) *Journal of Human Rights and the Environment* 13(1), 7–34.

Scotford, Eloise and Minas, Stephen, 'Probing the Hidden Depths of Climate Law: Analysing National Climate Change Legislation' (2019) *Review of European, Comparative & International Environmental Law* 28(1), 67–81.

Setzer, Joana and Higham, Catherine, *Global Trends in Climate Change Litigation: 2022 Snapshot* (Grantham Research Institute on Climate Change and the Environment and Centre for Climate Change Economics and Policy, London School of Economics and Political Science, 2022).

Setzer, Joana and Higham, Catherine, *Global Trends in Climate Change Litigation: 2023 Snapshot* (Grantham Research Institute on Climate Change and the Environment and Centre for Climate Change Economics and Policy, London School of Economics and Political Science, 2023).

Slobodian, Lydia, 'Defending the Future: Intergenerational Equity in Climate Litigation' (2019) *Georgetown Environmental Law Review* 32, 569–90.

Setzer, Joana and Vanhala, Lisa C, 'Climate Change Litigation: A Review of Research on Courts and Litigants in Climate Governance' (2019) *Wiley Interdisciplinary Reviews: Climate Change* 10(3), e580.

Smith, Don C, 'Editorial: Landmark Climate Change-Related Judicial Decisions Handed Down in the Netherlands and Australia: A Preview of What's to Come?' (2019) *Journal of Energy & Natural Resources Law* 37(2), 145–47.

Smith, Jeff and Higginson, Sue, '"Please Come in": Access to Justice and the Development of Jurisprudence in the Land and Environment Court of New South Wales' in Elizabeth Fisher and Brian Preston (eds), *An Environmental Court in Action* (Hart Publishing, 2022), 253–68.

Spijkers, Otto, 'The Urgenda Case: A Successful Example of Public Interest Litigation for the Protection of the Environment?' in Christina Voigt and Zen Makuch (eds), *Courts and the Environment* (Edward Elgar, 2018), 305–44.

Spijkers, Otto and Oosterhuis, Sofie, 'The Dutch Response to Climate Change: Evaluating the Netherlands' Climate Act and Associated Issues of Importance', in Thomas L Muinzer (ed), *National Climate Change Acts: The Emergence, Form and Nature of National Framework Climate Legislation* (Hart Publishing, 2021), 175–98.

Spoelman, Naomi, 'Urgenda: A How-to Guide for Enforcing Greenhouse Gas Emission Targets by Protecting Human Rights' (2020) *Ecology Law Quarterly* 47, 751–60.

Supreme Court of Ireland, *Supreme Court Practice Directions: Conduct of Proceedings in Supreme Court*, SC19.

UK Government, *International Aviation and Shipping Emissions and the UK's Carbon Budgets and 2050 Target* (UK Government, 2012).

UK Government, *Net Zero Strategy: Build Back Greener* (UK Government, 2021).

Umukoro, Brown Etareri and Omozue, Moses Ogorugba, 'Environmental Protection and the Role of National Policy and Guidelines in Nigeria' (2022) *Baltic Journal of Law & Politics* 15(1), 2016–29.

Umukoro, Brown Etareri and Omozue, Moses Ogorugba, 'Prosecuting Environmental Pollution Cases in Nigeria: The Head of a Carmel Passing through the Eye of a Niddle' (2022) *Baltic Journal of Law & Politics* 15(2), 2232–43.

Van der Veen, GA and de Graaf, KJ, 'Climate Change Litigation in the Netherlands: The Urgenda Case and Beyond', in Wolfgang Khal and Marc-Philippe Weller (eds), *Climate Change Litigation: A Handbook* (Bloomsbury, 2021), 363–77.

Verschuuren, Jonathan, 'The State of the Netherlands v Urgenda Foundation: The Hague Court of Appeal Upholds Judgment Requiring the Netherlands to Further Reduce its Greenhouse Gas Emissions' (2019) *Review of European, Comparative & International Environmental Law* 28(1), 94–98.

Verschuuren, Jonathan, 'Climate Change and the Individual in the Netherlands', in Francesco Sindico and Makane Moïse Mbengue (eds), *Comparative Climate Change Litigation: Beyond the Usual Suspects* (Springer, 2021), 75–90.

Villabona, Luis Armando Tolosa, 'Vanguardism and Environmental Justice Developments in Colombia', in Domenico Amirante and Silvia Bagni (eds), *Environmental Constitutionalism in the Anthropocene* (Routledge, 2022).

Villavicencio Calzadilla, Paola, 'A Paradigm Shift in Courts' View on Nature: The Atrato River and Amazon Basin Cases in Colombia' (2019) *Law, Environment and Development Journal* 15, 1–11.

Watts, John, Eveleigh, Ken, Manikas, Michael and Kite, Jeff, 'Environmental Law and Indigenous Issues: What You Didn't Know about the Landmark Rocky Hill Judgment' (2019) *LSJ: Law Society of NSW Journal* 57, 72–73.

Wegener, Bernhard W, 'Urgenda – World Rescue by Court Order? The 'Climate Justice' Movement Tests the Limits of Legal Protection' (2019) *Journal for European Environmental & Planning Law* 16(2), 125–47.

Westaway, Ned, 'Friends of the Earth: Implications for Planning Law' (2021) *Journal of Environmental Law* 33(2), 455–459.

Wewerinke-Singh, Margaretha and McCoach, Ashleigh, 'The State of the Netherlands v Urgenda Foundation: Distilling Best Practice and Lessons Learnt for Future Rights-Based Climate Litigation' (2021) *Review of European, Comparative & International Environmental Law* 30(2), 275–283.

White, Robert, 'Eco-justice and Destructive Mining in Australia: Lessons from the New South Wales Land and Environmental Court' in Yuliya Zabyelina and Daan van Uhm (eds), *Illegal Mining: Organized Crime, Corruption and Ecocide in a Resource-Scarce World* (Springer Nature, 2020), 529–58.

White, Robert, Hallinan, Jemilah and Rayment, Belinda, 'Environmental Law: Climate Change Takes Centre Stage in Land and Environment Court' (2019) *LSJ: Law Society Journal* 54.

Wonneberger, Anke and Vliegenthart, Rens, 'Agenda-Setting Effects of Climate Change Litigation: Interrelations across Issue Levels, Media and Politics in the Case of Urgenda against the Dutch Government' (2021) *Environmental Communication* 15(5), 699–714.

World Commission on Environment and Development, *Our Common Future* (1987) (Brundtland Report).

Yanguas Parra, Paola A, Ganti, Gaurav, Brecha, Robert, Hare, Bill, Schaeffer, Michiel, Fuentes, Ursula and Geiges, Andreas, *Global and Regional Coal Phase out Requirements of the Paris Agreement: Insights from the IPCC Special Report on 1.5°C* (Climate Analytics, 2019).

INDEX

www.ingramcontent.com/pod-product-compliance
Ingram Content Group UK Ltd.
Pitfield, Milton Keynes, MK11 3LW, UK
UKHW021037150926
475561UK00003B/155